D1085393

THE HUMANITY OF GOD

THE HUMANITY OF GOD

Edmond Barbotin

Translated by Matthew J. O'Connell

ORBIS BOOKS
MARYKNOLL, NEW YORK

Originally published by Editions Aubier, Paris, France
Manufactured in the United States of America

Library of Congress Cataloging in Publication Data

Barbotin, Edmond.
The Humanity of God.

Translation of Humanité de Dieu.
Includes bibliographical references.
1. God—Biblical teaching. I. Title.
BS544.B3713 231 76-304
ISBN 0-88344-1845

CONTENTS

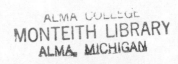

ABBREVIATIONS

Denz. Denzinger, H. *Enchiridion Symbolorum*, 32nd edition, revised by A. Schönmetzer, Fribourg:Herder, 1963.

PG *Patrologiae cursus. . . Series graeca*, Paris: Migne, 1857–1866.

PL *Patrologiae cursus. . . Series latina*, Paris: Migne, 1844–1864.

TCT Clarkson, John, et al., trans. and eds., *The Church Teaches: Documents of the Church in English Translation*, St. Louis: B. Herder, 1955.

For the biblical quotations the New American Bible translation has generally been followed. Exceptions are as follows:

JB *The Jerusalem Bible*, Garden City, N.Y.: Doubleday, 1966

NEB *The New English Bible with the Apochrypha*, New York: Oxford University and Cambridge University Press, 1970

RSV *The Holy Bible, Revised Standard Version*, Camden, N.J.: Nelson.

Smith-Goodspeed *The Complete Bible: An American Translation*. The Old Testament trans. J.M. Powis Smith, et al., the Aprochrypha and the New Testament trans. Edgar J. Goodspeed, Chicago: University of Chicago Press, 1939.

Vg. Vulgate reading.

THE HUMANITY OF GOD

INTRODUCTION

. . . the kindness and love of God
our savior appeared. . .
Paul to Titus 3:4

An anthropological approach to the Christian mystery requires some justification.

The enterprise can indeed seem paradoxical. After all, the God who reveals himself is the Most High, the Wholly Other; his transcendence is absolute and his plan of salvation, "hidden for many ages" (Rom. 16:25), continues to be mysterious at every stage of its unfolding. God does not cease to be God in making himself known to man, nor does the redemptive Incarnation of the Word in any way lessen his inalienable equality with the Father. Furthermore, man's faith in Christ the savior is not a purely human belief in whose attainment the Christian has the sole initiative; it is, instead, the commitment of a human freedom that has been called, enlightened, and moved by grace. In its origin, faith is God's gift (cf. John 6:44; 10:26–29; also Luke 17:5; Eph. 2:8; Phil. 1:6,29; Council of Orange, canons 5–6, *TCT*, pp. 226–227; Vatican I, session 3, chapter 3, *TCT*, p. 29). Every attempt, therefore, to approach the Christian mystery by way of man's knowledge about man—in particular with the aid of a concrete anthropology[1]—would seem rash if not irreligious, and at best doomed to failure.

However, without prejudice to further discussions, one decisive consideration imposes itself upon us. If the transcendent God reveals himself to Isarel, it is to come "nearer" to man than any god of the "nations" had ever come (Deut. 4:7; cf. 12:15; 1 Kings 8:10–29; Isa. 55:6; Ezek. 48:35; Pss. 119–151; 145:18). Even more significantly, the movement of divine prevenance finds a fulfillment beyond all expectation in the Word made flesh who has come to dwell "among us" (John 1:14); in him man and God meet in the closest possible proximity and forever. The one divine person of the Son holds the two partners in this encounter in an embrace so total that they constitute but one being. Christ is God's "Yes" to man and man's "Amen" to God (2 Cor. 1:20). God will not, indeed cannot, approach man in a more intimate way. Similarly, Christ's preaching is chiefly concerned with the "nearness" of the kingdom (Matt. 4:17; cf. 3:2; Mark 1:15; Luke 10:9–11). The result of the redemptive Incarnation is that pagan and Jew are drawn near to each other in order to be reconciled with God in one body (Eph. 2:13–22). It is now man's responsibility to approach God who has drawn near in Jesus Christ, so that the saving encounter may take place (James 4:8; Heb. 11:6; cf. Zech. 1:3; Mal. 3:7). In the man whom God's grace has touched, this process is the process of conversion (*metanoia*) which leads him to believe in the Good News (Mark 1:15).

This "turning around" of the spirit presupposes a knowledge of the salvation offered. That does not mean great learning or an esoteric wisdom, for the gospel is meant for all mankind (Matt. 28:19–20; Acts 1:8–9; 1 Tim. 2:4). Strictly speaking, only the hearing of the word is necessary (Luke 1:77; Rom. 10:14–15). But the proclamation of the Good News and the salvation it engenders become a historical reality in two different ways. Some men had the privilege of drawing near to Jesus Christ in his lifetime on earth, of living as his familiars, seeing him, and hearing the proclamation of salvation from his own mouth; in short, of resting their faith on personal experience (John 19:35; 1 John 1:1–3 cf. Acts 1:8,21,24; 2 Pet. 1:16–18). The vast majority of men, on the other hand, must come to know Jesus Christ through the testimony of eyewitnesses who became servants of the Word (Luke 1:1; Acts 4:20), and must believe without having seen (John 20:29). In both cases, knowledge of the message prepares for and evokes the commitment of faith, without making it any the less free.

The Christian Fact as Object of Science

As received from trustworthy witnesses (John 19:35) and transmitted by tradition down through generations of believers, the Christian fact is not merely the object of that initial proclamation (the *kerygma)* which makes possible a man's first adherence to Christian teaching and the conversion of his life; for the fact presents a plurality of aspects and a multiform intelligibility which open several avenues of approach to the mind, stimulating study and reflection.

Insofar as it is committed to writing in the inspired texts, the proclamation of salvation becomes the object of the philological disciplines: paleography, linguistics, textural and literary criticism. As an historical fact, Christianity offers another kind of intelligibility, and with all the resources of modern science the historian sets about building up a picture of Jesus in the context of his times. As a word spoken by God to men, the Christian message requires interpretation if God's meaning is to be determined as accurately as possible. Finally, theological science gathers the scriptural data and its interpretation by ecclesial tradition and by the magisterium which is the organ of that tradition, and tries to render a reflective account of the content of revelation and to impose a rational order upon it. All these diverse disciplines are intended to be no more than intellectual approaches to Christianity; they enlighten the mind without either dispelling the mystery of God as savior or forcing the commitment of faith upon men. That commitment takes place independently of the conclusions of science, not as a leap into the absurd but as a spiritual choice deliberately made in full awareness of both its rational grounds and its risks.

The disciplines thus devoted to the study of the Christian fact have in common that they are sciences; their aim, therefore, is the strict and impersonal objectivity of every scientific undertaking. This goal is determined by the object of the study and by the requirements of reason and faith alike. On the one hand, Christianity is an historical fact and, as such, has a real "objectivity." On the other hand, reason has the inalienable right and duty to acquire as exact as possible a knowledge of that fact under all its aspects and thus to determine its content and meaning. Christian faith, finally, calls for the same strict discipline and has always imposed it on itself, so as to avoid degenerating into formless religiosity or the fantastic aberrations of a gnosis (in the modern sense of this term). The apostle Paul's well-known instruction to Timothy, "Guard what has been committed to you," underlines the objective nature of the datum, while also stressing the need for genuine knowledge: "Stay clear of worldly, idle talk and the contradictions of what is falsely called knowledge. In laying claim to such knowledge, some men have missed the goal of faith" (1 Tim. 6:20–21). The progressive development of Christian science, in the sense explained, is an important condition for the fidelity and growth of God's people.

The rigorous standards of science call for one fundamental attitude in the scholar: objectivity. But notwithstanding certain present-day confusions, let us not understand by that the illusory refusal to take a position with respect to religious truth. The unbeliever, no less than the believer, has freely exercised a spiritual option: his state is not and cannot be that of a pure reason—discarnate, free of any bond with a concrete human subject and supposedly protected by that very fact against all danger of bias. In any case, this fallacious concept of scientific objectivity—which vitiates so many discussions of "Christian" science and philosophy—is contradicted *de facto* by the multiple interpretations of Christianity provided by non-Christian scholars: for if unbelief were a guarantee of perfect objectivity, should it not lead to unanimity?

Moreover, a science which would be satisfied with connecting the Christian fact with its historical antecedents and consequents, without seizing its religious vision, would not exhaust its whole intelligibility. Our earlier remarks[2] on the necessity of joining understanding to explanation showed that over and above purely objective scientific knowledge, there must be a grasp of concrete intentionality if we are to fully understand a cultural phenomenon. If a living comprehension is indispensable to the understanding of a philosophical system, how much more is it required in approaching a religious message of salvation—particularly one that presents itself as always contemporary? On the other hand, a superficial view might lead us to think that since the age of the great Christological controversies is over, the Incarnation is a datum which has been drained of its content of truth, that it is "finished business." On the contrary, apart from the fact that the Christian faith must always come to grips with its object, an existential approach based on the data of philosophical anthropology reminds us that the Christian mystery is a radical and abiding challenge to man and to the world. This fundamental truth calls for exploration at a deeper level.

The Christian Fact as Revelation of the Divine Subject to Created Subjects

The God who reveals himself in the Bible is not the Platonic idea of the Good nor Aristotle's First Mover or Thought of Thought, nor Taine's eternal Axiom; in short, he is not a solitary and impersonal first priniciple. The God of Israel and of Jesus Christ reveals himself as a Subject to other subjects. In the basic proclamation of Exodus, "I am who am" (Exod. 3:14), there is as strong an affirmation of the divine personality as there is of the supreme Being, and this is true whatever the translation adopted for the Hebrew words. Yahweh is the absolute Subject who addresses created subjects, that is, men. He is the God of the Fathers, of Abraham, Isaac, and Jacob, and through the mouth of Moses he extends an invitiation to the Hebrew people, offering a covenant which will make of it "his people" among all the peoples of the earth. Throughout the course of Israel's history, the prophets will ceaselessly call the chosen people back to "their God" and will condemn transgressions of the Law as infidelities. The mutual relations here involved are personal in character. Indeed, was not the marriage covenant the most perfect expression Israel could find for its relationship to the Most High?

In Jesus Christ the revelation of the personal God is continued and reaches its climax. "The Word became flesh and pitched his tent among us" (John 1:14; literal translation)[3] near to men and sharing their everyday existence. This man Jesus, the carpenter's son, whose mother, Mary, and "brothers" and "sisters" (Matt. 13:54–57) people know, deliberately applies to himself on several occasions the unqualified statement that God used in revealing himself to the Fathers: "I am." His hearers are not misinterpreting him when they accuse him of blasphemy and want to stone him.[4] Thus it is no longer through a borrowed humanity (that of the prophets) but through a humanity strictly his own that the Son reveals God (Heb. 1:1–2). The Most High thus introduces himself into the fabric of living, intimate relationships through which we are linked to the world and inscribed in the records of history.

But this physical nearness to men is only a means to an approach at a deeper level. For God also reveals himself by entering through his humanity into the dynamic interplay of personal relationships, into that living interrelatedness of man to man which makes of other persons the other existential pole of each man's being. If for the religious consciousness of Israel the events at Mount Sinai were the fundamental encounter of God with his people (Exod. 9:17; cf. 5:3; Hos. 12:10), all the more, then, does God's manifestation in the flesh (1 Tim. 3:16)—his effort, as it were, to make himself accessible to all of man's senses (1 John 1:1–3; Luke 24:38–40; John 20:24–29; etc.) and his total sharing of the human condition from birth to death (Phil. 2:6–8) and even beyond death in the resurrection (cf. Acts 1:3–4; 10:41 and also the Gospels)—constitute the perfect and definitive encounter. Rather, we might say: The perfect encounter is someone named Jesus Christ. Henceforth, between each man, on the one hand, and God manifested in the flesh, on the other, relations of a kind inaccessible to reason are established: these bonds nothing shall ever break (cf. Rom. 8:35–39). Every human consciousness, because it is in reciprocity with the human consciousness of Jesus, is called to enter into personal relations of faith and love with the personal God who calls men to salvation.

Thus all the human means of expression and communication are taken to himself by the Son authentically and with a sovereign freedom. In revealing himself to Israel through the prophets, God had already made use of all the languages with which he had endowed man. Word, gesture, symbolic action, silence, and the conjugal and familial life of the emissary all become expressive of what God wills to reveal.[5] In Jesus Christ these diverse means of communication are directly assumed with the humanity which the Word makes his own. Actions, gestures, declarations, silences, attitudes in the face of suffering, joy, and the death of others; work, rest, prayer, visits, shared meals, suffering, resurrection; and, in each situation, the living presence of this man with his face and gaze: everything in him is a sign and reveals God. Or, to put it better, the Sign of God par excellence is Christ. No other sign superior to this or independent of it can or will ever be given. Here there is inexhaustible depth of meaning, for the Most High declares himself in this presence which is accessible to the eyes of men. Two parallel declarations sum up the mystery: "Whoever looks on me is seeing him who sent me" (John 12:45) and "Whoever has seen me has seen the Father" (John 14:9).

In Jesus Christ, then, the human means of *expression* and *communication* become means of revelation and will be, for the disciples and the whole Church, means of *bearing witness*.

Thus God applies a pedagogy which the human mind would never have conceived; for, while surrendering nothing of his transcendence, he reveals himself to man in ways that are the most obvious and near at hand and the only ones which are universally accessible. God speaks the language of his human interlocutor. Just as a man must speak French to a Frenchman if he is to be understood, so God speaks "man" to man. Christ makes our experience his own, and his language grows out of that experience. Above and beyond all cultural, linguistic, and social divergences and on this side or the other side of discourse, God will henceforth reveal himself through the silent language afforded by similar physical structure, by mutual presence, and by the reciprocal intentionality of faces, gazes, hands, and attitudes; in short, through all those means of expression which manifest one man to another. The body and the human consciousness of Jesus Christ have now become the privileged place of encounter and of the living dialogue between the divine Subject and every human subject down to the end of history.[6]

Understanding of the Christian Fact

The understanding the Christian mystery calls for is, then, in its point of departure, of the anthropological order—an approach which all men, whether or not they are instructed in the findings of the religious sciences, can and always must adopt.

From the moment the Son of God becomes man and makes the plan of salvation known through the media supplied by his humanity, we must know man in order to discover the divine intentions. The living and lived meaning of our basic human behaviors must be grasped in order that their meaning in Jesus Christ should be discovered by faith. What is the point of saying that God has entered the world and history if you have not grasped what it means for man to be situated, willingly or not, in space and time? What is the point of saying that God has spoken to men through the prophets and addresses them in Jesus Christ if you do not have a very concrete grasp of what speaking means? How can you grasp the meaning of the Lord's Supper and the Eucharist if you do not grasp the existential meaning of shared bread with its implications for community? The Incarnation forces me to ask about man if I am to have access in faith to the Christian mystery. I must learn the language by which God reveals himself, that is, I must *learn man*, if I am to approach God. Once I am instructed in the various means of expression supplied by consciousness as the ever active source of meaning, I will be able to grasp the divine intentions which are manifested in the humanity of the man from Nazareth. Once I am capable of interpreting the universal sign which is man, I will be ready to decipher the privileged sign of God: the man Jesus Christ (1 Tim. 2:5). *I will move from the humanity of man to the humanity of God.* Each individual can thus discover in the God-Man the other pole, at once close at hand and transcendent, of his own fragile existence; he can experience the reciprocity between himself and Christ present, speaking, and acting; in Christ he can find his own life again, enriched with a new, divine meaning. In short, I recognize in Jesus Christ the fellow man beyond all others, the one who is, beyond comparison, a "man with me." I pass along this true and living way to reach the divine Thou who calls me to salvation (John 14:4–6).[7] We might sum up the anthropological approach to the mystery of God by adapting the Socratic motto: "know yourself in order to recognize yourself in Jesus Christ."

If we are thus to reach the God who is the Wholly Other, who is saving Love, we must in particular have a sense of the incalculable potentialities of the human, of love, and of the mystery of the person. An acquaintance with history and literature, therefore, is called for and a respect for art and for all the divers ways in which man's creativity and his capacity for disinterested love find expression. All this will be needed if we are to surmount the "epistemological obstacle" set up by the positivist mentality. A grasp of the meaning of man thus proves to be a "preamble of the faith"—that is, in the present context, a psychological condition required for the acceptance of the Christian mystery. Unless we have a living understanding of man (and this means a genuine humanism, wisdom, and profound culture) we shall not be able to enter into communion with the divine "philanthropy" that is manifested in Jesus Christ (Titus 3:4).[8]

Such a process is, however, only an approach; it can neither substitute for nor produce the act of faith, nor even lessen in any way its opposite characteristics of being both a free choice and a grace from God. Conversion is on the hither or further side of this process of understanding as it is of objective knowledge, for the human subject must recognize that he has been personally addressed by the divine Subject and must formulate the acceptance which faith is. Pascal notes the necessity of an anthropological approach (in the broadest sense of the word) when he writes: "A fine thing to yell at a man who does not know himself to find the way to God alone!"; but he hastens to stress the limitations and ambiguity of such an approach, by adding: "And a fine thing to say it to a man who does know himself!"[9]

In return, once Jesus Christ is recognized and accepted, he reveals man to himself. Pascal, once again, pointed this out.[10] Once God and man are forever united in the incarnate Word, the discovery of the one is inseparable from the revelation of the other. The meaning of God and the meaning of man go together. In Christ's humiliations man recognizes his own wretchedness; in the glory of the resurrection and ascension, the pattern presented for his own (cf. Phil 3:21; Rom. 8:29; Col. 3:4; 1 John 3:2).[11]

Beyond the new meaning which mankind as a whole receives from Jesus Christ, each individual human person receives an impetus to become more fully himself. Every human associate is for me something more than just someone like me or near me; he is also a source of my own being, insofar as he brings me to affirm my own uniqueness.[12] It is, in fact, only in confrontation with another person that I can consciously adopt an authentically personal attitude. Much more, then, does the divine Thou, having become a man, summon me to enter into my own innermost depths. The transcendent Subject develops in me, whether or not I am aware of it, the vital consciousness and powers of my subjectivity. I am never more fully my own, never more responsible for my own destiny, than when I take a position in face of God and his offer of salvation in Jesus Christ. Christ's consciousness and his humanity, which are reciprocal with my own, touch me at a depth to which no others have access. Those, therefore, who are commissioned to preach God to man must, if they are to fulfill their commission, preach man to himself.

The revealed datum can and must be read in the light of our own human experience. This is not, however, to say that the datum can be simply reduced to subjectivist interpretations. We would like to bring out this point in the face of the purely "existentialist" interpretations of a Bultmann or a Robinson.[13] Not only must historical method be respected, but *we can speak of Revelation only if we acknowledge that God has the initiative in creating meaning.*

Objections

An anthropological approach to the Christian mystery can be challenged on various grounds.

First, it will be objected that the dimensions of our experience of man are extremely narrow. If we take this limited experience as our point of departure, shall we not be running the risk of measuring the revelation God makes of himself according to our meager knowledge of ourselves? And will not God's word then be reduced to the scope of man's commentary on man?

In reply it must be said that we are offering here an approach and nothing more. But my own experience and the reciprocity that links me with Jesus Christ do not deform God's revelation any more than do the words which the whole Bible uses. Those words are points of departure which the thrust of faith must soon transcend. The humanity I see both in myself and in the God-Man is a way, the Way which God himself offers me for approaching him; it is not a terminus (cf. John 14:6).[14] It is a passage, a "Passover," and therefore a test, a sign offered to senses and spirit as support for a vision of faith. Man, who is flesh, must pass through the flesh of Jesus if he is to reach what he cannot attain by himself: the transcendent divine reality which condescends to open itself to him. It is true that the flesh of itself is only flesh (John 3:6; cf. 1:13); it is the source neither of revelation (Matt.

16:17) nor of life (John 6:63), and becomes a means of salvation only by the unpredictable, freely given, divine power of the Spirit *(ibid.)*.[15] The mystery of God thus loses none of its transcendence but on the contrary affirms it in an unparalleled way, when it adopts a means so lowly (frail mortal humanity) that it can have no pretensions with regard to God. If on the other hand the means adopted were great and wonderful in men's eyes, then they would indeed risk compromising the revelation of the divine transcendence by fixing men's attention on themselves.[16] An anthropological approach therefore simply follows the path opened up by God himself; it allows the infinite mystery of God to shed its light through the finite mystery of man. Unless we are to profess docetism and set limits to the living reality and full consistency of the humanity of Jesus Christ (cf. 1 John 4:2–3), then it is " in the flesh" that men are to reach the "Word" (cf. John 1:14). Finally, as we will have occasion to demonstrate, the limitations of the means of expression are necessary if revelation is not to be degraded into an "exhibition" and the mystery to be profaned.

Another objection can be raised which is really a particular instance of the first. It may be said that the use of anthropological data is illegitimate inasmuch as science, for all its spectacular progress, is still remarkably ignorant concerning man. The biological, psychological, and philosophical sciences discover new depths as they move forward, with the result that each new discovery is offset by the new evidence it provides of our ignorance. Whether we are dealing with our spatiality or temporality, word or gesture, life or death, there are countless unanswered questions which still call for years, even centuries, of research. Furthermore, who knows whether we shall ever have exhaustive and definitive answers? If, in such conditions, we discuss the meaning of human activities before inventorying the whole psycho-physiological and social substratum, are we not, as philosophers, supposing that answers exist where there are really still only problems? All the more, then, if we use such anthropological knowledge as an approach to the Christian mystery, are we not, as theologians, trying to clarify the obscure in terms of the more obscure, and the mysterious in terms of the unknown?

It is indeed certain that though the sciences which investigate man have learned a little, or even a great deal, there is much more of which they are ignorant. No one can claim to know perfertly "what is in man" (cf. John 2:25), whether the human organism or the psyche is in question or the highest forms of mental activity: art, morality, and religion. Man does indeed prove inexhaustible to himself and must largely remain an unknown. If it could be totally inventoried, the human would be only a thing; the manifold progress of civilization would have nothing to stimulate it and would even lose its fundamental conditions of possibility.

In fact, however, the scientist need not hesitate to publicize his knowledge, limited though it is, or refuse to exploit it for making new discoveries. If we do not know everything about something, that is not to say that we do not know it at all. But that is not the real answer to the objection just raised. The real answer is that the viewpoint of objective science is not the only one, nor the primary nor the most common one, that we can adopt in approaching the world and man. Long before acquiring a scientific knowledge of the body, we have a living experience of it. Before the body is "known" or "scientifically understood," it is "lived," experienced, felt from within in the very act by which I exist. In everyday life, whether or not I am a biologist, I rightly speak of my body as I experience it, and this without prejudice to anything I may learn about the body later on from science. Furthermore, there are immediate and universal experiential data which science must take as its starting-point, even if it later reflects back upon them to determine them more accurately.

I am, therefore, not prejudging the future progress of science or speaking of something of which I am ignorant, when I say: the Son of God became a human being, lived, suffered, toiled, spoke, extended his hand, raised his eyes to others, and died on the cross. As a man, I know what it means to live, suffer, speak, and die. The scientist may ask whether the criterion for death should be derived from the heart or the brain. But the fact is that men die every day, and that with the cessation of the vital functions and the disappearance of the body, vital relations with the world and other men are broken off forever. Similarly, I do not have to resolve the debate about the corpuscular versus the wave character of light in order to understand Christ's words: "I am the light of the world" (John 8:12). It is enough that I know from experience the value of light for human life. We are dealing in such instances with ordinary meanings which everyone immediately grasps who is aware of the world, himself, and others. It is this way of universal human experience, not the way of science, that God adopts in order to reveal himself. However estimable the way of science is, it is never finished and, in addition, always reserved to a few. If God had revealed himself through science, Christianity would be a gnosis—that is, it would offer salvation through pure knowledge or a more or less scholarly initiation; we would be faced with an esoteric cult, and salvation would be offered only to a coterie of privileged individuals. In fact, however, the saving love of God embraces the whole human race (1 Tim. 2:4); he presents himself therefore in a form with which everyone is familiar, as a living man. Henceforth it is impossible that any man, whoever he is, should fail to encounter Jesus Christ at some turn in life's road, at some unforeseen moment in his life-history.

A still more radical objection (an instance of the objection formulated at the beginning of this Introduction) can be raised against our project. An *anthropological* reading of the Christian mystery, it may be said, is necessarily also an *anthropocentric* reading: that is, it locks man up in himself by enclosing him in the minute circle of his empirical existence; it really treats of man under the pretext of talking about God. The very language which such a process is forced to use brings this home: phrases such as "word of God," "hand of God," and "face of God" maintain man in immanence—within his own world—instead of opening him to transcendence. An *anthropological* language is *anthropomorphic* and hence inevitably *anthropocentric*.

The difficulty is both obvious and basic; it raises the question of the possibility of discourse about God and, beyond that, of the very possibility of a revelation of God to man. Without pretending to treat so vast a question here, let us at least set up a few guidelines.

A form of religion in which man was the center and the term, in which the relationship to God as Creator, Savior, and ultimate End of all things was excluded or strained almost to the breaking point, would not be Christianity. But the "humanness" of the Judeo-Christian revelation is something quite other than this, and moreover comprises a multiplicity of aspects. God reveals himself at the outset not by disclosing the mystery of his inner being but by showing what he is *in relation to* man: He is the God of Abraham, Isaac, and Jacob.

The Christian tradition has always stressed the close connection between "theo-logy" and "economy": the God of the Bible declares the "in itself" of his being in the "for us" of his saving design. God speaks *for* man's sake, therefore, and not for his own. He speaks *with* man, who is raised to the dignity of partner in the saving dialogue. He speaks *of* man at the same time as he speaks of himself. He speaks *through* man: the prophets under the old economy, the incarnate Son under the new (Heb. 1:1–2). Finally, God speaks *as* man. That is, the divine interlocutor does not hesitate to speak of himself as though he were subject to the servitudes belonging to our nature: it is written that God is angered, repents, sleeps, rises up.

In speaking of himself in this anthropomorphic way, God indeed brings himself close to us, but is his transcendence not thereby compromised? The Fathers of the Church, the theologians, and even the philosophers have always been much exercised about this fundamental problem. They are agreed in recognizing in it an effect of the divine condescension. Leibniz and Malebranche both use, very significantly, the term "anthropology" where we would use "anthropomorphism": significantly, because are we not, after all, dealing with a fully human *logos* or discourse? Leibniz notes that God "is willing to suffer anthropologies, and that he enters into social relations with us."[17] Malebranche writes: "Since Scripture is intended for everyone, the uninstructed no less than the learned, it is full of 'anthropologies.' Not only does it ascribe to God a body, a throne, a chariot, a retinue, and the passions of joy, sadness, anger, repentance, and other movements of the soul, but it also attributes to him the ordinary ways in which men deal with men, so that he may speak to the uninstructed in the most vivid way."[18]

Yet, whatever our first reaction, this condenscension entailed in the manner of its expression does not distort the content of the revealed message. The God who speaks after the fashion of men asserts sharply, forcefully, and constantly that he is the Most High and the Wholly Other. Furthermore, on many occasions the inspired writers use anthropomorphism in such a way that it can aim at nothing but the expression of the divine transcendence. If we say that God is "in heaven," the anthropological category "high" or "up" serves to affirm the inaccessible majesty of God.[19] If God intervenes in history "with . . . strong hand and outstretched arm" (Deut. 4:34; 5:15;

etc.), if he hides Moses in the hollow of the rock and covers the hollow with his hand; passes by and then removes his hand so that he may be seen only from the back (Exod. 33:18–23), it is always the infinite grandeur of God that is signified.[20] For the word transcends the vocable; the spirit, the letter; and the intention exercises a sovereign liberty with regard to the materials it uses.

Under the new economy a decisive change takes place in the way revelation is brought about. In sending his Son, "born of a woman" (Gal. 4:4), God takes the *form of man.* Henceforth it is no longer a question of an anthropology in the sense of a very human discourse about God: now it is no longer a way of *speaking* but a way of *being.* Anthropomorphic language is thus brought to fulfillment. It is at the same time done away with and carried to its ultimate limits. It is abolished as a stylistic form in becoming a reality. Faithful to his own terminology, but still more so to Christian truth, Malebranche notes this change by recognizing in the Incarnation a "kind of authentic and real *anthropology.*"[21] Anthropomorphism has become Someone. In this fashion, God in Jesus Christ takes the side of a Xenophanes and in his own person condemns anthropomorphic language.[22] The risk of error which accompanies too human a way of talking about God is eliminated. In virtue of the union of God and man in one person and of the "communication of properties" such a union legitimizes, I can say that God truly has a body, a hand, a face. Through the humanity of Christ, which mediates revelation, God comes to man in a sovereign movement of prevenance. It is therefore fully legitimate for man to travel the same road "in the opposite direction." An anthropological approach thus understood is only man's response to the divine initiative.

The fact that it is a response also preserves such a procedure from the danger of anthropocentrism. One would succumb to that danger if one claimed to define Christianity on the basis of man. But the Christian mystery cannot in fact be inductively established on the basis of human reality, any more than it can be deduced from a philosophical idea of God. For one thing, Christianity is an encounter and, as such, cannot be defined in terms of only one partner in the meeting. For another, the initiative in the encounter lies entirely with God, who summons man to reach beyond himself in order to respond to a prevenient love. The anthropological approach is a search for

God, not a dialogue of man with himself. Consequently all danger of error is removed: not only do we go to the Father only through Jesus Christ, but through Jesus Christ we go only to the Father. The movement is thus grounded and justified by the very humanity of God.[23] Though anthropological in its procedure, the movement is strictly *theocentric* in its *principle* (the divine initiative which elicits and sustains it) and in the *term* to which it tends.

Biblical Revelation and Anthropological Categories

Further light will be thrown on the points we have been discussing if we consider the characteristics of some of the categories used in revelation. It would be a mistake, of course, to ignore or minimize the historical character of these categories, linked as they are with diverse cultures very precisely situated in space and time. Thus the culture of the patriarchal period and those which underlie the wisdom literature or the theology of the Letter to the Hebrews differ from one another, even though the same religious tradition runs through them all. Let us leave to the historian and the exegete the primary concern for undertaking research and reflection in this area. Here we wish to note that biblical thought also makes use of universal anthropological categories, the role of which in all human languages we have discussed elsewhere.[24]

Everyone recognizes today that the Bible is not a book of science and makes no claim to present a systematic treatment of man and the world. The various cosmological conceptions to be found scattered through it are in no way intrinsically connected with the message of salvation. The biblical writer simply describes the world as his senses perceive it, and speaks of man as man experiences himself in daily life. The space and time in which he moves are not those of the scientist but those of man as "a being-in-the-world." In the same way, man's own body and his personal relations with other men provide religious thought and language with a concrete logic. The Bible raises *anthropological categories* to the rank of *theological categories.*

These observations have several important consequences. First of all, anthropological categories give the biblical message part of its universality. The Bible's universality is due primarily to the "existential" nature of its themes. Man of every age with his joys, anxieties, and hopes finds himself reflected in the Bible. But precisely because the modes of expression stay so close to lived experience, they guarantee the essential message an unfailing intelligibility. This is a critical factor to be kept in mind in an age when people repeat, often without thinking, the charge that the proclamation of salvation is not accessible to contempory man. In fact, after due account has been taken of historically conditioned elements in the Scriptures, the biblical message continues to be a "catechesis" in the etymological sense of the word: it can ring and resonate in the soul and awaken endless echoes there.

A second consequence is that the human element which is a constant factor in biblical language sets limits to the attempt at "demythologization" advocated by a Bultmann. It is undoubtedly true that some conceptions to be found in the Book are bound up with one or another particular cultural context. It is the role of the exegete and historian to situate these collective representations even if it means showing their relativity. But has one the right to declare "mythical"—that is, fabulous and legendary—everything that is not in accord with our scientific vision of the world? This position is in fact both related and diametrically opposed to the concordism of the last century. Related because in both cases the same postulate is at work: biblical language must be understood in accordance with scientific findings. Opposed because whereas concordism seeks to discover agreements in order to "save" revelation, "demythologization" puts revelation into Procrustes' bed and cuts off everything that contemporary science cannot guarantee. Let us observe in the first place that the postulate common to the two positions neglects the fact that scientific concepts are in a constant process of evolution. How, then, could we expect biblical language to be in accord with this continual growth and change? Moreover, to reject as "mythical" everything that is not "scientific" is the act of an intellectualist and rationalist mentality devoid of any sense of language and the categories of experience. Often it considers *mythical* what is simply *anthropological*. This kind of mentality would like, for example, the space in which biblical man moves to be that of mathematical physics, whereas it is in fact the space of man as he lived yesterday and lives today and utters the world as he experiences it. In a religious language purely rational in character, man, the concrete existent, would not recognize himself. For the most part there is an unmistakable natural harmony between biblical language and the language of our experience. Therefore one of the limits is set for "demythologization" (and this is said without prejudice to the respect with which science must treat what is given in the text) by the existence of universal anthropological categories. Some of our later discussions will give substance to that observation.

This does not mean that even the ethnologist and the historian of religions cannot find something of interest in an anthropological reading of Christianity. The comparative method endeavors, quite legitimately, to detect mutual dependences between diverse religious forms: to determine, for example, the influences exercised or undergone by Judaism or Christianity. At one time, scholars even spoke of Christian borrowings from the mystery religions and pointed to suggestive similarities. The claim is a legitimate and necessary object of research, but the scholar would be remaining on the surface of things if he were satisfied with an investigation conducted on the "horizontal" level for the purpose of establishing the existence of interactions. In reality there is a common stock of prereflective representations in which comparable yet independently formulated religious conceptions have their origin. If numerous systems of belief localize divinity "in heaven" and other powers in the "lower world," or if followers of various religions have a ritual meal, this does not permit us to conclude immediately to reciprocal influences. At the root of such representations and rites there are constant and very general anthropological factors which would allow for the full originality of each religious form. An exploration "in depth" and a constant attention to the most common categories of lived experience are indispensable for the historian and the enthnologist concerned with grasping phenomena not only in their materiality but in their living signification.

In the matter with which we shall be dealing, references to nonbiblical religious conceptions would have been of real interest. We have had to sacrifice them, however, so as not to produce too weighty a book.

Complementarity of Anthropological and Rational Language

The views we have been proposing must not lead the reader to think that anthropological expression alone can suffice for the study and formulation of the Christian mystery. As we noted earlier the need for objective science, so now we must acknowledge the need of conceptual language, which is the instrument of rationally ordered knowledge. It is true enough that we find few abstract terms in the Bible and that the prophetic and apostolic preaching, as well as patristic literature, often uses the language of experience and image. Nonetheless the theologian finds in rational discourse a support and guarantee of scientific accuracy. The proclamation of the message is one thing, the rational study of its content another. This development may be compared to the evolution of writing. In the course of its history, writing gradually moved away from the image (pictogram, ideogram) to become purely conceptual. Similarly, theological thought emancipated itself from the symbol and acquired a rational, analytic mode of expression, wholly dedicated to conveying meaning. Even the catechist must keep this language in mind and deliberately use it.[25] It would be a mistake, then, to condemn the use of rational language on the grounds of its always possible and often real abuse, and to make the living quality of the Christian mystery a pretext for refusing all use of abstraction.

On the other hand, the theologian must not fail to realize the resources of concrete language, and especially the language of lived experience. For one thing, that kind of language conveys the existential implications of the Christian message. For another, the theologian must learn that an image can translate an idea in a strictly accurate way. Such elements of concrete theology as the New Testament uses have a very precise import. The "sitting at the right hand of God," for example, signifies, beyond any possible ambiguity, a perfect equality of nature and authority with the Most High.[26] Or again: nowhere in the Gospel does Jesus affirm his divinity in the language of rational theology, but he does do so in a concrete way, and so clearly that his adversaries are left in no doubt of his claim. Or again: in saying "I am the Way" and "I am the Door," Christ proclaims his universal mediatorship. These examples are enough to show that symbolic language opens the spirit to the superabundance of truth which the mystery contains and which no concept, however "open," can exhaust.[27]

We are faced here with the question, raised a few years back by Pie Duployé, of the relations between literature (poetic or symbolic language, in particular) and theology.[28] Future study will perhaps bring the elements of a solution of this difficult problem, but even now an *essay in concrete theology*, based on precise anthropological analyses, seems in some measure possible. Whether we are dealing with a rapid sketch or a more elaborated expression of the faith, all the resources of language can be employed (according to the circumstances of study or exposition) to give expression to a mystery which is to be the salvation of all men.

Limitations

The limitations of our project must be clearly defined.

Since the Word has assumed a complete humanity, the multiple aspects of human reality constitute as many ways to God. Since the very beginnings of Christianity, several anthropological approaches have in fact been used. The effort has always been made, for example, to make man aware of his deep needs and to show him that only the God of Jesus Christ can satisfy them. Was it not an approach of this kind that the apostle Paul was taking in his speech on the Areopagus, when he proclaimed to the Athenians the unknown God of whose existence they had a groping awareness without being able to name him? (Acts 17:16–33). An unbroken tradition in Christian apologetics, from the *Confessions* of St. Augustine down to Pascal and the Blondelian system of immanence, explores in man the desire for a supernatural order of salvation that is revealed in Jesus Christ.[29] Here we are limiting ourselves to a very modest undertaking: to help man to recognize in himself and in the Word made flesh that common experience of the world, of the body, and of the means of communication, that relationship to other men, which together constitute a bridge flung across the gulf between God and men.

The reader will not find an exegetical study in this book. Without in any way—need we say it again?—challenging the basic role of philological, literary, and historical criticism and of all the other forms of "objective" research, we shall confine ourselves to approaching the mystery in the light of living experience. Technical analyses and specialist discussions will therefore be omitted. The texts will be gathered and ordered exclusively in view of the goal which is sought. This necessity of selection will preserve us both from the illusory concern for being exhaustive and from that kind of literalism which is a betrayal of the authors' thought. We shall not be using either all the texts or only the texts in which terms like word, hand, or face are expressly found. The anthropological commentary also will be kept under restraint, given that *The Humanity of Man* has provided sufficient detail. On the other hand, the biblical texts will be liberally quoted for the convenience of the reader.

The Fathers of the Church, spiritual tradition, and the liturgies of the East and West all offer immense treasures for concrete reflection. We have had to limit ourselves to a few quotations, but these, we hope, will stimulate the reader to pursue the matter himself.

We must insist again—the issue is important—on the limitations of our project in relation to rational theology. There is no question of debating the necessity of the latter—indeed, the notion of trying to substitute for the effort of "explanation" a reading with a view towards pure "understanding" would be an aberration. The revealed datum has a manifold intelligibility which legitimates the various approaches the mind can and ought to take to it. Our purpose is simply to show, with the help of some particular themes, the anthropological intelligibility of Christianity.[30] A further project would be to establish systematically the harmony between the two outlooks and the two linguistic registers: objective and subjective, abstract and concrete, rational and imagistic.

Finally, we must avoid reading into the biblical datum a metaphysics, ancient or modern, that would be alien to it. More particularly, we cannot set up any philosophical doctrine, whether Platonism, Aristotelianism, Hegelianism, or any other system, as a *criterion* of the revealed datum. Objection has been raised on this account, and with justice, to Bultmann's proposed interpretation of Christianity in terms of Heidegger's philosophical categories.[31] This kind of approach is unacceptable from the viewpoint of historical criticism, for which interesting but always debatable philosophical principles can be taken as interpretive norms only by arbitrary fiat. It would be just as much of an abuse in the eyes of the believer, since a philosophy, being man's word, cannot arrogate the right to pass judgment on the sovereignly free word of God. The theologian in fact mistakes the services philosophy can render him if he asks too much or too little of it. The attitude of a Thomas Aquinas, for example, is quite different from the one we have just been describing, for he accepts revealed truths as unassailable first principles of theological science and uses the contributions of reason to manifest the intelligibility of the principles.[32] Aristotelianism is undoubtedly not the sole supplier of the rational instruments which the theologian requires; the Greek Fathers and Augustine, for example, sought them elsewhere. What is beyond question is that the philosopher's function is not to be judge of the revealed data and to decide what is to be kept and what rejected, but only to help faith to make a more precise inventory.

We shall make the effort, therefore, not to distort the biblical texts which we cite by introducing fanciful personal views. Our undertaking will consist in a very simple analysis of lived experience, to the exclusion of every systematic approach. We shall even avoid using the reflective method as we have used it elsewhere to pave the way to a theological understanding of Christian witnessing.[33] Such a sketch of a concrete theology will, we hope, be accessible to the reader, whatever his philosophical preferences might otherwise be. We must also note that, given our intention, there can be no question of a methodical study of biblical anthropology in its specificity, however useful such a study might in general be. While we occasionally draw attention to points in that area, we draw primarily on permanent and universal anthropological data.

The arrangement of the chapters will be parallel to that used in *The Humanity of Man*. A correspondence like that between the leaves of a diptych permits the use here of the analyses made in the earlier book. Since God in Jesus Christ takes to himself a complete humanity with the countless relationships in which it is involved, we shall be showing how man's situation in the world, his means of expression and communication, and certain interpersonal activities (the visit, the meal) are raised to a new level of meaning in the Christian mystery.

The internal structure of the chapters will not be uniform throughout. In most chapters the exposition follows the division of Old and New Testaments, so that the full scope of the progress of revelation emerges. In the two chapters on the word and the hand of God, however, the material is divided according to doctrinal themes, while the distinction between the two economies is used within each development of theme. The second procedure, which is made possible by the biblical data, offers another kind of analysis. In every case, the numerous perspectives in which the Christian mystery is viewed, and the various reading of the same texts and episodes should not be thought useless. For, whatever the viewpoint adopted, all the approaches converge upon the single, living center in which the Christian mystery is gathered up: Jesus Christ, Son of God, revealer and Savior.

NOTES

1. In the sense defined and applied in *The Humanity of Man.*
2. *The Humanity of Man*, pp. 5 ff.
3. On this text, cf. below, Chapter 1, note 27.
4. Cf. below, Chapter 3, note 51.
5. Cf. below, Chapter 3, section 7, "The Prevenient Word."
6. Cf. Yves Congar, O.P., *Jesus Christ*, trans. Luke O'Neill (New York: Herder and Herder, 1966), pp. 56–58, and, very especially, Antoine Chavasse, ed., *Eglise et apostolat* (Tournai-Paris: Casterman, 1957), pp. 54–85, 102–105.
7. St. Augustine, *Sermo* 181:4,4 (PL 38:777); "Walk by way of the man and you will reach the God."
8. Cf. Paul VI, Closing Discourse at Vatican II (December 7, 1965): "To know God we must know man." John A. T. Robinson, *The New Reformation?* (London: SCM, 1965), pp. 32–53, rightly insists on the special opportuneness of the anthropological approach today. We can agree with Robinson on this point even though the positions taken throughout the book call for very explicit reservations.
9. Pascal, *Pensées*, Fr. 509 (in Brunschvicg's numbering), trans. Martin Turnell, Pascal's *Pensées* (New York: Harper, 1962), Fr. 279, p. 183. (Henceforth, Pascal will be cited by the fragment number according to Brunschvicg, with Turnell's number and page in parentheses.)
10. Cf. Pascal, *Pensées*, Fr. 548 (Turnell, Fr. 602, p. 287).
11. Cf. Pascal, *Pensées*, Fr. 527 (Turnell, Fr. 383, p. 212): "Man's knowledge of God without awareness of his own wretchedness leads to pride. An awareness of his wretchedness without the knowledge of God leads to despair. The knowledge of Jesus Christ represents the middle state because we find in it both God and our wretchedness."
12. Cf. Maurice Nédoncelle, *La réciprocité des consciences* (Paris: Aubier, 1942), pp. 67ff.
13. The same subjectivist orientation characterizes Louis Evely, *The Gospels without Myth*, trans. J.F. Bernard (Garden City, N.Y.: Doubleday, 1971).
14. Cf. below, Chapter 1, section 12, "Christ the Way."
15. The same holds for the concepts with which we attempt to name God: they must be purified in the crucible of radical negation. The issue here is the important question of analogical knowledge. Cf. below, Conclusion, note 2,

and Charles de Moré-Pongibaud, *Du fini à l'infini* (Paris: Aubier, 1957).

16. Recall here Christ's numerous refusals of a messiahship in the temporal order. Cf. also 1 Cor. 1:17–3:4.

17. Gottfried Wilhelm Leibniz, *Discourses on Metaphysics*, trans. George Montgomery (Chicago: Open Court, 1902), Chapter 36, pp. 61–62.

18. Nicolas Malebranche, *Traité de la nature et de la grâce*, I, 58, in *Oeuvres complétes* (Paris: Vrin, 1958), Vol. 5, p. 62.

19. Cf. below, Chapter 1, section 2, "Yahweh Is 'in Heaven' " and section 10, "The Father Is 'in Heaven.' "

20. Cf. pp. 200–04.

21. Malebranche, *Traité*, Vol. 5, p. 62.

22. Cf. the statements of Xenophanes quoted below at the beginning of Chapter 5.

23. Cf. Karl Barth, *The Humanity of God* (Richmond, Va.: John Knox, 1960). Barth here corrects his earlier views of divine transcendence, which had been one-sided and too exclusive; he rightly observes that God is human in his very divinity: "It is precisely God's *deity* which, rightly understood, includes his humanity" (p. 46).

24. *The Humanity of Man*, Introduction, pp. 18 ff. and *passim*.

25. Cf. Edmond Barbotin, "Connaissance rationnelle et éducation de la foi," in *Catéchèse: Esprit et langage* (Paris: Fayard-Mame, 1968), pp. 111–21.

26. Cf below, Chapter 1, section 14, "Christ, 'Seated at the Father's Right Hand.' "

27. Cf. St. Thomas Aquinas, *Summa theologiae*, I, q. 1, a. 8.

28. Pie Duployé, O.P., *La religion de Péguy* (Paris: Klincksieck, 1965), pp. 1ff. Cf. also Hans Urs von Balthasar, *La gloire et la croix: Les aspects esthétiques de la révélation*, I: *Apparition* (Paris: Aubier, 1965); II: *Styles*, 1: *D'Irénée à Dante (ibid.*, 1968). Our study was almost completed before we discovered our frequent agreement with Balthasar's basic perspectives.

29. On Blondel, cf. Robert Saint-Jean, *Apologétique philosophique: Blondel, 1893–1913* (Paris: Aubier, 1966).

30. Other basic anthropological categories taken up by Christianity, e.g., fatherhood and sonship, call for more extensive study.

31. Cf. Léopold Malevez, *The Christian Message and Myth: The Theology of Rudolf Bultmann*, trans. Olive Wyon (London: SCM, 1958); René Marlé, *Bultmann and Christian Faith*, trans. Theodore Dubois (Westminster: Newman, 1968).

32. St. Thomas Aquinas, *Summa theologiae*, I, q. 1, aa. 1, 5, 6.

33. Edmond Barbotin, *Le témoignage spirituel* (Paris: Editions de l'Epi, 1964). This approach to the Christian mystery, which starts from a phenomenological and refletive study, is widely used today. Thus, to note but one instance among many, Jean Mouroux, *The Mystery of Time: A Theological Inquiry*, trans. John Drury (New York: Desclée, 1964), bases his theological study on an analysis of human time (pp. 61–81). The title of Maurice Nédoncelle's *Prière humaine, prière divine* shows a similar approach (the published English translation by A. Manson bears the titles *The Nature and Use of*

Prayer [London: Burns, Oates, 1962] and *God's Encounter With Man: A Contemporary Approach to Prayer* [New York: Sheed & Ward, 1964]). Several essays in *Problèmes actuels de Christologie* (Paris: Desclée de Brouwer, 1960) follow the same pattern. Here, as in *The Humanity of Man*, we are striving for "realism" through fidelity to the prereflective and empirical phenomenology of common sense which goes immediately "to the things themselves."

PART I

MEASURES OF EXISTENCE AND CHRISTIAN MYSTERY

Christian revelation occurs within the space and time that measure all aspects of human existence. Using the spatial and temporal categories of language, the Bible expresses the world as man experiences it. But the constant exchanges of meaning between man and the world are the vehicle here for expressions of a transcendent meaning. Above all, however, the Son of God through his incarnation makes his own all the relations we have with the universe; his human consciousness shares our experience and uses our languages and through these reveals the Father.

CHAPTER 1

HUMAN SPACE AND CHRISTIAN MYSTERY

Christianity requires of the person a radical existential reorientation, a conversion to himself which alone makes possible a conversion to God and the acceptance into himself of the divine presence.[1] From this point of view, Christianity seems indeed to be pre-eminently an interior religion, alien to spatiality as to a reality belonging to another order. Yet if Christianity is a mystery of interior conversion, it is also a mystery of incarnation in which spatiality is involved along with all the other aspects of human existence. The God of the Bible does not undergo any diminution of his transcendence when he assumes a humanity subject to the measures of space and time.

I. THE OLD TESTAMENT

God Transcends Space

When it states that in the beginning God created "the heavens and the earth" (that is, for biblical man, the whole universe), Genesis teaches in a definitive way the absolute transcendence of God in relation to cosmic space. The earth was created as "a formless wasteland." Heaven and earth together form a kind of empty space which the divine power will gradually fill and put into order (Gen. 1–2). The biblical tradition will never tire of repeating that God created "the heavens and the earth and . . . all that is in them," the vast container no less than what it contains (Exod. 20:11; Neh. 9:6; Ps. 24:1–2; 146:6; Isa. 42:5; Bar. 3:32–35; Acts 4:24; 14:15; Rev. 10:6). As creator, God transcends space.

Such transcendence does not mean separation or absence. On the contrary, since God the creator is sovereign lord of the universe, he is also present in all places. What Western philosophy will later call the divine "omnipresence" or "ubiquity" is expressed in the book of Wisdom in a forceful experiential and concrete way: "For the spirit of the Lord fills the world, is all-embracing, and knows what man says" (1:7).[2]

The inspired writers delight in mentally traversing the whole cosmos and finding God everywhere present: "Can a man hide in secret without my seeing him? says the Lord. Do I not fill both heaven and earth? says the Lord" (Jer. 23:24; cf. Bar. 3:24).

Wonderful above all is the meditation of the psalmist when he is seized with terror in face of the divine omnipresence:

> Where can I go from your spirit?
> from your presence where can I flee?
> If I go up to the heavens, you are there;
> if I sink to the nether world, you are present there.
> If I take the wings of the dawn,
> if I settle at the farthest limits of the sea,
> Even there your hand shall guide me,
> and your right hand hold me fast (Ps. 139:7–10).[3]

By the constant use of a literary device—the *dialectic of opposites*—the biblical writer sets the ultimate points of reference of our universe over against each other by pairing them. The heights and the depths, the regions of the sun's rising and its setting—all alike are filled with God.

With equal power and literary elegance, the psalmist acknowledges Yahweh's sovereign rule over the created world: "All that the Lord wills he does in heaven and on earth, in the seas and in all the deeps"

(Ps. 135:6; cf. Pss. 29 and 47),[4] and again: "In his hands are the depths of the earth, and the tops of the mountains are his. His is the sea, for he has made it, and the dry land, which his hands have formed" (Ps. 95:4–5; cf. Ps. 108:9–10; 1 Chron. 21:11).

Biblical thought thus embraces the universe in its totality by traversing its vertical and horizontal dimensions; it ranges from pole to pole in its play of contrasts between the ultimate points of reference of the world in order to report and, as it were, to exalt the God whose immensity transcends the whole earthly domain and every created dwelling place. Yahweh's sovereignty extends over all the paths the human spirit marks out for itself, and with them the whole space which these paths delimit. In short, we can say equally that God is everywhere or that he is nowhere: he is not in any place because no point can circumscribe him as in the case of man, who cannot be separated from place; he is present everywhere because his transcendence envelops the whole space.[5]

There is more to be said. These same spatial grandeurs supply a point of rest, a fulcrum as it were, for the vision of faith in its desire to raise itself to contemplation of the splendors of the divine perfections: "O Lord, your kindness reaches to heaven; your faithfulness, to the clouds. Your justice is like the mountains of God; your judgments, like the mighty deep" (Ps. 36:6–7)[6] or again: "his name alone is exalted; his majesty is above heaven and earth" (Ps. 148:3).

It is this very lesson which Zophar the Naamathite is concerned with teaching the unfortunate Job when he says, in a tone of sharp reproach: "Can you penetrate the designs of God? Dare you vie with the perfection of the Almighty? It is higher than the heavens; what can you do? It is deeper than the nether world; what can you know? It is longer than the earth in measure, and broader than the sea" (Job 11:7–9).

Thus all the dimensions of our world—height and depth, length and breadth—cancel each other out and disappear before God, for the divine perfection passes out of range of any known standard of measurement.

In the book of Isaiah, the same spatial imagery admirably expresses the mysterious grandeur of God's intentions towards his people: "My thoughts are not your thoughts, nor are your ways my ways, says the Lord. As high as the heavens are above the earth so high are my ways above your ways and my thoughts above your thoughts" (Isa. 55:8–9; cf. 40:12–20).

He who dwells in the inaccessible heavens is the God who is great above all the gods, who has no measurement in common with man and the world: the "transcendent One."

This is not an artificial language or one empty of intelligible content. Although abstract speculation is wholly lacking in it, this mode of expression has nevertheless a technical value since it is sanctioned by precise and constant usage. It speaks to every man because it is rooted in universal everyday human experience. Lastly it is an existential language, since it has for its substructure the primordial relations linking man to his world. But the thought is not the captive of its own instruments. By the use of literary devices adapted to the purpose, spatial language succeeds in expressing the nonspatial, what is "without measure." With the aid of imagery borrowed from the world of "immanence" biblical man conveys the meaning of authentic "transcendence."

The sovereign rule of God over created space is asserted again, and in the same fashion, when the issue is the economy of the *plan of salvation* and the preaching of the *judgment* in which that plan will culminate.

The divine plan of salvation transcends and envelops the universe in all its dimensions. Yahweh asserts his mastery of the whole world by liberating Israel from the Egyptian captivity and promising, then giving, it a land which will be its own, whether or not it is now the possession of neighboring peoples (Gen. 12:1,7; 17:8; 28:13; Exod. 3:8,17; cf. Exod. 19:5; Deut. 6:3; 8:7–8; Josh., *passim;* Ps. 60:8–10). Yahweh also affirms his mastery by proclaiming the return and reunion which will follow upon the testing of dispersion and exile (e.g., Isa. 60 and 62; Ezek. 11:16–21; 40–48). A constant theme of prophetic preaching is that Yahweh will gather his people from all the points of the horizon, however distant they may be. Recall the beautiful passage in the *Book of Consolation:* "From the east I will bring back your descendants, from the west I will gather you. I will say to the north: Give them up! and to the south: Hold not back! Bring back my sons from afar, and my daughters from the ends of the earth" (Isa. 43:5–6; cf. 49:12; 60:4; Jer. 29:14; 31:8; Bar. 4:37; Zech. 8:7–8).[7] In like fashion, Yahweh's judgment falls upon the whole vast universe, and all creation is summoned before his tribunal: "God the Lord has spoken and summoned the earth, from the rising of the sun to its setting. From Zion, perfect in beauty, God shines forth. . . . He summons the heavens from above, and the earth, to the trial of his people" (Ps. 50:1,4; cf. Ps. 65:6–8; 75:7–8; 76:9–10).

Thus every man, where he is, even in the inaccessible retreats of sky or abyss, is reached by the hand and the decrees of the sovereign judge. The idea is given forceful expression by the prophet Amos: "No survivor shall escape. Though they break through to the nether world, even from there my hand shall bring them out; though they climb to the heavens, I will bring them down; though they hide on the summit of Carmel, there too I will hunt them out and take them away; though they hide from my gaze in the bottom of the sea, I will command the serpent there to bite them"(Amos 9:1–3).

The wise man, therefore, has no difficulty in showing how foolish man is to think he can elude God's gaze: "Say not: 'I am hidden from God; in heaven who remembers me?' . . . The roots of the mountains, the earth's foundations, at his mere glance, quiver and quake" (Ecclus. 16:15,17).[8]

He whose masterful presence fills all the dimensions of cosmic space is also present in the world of men to raise up the weak and oppressed: "From the rising to the setting of the sun is the name of the Lord to be praised. High above all nations is the Lord, above the heavens is his glory. Who is like the Lord, our God, who is enthroned on high and looks upon the heavens and the earth below? He raises up the lowly from the dust, from the dunghill he lifts up the poor to seat them with princes, with the princes of his own people" (Ps. 113:3–8; cf. Ps. 138:6; Isa. 57:15). Anna, the mother of Samuel, voices the same act of faith (1 Sam. 2:1–10; cf. Luke 1:51–52).

In short, divine transcendence and divine condescension are inseparable. He who rules in the heights of heaven and the depths of sea or earth, also rules the whole *ordered body of society* and molds it at will to the advantage of the humblest.

The spatial universe, then—heaven and earth and distant isles—and all creatures are invited to rejoice and to praise the sovereignty and judgments and the salvation which these bring: "Say among the nations: The Lord is king. He has made the world firm, not to be moved; he governs the people with equity. Let the heavens be glad and the earth rejoice; let the sea and what fills it resound; let the plains be joyful and all that is in them! Then shall all the trees of the forest exult" (Ps. 96:10–12; cf. Ps. 97:3–6,9). Or again: "All the ends of the earth have seen the salvation by our God. Sing joyfully to the Lord, all you lands; break into song; sing praise" (Ps. 98:3–4, cf. 7–9; Ps. 66:1–4; 100:1; 148; Dan. 3:52–90).

Not only the universal prayer of praise but the universality of the sacrificial cult should respond to the omnipresence of God: "From the rising of the sun, even to its setting, my name is great among the nations; and everywhere they bring sacrifice to my name, and a pure offering" (Mal. 1:11).[9]

We may conclude by saying that the whole of cosmic space, in all its dimensions, is dominated by the God of infinite majesty. But this mastery of the Creator is experienced as at once sovereign lordship and intimate presence. The more total God's dominion over his creatures, the closer he is to them. This intuition is accurate and profound. Later on, the language of rational theology will say that transcendence and immanence are directly proportionate to each other: the two attributes are but complementary and inseparable expressions of the infinite excellence of God.

Yahweh Is "in Heaven"

The human body is orientated in space. My feet steady me on the earth, my head is lifted towards the firmament. This orientation reproduces in my being itself the structure of the universe; and I, in return, give these structures a well-defined existential meaning. Language, therefore, having the source of its being in man himself, bears the impress of spatiality.[10]

Biblical man is subject to these universal laws and his faith is spontaneously expressed in anthropological categories. Yet a mastery of the resources of language enables the writer also to express the irreducible originality of the revealed message.

The limitless excellence of God finds its natural expression in terms of elevation. Yahweh is so far superior to his creatures in perfection, power, wisdom, and so on, that it is his nature to be the "Most High," "elevated" above all else. These attributes even yield a proper name for Yahweh: "You alone bear the name Yahweh, Most High over the whole world" (Ps. 83:18,JB).[11]

The dwelling of the Most High, therefore, is necessarily the inaccessible heavens, unlimited and everywhere present (cf. Ps. 19:5), while man's dwelling place is the earth: "Heaven is the heaven of the Lord, but the earth he has given to the children of men" (Ps. 115:16).[12]

In this conception there is an affirmation of the creator's sovereign mastery in bending to his will the tremendous powers of the cosmos: "You have spread out the heavens like a tent-cloth; you have constructed your palace upon the waters. You make the clouds your chariot; you travel on the wings of the wind. You make the winds your messengers, and flaming fire your ministers" (Ps. 104:2–4).

If there is to be any place in the universe where the Most High makes himself especially present, that place will evidently be the most inaccessible summit, the privileged point where heaven seems to touch earth: the *mountain*. God's grandeur, his unassailable power, his fearful and compelling majesty all are "naturally" expressed by the mountain and find in it the most effective setting for any supernatural manifestation. The God of the Bible takes this anthropological constant into account. Sinai is thus the place where Yahweh reveals his glory and promulgates his law (Exod. 19–24). On many occasions, too, men offer sacrifice on the mountains, [13] while they wait for Yahweh to establish his dwelling on Sion, the holy mountain (1 Kings 3:1–3).[14] But however mighty and unshakeable they seem to be (Ps. 36:7), the mountains are still creatures. On the day of judgment, they tremble, melt like wax, and are broken up (cf., e.g., Ps. 97:5; 114:4–7; Jer. 4:24; Hos. 10:8 [cf. Luke 23:30; Rev. 6:16]; Hab. 3:6). Yahweh remains sovereign master of the heights no less than of the abyssal depths (Ps. 95:4).

Since God is so exalted in his perfection, religious man delights to acknowledge this limitless superiority; he "ex-alts" Yahweh in prayer of praise, even as he realizes that he can never raise Yahweh "high enough" in his own esteem or that of others: "Glorify the Lord with me, let us together extol his name" (Ps. 34:3; cf. Ps. 30:2; 145:1–3; 118:28; Exod. 15:2; Tob. 13:6; Jth. 16:1; Ecclus. 43:30). Or again: "be exalted above the heavens, O God; above all the earth be your glory!" (Ps. 57:6 [=Ps. 108:6]).

Unable to find words adequate to express how far God is exalted over himself and the world, man will make himself as little as possible in a total gesture which embraces his whole being, body and soul; before the Most High he bows, kneels, prostrates himself: "Come, let us bow down in worship, let us kneel before the Lord who made us" (Ps. 95:6); and elsewhere: "Extol the Lord, our God, and worship at his footstool; holy is he!" (Ps. 99:5).

The two approaches are correlative, or really only one. The more conscious man is of God's grandeur, the more he seeks to acknowledge it by making himself smaller before it. The abasement of the creature signifies the elevation of God by way of contrast. Even an inclination of the head lessens my stature and hides my face. If I kneel down, I reduce my height by a third. Yet, seeking a more radical avowal of my nothingness, I stretch out on the ground, renouncing the upright stance which is the specific sign of my dignity. Thus reduced to being almost nothing, I am yet at pains to apply my face to the ground in order to sacrifice my countenance itself, from which my human dignity radiates. I am now no more than an anonymous form, and I would like to sink into the earth, to permit myself to be absorbed in the abyss of my own nothingness. I "humble myself"—that is, I willingly make myself indistinguishable from the *humus* from which I was taken and to which I must return (Gen. 2:7; 3:19).

Abraham therefore sinks with his face to the ground when Yahweh appears to him (Gen. 17:3).[15] Tobias and his son prostrate themselves before Gabriel (Tob. 12:16), Ezekiel before the glory of Yahweh (Ezek. 1:28–2:1), and Daniel before the divine messenger (Dan. 8:17; 10:7–9,15). In this behavior, as in the liturgical rite of prostration, we have man's avowal of his own nothingness before God as expressed in an abasement of his whole being.

The presence of the Most High "in the heights," "in the heights of heaven" (cf. Luke 2:14; Matt. 21:9) determines another gesture of praying man, a gesture sometimes spontaneous, sometimes ritual, but always full of meaning: the lifting of hands or eyes. We know that between human subjects the encounter of hands and gazes, reciprocal with one another as they are, establishes a presence that is both physical and intentional and expresses the gift of self to one another.[16] In my desire to encounter the Most High, I must somehow raise myself above myself and the world, turn my heart, my hands, and my gaze to the place on high where God dwells: "Let us stretch out our hearts and hands to God in heaven" (Lam. 3:41,JB).

Thus the psalmist lifts his eyes to Yahweh in order to draw down his mercy: "To you I lift up my eyes, to you who are enthroned in heaven. . . as the eyes of servants are on the hands of their masters" (Ps. 123:1–2). At other times it is the hands that are raised up in supplication: "On the day of my distress I seek the Lord. By night my hands are stretched out without flagging" (Ps. 77:3; cf. Ps. 63:5; 119:48; 141:2). In this movement of hands and eyes, it is the prayer, it is the whole man in his deepest inwardness—his heart and soul—that are raised towards God (Ps.25:1; 86:4; 143:8).[17]

But it is not only towards heaven but also towards the "mountains" where Yahweh dwells, towards Jerusalem, that the faithful Israelite turns in fervent expectation of divine help: "I lift up my eyes toward the mountains: whence shall help come to me?" (Ps. 121:1). This, until the day when prayer "from a distance" no longer satisfies him and the movement of eyes and hands spreads to the whole body, drawing him to the ritual "ascents." Then the believer can, in a sense, "see" and encounter the Most High (Ps. 42:3). The effort is rewarded with joy, the joy of departure and of arrival as well: "I rejoiced because they said to me, 'We will go up to the house of the Lord.' And now we have set foot within your gates, O Jerusalem" (Ps. 122:1–2).

To this movement on the part of man, in his effort to raise himself up towards God, corresponds the inverse movement of "condescension" by which the Most High leans towards his servant. How often biblical man asks God to look upon his wretchedness, and how often he rejoices that the Most High has lowered his gaze to him! (1 Sam. 1:11; Ps. 33:13; 113:6).

This, too, should be said. In accordance with the logic of language, the interventions of the Most High in history are represented as "descents." If Yahweh comes to inspect the work at the Tower of Babel (Gen. 11:5), or manifests himself on Sinai (Exod. 19:18) or in a column of cloud at the opening of the tent (Num. 12:5), he "descends." Thus the psalmist prays when he invokes God's help: "Incline your heavens, O Lord, and come down" (Ps. 144:5; cf. Isa. 63:19). Thanksgiving for favors received often takes the same form (Ps. 18:10; 113:6). To the heavenly "up there," where God dwells, is opposed the "down here" of mortal men.

Finally, on the last day, when the sinner is forever abased, the Most High will be forever exalted:

> The haughty eyes of man will be lowered,
> the arrogance of men will be abased,
> and the Lord alone will be exalted, on that day.
> For the Lord of hosts will have his day
> against all that is proud and arrogant,
> all that is high, and it will be brought low.
> Yes, against all the cedars of Lebanon
> and all the oaks of Bashan,
> Against all the lofty mountains
> and all the high hills,
> Against every lofty tower
> and every fortified wall. . . ,
> and the Lord alone will be exalted, on that day (Isa. 2:11–17).

The orientation of the human body upwards and the meaning this gives to every natural elevation provide a basis for the felicitous expression of the eschatological mystery.

God Makes Certain Points in Space Privileged Places

Without ceasing to be present to the whole universe and without losing any of his transcendence, God reveals himself to men whom he has put into space and time. In so doing, the divine penetrates into human space and gives certain places a privileged character. These places bear the imprint of the encounters between man and the God who calls him to salvation.[18]

During their nomadic life, the patriarchs hear God's voice and worship him in many places whose memory is jealously preserved in the biblical tradition: Abram at the oak of Moreh near Sichem (Gen. 12:6–7), Isaac at Beersheba (Gen. 26:23–25), Jacob at "Bethel" (Gen. 28:10–22; 35:1–7), at "Peniel" (Gen. 32:31–32), and at Sichem (Gen. 33:18–20). During the Exodus, the great manifestations of Yahweh to his people, his glory shown in peals of thunder and lightning, consecrates Horeb forever as the "mountain of God." Here Israel is born as the people of Yahweh. The sovereign power of God, hitherto everywhere present but also everywhere hidden, bursts perceptibly and publicly into cosmic space and human space.

In the long pilgrimage of the Hebrews through the desert, the Tabernacle accompanies them from camp to camp. It is in this Tent, upon the outspread wings of the cherubim over the Ark, that Yahweh dwells invisibly and gives his oracles. Now that he makes use of this sanctuary which is moved from place to place, God is no longer satisfied with fleeting manifestations: now he dwells among his people (Exod. 25:8; cf. 2 Sam. 7:6–7), sharing their restless journeying over the face of the earth.

God Establishes His Dwelling in the Temple at Jerusalem

When Israel had conquered Canaan, the sanctuary acquired a fixed location after many vicissitudes, at Shiloh (Josh. 8:30–31; 24:1–18; cf. 18:1; 1 Sam. 1–4), and finally at Jerusalem, which had been taken by David (2 Sam. 6). It was left to Solomon to build the Temple of Yahweh (2 Sam. 7; 1 Kings 5:15–7:51).[19] Henceforth, the Glory and the Name dwell in this place that is privileged beyond all others; here is the abiding presence of Yahweh's eyes and ears and heart (1 Kings 8:10–9:9; Chron. 5–7); it is here that he listens to the prayers of his people and answers them and receives the homage of their sacrifices. Thus, here also is the center of the land that yesterday was promised and today is given; the focal point to which the eyes, the yearning, the faith, and the hope of Israel are drawn, and the goal of the periodic ritual pilgrimages (Exod. 23:14–19; Neh. 13:14; Tob. 13:9–17; Ps. 24; 26:8; 42; 43; 84; 122; 137; 138:2).[20] It is the privileged source of national and religious meaning for the whole of Israel.

But in thus penetrating into man's space, God loses nothing of his transcendence; he remains the God who is ruler of heaven and earth. Thus he declares through the prophet: "The heavens are my throne, the earth is my footstool. What kind of house can you build for me; what is to be my restingplace? My hand made all these things when all of them came to be, says the Lord" (Isa. 66:1–2).[21]

As a matter of fact, at each stage of Israel's history God initiates a more intimate manner of presence to his people. But this ever deepened presence is always accompanied by some indication of inviolable transcendence. Thus, for example, the very diverse manifestations of Yahweh to the patriarchs show his sovereign independence of the places where they worship him. The travels of the Ark through the desert help the Hebrews to understand that God is present not so much at this or that geographic point as where a believing and trusting people are found. Even the Temple could not make a prisoner of Yahweh, as Solomon humbly admits: "Can it indeed be that God dwells among men on earth? If the heavens and the highest heavens cannot contain you, how much less this temple which I have built!" (1 Kings 8:27). (The exclusive place for sacrifice does, however, effectively symbolize the fact that Yahweh is unique and superior to the numerous, quite "localized," gods of the "nations" [Deut. 12:1–14]). Finally, God himself tells Solomon that if Israel is unfaithful, the divine presence will abandon the Temple and leave it to be mocked by passersby (1 Kings 9:6–9; cf. 2 Kings 23:27). The preaching of the prophets will reiterate the same fearful threat (Mic. 3:12; Jer. 7:1–15; 26:1–24; Ezek. 10:18–19; 11:22–23).

The events of the destruction of the Temple and the ordeal of exile, therefore, combine in helping religious consciousness to achieve a fuller grasp of God's transcendence. Aided by the prophetic preaching, a displaced people sees the necessity of a worship that is more interior and spiritual, more detached from material supports. Yahweh himself now becomes the sanctuary of his people in a foreign land (Ezek. 11:16). The consequence is that when the return takes place and the Temple is rebuilt, monotheism (that is, the worship of a transcendent Yahweh) comes more strongly to the fore in Judaism (cf. Ezra and Nehemiah; Hag. 1:14–2:9; Zechariah, *passim).*

The Deuteronomist tradition, on the other hand, likes to insist on God's closeness to his people (Deut. 12:5–7, 11–12; cf. 30:11–14). The result is a certain tension between the distant God and the near God, between inviolable transcendence and benevolent closeness.

II. THE NEW TESTAMENT

In the Incarnation God Enters Personally into Human Space

With the same vigor and in the same terms as the Old Testament, Jesus teaches the transcendence of God and his unconditioned sovereignty over created space and all that it contains. The Father is

"Lord of heaven and earth" (Matt. 11:25); as Isaiah had preached, "heaven . . . is God's throne,. . . earth. . . his footstool" (Matt. 5:34–35; cf. Isa. 66:1).[22] He whom no place can contain is present through his sovereign power to the whole extent of the universe.

Nonetheless, without losing any of his transcendence, God assumes a human body that is situated in space and in time. The incarnation of the Son marks the mysterious personal entrance of God into cosmic space and man's world. The Word is therefore able to adopt for himself the anthropological categories of human language and to represent his action as a "coming": he had to cross not interstellar space but the infinitely more awesome distance which separates the Creator from the creature, the Holy one from the sinner.[23]

We have said that to be born is to enter into a spatial world by means of a body to which little space is meted out. In becoming man (John 1:14), in being born in a particular geographical place, Bethlehem, the Word accepts the limitations of spatiality. God is no longer content to honor one or other point on the earth's surface as in the divine manifestations to the patriarchs, or even to consecrate some portion of the world enduringly, to make it his Temple. By means of a humanity like ours, minute in its material dimensions and strictly localized in space, God in person assumes a "bodily place." After having been carried in Mary's womb, Jesus is born with the body of an infant; a few swaddling bands suffice to wrap him in and a manger is big enough to hold him (Luke 2:7). This smallness—so disproportionate—is even the distinctive sign, the criterion for identification, given to the shepherds (Luke 2:12, 16–17). The infant is carried to Egypt and brought back to Palestine; as an adult, he journeys from one village to another in the accomplishment of his mission: wherever he is, at rest or in movement, Jesus preempts for himself the portion of space required for any authentic human presence. At the end, a cross and a tomb like those of other men will take the measure of the man Jesus.

The thought of the believer, therefore, spontaneously resorts to the experience of the body as a "within" in order to express the mystery of Jesus. The term "in-carnation," which has its basis in Scripture (cf. 1 John 4:2; 2 John 7:1; Tim. 3:16; 1 Pet. 4:1) and is "objectively" appropriate, [24] is well adapted to convey the condition of a human consciousness which is involved in a body and experiences itself as an incarnated interiority. In opposition to an incipient docetism, the apostle John, and the Church with him, acknowledge as a true disciple only one who confesses "Jesus Christ as coming in the flesh" (2 John 7). The early Christian hymn recorded by Paul likewise commemorates Jesus "manifested in the flesh" (1 Tim. 3:16). Within a manhood as limited as any other "the fullness of deity resides in bodily form" (Col. 2:9).[25]

The Word made flesh submitted to the necessities of the human condition. Like any child, he progressively distinguished his bodily "I" from the environing "not-I" and became aware of his bodiliness through daily experiences: breathing, eating, moving about, working, becoming weary, and resting. He made his own the universal laws of growth and grew in stature as well as in wisdom and grace; he developed with reference to things and to other people (Luke 2:40,52). Present in the universe as an incarnated subject, he was constantly in the process of detaching himself from things through the consciousness he had of himself and, conversely, moving towards things in the use of them and in the achievement of his projects. Through all the vital powers of his being, Christ acquired an experience which was authentically human: the experience of being in the world by means of a body in which the circulation of meaning is incessant.[26]

Thus God entered personally into human space. The Temple at Jerusalem, holy and splendid though it was, was but a thing among other things; for, although the divine Glory dwelt there, it remained a building of stone and wood, devoid of ontological reciprocity with the man of faith. The Son of God, on the other hand, in becoming incarnate, takes to himself a body like ours and reciprocal with it. He enters not only the world of things but also, and above all, the world of men—that is, the field of our personal relations: the new, irreducibly different kind of space which the presence of man gives rise to in the heart of cosmic space. Here countless relations involving distance, neighborhood, moving away and coming together, constitute the substructure of the bonds of knowledge, love, and hostility between men. "The word became flesh and pitched his tent among us" (John 1:14; literal translation).[27] By the very fact of his birth the God-man asks men to welcome him into their midst, into that area, at once geographical and spiritual, which is their "world." But immediately—or rather, even before his birth—Jesus' request to share our human dwelling-place meets with refusal: Mary "laid him in a manger, because there was no room for them in the place where travelers lodged" (Luke 2:7). Pursued by Herod's hatred and forced into exile; later, in his public life, walking from village to village, having no place where he might lay his head (Luke 9:58); welcomed by some into the intimacy of their homes and rejected by others;[28] and, finally, thrust out of the world of the living, crucified outside the gates of Jerusalem (John 19:30; Heb. 13:12; cf. Matt. 21:39, and the instance of Stephen in Acts 7:58) and relegated to a tomb in the world of the dead—in all this, Jesus never paused in the acting out of his mission as a drama of acceptance or rejection that was simultaneously physical and spiritual. "He was in the world . . . yet the world did not know who he was. To his own he came, yet his own did not accept him. Any who did accept him he empowered to become children of God" (John 1:10–12).[29] In making room for Jesus Christ or excluding him from their world, men are deciding their own destiny.[30]

Objectivity and Subjectivity of the Man Jesus

The humanity of Jesus thus presents a reality which is at once objective and subjective. Inasmuch as he is situated in space and subject to all the measurements, limitations, and necessities belonging to bodies, Jesus exists side by side with things and lives among men as a fully objective reality. Before and after his resurrection, men see him, watch and stare at him, hear and listen to him, touch him and even feel of him: he falls under all the senses of man. For some of his contemporaries this was more than a matter of observation and experience: it amounted to experimental knowledge. With a testimony which is extraordinarily forceful the evangelists, as direct witness, assert this objective reality and condemn any tendency towards docetism (cf. especially 1 John 1:1–4). More than that: in being made flesh the Word accepts the supreme risk of corporal objectivity and carries it to its ultimate limits in the passion: the risk of being treated in actual fact as an object, cut off from the world of the living,[31] and consigned to the tomb in the world of things.

But at the same time the human body of Jesus is ensouled by a living consciousness which is in tension towards the world, is the source of meaning for all his actions, is reciprocal with every other human person, and is constantly turned towards God in an extraordinary relationship. Jesus is "someone," and the question recurrent throughout the Gospels—especially John's—involves the effort to penetrate the mystery of his identity. This objectively measurable being who has entered into space and into the field of human relationships has declared that he is God. Here the mystery of subjectivity attains an unfathomable depth. Every man who approaches Jesus—whether by direct encounter in Jesus' own time or since then, thanks to history and faith—seeks to take a position in relation to him. Men try to sound the depths of his person, become lost in the mystery of his subjectivity, regain a certain perspective by virtue of objective erudition, then let themselves be seized all over again and held by the fascination of this extraodinary "other" who calls them to a very special reciprocity. The reason for all this is that the reality of Christ is objective and subjective at the same time: it calls for both explanation and understanding. Each of these points of view is necessary; neither is exhaustive. The permanent temptation of unbelief is to refuse the Nazarean either his identity as divine Subject or his objective reality as a being-in-the-world. In either case, Jesus Christ is "dissolved" (1 John 4:3, Vg. reading).

Without entering here into the dogmatic developments of this datum, let us note briefly the major importance for ecclesiology of the objective reality of Jesus' humanity. On one hand the Church as the Body of Christ, endowed with life by his Spirit, presents a reality which is at once "worldy" and spiritual. Provided with a substantial objectivity, it is inserted into space and time—visible, audible, and tangible, after the manner of Jesus Christ, its Head and its norm. Though it is a communion of subjects, it is also a social institution. Composed of men and not simply of souls, the Church has received in trust the objective means of salvation which actualize in the here-and-now God's eternal intention of saving all men in Jesus Christ.

Furthermore, if the manhood of Jesus is not a mere appearance, a deception, a phantom, but possesses an objective fullness of reality, then the Father has given men a real and not a fictitious gift in the person of the Son appearing in the flesh. The multiform gifts of God, which all derive from the perfect gift which is Jesus Christ (cf. 1 John 3:16; 1 Cor. 1:45), received from him a fullness of reality. The graces of salvation, earned by Christ and poured out by his mediation (Acts

2:33; cf. 1 Tim. 2:5), are in man "something" as objectively received as they are gratuitously given.[32]

To Live "in Christ"

It has been observed that love gives rise to the desire for physical closeness;[33] indeed the ultimate implications of love are the dream of coincidence—coinherence in the same bodily place: my hands, my arms, are adapted to the gesture of opening wide to make room for the other within my very being. The body which the Son of God assumes allows him these gestures familiar to every man. With hand opened wide to bless, heal, and raise to life, Jesus welcomes to himself the most varied needs and concerns;[34] he embraces children (Mark 9:36; 10:16); at the Last Supper he allows "the disciple whom he loved" to lay his head on his breast (John 13:23; 21:20); he dies with his arms extended, fixed in a gesture of universal welcome, as though to take the whole universe into himself.

Christ uses the language of coincidence in the same bodily place to express, above all, the close union which should exist between himself and his disciples: "Live on in me, as I do in you" (John 15:4). Doubtless the substructure of this precept is the idea of the living union between the vine and the branches which is being developed in the passage. Doubtless, too, this kind of mutual immanence between Christ and his own is elsewhere presented as the result of eating his flesh and blood: "The man who feeds on my flesh and drinks my blood remains in me, and I in him" (John 6:56). The fact remains, however, that the two declarations, when taken literally, state a physical impossibility. Nothing can be a container—of whatever sort—and at the same time be inside what it contains. No matter how close the relation of inclusion is, it always involves a material distinction between the two terms, a certain degree of mutual exteriority which eliminates reciprocity. But here the technique of setting the two opposite ideas over against each other—"you in me, I in you"—cancels out any representation of a strict material relationship: the self-evident impossibility of a reciprocal inclusion forces the mind to go beyond a physical interpretation of the words towards the conception of a mutual presence which is deeper than any bodily presence. What we find here is a method of expression analogous to that used in the Old Testament to point to the divine transcendence: when the biblical writer (as we noted earlier) set the ultimate points of reference of our universe over against each other by pairing them, he was canceling out and transcending all spatial representation; he was casting the divine presence and grandeur into a sphere above and beyond all measurement.

Similarly, the words of Christ which we have been quoting use the language of mutual inclusion to support the thought and, at the same time, to force it, owing to the impossibility which the words express, to move beyond all literalism. So Paul, in his turn, can without risk of contradiction express the desire that Christ should dwell in the hearts of the faithful through faith (Eph. 3:17; cf. Gal. 2:20) and then elsewhere describe Christian life as a life "in Christ" (e.g., Rom. 6:11,23; 8:39; 1 Cor. 1:2,4,30; 3:1; 4:15; Gal. 3:26,28; Eph. 1:1,3,10; 2:5–6; Col. 1:2,4).[35] We cannot overemphasize the skill involved in such a literary device: with the aid of the language of spatiality, it is in fact a nonspatial union and a reciprocal immanence of the spiritual order that is stated.

Moreover, the idea of a mutual incorporation of subjects united by love throws light on the Pauline doctrine of the Body of Christ. The incarnate Son of God, who through his manhood is reciprocal with every human being, really "incorporates" his faithful "into himself," assumes them as his own members, and gives himself to them as their sole and common Head, their source of unity and life (Rom. 12:4–8; 1 Cor. 6:15; 12:12–30; Eph. 1:22; 4:4, 12–16; Col. 1:18; 2:19). Let us take careful note of the fact that the body and the incorporation in love are not simply images here—not merely pedagogical means adapted to gaining access to the mystery. These humble human realities are the substructure of the supernatural reality itself which, in turn, transfigures them. The mystical body of Christ is a real supernatural organism in which the corporeity of the Head and that of his members hold an essential place.[36] In becoming really incarnate, the Son of God makes his own the language of bodily reciprocity; but he also makes his own the relationships, desires, and needs which correspond to this language and bring it into being.

The Gospel uses the same experiences and the same procedures for expressing the unique, transcendent union of Father and Son. The mutual immanence of the divine persons is expressed in this fashion: "I am in the Father and the Father is in me. . . . It is the Father who lives in me accomplishing his works. Believe me that I am in the Father and the Father is in me" (John 14:10–11; cf. 10:30). John does not even hesitate to use an image from our human bodily space, the image of the "lap" or "bosom," to signify the same mystery: "No one has ever seen God; the only Son, who is in the bosom of the Father, he has made him known" (John 1:18,RSV).[37] The metaphor brings home quite effectively the most perfect communion in knowledge, life, and love, and is more suited than any other to accredit the Son as the perfect Revealer of the Father.

Since, finally, one person cannot possess another or be possessed by another more fully than through mutual immanence, the relationships between the faithful and the divine persons are defined by the same methods of expression. Thus, of the presence of the Holy Spirit: "the Spirit of truth. . . you can recognize. . . because he remains with you and will be within you" (John 14:17). The disciples are in this way introduced *within* the mystery of the relations that unite Father and Son: "You will know that I am in my Father, and you in me, and I in you" (John 14:20). There they will find the model and source of their own unity: "That all may be one, as you, Father, are in me, and I in you; I pray that they may be [one] in us. . . . I have given them the glory you gave me that they may be one, as we are one—I living in them, you living in me—that their unity may be complete" (John 17:21–23; cf. 17:26).

We can sum up by saying that from this moment forward God's dwelling among men is no longer the splendid building at Jerusalem, but the body of a man who lives among men and in whom dwell the Glory (cf. John 1:14) and the Name.[38] The substitution of the new temple for the old takes place in a series of events, obscure to the eyes of the crowd but decisive in God's plan; faith discerns in them a continuity and a break, which are both elements in the development of the economy of salvation.

A continuity: Jesus is presented in the Temple by his parents, who were concerned to follow the precepts of the Law (Luke 2:22, 39); at the age of twelve, when taken on the ritual pilgrimage, he deliberately presents himself in the Temple school in order to be engaged in his Father's business (Luke 2:41–50).[39] During his public life, he observes the traditional "ascents" (John 2:13; 5:1; 7:1,10; 10:22; 12:1,12); He requires of anyone making an offering in the Temple something better than a merely external and legal purity, namely, the forgiveness of offenses (Matt. 5:23–24; he expels those engaged in buying and selling, to avenge the holiness of the place (Matt. 21:12–13; cf. John 2:13–17).

But a break, too: Jesus prophesies that his own body, "destroyed" and then "raised up" in the resurrection, will be the new sanctuary (John 2:19–22; cf. Matt. 26:61);[40] he foretells a worship "in spirit and truth" emancipated from any ties with an exclusive place (John 4:20–24); he predicts the destruction of the ancient Temple (Matt. 23:37–24:3) and his entry into it is attended by messianic acclamations from the crowd (Mark 11:1–11).[41] Finally, at the moment of Jesus' last cry on the cross, the veil of the Temple is rent (Mark 15:38): the old dispensation has come to a close. Henceforth the new sanctuary will be the manhood of the risen Christ itself. Liberated from all spatial determinisms, the paschal body of Jesus frees God's dwelling place from all specific geographical localization. What was signified by the Tent of gathering and the Temple is fulfilled and transcended.

Through the paschal appearances God's transcendence of the universe is affirmed with a new splendor. The Lord does indeed manifest himself in places; for his humanity, far from being an evanescent phantom or the projection of a purely subjective vision, is an objective reality. Jesus keeps the initiative in his presence to others, and the personal, experimental verification which was first needed, then accomplished, by a doubting Thomas is highly significant. But if he situates himself in places, the risen Christ is not subject to the limitations of place: he exercises a sovereign mastery over concrete space and time.

We see, for example, how Jesus is suddenly present where he is least expected: on the road where the holy women are walking (Matt. 28:9–10), with the travelers to Emmaus (Luke 24:29–32), in the room where the Eleven are gathered (Luke 24:36–45), on the shore of Lake Tiberias (John 21:4). This paschal presence of Christ, multiplied with sovereign freedom at various points in space, doubtless increases the number of witnesses to the resurrection; it also reveals that God, the Wholly Other, is present to the universe in its totality and that, far from being contained by space, he contains it.

Each Christian in turn, as a member of Christ, becomes the "temple" (1 Cor. 6:15, 19–20; cf. Rom. 8:11)[42] in which God receives spiritual sacrifices (Rom. 12:1; 1 Cor. 3:16–17). The whole Church, as body of Christ, forms a spiritual edifice made of living stones (1 Pet. 2:4–6). But the day will come when the heavenly Jerusalem will descend from heaven to meet the faithful (Rev. 21:2–4): then the temple will be God himself and the Lamb (Rev. 21:22).[43]

The Humanity of Jesus at the Center of the World

Like every man, Christ experienced in his body the force of the multiplicity of relations which bind us to the universe. The elements and the lower realms of being are gathered and ordered hierarchically in his being: cosmic influences from far and near play upon him—the alternation of the seasons (John 10:22; Matt. 24:20, 32), storms (Matt. 8:23–27; 14:22–25), the rhythm of days and nights (Matt. 4:2; 16:2–3; John 9:4). Sun, air, water (John 4:7), and food sustain his life.[44] Through these needs and their daily satisfaction the whole universe is summed up in Christ's body as it is in every human microcosm.

Moreover, Jesus is situated in the world as a center of perspective; his incarnated consciousness, like ours, orders the universe around itself. Christ therefore uses the ready-to-hand, empirical language of any man who opens his eyes to the light of day; he speaks of the world as he sees it from that center of perspective which necessarily defines his outlook. Thus, for Jesus as for all other men, the sun "rises" and "sets" (Matt. 5:45; 13:6; cf. 8:11; Mark 1:32); the heavens present a face to him that is sometimes a fiery red, sometimes red and gloomy (Matt. 16:2–3). In this daily intercourse with things, the human consciousness of Christ is the living source of a plan which undergoes constant renewal. But through this consciousness it is God himself who is taking the whole universe to himself.

In a decisive situation, Jesus saw the whole of creation offered to him, gravitating around him as the matter of a possible choice. The Christ had then to assert the spiritual meaning of his relation to the world. In the temptation in the desert, creation is offered to Jesus as an immense field open to his domination: from the top of a very high mountain the tempter shows him all the kindgoms of the earth in their glory and says to him: "All these will I bestow on you if you prostrate yourself in homage before me" (Matt. 4:9). But Christ refuses to center the universe on himself with a view to the egoistic enjoyment of it and at the cost of idolatry and the rejection of God's plan: he wills that his relation to the world shall be not one of temporal domination but one of service, even to the giving of his life itself (Matt. 4:10; 20:28; Luke 22:27; John 13:1–10).

This same will is reaffirmed throughout his public life. Without going into all the details of its expression, we may concentrate our attention on the supreme affirmation of Calvary. It is at Jerusalem, the national and religious center, that in the divine plan Jesus must carry out his sacrifice. The third evangelist arranges a good part of his material as an ascent to the Holy City (Luke 9:51 ff.). Christ himself declares: "No prophet can be allowed to die anywhere except in Jerusalem" (Luke 13:33).

These last words are perhaps, as Lagrange observes, "painfully ironic" ones intended for Herod's ears.[45] But it is not difficult to glimpse something of their meaning in God's plan. It is in the place of so many similar dramas that the sacrifice of the Prophet of prophets will most fittingly complete the list of prophet-martyrs (cf. Luke 13:34; Matt. 23:29–31); it is there that the rejection of Jesus by established religious authority and a part of the people will bring out the full spiritual tragedy of such an ending; it is there, too, that the Israelite's passionate love for the Holy City, finding its supreme form in the consciousness of Jesus (Luke 13:34–35; 19:41–44), brings him to finish his course (Luke 13:32). It is there, before the High Priest and the Council, that Christ's witness manifests its full depth of meaning; there, at the center of worship, that the new sacrifice is to fulfill and forever replace all the old sacrifices (cf. Hebrews, especially 10:1–18). It is there, finally, at the active center of Israel's national and religious unity, that the entire old dispensation comes to its climax and yields place to the new. From this focal point, the salvation which yesterday was promised and today is given breaks through the boundaries that were necessary until now and reaches out to embrace all mankind and the whole universe. Jerusalem and Calvary thus become the center from which the consciousness of Jesus and, through it, God himself embrace the whole of creation in a single saving will. Present through his body at this single point, the Savior is present through his intentionality to the whole of creation. Thomas Aquinas writes: "By suffering in a single place on earth, he delivered the whole world through his passion."[46]

Around this one cross, whose elevation above the earth deepens its import as "center," the redeemed universe is gathered and ordered as around a new focal point. Human space, rent by countless divisions, is unified at last; the walls are brought down and the rifts healed. Specifically, the religious opposition between Jew and Greek, signified in the Temple at Jerusalem by the wall separating the two courtyards, is no longer valid; the whole of mankind is brought into one: "Now in Christ Jesus you who once were far off have been bought near through the blood of Christ. It is he who is our peace, and who made the two of us one by breaking down the barriers of hostility that kept us apart . . . reconciling both of us to God in one body through his cross" (Eph. 2:13–17; cf. Gal. 3:28; Col. 3:11; Rev. 5:9–10).[47]

This is why it is at Jerusalem that the apostles receive the outpouring of the Holy Spirit, which is the fruit of Christ's sacrifice; why they set out from there to evangelize the world (Luke 24:46–53; Acts 1:4,8; 2, *passim*).[48] In this center of unity, where all new developments have their starting-point, the redeemed world attains a new equilibrium.

The Humanity of Christ Measures and Qualifies Space

Though infinitesimal in comparison with the immensity of cosmic space, the Christ-Man nonetheless measures space with his body as does every human being. Gestures of the hand,[49] glances of the eye (e.g., Luke 19:5; John 11:41), daily goings and comings, pilgrimages to Jerusalem, and apostolic journeys all give him the basic experience of distance. In thus measuring the world, Jesus also takes the measure of his own humanity. The same God who had once reproached Job for his presumption and recalled him to such a lively sense of his own insignificance before the divine grandeur (Job 38–41), now has personal experience, in the consciousness of Jesus, of this littleness of man.

In entering into our vital space, the Word also acquires experience of our human roots. In every fiber of his being Jesus is a Palestinian. He belongs to a soil no less than to a people and a period. He is nourished by the produce of this land, breathes its air, is filled with wonder at its marvelous light, its vegetation, and its seasonal rhythms. He became a student in nature's school and willed to be formed in it. None of his gestures and words can be understood without being situated in this vital context. The lowly realities of his land—vine, fig tree, wine, oil, and flowing water, seed and harvest, hen and chickens, lambs, the ass and the ox that must be led to water, the well rising to the level of the ground, the net and the fish, lake and mountain, sun and wind—are all present in his teaching; his sentences, discourses, and parables receive from them their realistic power. In addition to the religious culture supplied by the Jewish tradition, Jesus inherited the human culture and wisdom, the mentality, the specific way of approaching men and things, which only the land can give. He wanted to become familiar even with the desert, for, as new Israel, he fulfills in his person the Exodus of his people; he submits to the temptations that arise in solitude, for without them he would not be fully a part of this land and its history. In short: through the human consciousness of Jesus, God personally makes his own the links—hidden but living and immensely strong—which bind a man to his native soil.

In return the humanity of Jesus gives new meaning to geographic space. Just as the manifestations of Yahweh to the patriarchs, the theophany at Horeb, and the Presence in the sanctuary had communicated to physical places something of the divine *holiness*, so too the places where Christ was born, lived, suffered, and, finally, manifested his paschal glory, acquire a profound religious meaning from his presence.

Thus Bethlehem, city of David but small village nonetheless, is to receive a wholly new greatness from the Messiah's birth there. According to the evangelist, the scribes were well aware of Micah's prophecy: "And you, Bethlehem, land of Judah, are by no means least among the princes of Judah, since from you shall come a ruler who is to shepherd my people Israel" (Matt. 2:6; cf. Mic. 5:1; John 7:42). Nazareth, however, can bring credit to no one: "Can anything good come from Nazareth?" Nathaniel asks (John 1:46); and everyone knows that "you will not find the Prophet coming from Galilee" (John 7:52). But if Nazareth cannot bring credit to Jesus, he, on the contrary, immortalizes the village where he grew up. The death sentence attached to the cross forever designates the crucified man as "Jesus the Nazorean" (John 19:19), and thus the prophecy is fulfilled: "He shall be called a Nazorean" (Matt. 2:23).[50] The land is part of the man as the man is part of the land.

Even the desert where Christ willed to be tempted receives a new meaning from him. The place empty of presence is henceforth rich with the presence and mystery of the God-man, his struggle, and his victory. We can understand, therefore, the important place the desert has had in the Church's life, why so many Christians went to live in the Thebaid, and why others built places of retreat or created an interior solitude in themselves: all wanted to encounter Jesus Christ and to share in his struggle.

In the same way, in the country which Jesus constantly traversed, certain places became "high places" of the Christian faith, privileged centers of humanity's religious history, a Holy Land and a Holy City; the places in which he went about doing good (Acts 10:38) and where he made the message of salvation resound; the city of Jerusalem where the "Holy and Just One" (Acts 3:14) finished his course (Luke 13:32), where he was raised from the dead, whence he left the world to return to the Father, where the Church was born under the outpouring of the Spirit, whence the gospel went forth to the ends of the earth (Acts 1:18; cf. Matt. 28:18) and of history (Matt. 23:20). Jesus Christ completes that prophetic and inchoative holiness which these places already possessed under the old dispensation, looking forward to the definitive consummation in the heavenly Jerusalem (Rev. 21:1f.) Without in any way detracting from the meaning of transcendence or from worship "in spirit and in truth," the idea of the "holy place" rests on a universal anthropological truth; it testifies to the immanence of God-made-flesh to the world and to human history.

Moreover, since each person, from the center in which he is placed, intentionally makes his own the whole of space, the universe which is suffering birth pangs and hoping for redemption receives from the humanity of Jesus a new determination, a new quality, and a new meaning (Rom. 8:19–23).

The Father Is "in Heaven"

Faithful to man and his language no less than to biblical tradition, the New Testament sets earth, man's dwelling-place, over against heaven, the dwelling-place of God. Above the stable of Bethlehem, for example, the heavenly spirits praise God with the Words: "Glory to God in high heaven, peace on earth to those on whom his favor rests" (Luke 2:14).

Thus, too, the God of Jesus Christ is the "heavenly Father" (Matt. 6:14, 26; 15:13; 18:35; cf. Luke 11:13). The disciples are instructed to say: "Our Father in heaven" (Matt. 6:9; cf. 7:11; 10:32; 16:17; 18:10,19; 23:9; Mark 11:25–26). The expression "kingdom of heaven" in Matthew is equivalent to the other evangelists' "reign of God" (Matt. 3:2; 4:17; 5:10,20; 7:21; 8:11; 10:7: all in, e.g. JB).[51] To "sin against heaven" is to sin against God (Luke 15:21,JB). What Peter binds or looses on earth will be bound or loosed in heaven, that is, by God himself (Matt. 16:19). At the baptism of Jesus the heavens open and the voice of the Father is heard (Matt. 3:16–17), as is the Father's testimony to Jesus shortly before his passion (John 12:28). The whole of the Apocalypse, finally, takes place in heaven where God, the Lamb, and the elect dwell.

It is thus in complete continuity with, as well as in fullfilment of, the biblical tradition that Jesus proclaims the new law of the beatitudes from the place that rises up towards heaven: the mountain (Matt. 5:1).[52] On the mountain, too, the Master reveals his glory to the three disciples at the transfiguration (Matt. 17:1–9); his earthly life is punctuated by various ritual "ascents" and climaxed by the ascent for the Passover, by his agony on Mount Olivet, by his sacrifice on the hill of Golgotha (Luke 2:41–42,51; John 1:13; 5:1; 7:8–10; Matt. 20:18; 27:33), by the post-resurrection meeting with the disciples on a mountain in Galilee (Matt. 28:10,16), and finally by his ascension from the same high place which had been the scene of the mortal struggle of his agony (Acts 1:6–12). But while mountains may continue, under the new law, to provide a support for religious vision, they cannot localize that vision. Adorers of the Father in spirit and truth will not have to come to Mount Garizim or to Jerusalem (John 4:20–24).

Since Christ is himself God, he receives from those who acknowledge him the homage of prostration—thus, in addition to the Magi (Matt. 2:11), there are the examples of Peter at the miraculous draught of fishes (Luke 5:8), the three apostles confronted by the transfigured Master (Matt. 17:6), and the cured blind man at his benefactor's feet (John 9:38).[53] But, in a mysterious counterpart of these demonstrations, Jesus lies face to the ground in his agony, proclaiming his weakness as man and imploring the Father's help (Matt. 26:39 and parallel places). The same basic human instincts cause him to raise his eyes to heaven when he prays: as before multiplying the loaves (Matt. 14:19 and parallel places), before curing the deaf man of Decapolis (Mark 7:34), before raising Lazarus (John 11:41), and before uttering his "priestly" prayer (John 17:1).

Conversely, the coming of the Son of God among men is constantly presented as a "descent." Jesus himself declares: "I have come down from heaven" (John 6:38; cf. 3:13), and gives himself as the bread which comes down from heaven (John 6:33,35,58). The Jews are not being misled when they protest against this as a claim to a divine origin (John 6:41–42) but, far from retracting the claim, Jesus insists: "I myself am the living bread come down from heaven" (John 6:51). The Council of Nicaea will later on use the same language: "for our salvation he came down" (*TCS*, p. 2; cf. Creed of Council of Constantinople I, *TCS*, p. 2).

We may recall, too, that at the baptism of Jesus, the Spirit "descended" on him like a dove (Matt. 3:16; cf. Luke 20:4–5). James teaches that "every genuine benefit comes from above, descending from the Father of the heavenly luminaries" (James 1:17). Finally, the heavenly Jerusalem will "come down" from heaven (Rev. 21:2, 10).[54]

The Christian liturgy makes use of the gesture of extended arms and hands and of eyes raised to heaven. Many a prayer of the Roman Missal asks God to "cast" his eyes upon his servants or to "lower his gaze" to them: "Look, Lord, upon. . . . " The value of such rites and prayers is grounded in their evident anthropological truth. Any saving intervention of the Most High, the Transcendent One, can only be an act of gracious condescension, any prayer an upward thrust of man towards God.[55]

Jesus Christ "Here Below" and in "Heaven Above"

If Christ has thus come down from heaven to live among men, he is not therefore shut up within the confines of earth. On the contrary, his existence has two distinct, even opposed, levels. Unlike his hearers, Jesus does not have his origins within the world: "You are from below; I am from above. You are of this world; I am not of this world"

(John 8:22–23, JB). Although he "came from" the Father and came into the world (John 16:27–28; cf. 17:8), Christ remains in a mysterious fashion with the Father. He who makes the Father known to men is "the only Son, who *is* in the bosom of the Father" (John 1:18, RSV; italics added). "No one has gone up to heaven" except "the Son of Man [who *is* in heaven]" (John 3:13; italics added).[56] When Jesus tells the Jews that he will soon "go away," he makes it clear that in some fashion he is already with the Father: "You will look for me, but you will not find me; where I am you cannot come" (John 7:34).[57] He will express the same ideas to his disciples on the eve of his death: "You will look for me, but I say to you now what I once said to the Jews: 'Where I am going, you cannot come' " (John 13:33).[58] If we compare these last two statements, which are really one in the mind of Christ, we see that he already *is* in the place to which he *is going*. Even while "here" among men, he is also in a mysterious "beyond."

Similarly, the Master's desire is that some day his disciples should also be "there" where he is now: "where I am, there will my servant be" (John 12:26), that is , with the Father, as the context shows (cf. 12:26b). The same desire is expressed more fully in the farewell conversations: "I shall come back to take you with me, that where I am you also may be" (John 14:3) and in his "priestly" prayer to his Father: "all those you gave me I would have in my company where I am" (John 17:24).

Christ the Way

During his earthly life, therefore, Christ dwells in two seemingly incompatible spheres. On the one hand, he shares the life of men and is plunged into the daily life and the history of his time. On the other hand, he is present to the Father in an extraordinary way, in a mysterious relationship of knowledge and love. Christ is both among men and in the bosom of the Father, "here below" and "in heaven above." In his being which is both human and divine, he unites heaven and earth, far and near, eternal and temporal. In him the distance is bridged which separates creature from Creator and the sinner from the Holy One. Being thus in tension (so much so as to die of it) between the two extremes of the human and the divine, Christ Jesus the man is Mediator and Way. To Thomas's question: "Lord, we do not know where you are going. How can we know the way?," the Master answers: " I am the way, and the truth, and the life; no one comes to the Father but through me" (John 14:6; cf. Eph. 2:18).

In this passage we have both the goal to be reached and the way to it. Christ is the sole and exclusive Way; all other ways are dead ends if they do not converge upon him. His call to men is an invitation to go forth and requires a constantly renewed abnegation: each person must go out of himself, follow the Master in unreserved commitment, and carry the burden of his cross (Matt. 16:24–26).[59] But it is not his own fallible senses that guide the traveler: the Way is also the Truth; it leads undeviatingly; the pilgrim is in no danger of walking in darkness but will have the light of life (John 8:12).[60] Unlike the paths of our human experience, this Way is life; it is not something, but someone. In addition, Jesus gives himself as the food we truly need for the journey, the genuine manna of which the first was only a symbol (John 6:48–51). He manifests himself to the pilgrims at Emmaus as the traveling companion whose presence and words enlighten and warm the heart (Luke 24: 13–35).Finally, he is at the journey's end with the Father (cf. John 6:44; 10:30; 14:7; 17:21–24),[61] in that "beyond" which is so far away without him, so near with him. Jesus Christ is the Way, the origin and goal of all things, the Alpha and the Omega; in him the goal is given along with the beginning; in him, the Mediator and not an intermediary, each man is already made present in the place to which he is traveling. The "here below" of men coincides with the "on high" of God.

Humiliation and Exaltation of Jesus Christ

In assuming a manhood like ours, the Son of God takes to himself an orientated human body, so that the fundamental divisions of above and below, before and behind, right and left, are rich in meaning for him as for every other man. These divisions then become supports and means of expression for the redemptive mystery.

As we have already pointed out, the incarnation of the Most High is an abasement, a "descent," not in the sense that the Son of God ceased to be God, but in the sense that he makes the human condition his own and renounces the manifestation in his humanity of the radiance of the divine Glory. Furthermore, in a very literal and nonmetaphorical way the earthly life of Jesus is played out, as every human existence is, between the two poles of up above and down below.

Before achieving the upright stance which is the sign of his stature as a man, Jesus experienced the weakness of infancy. At birth, his mother "laid" him in the manger (Luke 2:7, 10); at his presentation in the Temple, she carried him in her arms (Luke 2:22, 28). For him, as for other men, a vertical posture is something to be achieved and his body passes through the slow stages of growth (Luke 2:40,52). As an adult, Jesus stands up in the posture of the orator (John 7:37), but sits down when overcome with fatigue (John 4:6; cf. 6:3) and submits to the common necessity of lying down and sleeping (Mark 4:38; cf. Matt. 8:20). On the eve of his death, he gives his disciples a practical lesson in humility by bending down before them to wash their feet (John 13:1–12). During his agony he lies prostrate on the ground in extreme depression; under the weight of anxiety he "went down on his knees" (Luke 22:42) and "fell to the ground" (Mark 14:35) "on his face" (Matt. 26:39, RSV). Thus overwhelmed, Christ acknowledges his human weakness, with the sweat of blood adding a final note of horror to his state. The requistioning of Simon the Cyrenean suggests that the cross was too heavy and forced Christ to his knees (Luke 23:26). The crucifixion, finally, brings the Son of the Most High (Luke 1:32; Mark 5:37) to a humiliation which is the equivalent of an annihilation, an "emptying" (Phil. 2:7): the death penalty reserved for slaves. Once dead, he is carried away and laid in the tomb in the posture of irreversible defeat: the posture of a man who has forever lost his upright stance and, with it, life, nobility, everything belonging to human existence—lying dead and soon to be indistinguishable from the earth on which he rests (Matt. 27:59–60).

In God's intention the torment of the cross and the ultimate abasement of the tomb have a mysterious meaning. In men's eyes the raising of the condemned person on the cross is the supreme humiliation. A man is raised from the earth, "displayed" (Gal. 3:1), so that the eyes of all may be drawn to his suffering, his punishment, his disgrace. In the case of Christ the place of his torment and the nearness of Passover with its crowds of pilgrims guaranteed his shameful death a tragic publicity. The trilingual inscription nailed to the cross is the crowning mockery, suggesting as it does that the King of the Jews has a gibbet for his throne (John 19:19–22).

In God's plan, however, the raising of Christ onto the cross has a wholly different significance, one that is a direct challenge to the evil intent of men. The same torment that in men's eyes consummates the shameful failure of the condemned man is the assertion in God's eyes of his victory and his glorification. The elevation onto the cross, seemingly a lifting in dishonor, is in fact an exaltation to glory.

In his conversation with Nicodemus, Jesus had alluded to his future suffering. Just as the bronze serpent, like any emblem raised on high, drew the eyes of men almost irresistibly, so the Son of Man must be "raised up" so that the gaze of believers may turn to him and plead for eternal life. "Just as Moses lifted up the serpent in the desert, so must the Son of Man be lifted up, that all who believe may have eternal life in him" (John 3:14–15; cf. Num. 21:4–9; Wisd. 16:5–7). Later, a few days before his death, Christ referred to the mystery of his exaltation in analogous terms: Satan will be overcome, while Jesus, lifted up from the earth, will become sole center and universal gathering-point: "Now has judgment come upon this world, now will this world's prince be driven out, and I—once I am lifted up from earth—will draw all men to myself." The evangelist adds: "This statement indicated the sort of death he had to die" (John 12:31–33).

The tree of the cross is orientated like the human body of Jesus; the cross was made for a man, and like him has a top, or head, a foot and arms. The crucified man dies standing.[62] In espousing each other in a mutual embrace, this tree and this living body become one and heighten the signification of their respective orientation. Both stand up vertically, along the axis that links the zenith to the depths of the earth; both extend their arms horizontally to link one end of the world to the other.

Fixed in the soil, the cross takes possession of it and hands over to the Crucified the earth, the lower regions, and the realm of hell. But though rooted in the depths, the tree shoots towards the heights of heaven, conquers for Jesus Christ the vast uppermost reaches of the cosmos and the highest ranks in the hierarchy of creatures. The abysses of the lower regions, man's earth, and the luminous heavens are in this way reunited, reconciled, and gathered up in the body, now strained to the limits of its endurance, of the one Mediator.[63] Down below and up above are linked in submission to a single Lordship. Moreover, the arms of the cross and the arms of the

Crucified, stretched out horizontally, reach intentionally to the limits of the world and bring them together, eliminating all the distances between them. The immobility of the Crucified, far from condemning him to final powerlessness, eternalizes his gesture of universal appeal and opens it upon the totality of creation. Jesus Christ is crucified to the world and the world to Jesus Christ (cf. Gal. 3:19).[64] Present physically at this single point in the universe, he envelops through his efficacious redemptive intention the whole immensity of creation.[65]

The meaning of the humanity of Jesus as universal center and Head thus finds its full expression in his elevation on the cross. And when we say that Christ is center and summit of the redeemed universe we are speaking not only of the subjective vantage-point of his human consciousness but also of the objective vantage-point of God's will (cf. Eph. 1; Col. 1:15,20, etc.). Since all the vertical and horizontal dimensions of the cosmos are gathered together and, in a sense, eliminated, the crucified Christ must draw and in fact does draw all men and all things to himself: his grace "as Head" is to sum up the whole creation, "bring all things under himself" (John 12:31–32; cf. 1 Tim. 3:16).[66]

The exaltation of the Crucified becomes a revelation to many; in the very depths of total abasement he manifests himself as Son of the Most High. It is at this moment, according to John, that Zechariah's prophecy begins to be fulfilled: "They shall look upon him whom they have thrust through" (Zech. 12:10; cf. John 19:37); the prayer of the repentant thief (Luke 23:40–42), and the profession of the faith of the centurion (Luke 23:47) bear out the evangelist's words. Christian art, in turn, aware of the providential meaning of Christ's exaltation, delighted, especially in the Carolingian period, in giving the Crucified the trappings of royalty.

It is through his resurrection and ascension that the Lordship of Christ finds its clearest expression in the world's eyes. The buried Jesus is apparently forever the victim of death; as a new Jonah he is swallowed up by the abyss (cf. Matt. 12:39–40);[67] lying in death, he is forever conquered; thrust into the solitude of the tomb, he is in the ultimate sense the absent man. But then, on the third day, the man who yesterday lay dead stands up. Without experiencing corruption

Jesus escapes the power of death (Acts 2:24–32)[68] and passes from darkness to light, death to life. By God's power, the man who was thrown down is "re-suscitated"—that is, raised up, set upright again.[69] According to an anthropological law often appealed to in the biblical tradition,[70] this raising up is the sign of salvation, this setting upright the very embodiment of victory. The reason is that in being thus raised up the dead person recovers that natural orientation of living man—namely, upright stance—by which he asserts his own dignity and his mastery over the universe. At the same time, the man who had disappeared now appears to his friends in varying circumstances and multiplies the sensible proofs of his victory (cf. Gospel narratives of risen life; Acts 1:3–4; 1 Cor. 15:1–11). He who was thrust into the tomb, the absent one, now becomes present once again to men; he re-enters the world and history, and there carries on a new activity. It is there that he is henceforth to be sought; you do not seek the living among the dead (Luke 24:5). This presence and this activity are extraordinary in their quality, for they assert their emancipation from the limitations of spatiality. The risen Christ is master of physical distance and manifests himself where he is least expected but where his concern for his own brings him. Without ceasing to be genuinely human (too many witnesses saw, heard, and touched him, and even shared food with him for this to be denied),[71] the body of Christ shares in the divine mastery of space and time and enjoys a kind of omnipresence. The orientational structures of living man, bestowed by the Creator on the first Adam, are not only recovered but acquire a new meaning in the Easter body of the second Adam: through them, man and God, conquerors of death, lay "bodily" hold on the entire universe and, each in his degree, fill them with their presence (cf. Col. 2:9).

Begun in a hidden manner on the cross, accomplished and already manifested in the resurrection, Christ's exaltation must reach a final fulfillment. Making no concessions to the popular imagination with its avid interest in the marvelous and fantastic (shown, for example, in the apocryphal gospels), but conforming to the demands of anthropology and of the biblical tradition, the New Testament presents Christ's exaltation as an *ascension.* The resurrection did not, of course, consist simply in a coming forth from the tomb, a raising up of the one who had been laid there: it was already the rising of Jesus in his glory. Doesn't the Master himself inform Mary Magdalene that new relations are being established between himself and men because he is "ascending" to the Father (John 20:17; cf. Rom. 10:6–7)? Jesus must reveal himself in a definitive way as the Most High by entering into the dwelling of God itself: "heaven."

As with the theophanies of the Old Testament and the transfiguration, it is on a mountain that the final event of Jesus' earthly life finds its appropriate setting (Matt. 28:16). By raising himself a short space above the earth, the Master signifies that he is above the whole created order. A cloud, corresponding to the cloud on Sinai, veils the humanity of Jesus from men's eyes and reveals his definitive passage to God (Acts 1:9–12). This ascension is in fact the "return" of which Christ himself had spoken, the theophany which establishes the authenticity of his divine mission and his divine identity forever: "No one has gone up to heaven except the One who came down from there—the Son of man [who is in heaven]" (John 3:13).

Thus Christ ascends "to where he was before" (John 6:62); he ends the journey which, after leading him into the abyss, now raises him above the whole created universe: " 'He ascended'—what does this mean but that he had first descended into the lower regions of the earth? He who descended is the very one who ascended high above the heavens, that he might fill all men with his gifts" (Eph. 4:9–10; cf. Ps. 68:19, quoted in verse 8).[72] It was his providential destiny to traverse the whole of the universe in order to conquer it for God. Since it is by movement that man appropriates space to himself,[73] it is in this fashion that Christ subjects to himself the "lower world" and the "high places,"[74] the depths and the heights in the hierarchy of creatures, and the men of the past with their history who are apparently swallowed up in death; it is in this fashion that he bestows upon the universe a mysterious fullness—doubtless the fullness of his Lordship which gathers all things into unity (cf. Eph. 1:23; Col. 1:19).

The Christological hymn in Philippians traces the same arc described by the destined course of Jesus Christ. Passing from the divine condition to that of a slave, from the latter to death—even to death on a cross—Jesus descends into the uttermost depths, to be in return exalted by the Father (Phil. 2:6–11)[75] and given the Name above every name: the rightfully divine name of "Lord." In response to this supreme exaltation, the created universe prostrates itself in adoration: "every knee must bend in the heavens, on the earth, and under the earth" (Phil. 2:10), while every tongue confesses that Christ is Lord. We have here essentially the same course of conquest described in the profession of faith in 1 Timothy: from manifestation in the flesh to exaltation in glory (1 Tim. 3:16).[76]

All the texts affirm the same basic truth: by his "descent" and his victorious "return" Christ subjected the whole universe to himself. The spatial image of a triumphal journey supports the vision of faith but does not limit or distort it.

Christ "Seated at the Father's Right Hand"

The biblical tradition, along with other religious traditions, considers sitting in the heights, on the most elevated throne, to be an attribute of divinity.[77] Sitting and exaltation combine to express the idea of unqualified power. Thus it is the sovereign power and the repose of blessedness that are expressed in Yahweh's sitting above the cherubim (Ps. 80.2 [cf. Exod. 25:18–24]; 99:1; 103:19; Dan. 3:54–55), on his holy throne (Ps. 47:9), or on the lofty throne which Isaiah saw in the Temple (Isa. 6:1).[78] Supreme judicial power is attributed by Daniel to the Ancient One seated on his throne and surrounded by his council (Dan. 7:9–10; cf. Ps. 9:5).[79] In like manner, Christ reminds his hearers that "heaven . . . is God's throne . . . ,the earth . . . is his footstool" (Matt. 5:34; 23:22). In the letter to the Hebrews the "throne of grace" is a symbol of God himself (Heb. 4:16). Especially in Revelation do we find a very significant text which records a vision the writer had: "I saw a throne standing in heaven, and the One who was sitting on the throne . . . " (Rev. 4:2,JB).

Whereas Isaiah recognized and immediately named "the Lord Yahweh" and Ezekiel discerned "one who had the appearance of a man" (Ezek. 1: 26–28), John refrains from naming or describing what he saw; he only experiences its luminous splendor.[80] This reserve is in striking contrast to the minutely detailed description of the heavenly court which follows the text cited above. He is satisfied to designate the personage as "sitting"—in itself a means of conveying with rigorous exactitude the position of the one described and of permitting immediate identification. The one who is "seated," whose splendid court reflects his ineffable majesty, possesses absolute power, sovereign kingship, blessedness, and supreme judicial authority: he is God.[81]

The glorious exaltation of Christ terminates in his "sitting at the right hand of the Father." Mark affirms it explicitly (16:19). Peter testifies to it in his first sermon on the morning of Pentecost and sees in it the fulfillment of Ps. 110:1: "The Lord said to my Lord, 'Sit at my right hand until I make your enemies your footstool' " (Acts 2:34–35).[82] Paul in turn proclaims it with passionate conviction: the Father used his power "in raising Christ from the dead and seating him at his right hand in heaven" (Eph. 1:20; cf. Rom. 8:34). Thus, having taken "his seat at the right hand of the Majesty in heaven" (Heb. 1:3; cf. 1:8,13; 8:1; 10:12–13; 12:2), Christ occupies a place superior to that of the angels (Heb. 1:4–13; 2:5–9; cf. Col. 2:15); he is "King of kings and Lord of lords" (Rev. 19:16).

The sitting posture signifies, for the glorified Christ, rest after conflict, calm possession after victory, and power that is uncontested and serenely exercised. It was in such terms that Jesus himself had foretold the final judgment: "When the Son of Man comes in his glory, escorted by all the angels of heaven, he will sit upon his royal throne" (Matt. 25:31).[83]

But all sitting is not equally significant. By the fact that Jesus sits "at the right hand of the Father," his merits are acknowledged by God himself. Christ shares, as fully God's equal, in the sovereignty, majesty, royal and judicial authority which belong to God alone (Matt. 26:64; cf. Mark 16:19; Col. 3:1; Wisd. 9:4). Consequently the heavenly court renders one and the same adoration to God and the Lamb (Rev. 5:13). In short, "sitting at the right hand of the Father" is a consecrated formula which designates the relationship of equality between Christ and God.[84]

The Scriptures establish a close correspondence between the exaltation of Jesus on the day of his ascension and his glorious return at the end of time (Acts 1:11). The Lord will return "on the clouds of heaven" (Matt. 24:30 and parallel places; cf. Dan. 7:13) and will take his place "on his throne of glory" (Matt. 25:31; cf. John 5:25–30) in the posture of the supreme judge. Thus the anthropological data offer constant support to the expression of the Christian mystery.[85] But such anthropomorphisms, far from obscuring the divine transcendence, are on the contrary the most deliberate affirmation of it.

The "Upright-ing" of Man in Jesus Christ

In God's plan the career of Jesus Christ is the perfect exemplar of every human destiny (cf. Rom. 8:29). The humiliations of the Savior are a divine condescension to lost man; his exaltation draws a new mankind into its irresistible movement.

Adam had been created innocent, in splendid integrity of soul and body; sin meant his "fall." Henceforth man is subject to weary toil which bows his back, to illness which puts him on his bed, and to death which lays him low and plunges him into the abyss: "You are dirt and to dirt you shall return" (Gen. 3:19). In keeping, then, with the universally accepted significance of the nether pole, biblical man expresses his distress in terms of a fall into the depths: "I am sunk in the abysmal swamp where there is no foothold; I have reached the watery depths; the flood overwhelms me" (Ps. 69:3).[86] Salvation, consequently, consists in being drawn forth from the abyss: "Rescue me out of the mire; may I not sink! May I be rescued from my foes, and from the watery depths. Let not the flood-waters overwhelm me, nor the abyss swallow me up, nor the pit close its mouth over me. . . . I am afflicted and in pain; let your saving help, O God, protect me" (Ps. 69:15–16, 30).[87] Again: "Out of the depths I cry to you, O Lord" (Ps. 130:1). If Yahweh hears the prayer of his faithful one, the latter escapes from *below:* "He drew me out of the pit of destruction, out of the mud of the swamp; he set my feet upon a crag; he made firm my steps" (Ps. 40:3).

Along with his upright stance, man regains security, life and the joy of living, and his original dignity; once liberated, he can raise his head[88] and sing the praises of his God (Ps. 40:4).[89] In short, the God who saves is he who straightens the man who is bowed down (Ps. 113:7–8; 145:14; 146:8; cf. Isa. 35:3; 40:29–31; Heb. 12:12), sets his feet firmly upon the earth, and leads him to the tops of the mountains (Ps. 18:34; 27:5; 61:3; Hab. 3:19) or of the social hierarchy (1 Sam. 2:6–8; Ps. 113:7–8; cf. Ps. 75:11; 92:11). The whole history of Israel is a series of falls and of recoveries through the interventions of Yahweh's powerful hand.

In Jesus Christ, however, God personally abases himself in order to seek man out in the depths of his degradation. On many different occasions Jesus presents himself as the one who raises up the man prostrate in the suffering which is a result and sign of sin. Every healing is thus a "raising up" and has, by opposition to illness, the meaning of a salvation for soul and body.[90] Let us note here some instances which are "revelatory," in the full sense of the word, of the mission of Jesus. There is the cure of Peter's mother-in-law, victim of a fever which confines her to her bed: "He went over to her and grasped her hand and helped her up, and the fever left her" (Mark 1:31).[91] To the bedridden paralytic of Capernaum the Master says first that his sins are forgiven; then, in face of the murmering of the scribes, who challenge his right to say this, he issues a command to the sick man: "Stand up! Roll up your mat, and go home." And "the man stood up and went toward his home" (Matt. 9:1–8). This physical "setting upright" is offered as an outwardly manifest sign which proves the recovery effected interiorly in the conscience. Finally, the cure of the bent and crippled woman is very much to our purpose: here is a woman "who for eighteen years had been possessed by a spirit which drained her strength. She was badly stooped—quite incapable of standing erect." Jesus laid his hand on her, "and immediately she stood up straight and began thanking God" (Luke 13:11–13). To this unhappy woman, victim of Satan, Christ restores her upright position, the sign of her twofold nobility as creature and as daughter of Abraham (Luke 13:16); in the same way he raises up the epileptic who was possessed (Mark 9:26–27).

But illness is not the definitive loss for man; his loss is, to all appearances, made final by death. The dead person is the person lying down, recumbent forever, without any hope of regaining that vertical balance associated with life. The Savior must therefore go to seek man out even in the prostration of death and raise him up again. Brought to Jairus's daughter, "taking her hand he said to her, '*Talitha, koum*,' which means, 'Little girl, get up.' The girl . . . stood up immediately and began to walk around" (Mark 5:41–42). The same command is given to the widow of Naim's son: " 'Young man, I bid you get up.' The dead man sat up and began to speak" (Luke 7:14–15). Finally, if the narrative of the raising of Lazarus does not report exactly the same words (Jesus calls the dead man "forth" and he "comes forth" from the tomb [John 11:43–44]),[92] the meaning of the event is identical: Jesus raises up man who lies in death, sets him upright, and restores his upright stance. The Greek word, *egeirein*, like the Latin *resuscitare*, has the meanings of awaken, set upright, raise up, and restore to life.[93]

All these gestures and words receive their full meaning from the resurrection of Jesus Christ himself and are anticipations of its saving effectiveness. In "setting himself upright" on Easter morning, the dead man in his own person restores to all mankind the orientation proper to a living man, with what it implies of mastery over the lower realms and of thrust towards the summits for which he is destined. As in Adam all fell into death, so in Jesus Christ all are called to raise themselves up and live in the light (cf. 1 Cor. 15:22, and 15, *passim;* 6:14; 2 Cor. 4:14): "Awake, O sleeper, arise from the dead, and Christ will give you light" (Eph. 5:14b).[94]

During his public life the Master gave the apostles the mission of curing the sick and raising the dead (Matt. 10:8). After the ascension and Pentecost the newborn Church carries out the mission: Peter and John restore the crippled man in the Temple (Acts 3:1–10); Paul sets on his feet the cripple of Lystra who had never walked (Acts 14:8–10); and at Joppa, Peter raises Tabitha to life (Acts 9:36–42). All of these are effective signs of the salvation that is to come.

Only one requirement is laid on the man to be set upright: he must recognize his littleness before God. Whereas pride "raises up" the heart of the creature against the Creator (1 Macc. 1:3; Prov. 16:18; 18:12; cf. Ps. 75:5–6; Isa. 14:13–14; Obad. 3–4), humility keeps it in a state proper to it (Ps. 131:1). God, therefore, resists the proud and abases them (James 4:6; 1 Pet. 5:5; cf. Ps. 75:8; 89:20, 25; Ecclus. 7:11) but exalts the humble: "Whoever exalts himself shall be humbled, but whoever humbles himself shall be exalted" (Matt.23:12; Luke 14:7–11; 18:9–14).[95] Mary sees in her own mysterious vocation this constant feature of God's dealings with men: "He has confused the proud in their inmost thoughts. He has deposed the mighty from their thrones and raised the lowly to high places" (Luke 1:51–52).

Once established in a new life by the risen Christ, the Christian is a man who stands; the attitude proper to such a man when he prays is the upright stance, not as an insolent assertion of supposed equality with God, but as homage paid to God by a man who has regained his dignity by God's favor. In Jesus Christ man can approach God with the candor of an adopted son who has been rescued forever.[96] The Christian pursues this movement of ascent throughout his whole life; for, once restored to life with his victorious Head, he is carried to the celestial heights and is already seated there with him (Eph. 2:6). Thus, though involved here below in the world of men, the believer is "intentionally" present, by faith and hope, "where Christ is seated at God's right hand" (Col. 1:1–3).[97]

Salvation will be complete only on the last day, at the Son of Man's coming in glory. Then mankind, still disturbed by the powers of evil, will be raised up by hope of imminent redemption: "Stand erect and hold your head high, for your deliverance is near at hand" (Luke 21:28).[98] Then Christ's followers will be associated with his royal estate: "I give you my solemn word, in the new age when the Son of Man takes his seat upon a throne befitting his glory, you who have followed me shall likewise take your places on twelve thrones to judge the twelve tribes of Israel" (Matt. 19:28). Revelation repeats the promise: "I will give the victor the right to sit with me on my throne, as I myself won the victory and took my seat beside my Father on his throne" (Rev. 3:21). And finally, while the sinner will be definitively "cast down," God will be forever "exalted," according to Isaiah's prophecy: "The haughty eyes of man will be lowered, the arrogance of men will be abased, and the Lord alone will be exalted, on that day" (Isa. 2:11; cf. verses 6–22; 5:14–15; Ps. 9:16–20).[99]

Thus religious language relies on the concrete categories supplied by daily experience and by the empirical phenomenology issuing from common sense. Faith lays hold of the incarnated subject in his totality: spirit, flesh, and highly differentiated network of relations with the world.

Conversion

The anatomical differentiation of my body into "front" and "back" divides my world into two parts that are not only distinct but opposed in meaning: the front or "before" ("ahead") is the direction of action and the future, the back or "behind" ("after") is the direction of forgetfulness, refusal, and negation. But it is also possible for me to reject goals hitherto pursued and, by a bodily turning, to direct myself to a region of the world to which I formerly paid no heed. This about-face maneuver, essentially connected with the body's spatial character, is quite naturally transposed to the moral order where it expresses a basic shift in existential purpose.[100] Biblical language has not neglected this mode of expression: in fact, whatever their cultural milieu, the sacred writers have recourse to the images of "turning away" and "turning around" in order to express the ideas of sin and religious conversion.[101]

To begin with, without entering into any detailed philological and semantic analysis, we may note the importance of the movement of "conversion" in interpersonal relationships. To speak only of the New Testament, we find numerous texts in which "turning" means simply the physical, almost chance, about-face. Thus Mary Magdalene turns and finds the risen Jesus near her (John 20:14). Similarly, after the meal by the lakeside, Peter turns and sees the disciple whom Jesus loved (John 21:20). But in many contexts the turning is more than an involuntary movement and, instead, is filled with intersubjective meaning. The most striking text is surely the one describing Christ's attitude to Peter at the first prediction of his passion. Jesus turns and says to Peter: "Get behind me, Satan! You are an obstacle in my path" (Matt. 16:23,JB). Exegetes have rightly noted how harsh a reproof this is by contrast with the words of praise with which, shortly before this, Christ had rewarded Peter's profession of faith and conferred the primacy and power of the keys on him (Matt. 16:17–19). But, even apart from the contrast, the present text is forceful in a way not easy to translate. By his very human refusal of a suffering Messiah, Peter had presented himself to Jesus as an obstacle in the path which makes the traveler stumble or else closes the road to him. The apostle had thus blocked God's path and opposed the Master's providential destiny. Christ orders Peter, with gesture and words, to "get behind" in order to leave the way clear. The apostle is thus put behind Jesus, in that region of the world which is, for men, the region of refusal, forgetfulness, nonexistence; there is the threat of a breaking off of friendship and intimacy if Peter persists in his views. The teaching that follows, on the need of renunciation, confirms the meaning of the reprimand. During the passion, however, in relation to the same Peter who is now guilty of the threefold denial, Christ adopts a diametrically opposed attitude, but in service of the same goal; that is, to bring him to repentance: "The Lord turned around and looked at Peter" (Luke 22:61). Instead of turning in a gesture of rejection, the Master turns to the apostle in order to direct to him the reproach and the summons of his gaze. The action, though wordless, is clear enough in its meaning, for Peter goes out and weeps for his failure.

We may note two further instances in the New Testament of a "turning," or "conversion" in the literal sense, inspired by benevolent intentions. On the way to Calvary, Christ forgets his own suffering, turns to the women of Jerusalem who weep for him, and declares prophetically that they will be still more unhappy later on (Luke 23:28). At Joppa, Peter will turn to the corpse of Tabitha, laid out on its bier, and order her to arise (Acts 9:40). In this turning, the subject—Jesus, Peter—renounces himself and gives himself to another in an effective *act of presence.* The bodily turning is then decisive action which creates a new relationship to another.

It is natural, then, that the word should come to signify the interior act by which a man, recognizing that he has gone astray in pursuit of illusory values, radically reverses the direction of his life. That is what moral and religious "conversion" is in the Old Testament: a man turns from his evil ways (2 Kings 17:13; Ezek. 33:11; cf. 33:7–20; Jer. 18:11; 25:5; 36:3,7), from idols (Ezek. 14:6; 1 Thess. 1:9), from wickedness (Ezek. 3:19; Jon. 3:10; cf. Acts 3:26) from sin (Job 36:10; Ezek. 18:30; etc.); he deliberately engages in penance through fasting, tears, and mourning (Joel 2:12; Jon. 3:5–10). More importantly, if the sinner renounces himself and turns from something, it is in order to turn to someone, to God whom he accepts henceforward as Creator, Lord, and Savior. Conversion is a *turning back* to the living and true God (Ps. 51, *passim;* Ecclus. 17:26; Isa. 9:13; 44:22; 45:22; 55:7; Jer. 3, *passim;* Lam. 3:40; Hos. 3:5; 6:1; 7:10; 14:2–3; Hag. 2:18). The asceticism which liberates a man from his sinful habits helps him achieve a new heart and spirit (Ezek. 18:30–32)[102] and draws down on him the mercy of the God who saves the sinner from death (Ezek. 18:27–28,32). In the New Testament the interior change in the heart is expressed in a very vivid way by the return of the prodigal son to his father's house (Luke 15:11–32; cf. Acts 14:15). Conversion prepares a man to believe in the Good News (Mark 1:15); it obtains the forgiveness of sins (Acts 3:19; 2 Pet. 3:9), entrance into the kingdom (Matt. 3:2; 4:17; 18:3), and the gift of the Holy Spirit (cf. Acts 2:38);[103] it links the believer to Christ, shepherd and guardian of souls (1 Pet. 2:25; cf. Luke 5:32). In short: conversion is a turning about of the spirit *(metanoia)* and the whole being; it radically reverses the existential project.

But the false impression must be avoided that conversion is the work of unaided man. Rather, the same God who is at the term of the process, as the unique pole of our new existence, is also in a mysterious way at the origin. Man's freedom remains intact—can he not voluntarily harden his own heart?(Pharaoh in Exod. 7:13; 8:15; 9:7,34; the Israelites: Exod. 17:1–7; Ps. 95:8; Isa. 6:10 [cf. Mark 4:12]; etc.);[104] yet God converts the heart (1 Kings 18:37), "makes" his erring people "return to him" (Jer. 31:18–19; Lam. 5:21) and gives them a new heart and a new spirit (Ezek. 36:25–32). We may, therefore, without doing any violence to the Gospel narrative of Peter's denial (Luke 22:61), see in it an illustration of God's prevenient role in conversion: Peter's repentance begins with Jesus' turning to him and summoning him, with a look, to repent. Furthermore, if the first Christian sermons lead to the conversion of great numbers of believers, this is because the hand of God was with the apostles (Acts 11:21). Conversion has its origin in God's grace.

In a second phase, the existential about-face by which man dedicates himself to God makes the divine partner disposed to turn to his creature: "Return to me . . . and I will return to you, " says Yahweh (Zech. 1:3; Mal. 3:7; cf. Jer. 15:19; Tob. 13:6). The man, therefore, who is tormented by awareness of his weakness or sin asks God to "return": this "return" of God brings deliverance to the repentant believer (Ps. 6:5; 80:15; 90:13; Isa. 63:17; Joel 2:14; Jon. 3:9), life (Ps. 71:20–21), and joy (Ps. 85:7–8).

The obvious meaning of the movement of turning is brought into play in the baptismal rite as reported by Cyril of Jerusalem in a text to which we have already referred.[105] The catechumen first stands facing the west, where the Prince of Darkness dwells, and extends his hand in that direction. Here, all the factors in an intentional presence are to be found; upright stance, facing position, and extended hand effect a genuine confrontation. Then the catechumen can address the enemy in order to reject him *as if he were present.*[106] Then the man makes an about-face to the east, the region of Paradise and light, and makes his trinitarian profession of faith.[107] In this way, expression is given to the total existential turnabout which adherence to Jesus Christ supposes. "You turn toward the east. For he who renounces the devil, turns toward Christ, recognizes him by a direct glance" (Ambrose).[108] From this point on, the two partners, man and Christ, can encounter each other in the mysterious face-to-face of faith.[109]

Having and the Christian Mystery

As we have said, in becoming man the Son of God makes his own the countless mysterious bonds that link us to our cosmic environment. He assumes fully the complex relationship "of man to world." At times, the spontaneous movement of perception draws Christ to the observation of men and things; at times, no less spontaneous needs lead him to use and consume things. At his birth Mary and Joseph try to find some sort of shelter for the child; the first thing his mother gives him is the most elementary of possessions, some clothing ("She wrapped him in swaddling clothes") and a makeshift crib ("and laid him in a manger": Luke 2:7). Throughout his life Jesus has to make use of the material things most indispensable for work and domestic life. During the years of his ministry he accepts hospitality. Like every man, he incorporates into himself foods drawn from the earth and makes them his own in the most complete way possible by "consuming" them. Such use of basic possessions is a condition for any authentic human life; to refuse it is to refuse to be a man. Consequently, even in the post-Easter period, Jesus shares meals with men.[110]

But even while he thus sinks his roots into human space by this use of indispensable goods, Christ constantly and forcefully challenges the relation of owership. The point is not that he accepts degrading poverty for his fellowmen. On the contrary, he energetically orders his disciples to struggle against it by sharing their goods; for proof of this we need think only of the parable of the evil rich man (Luke 16:19–31) or the importance given by the sovereign Judge, at the final judgment, to the practice of sharing (Matt. 25:31–46). Unlike the scribes, Jesus gives the satisfaction of basic needs priority even over observance of the Law (Matt. 12:1–8). The point we want to make is rather that, in opposition to the spontaneous tendency towards appropriation, Christ constantly urges the quest for detachment and voluntary poverty. Thus he refuses for himself even a legitimate owership which could make a man a prisoner of this world: the owership of a shelter, for example; he had been born under a chance-found roof, and throughout his public life he had no permanent dwelling to which he could go: "The foxes have lairs, the birds of the sky have nests, but the Son of Man has nowhere to lay his head" (Luke 9:58).

In his fast in the desert, Jesus deliberately opposes the spontaneous primordial movement by which man seizes food for his body: "Not on bread alone is man to live but on every utterance that comes from the mouth of God" (Matt. 4:4); his real food is to do his Father's will (John 4:32–34; cf. 6:27). With his disciples he shares his food; in fact, not only does he give away the food for his own body to others, but, in a movement of unqualified disappropriation, he gives that very body as food: "Take this and eat it . . . this is my body. . . . This is my blood" (Matt. 26:26–28).[111] On Calvary he allows the soldiers to strip him of his clothes (Matt. 27:35), thus surrendering the first possession he received from Mary on his birth. Finally, death consummates the self-dispossession; for in death Christ surrenders life and his very being (Matt. 27:50).

In all these ways, then, Jesus wanted to depend on things and the elements enough to be fully a man with roots in this world, but free enough to be constantly turned to God; he is in the world without belonging to it; he pitches his tent among men, but never takes up a permanent abode in empirical reality. Consequently he can reveal to men God's transcendence over created space and what fills it.

Without entering in detail into the problem of earthly values and poverty according to Christianity, let us recall at least some of the principal features of Christ's teaching. A certain tension between earthly goods and those of the kingdom is a component of Christian existence. Jesus pronounces the poor in spirit happy (Matt. 5:3) and insistently emphasizes to his disciples the need of detachment, the impossibility of serving both God and money, and the disorder inherent in immoderate concern for material things (Matt. 6:24–34); he gives the Twelve very precise instructions on poverty as they set out on their missionary journey (Matt. 10:8–10); he urges his hearers to give everything away for the sake of the kingdom (Matt. 13:44–46; 19:16–29; cf. 16:24–26); and identifies himself in a mysterious fashion with the poor and the unfortunate (Matt. 25:31–46). And it is indeed true that possessions give a man stability in the world and have a dangerous capacity for making him its prisoner. It is not so much our body that determines our true dwelling-place as it is the possession we regard as most precious: "Where your treasure is, there your heart is also" (Matt. 6:21). It is crucial, therefore, to store up treasure not on earth, but in heaven (Matt. 6:19–20).[112]

In addition, in order to resolve the basic paradox of Christian existence: being in the world (John 17:11) without being of the world (John 17:16), Christ transforms the material goods which might be an obstacle into means of approaching God. Through the Savior's words of institution, the basic material realities become efficacious signs of salvation. In the sacramental symbols the imperishable goods of the kingdom are rendered present to the immanence of history; instead of holding the believer captive to what is accessible to the senses, the world and the use of the things of the world are opened into invisible values, the human to the divine and the temporal to the eternal.[113] By his glorious ascent to the Father's right hand, Christ himself leads the believer to live intentionally, through faith, hope, and love, where he himself now is (Col. 3:1–3). Far from leaving the visible world, the Christian wins new mastery over it and, because he is liberated from all enslaving attachments, restores that world to its Creator: "All things are yours, and you are Christ's, and Christ is God's" (1 Cor. 3:22–23).

Christian Language and Spatiality

The preceding analyses allow us to draw some conclusions about the expression of the Christian mystery.

We have shown that human language necessarily depends on the daily renewed experience of the world in which we live. The legitimate ways of expressing the experience of space are therefore valid for giving expression to the mystery. The logic of religious language is, in large part, the same as the logic of experience.

The Bible and, after it, the Church bring men an existential message of salvation, not a scientific knowledge of the universe; they therefore speak to humanity its own spontaneous language—that is, the language of experience, which bears the deep impress of spatiality. But the biblical writers know how to express, through this *empirical phenomenology* and the *concrete logic* of which it is the substructure, the transcendent mystery of God. In saying that God is in heaven, the Bible is not in any way claiming that the divinity is localized somewhere in the stratosphere. Even the simplest of Christians is not tempted to locate God in an orbit, even in Aristotle's "first heaven," or to think of him as a kind of spaceship. The reason for this is that biblical language, in setting the poles of our universe over against each other, projects God outside the universe and beyond all spatiality. For anyone who knows how to interpret speech, the empirical language of the Bible authentically signifies the absolute transcendence of God in the order of being.

We can see, then, how little foundation there is, from this point of view, for a critique of Christian language like that proposed by Robinson, with its basis in Tillich, Bonhoeffer, and Bultmann.[114] To say that the idea of a "three-story" universe is scientifically outdated, mythical, and therefore unacceptable to a modern mind is to give evidence of confusion and fail to recognize the basic anthropological data which we have been explaining. It is, of course, true that the biblical writings show traces of cosmological ideas which were connected with a primitive stage of knowledge and have, to that extent, become invalid; such would be, for example, the picture of the earth as a flat surface resting on pilings that are sunk into "the waters beneath"; or of the firmament as a solid vault holding back "the waters above" (cf., e.g., Gen. 1:1–8; 1 Sam. 2:8; Job 9:6; 26:7–8; 38:6; Ps. 75:4; 104:5; 148:4). But such rudimentary scientific ideas, which in any case are in evolution all through the Old Testament, are not essentially connected with the message of salvation. On the other hand, the divisions of "high and low," "right and left," standing upright and sitting, with the natural meanings they carry, are not bound up with any particular state of scientific knowledge; they belong rather to universal human experience and are valid for man yesterday, today, and tomorrow. The "three-story universe" (depths of earth or sea, surface of the earth, and the sky) does not have its basis in "prelogical" thinking; not only do our senses find it acceptable, but it is inscribed in our bodies and minds. *Man carries that universe in himself*, whatever his level of education or the variations of meaning assigned to that universe in different cultures. Such representations can, therefore, legitimately be employed in expressing the Christian faith, since their meaning belongs to everyone's living experience.

Shall we substitute for the representation of heaven as God's dwelling that of depth, as Tillich and Robinson suggest? But depth is no less a spatial dimension than height and keeps us just as much within "a three-story universe." A change from height to depth is simply a change in perspective; the Romans recognized this when they used the same word *(altitudo)* for both dimensions. And should we forget that the biblical writers, far from ignoring the idea of depth, oppose it to that of height in expressing the fact that God is present to both—that is, to the totality of creation which can neither measure nor enclose him? Height and depth, then, in biblical language, which so faithfully mirrors man's experience and makes such skillful use of it, effectively signify the ideas of "transcendence" and "immanence." The images of high and low, opposed to each other and transcended by the mind, support the idea of God's infinite excellence.

Would it be better if the language of preaching or catechesis were to reject all concrete points of reference and to use only the language of a more abstract theology? if, instead of saying "God is in heaven," one were to teach: "God is transcendent"? But the very word "transcendence" is borrowed from our experience of space, since *trans-scandere* means "to step over, " "to go higher than." Even the subtlest metaphysical language has strong, unbreakable bonds with experience.

Shall we *create* an entirely new language to express revealed truth? The suggestion may be attractive at first glance, but it cannot be implemented. You cannot deliberately invent a language the way you invent a household appliance. A language is not a thing, a simple external possession; it is rooted in man's *being*. And even if it were possible to invent a complete set of symbols out of whole cloth, it would make of the Christian message, which is intended for all mankind, the esoteric possession of a small band of initiates, comparable to the few people who know Volapük or Esperanto. Wouldn't it be ironic, in an age that finds the language of traditional theology too technical, to substitute one scholasticism for another?

The objections to biblical language, then, have force only for the man who forgets his own humanness and the existential roots of language. The preaching of the gospel cannot afford to make a mistake about how man approaches the world and situates himself in cosmic space. The pedagogical need is not to break away from the concrete but to bring man to full awareness of himself. In any event, the great diversity of cultural levels forbids any uniform approach. The concrete language of experience and conceptual expression must always be carefully combined, with an eye to different age brackets and backgrounds, so that they will support one another.

The expression of the Christian mystery is a very complex problem; we have been dealing with only one limited aspect of it. Our intention has been to emphasize the critical justification (existential rather than reflective) and the universality (in fact and by right) of anthropological language.

NOTES

1. Conversion will be studied further on in this chapter. For the presence of God in the disciple of Christ, cf., e.g., John 6:56–57; 14:16–17; 15, *passim;* 1 John 4:12–16; 2:24; Eph. 3:17.

2. In other passages it is the *Name* of Yahweh that is "glorious over all the earth": Ps. 2:8, 10; cf. Ps. 48:11.

3. For the Palestinian, the East, on the one hand, and the western end of the Mediterranean, on the other, were the extremities of the visible universe, that is, of man's world. Thus the divine presence fills all dimensions, vertical (Ps. 139:8) and horizontal (9), of the cosmos. Cf. Ps. 108:6: "Be exalted above the heavens, O God; over all the earth be your glory!" and Job 23:8–9.

4. Cf. St. Augustine, *De Genesi ad litteram*, V, 3 (PL 34:322): "The inspired Scriptures usually express the totality of creation by referring to heaven and earth, adding at times the sea."

5. Cf. Origen, *De oratione*, 23 (PG 11:486–87); St Augustine, *Epistolae*, 140:3,6 (PL 33:540); *De diversis quaestionibus*, 20 (PL 40:15–16).

6. Cf. also Ps. 103:11–12: "For as the heavens are high above the earth, so surpassing is his kindness towards those who fear him. As far as the east is from the west, so far has he put our transgressions from us." Cf. Deut. 30:11.

7. Cf. also Ps. 107:2–3: "the redeemed of the Lord . . . those whom he has . . . gathered from the lands, from the east and the west, from the north and the south."

8. Cf. below, pp. 203–05.

9. Christian tradition has seen in this text a prophecy of Christ's sacrifice, which is both once-for-all and rendered universally present by the Eucharist.

10. Cf. *The Humanity of God*, pp. 84–85.

11. The texts in which God is called "the Most High" are so numerous that there is no point to multiplying references.

12. Cf. Isa. 66:1: "The heavens are my throne."

13. For example, Abraham (Gen. 22:2; cf. 2 Chron. 3:1), Moses (Exod. 24:3–8), Gideon (Judg. 5:26), Samuel (1 Sam. 9:12).

14. Cf. Isa. 2:2: "The mountain of the Temple of the Lord will be *raised up!*"

15. Cf. Gen. 33:3: Jacob prostrates himself seven times before his brother Esau.

16. Cf. *The Humanity of Man*, pp. 211–16, 267–68.

17. Cf. Exod. 2:23: The cry of the oppressed Hebrews "went up" to God.

18. On this and the following section cf. Yves Congar, *The Mystery of the Temple*, trans. Reginald F. Trevett (Westminster, Md.: Newman, 1962).

19. Ps. 68:1–20 describes in epic style the pilgrimage of Yahweh to the sanctuary on Mount Zion.

20. Jerusalem is "the navel of the earth," according to Ezek. 38:12; cf. 5:5.

21. Allusion is often made to this text in the New Testament tradition: by Christ himself (Matt. 5:34–35), by Stephen (Acts 7:48–50), by Paul on the Areopagus (Acts 17:24).

22. Cf. Matt. 6:10: The disciples are to pray that God's will be done "on earth as it is in heaven."

23. The Old Testament also speaks of God's interventions as "comings"; cf.,e.g., Ps. 80:3; 96:13; Isa. 35:4; Zech. 9:9. From the vantage point of the human "here" in which he finds himself, Jesus sees the movement of his coming as climaxed, in a first stage, in this particular point of space and time. This is what is meant by the "I come" *(erchomai)* of John 3:19; 7:28; 8:14; 16:28; 18:37 cf. Matt. 11:3; 21:9; John 1:9–11. Following the same logic Jesus speaks of his passage to the Father as a "departure" and a "journey to be made," sometimes using the Greek verb *hypago*: John 8:14, 21; 13:33, 36; 14:4, 28 (note here and in verse 3 the use of "I come" to designate the second "coming" of Christ); 16:5, 17; sometimes the verb *aperchomai:* John 16:7. On the other hand, in John 17:11, Jesus in speaking of his Father considers himself to be already present with him in that "beyond" which is so mysterious for men but which is Christ's proper "here" as God; from this standpoint his passage is "coming": "I am in the world no more, but these are in the world as I come to you (*erchomai*)." On the category of "descent," cf. later in this chapter; on "going" and "coming," cf. *The Humanity of Man*, p. 39.

24. On the history of the term cf. "Incarnation," *Dictionnaire de théologie catholique*, 7:1445–1539. Ordinarily the stress is laid on the full meaning of the word "flesh" *(caro, -carnation);* here, however, we are emphasizing the depth of meaning in the prefix *in*.

25. We should not pass too quickly over this deeply meaningful formula and its powerful *somatikos* ("in bodily form"). The "fullness of deity" in Jesus Christ will be affirmed in all its splendor at his glorification. Christian thought has often meditated on this unlimited presence of God within the limits of our humanness. Cf., for example, St. Augustine in his letters to Volusianus, *Epp.* 135:2, and 137:2 (PL 33:513, 516–17); St. Thomas Aquinas refers to these texts in his *Summa theologiae*, III, q.l, a. l, ad 4; cf. St. Leo the Great, *Second Sermon on the Lord's Nativity (=Sermo 22)* 2 (PL 54:195): "incomprehensible, he desired to be comprehended." This last text reminds us in turn of Pascal, *Pensées*, Fr. 348 (Turnell, Fr. 217, p. 162): "By means of space

the universe contains me and swallows me up like a speck; by means of thought I comprehend the universe." But if the consciousness of Christ, like every human consciousness, "comprehends" the universe by means of thought, his divine power "comprehends" it in quite a different way, by means of an infinite creative embrace.

26. The evidence is provided by the Gospels in their totality. On Christ's experiential knowledge, cf. St. Thomas Aquinas, *Summa theologiae*, III, q. 9, a. 4; q. 3, a. 12. On the circulation of meaning, cf. *The Humanity of Man*, p. 19 and *passim*.

27. It is common knowledge that John did not write: "he dwelt among us," but used the verb *eskenosen* ("pitched his tent"). For a people whose ancestors were nomads and, during the Exodus, saw the sacred Tent pitched near their own, this verb was richer in meaning than it is for us, even if use had gradually obscured the original connotations. It has also been noted that the consonants of the Greek verb suggest the Hebrew *shekinah* or "presence" of Yahweh as elaborated in Jewish theology. In addition, John seems to be referring to the presence of divine wisdom in Israel according to Ecclus. 24:7–22; Bar. 3:36–44.

28. Jesus was received by Simon Peter (Mark 1:29; 2:1; 3:20), by Levi, son of Alphaeus (Mark 2:15), by Martha and Mary (Luke 10:38), by Zacchaeus (Luke 19:5–6); he was rejected by his fellow-townsmen of Nazareth (Luke 4:29–30) and by a Samaritan village (Luke 9:51–53).

29. It is of interest to compare the different usages of the term "world" in English and in John's vocabulary. By and large, "world" can mean, for John the universe, the earth, mankind, and the powers hostile to God and Christ.

30. This drama of acceptance or rejection of God will be taken up again, in Chapter 7, in connection with the "visit."

31. Cf. Jer. 11:19, which the Passion liturgy applies to the persecuted Christ.

32. The objectivity of God's gifts in no way affects the divine transcendence. If God is truly the Wholly Other, infinitely above creatures, then neither the reality of man nor the objectivity of the gifts of grace can lessen in the slightest the infinite fullness of God. It is the *uncorrected* anthropomorphism based on human "giving" that leads us to think that the creature or God's gifts could affect the plenitude and transcendence of the Creator.

33. Cf. *The Humanity of Man*, p. 31.

34. Cf.pp. 182–85.

35. The same method of expression is used in connection with the word of God; cf. below, Chapter 3, note 36.

36. Cf. the patristic texts cited below in Chapter 7, notes 31 and 34; cf. also St. Thomas Aquinas, *Summa theologiae*, III, q. 8, a. 2.

37. The image of the "bosom" throws light on John 1:1–2: "The Word was close beside God *(pros ton theon)*" (author's version); cf. John 6:46.

38. Cf. pp. 150–51.

39. Cf. René Laurentin, *Jésus au Temple* (Paris: Gabalda, 1966).

40. Note that here and in some other texts concerning the body of

Christians Scripture uses *naos,* which, in its primary meaning, refers to the Holy of Holies. Cf. below, note 42.

41. The evangelist notes how when Jesus enters the Temple he "looks around." This is doubtless an attitude and affirmation of authority; cf. *The Humanity of Man*, pp. 250–51.

42. Cf. St Augustine, Sermo 82:10 (PL 38:512); "Now you yourself are God's temple. As temple you go in and go out, as temple you abide at home, as temple you rise up."

43. Cf. Congar, *The Mystery of the Temple.*

44. On Jesus's meals, see Chapter 7, New Testament part.

45. Cf. Marie-Joseph Lagrange, *Evangile selon Saint Luc* (Paris: Gabalda, 1948[7]), p. 393.

46. St. Thomas Aquinas, *Summa theologiae*, III, q. 52, a. 2, and trans. Richard T.A. Murphy, O.P., *Summa theologiae*, 54 (3a, 46–52) (New York: McGraw-Hill, 1965), p. 159.

47. Cf. *The Humanity of Man*, pp. 50–51.

48. In Christianity, however, the eastward position of the believer at prayer, of the worshipping congregation, or of the church building is not determined by the idea of reference to Jerusalem. Unlike the Israelite who turns towards the Holy City and the Muslim who turns towards Mecca in prayer, the Christian looks to the "cosmic" or solar east. The difference between the two kinds of orientation is, in the opinion of Cyrille Vogel, "basic and irreducible." The element common to all special orientations, we might add, is a universal anthropological constant, whatever the particular direction prescribed for the ritual gesture: in turning to a particular point of the world, man becomes intentionally present to it. Why, in fact, does the Christian choose to turn to the east? It seems that the idea of a return to the origins of the world (an idea that inspires cosmic orientations even outside of solar cults) was taken up in the cultural milieu of the Mediterannean world and given a Christian meaning. Just as the earthly Paradise lay in the East (Gen. 2:8), so from the east the Christian awaits the return of Christ, the sun of salvation, regenerator of the world and mankind. Cf. Origen, *Prayer*, 32, tr. John J. O'Meara *(Ancient Christian Writers*, 19; Westmininster, Md.: Newman, 1954), p. 136: facing the east in prayer is "an act which symbolizes the soul looking toward where the true light rises"; or the ritual of baptismal profession of faith which St. Cyrii of Jerusalem describes and comments on in his *Catechesis* 19 (=Mystagogic Catechesis 1):2,4 (PG 33:1068–69): in renouncing Satan the catechumen turns to the west as the place of visible darkness and therefore the symbol of the dwelling of the prince of darkness; after the renunciation an about-face turns the catechumen to the east, the region of Paradise and light, as he professes faith in the Trinity (cf. 19:9, 1–8). Cf. St. Ambrose, *De mysteriis*, 2:7 (quoted below,); *Constitutiones apostolicae*, 2:57 (PG 73 1:33-36); St. Gregory of Nyssa, *De oratione dominica*, 5 (PG 44:1384B-C); St. Basil, *De Sancto Spiritu*, 27:66 (PG 32:188B, 189C–192A); St. John Chrysostom, *In Danielem*, 6 (PG 56:226–27). On this large question, extensive historical documentation is available in: Franz Joseph Dolger, *Sol salutis*

(Liturgiegeschichtliche Quellen und Forschungen 16–17; Münster: Aschendorff, 1925); Cyrille Vogel, "*Versus ad Orientem:* L'orientation dans les *Ordines Romani* du haut Moyen Age," *Studi medievali,* 3rd series, 1 (1960) 447–69; "*Sol aequinoctialis:* Promblèmes et technique de l'orientation dans le culte chrétien," *Revue des sciences religieuses* 36 (1962) 175–211; "L'orientation vers l'est du célébrant et des fidèles pendant la célébration eucharistique," *Orient syrien* 9 (1964) 3–37; Louis Bouyer, *Architecture et Liturgie* (Paris: Editions du Cerf, 1967), *passim.*

49. Cf. below, Chapter 4.

50. It is difficult to determine the prophetic texts to which the evangelist is referring.

51. Note, however, Matt. 12:28: "kingdom of God" (JB). Cf. Mark 4:11; Luke 4:43; 9:62; 10:9; 17:21; John 3:3–5. Matthew's formula follows the rabbinical tradition in avoiding the ineffable Name.

52. Jesus also prays on a mountain in Matt. 14:23.

53. In addition to *prospiptein* ("fall at the feet of . . . "), classical Greek and the texts of Matthew and John to which we are referring use a very vivid term to express prostration: *proskynein*—literally, "play the part of the dog before someone," and figuratively, "adore." The image of a suppliant or guilty dog creeping towards his master with head to the ground and tail between his legs is certainly an apt one for expressing man's lowliness before God.

54. The Greek Fathers speak of God's "condescension," his "coming down with us."

55. The Virgin Mary "extols the Lord" (Luke 1:46, Smith-Goodspeed), "for he has looked upon his servant in her lowliness" (1:48). The Latin *respicere* means "to look from above" and "to look favorably." *Despicere* expresses the idea of looking from above or with scorn. As for the ascensional movement of prayer, cf. Acts 10:4: the prayers and alms of Cornelius "have risen in God's sight"; Rev. 8:4: "The smoke of the incense went up before God, and with it the prayers of God's people"; cf. Ps. 141:2. Some texts of the Roman Liturgy which are particularly faithful to biblical language: prayer of blessing of incense at Solemn Mass, "May this incense which you bless arise to you, Lord, and your mercy descend upon us"; versicle and response for the Magnificat at Saturday Vespers, "Let our evening prayer ascend to you, Lord, and your mercy descend upon us"; invitation to the people just before the Preface of the Mass, "Lift up your hearts! "

56. Cf. St. Augustine, *Sermo* 123:4, 4 (PL 33:686): "He is above, he is below: above by his own nature, below in his followers; above in the Father, below in us. Reverence the Christ who is above, recognize the Christ who is below."

57. The remarks of the Jews (verses 35–36) highlight the force of Christ's statement.

58. Peter's inability to understand (verses 36–37) parallels that of the Jews in 7:35–36.

59. Cf. Origen, *Commentarium in Matthaeum,* 12:21–22 (PG 13:1032–33) on the phrase "after me." Origen elsewhere notes that Christ is a way on

which the traveler needs no luggage (*Commentarium in Johannem*, 1:26; 6:11 [PG 14:73, 233]). The whole Church must be a pilgrim, according to Heb. 13:14.

60. Cf. St. Augustine, *Sermo* 91:6, 7 (PL 38:570): "Why do you look for a way? Cling to Christ who by descending and ascending made himself the way"; *Sermo* 141:4, 4 (PL 38:777): "The Son of God who, being always with the Father, is truth and life, by taking manhood to himself became the way as well." More than that, the Way comes to meet us: "I do not say: 'seek the way,' for the way itself comes to meet you; arise and walk!" (*ibid*.).

61. Cf. St. Augustine, *Sermo* 123:3,3 (PL 38:685): "Christ-God is the fatherland to which we go; Christ-man is the way by which we go. We are going to him, we are going through him." Cf. *Sermo* 346 (PL 39:1522–26). The theme of the "way" could be followed through the Bible, especially in the events of the patriarchal period and of the Exodus, as could the theme of the "two ways" (cf. Deut. 30:15–20; Ps. 1; 107:4–9; 119; Prov. 4:11–19; Jer. 21:8; Matt. 7:13–14). Christianity is called "the way" in Acts 9:2; 18:25–26; 19:9, 23; 22:4; 24:14,22. The *Didache* picks up the theme of the two ways.

62. The likeness between tree and man is observed in Isa. 11:1, where the messianic king is represented as a shoot from the stump of Jesse, a bud flowering from his roots. In Isa. 53:2 the servant of Yahweh is again likened to a shoot and a sapling. Cf. Hos. 14:6–8, and *The Humanity of Man*, p. 53.

63. Cf. Col. 1:19–20: "It pleased God . . . by means of him, to reconcile everything in his person, both on earth and in the heavens, making peace through the blood of his cross."

64. Cf. below, Chapter 4, section 7, "God's Hand and Man's Praying Hand."

65. Cf. St. Thomas Aquinas, *Summa theologiae*, III, q. 52, a. 2.

66. The cosmic meaning of the cross could be illustrated by numerous texts from the Christian tradition. Cf., e.g., Irenaeus, *Adversus haereses*, 5:17,4 (PG 8:1171–72); 5:18, 3 (PG 7:1174); St. Gregory of Nyssa, *In Christi Resurrectionem*, I (PG 46:621C–625B); *Contra Eunomium*, 3:3, 39–40, ed. Jaeger, Vol. 2, pp. 121–22); *Oratio catechetica*, 32:6–7 (PG 45:80–81, These texts have been studied by Jean Daniélou, "Le symbolisme cosmique de la Croix," *Maison-Dieu* n. 75 (1963) 23–36; Daniélou notes Gregory's efforts to find an allusion to the four dimensions of the cross in Eph. 3:18. Cf. also Daniélou, *The Theology of Jewish Christianity*, trans. John A. Baker (Chicago: Regnery, 1964), pp. 279–92; St. Cyril of Jerusalem, *Catecheses*, 13:28 (PG 33:805); St. Athanasius, *Oratio de Incarnatione Verbi*, 25 (PG 25:140); and Gérard de Champeaux and Sébastien Sterckx, *Introduction au monde des symboles* (St.-Léger-Vauban: Zodiaque, 1966), pp. 365–66 (henceforth: Champeaux-Sterckx, *Symboles*).

67. The prayer of Jonah (Jon. 2:3–10) is a fine illustration of the anthropological meaning of the depths.

68. Peter's use of Ps. 16:8–11, and the opposition between Jesus "freed from death's bitter pangs" (verse 24) and David whose "grave is in our midst to this day" (verse 29), are especially to be noted.

69. The one Greek verb *egeirein* has these various meanings.

70. Cf. pp. 183–84.

71. See the references, pp. 230–31.

72. Cf. Origen, *In Genesim homiliae*, 4:5 (PG 12:186–187); *Commentarium in Mathaeum*, 13:3 (PG 13:1100).

73. Cf. *The Humanity of Man*, pp. 72 ff.

74. On the desent into hell, cf. 1 Pet. 3:19–20; Louis Bouyer, *The Paschal Mystery*, trans. Sr. Mary Benoit, R.S.M. (Chicago: Regnery, 1950), pp. 249–57, Yves Congar, *Jesus Christ*, trans. Luke O'Neill (New York: Herder and Herder, 1966), pp. 82–85, with bibliographical note on p. 82.

75. Cf. detailed commentary on this text in Joseph Schmitt, *Jésus ressuscité dans la prédication apostolique: Etude de théologie biblique* (Paris: Gabalda, 1949), pp. 93–99. Cf. Acts 2:33; 5:31; on the name of Jesus, 4:12.

76. Cf. commentary in Schmitt, *op. cit.*, pp. 99–105.

77. The Fangs (or Boulous) of South Cameroun, for example, designate God simply as "he who is eternally seated." For the Bamilékés of West Cameroun the seat is the symbol of divinity and provides a favorite theme for art. (We owe these remarks to J.M. Ela.)—Among numerous biblical texts, cf. Ps. 9:8; 29:10; 102:13; Lam. 5:19. Cf. Champeaux-Sterckx, *Symboles*, pp. 382–86.

78. In another text it is the heavens which form God's throne: Isa. 66:1.

79. Cf. Ps. 9:8 "The Lord sits enthroned forever; he has set up his throne for judgment"; Ps. 29:10; 45:7; 122:5; Prov. 20:8.

80. The biblical writers frequently describe a theophany in an indirect way by describing its reflection in the mirror of creatures: upheaval of nature, man's fright and prostration; cf. Chapter 2, note 7, and pp. 202–03.

81. Cf. Pseudo-Dionysius, *De divinis nominibus*, 9:8 (PG 3:916); St. Thomas Aquinas, *In librum beati Dionysii De divinis nominibus expositio* (Rome: Marietti, 1960), *in loc.*

82. Jesus had applied the prophecy to himself in Matt. 22:44; 26:64. Cf. 1 Pet. 3:22. The prediction of the sitting on the Davidic throne in Luke 2:32–33 was fulfilled in a superior way. Cf. Jean Daniélou, *Etudes d'exégèse judéo-chrétienne (Les Testimonia)* (Paris: Beauchesne, 1966), pp. 42–49.

83. In Luke 2:46 Jesus is seated while listening to and questioning the teachers. During his public life he sits seeking rest after a journey (John 4:6), and while teaching magisterially (Matt. 5:1–2; 13:1–2; 24:3; 26:55 [cf. 23:2]; Luke 5:3; John 8:2 [but cf. 7:37: a prophetic proclamation issued standing]). Sitting is also the posture of receptive listening on the part of the disciple: Luke 10:39. To sit at the Master's side was regarded as the highest honor: Matt. 19:28 and 20:20–23; the unchanging significance of this sitting is highlighted by the very different character of the two contexts (proclamation of eschatological judgment and naive dream of temporal advancement).

84. On the sitting of God and on the sitting of Christ at the Father's right hand, cf. St. Augustine, *De fide et symbolo*, 7:14 (PL 40:188); *De agone christiano*, 26:28 (PL 40:304); *De symbolo ad catechumenos*, 4:11 (PL 40:634); *Sermo* 213:4,4 (PL 38:1062); St. Thomas Aquinas, *Summa theologiae*, III, q. 3, a. 1, ad 4 q. 58;

Quaestiones quodlibetales, 3:76: "What position is for bodily things, order is for spiritual ones"; Pascal, *Pensées*, Fr. 687 (Turnell, Fr. 506, p. 252).

85. We may note as a curiosity that the various properties and meanings of the throne—elevation, stability, etc. (cf. *The Humanity of Man*, p. 64)—are invoked by Pseudo-Dionysius to justify the name "thrones" for the third order in the first angelic hierarchy; cf. *De hieraracbia caelesti*, 7 (295D). St. Thomas Aquinas repeats the same arguments in *Summa theologiae*, I, q. 108, a. 5, ad 6; cf. q. 108, a. 6, ad 2.

86. For biblical man the subterranean regions, the pit, and the marine depths have the same existential meaning as they have for man of every age: they are the realm of irreversible defeat, of loss, of death. Salvation therefore consists in being snatched from the pit and from the hands of the infernal powers. Among many texts on the pit, cf. Ps. 7:16; 28:1; 30:4; 55:24; 57:7; 94:13; Jer. 18:20–22; 48:44; on the depths, Ps. 71:20; on the marine abyss: Ps. 18:5–6, 17; Isa. 5:14; 14:13–15; Jon. 2:1–11.

87. The same hope is forcefully expressed in Job 19:23–27.

88. At the departure from Egypt "I freed you from their slavery, breaking the yoke they had laid upon you and letting you walk erect" (Lev. 26:13).

89. Cf. Ps. 118:16–17 in the Vg.: "The Lord's right hand has exalted me. . . . I shall not die but live, and I shall tell the works of the Lord."

90. In addition to the passages to be cited in the next part of the text, cf. John 5:1–15; 9:2; and cf. Xavier Léon-Dufour, *Etudes d'èvangile* (Paris: Editions du Seuil, 1965), pp. 125–26.

91. Cf. Léon-Dufour, *op. cit.*, pp. 133–34.

92. Note the corrrespondence between the event and the prediction made in 5:28: "An hour is coming in which all those in their tombs shall hear his voice and come forth."

93. Similarly the verb *sozein* (to save) is used in very varied contexts: peril of the sea (Matt. 8:25; 14:30), illness (Matt. 9:21–22; Mark 3:4; 6:56; Luke 17:19; 18:42; John 11:12; etc.), inescapable death (Matt. 27:42), sin (Matt. 1:21); and with a global meaning (Luke 19:10; John 3:17; 10:9).

94. On this fragment of an early Christian hymn, cf. Schmitt, *Jésus ressuscité*, pp. 86–87. The hope of Job 19:25–26 is now fulfilled. Cf. Roman Missal, Collect for the Second Sunday after Easter: "God, who through the abasement of your Son raised up a prostrate world. . . "

95. Cf. James 4:10: "Be humbled in the sight of the Lord and he will raise you on high"; 1 Pet. 5:6: "Bow humbly under God's mighty hand, so that in due time he may lift you high." In many theophanies man's prostration quickly leads to his being raised up by God or the divine Messenger; e.g., Ezek. 1:28–2:1; 3:22–24; Dan. 10:10; Matt. 17:6, where the apostles fall to the ground before the transfigured Jesus, who then touches and raises them; John 18:6, where, in words that recall the divine name revealed to Moses, Jesus answers the guards who are searching for him: "I am he," and they fall to the ground. Cf. also Saul on the road to Damascus, Acts. 9:4–8.

96. Standing for prayer was already a Jewish practice (Mark 11:25); in Christianity it takes on a specifically paschal and eschatological meaning. Cf.

St. Basil, *De Sancto Spiritu*, 27:66 (PG 32:192); in particular, the genuflection followed by standing asserts that we were cast down by sin and that the Creator's "philanthropy" called us once again to a heavenly destiny *(ibid.)*. On the various postures for prayer, cf. Origen, *De oratione*, 31 (PG 11:549–50). On candor or frankness in speech *(parrhesia)*, cf. Eph. 3:12; 1 Tim. 3:13; Heb. 3:6; 1 John 2:28; 3:21; 4:17. Cf. *The Church at Prayer: Introduction to the Liturgy*, ed. Aimé-Georges Martimort, trans. Austin Flannery, O.P., and Vincent Ryan, O.S.B. (New York: Desclée, 1968), pp. 150–54.

97. Cf. St. Augustine, *Sermo* 123:4,4 (PL 38:686), quoted above, note 56.

98. This text is used in the Roman Breviary as the fifth antiphon for First Vespers of Christmas.

99. Cf. Luke 10:14 "And as for you, Capernaum, 'Are you to be exalted to the skies? You shall be hurled down to the realm of death.' " Cf. Isa. 14:13–15.

100. Cf. *The Humanity of Man*, pp. 66–70.

101. In the Hebrew Bible, the idea of "turning oneself back (around)" is expressed by various verbs, most often by *sabab* and especially *shub*. The Septuagint and the New Testament use *epistrephein* and *metanoein*, the first referring rather to a change in outward conduct, the second (as the etymology indicates) primarily to the inner turning back, or around, of the spirit. Acts 3:19 combines the two. Cf. Paul Aubin, *Le problème de la "conversion": Etude sur un terme commun á l'hellénisme et au christianisme des trois premiers siécles* (Paris: Beauchesne, 1963); cf. pp. 26–29 on the biblical vocabulary.

102. The "heart" is the innermost center of personality where the decisive existential choices are made.

103. Cf. Acts 3:16: if they turn from *(apostrephein)* their evil ways the "converts" will receive the blessing of God in Jesus Christ.

104. If Yahweh himself is said to harden man's heart (Exod. 4:21; 14:4), the meaning is that he passes judgment on man's sin and allows it to bear its deadly fruit.

105. St. Cyril of Jerusalem, *Catechesis* 19 (=Mystagogica 1): 2,4,9. Cf. above, note 48.

106. Cyril twice stresses the intentional presence to Satan, *Catechesis* 19, 2,3 and 4, 1.

107. *Ibid.*, 9,1–8.

108. St. Ambrose, *The Mysteries*, trans. Roy J. Deferrari, in *Saint Ambrose, Theological and Dogmatic Works*, Fathers of the Church, 44 (Washington, D.C.: Catholic University of America Press, 1963), p.7.

109. Cf. below, Chapter 5, section 16, "The Face-to-Face Relationship of Faith."

110. Cf. below, Chapter 7, section 10, "The Paschal Meals."

111. Cf. below, Chapter 7, section 9, "The Institution of the Eucharistic Meal."

112. Cf. St. Augustine, *Sermo* 86:1, 1 (PL 38:524): "A man cannot fail to think of his treasure and to pursue his wealth in a journeying of the heart. . . . if, therefore, you want your heart to be lifted up, it is there that

you must put what you love; be on earth as far as the flesh goes, but let your heart dwell with Christ." This "journeying of the heart" expresses in a very concrete way the movement of "intentionality."

113. Cf. *The Humanity of Man*, pp. 35–36.

114. John A. T. Robinson, *Honest to God* (London: SCM; Philadelphia: Westminster, 1963). Robinson refers to Paul Tillich, *The Shaking of the Foundations* (New York: Scribner's, 1948), especially p. 57; to Dietrich Bonhoeffer, *Prisoner for God*, trans. Reginald H. Fuller (New York: Macmillan, 1953), reprinted as *Letters and Papers from Prison* (New York: Macmillan, 1962; greatly enlarged edition, 1971); and to Rudolf Bultmann, "New Testament and Mythology," in Hans Werner Bartsch, ed., *Kerygma and Myth: A Theological Debate* (London: SPCK, 1953; reprinted as Harper Torchbook, Harper & Row, 1961), pp. 1–44.

CHAPTER 2

HUMAN TIME AND CHRISTIAN MYSTERY

God's plan for man's salvation unfolds in history: the old covenant is the age-long preparatory stage; the incarnation of the Son, God's entrance into man's duration, is the decisive moment in the plan; finally, the Church carries on until the end of time the divine work of salvation. Man's experience of time is thus inseparable from the Christian experience: the former is the matrix of the latter and constitutes one of its fundamental dimensions. The experience of temporality therefore provides the Christian mystery with more than a means of expression.

Yet the experience of time does not make as important a contribution to language as does the experience of space. The reason for this is that extension, as a property common to our bodies and to things, falls under the outer senses of sight and touch, while distance affects many of our perceptions and is accessible to us through movement. Time, on the contrary, is neither visible nor tangible; it is accessible only through the inner experience of consciousness.

In keeping with our special purpose, we will not study Christian time in all its aspects. Other books provide a reliable theological approach to the problem from an "objective" point of view.[1] Our intention here is to foster understanding of the Christian mystery in the light of the experience of time as a lived reality.

I. THE OLD TESTAMENT

God Transcends Time

Unlike the mythical gods whose heroic deeds take place in a primordial time before that of the world,[2] the God of the Bible does not exist in any duration, however privileged. On the contrary, it is his sovereign creative act that creates the beginning of time along with the beginning of the world: "In the beginning, when God created heaven and earth . . . . " (Gen. 1:1). The timeless God created a temporal world. The distribution of the creative activity over six successive "days" is not intended, therefore, as a measurement of that activity itself. It is, instead, a pedagogical procedure for impressing upon the Israelites the commandment of the Sabbath rest. The writer provides the believer with a supreme archetype for his conduct, a model inseparable from the creative activity of God himself.[3]

Involved as he is in duration, man cannot express God's infinite superiority to, or "transcendence" over, becoming except with the help of his own temporal experience. That experience yields modes of expression which, if taken literally, are very imperfect; yet the intention is always unambiguous: to signify the divine changelessness. God's incommunicable privilege in this respect gives rise to a name that is wholly proper to him: God is the "Eternal One."[4]

This divine attribute, which inspires biblical man with fear, wonder, and desire, is expressed through opposition to cosmic becoming. Man affirms the divine eternity in terms of *anteriority:* "Before the mountains were begotten and the earth and the world were brought forth, from everlasting to everlasting you are God" (Ps. 90:2). We may also quote a few verses of the splendid passage in Proverbs in which divine Wisdom unveils the mystery of its "eternity": "The Lord begot me, the firstborn of his ways, the forerunner of his prodigies of long ago; From of old I was poured forth, at the first, before the earth. When there were no depths I was brought forth, when there were no fountains or springs of water; Before the mountains were settled into place, before the hills, I was brought forth; When as yet the earth and the fields were not made, nor the first clouds of the world" (Prov. 8:22–26; cf. 22–31; cf. Wisd. 24:9).

In creating a temporal universe God also creates the rhythms which mark duration. The divine command given to the light to appear and separate itself from the darkness brings about the alternation of day and night, morning and evening (Gen. 1:3–4). The lights placed in the firmament illumine the earth, mark the divisions of time, and "serve as signs both for festivals and for seasons and years" (Gen. 1:14, NEB). These basic rhythms will not be destroyed; the same God who created them keeps them in existence after the flood, as he does the alternation of seasons with their growth (Gen. 8:22). The Eternal One thus stands outside the divisions of time; he assigns them their measure but is not measured by them in turn, for he is absolute master of them; before him, day and night are as though they were not.[5]

The universe does, however, offer one striking image of changelessness: the mountain, present there as far back as man can remember and challenging time with its immovable bulk. But God, who created the mountain,[6] precedes it in existence (cf. Ps. 90:2, quoted above [cf. Matt. 17:20; 21:21]; Ps. 125:1–2).[7] In a similar fashion, Yahweh is not only anterior to the whole universe but will continue in existence after it: "Of old you established the earth, and the heavens are the work of your hands. They shall perish, but you remain though all of them grow old like a garment. Like clothing you change them, and they are changed, but you are the same, and your years have no end" (Ps. 102:26–28; cf. Ps. 96:10b; 104:3). Consequently God, who exists *before* and *after* all things, cannot be measured by cosmic time; he exists beyond becoming in an absolute transcendence.

Much more, then, does God dominate the precarious duration of mortal men, and it is primarily by contrasting it with his own existential fragility that biblical man expresses God's eternity. In this context, too, eternity is conceived as a total anteriority. He whom no god preceded[8] precedes mankind in an inconceivable "before." Did he not form man out of the clay of the ground? (Gen. 1:27; 2:7). Has he not formed each man's body in his mother's womb, and does he not know each of his actions and the length of his days before they exist? (Ps. 139:13–16). Take Jeremiah for an example: before he was conceived, Yahweh knew him; before he was born, Yahweh consecrated him

(Jer. 1:5). Most striking of all is the case of Job. In his final "discourse," Yahweh confounds his servant's presumption with one simple question: "Where were you when I founded the earth?" (Job 38:4).[9] Job was, in fact, already quite aware of his own littleness. The experience of extreme distress and the fear of imminent death had sharpened the sufferer's sense of man's fragility and, by contrast, of God's eternity: "My days are swifter than a weaver's shuttle, they come to an end without hope. Remember that my life is like the wind" (Job 7:6–7); "Are your days as the days of a mortal, and are your years as a man's lifetime?" (10:5). Yet it is God who determines the short span of man's life: "Since man's days are measured out, since his tale of months depends on you, since you assign him bounds he cannot pass, turn your eyes from him, leave him alone, like a hired drudge, to finish his day" (14:5, JB).

The psalmist, too, gives poignant expression to man's plight. Man lives only for a short while, for a few breaths: "All our days have passed away in your indignation; we have spent our years like a sigh. Seventy is the sum of our years, or eighty, if we are strong" (Ps. 90:9–10). Only he, then, who has power to add to man's days (Ps. 21:5; 61:7; 91:16) can extend King Hezekiah's life by fifteen years (2 Kings 20:1–11; Isa. 38:1–20).[10] In contrast with man, whose days are but smoke, a lengthening shadow, quickly withering grass (Ps. 102:4,12; cf. 103:15–16; 144:4), "God is great beyond our knowledge; the number of his years is past searching out" (Job 36:26). "For," as the psalmist confesses to the Lord, "a thousand years in your sight are as yesterday, now that it is past, or as a watch of the night" (Ps. 90:4; cf. 90:5–6; 2 Pet. 3:8).

In short, he who is before all things and manifests himself to Daniel as the "Ancient of Days" (Dan. 7:9,13,22,RSV), is also, according to Habbakuk, "he who never dies" (Hab. 1:12,JB; cf. 1 Tim. 6:16).[11]

The duration which man experiences within cosmic time is often measured in terms of generations, as we have pointed out elsewhere.[12] But the succession of human generations forms a kind of living, unbreakable network to which no limits can be assigned: before and after me, this duration is lost in the night of time. Biblical man, particularly aware of ancestral solidarities and proud of posterity and ancestry as well, turns readily to the experience of duration of the generations (*toledoth*) to suggest the idea of God's everlastingness. Thus the name of Yahweh (Ps. 135:13),[13] his rule (Ps. 146:10; 3:33; 4:31), his thoughts (Ps. 33:11), his love (Ps. 100:5; cf. 136), and, above all, his fidelity to the covenant lasts "a thousand generations" or "from generation to generation" (cf. Ps. 136; Deut. 7:9; Ps. 105:8). And in even more radical fashion the God of Israel presents himself as the one "who has called forth the generations since the beginning. I, the Lord, am the first, and with the last I shall also be" (Isa. 41:4). To say that God is thus present at the beginning and at the end of the human generations, that he is "the first and. . . the last" (Isa. 44:6; 48:12), is to say that he is unbegotten and immortal; it is, by bringing into play the opposed extremes of our duration, to situate him beyond all becoming.

The experience of lived time also leads men to use the idea of the *century* in order to express God's eternity. A hundred years are far more than the average man lives, for he reaches only seventy or, if he be especially healthy, eighty (Ps. 90:9–10). If then a century is a measure of time which rarely applies to a man, centuries of centuries suggest a duration of which we can have no concrete idea. Confronted with such enormous measurements, the mind reels and the very awareness of such measurements as temporal is suppressed; to a man, such lengths of time are not a duration but the negation of duration. God is he who rules "throughout all ages" (Tob. 13:1,6,10, JB; cf. 1 Tim 1:17).

God's "transcendence" over time finds its supreme expression in the carrying out of his saving will and in the preaching of final judgment. The prevenient action of God as savior not only unfolds in time, but embraces time in its totality. A few basic references will suffice for our purpose. The first words that God addresses to sinful man: "Where are you?" (Gen. 3:9), contain in germ the whole history of salvation down to its final completion. Furthermore, throughout the history of Israel, Yahweh is always the "God of the fathers," who spoke formerly to the eponymous ancestors and, in their persons, chose the people of the promise (cf. the texts of Gen. 12 ff.; and, e.g., Deut. 15:15).[14] His fidelity is unfailing, and, throughout all the vicissitudes of history and despite the opposition of men or without their being aware of it, he infallibly implements a single saving plan: "The Lord brings to nought the plans of nations; he foils the designs of peoples. But the plan of the Lord stands forever; the design of his heart, through all generations" (Ps. 33:10–11; cf. Ps. 2; Prov. 21:30; Isa. 8:9–10).[15] Thus while the projects of mortal man come to naught and his works vanish, God's mastery of time is brilliantly affirmed in the prediction and fulfillment of his plan: "At the beginning I foretell the outcome; in advance, things not yet done. I say that my plan shall stand, I accomplish my every purpose . . . . Yes, I have spoken, I will accomplish it; I have planned it, and I will do it" (Isa. 46:10–11).[16]

Moreover, the existence of prophetism in Israel is a constant and singularly powerful reminder of a divine intention transcendent to history and in the course of realization in the development of history. The prophet is the visible, audible, tangible sign among men of a thought which rules all events and history as a whole (cf. especially the vocation-narratives: Moses, Exod. 3:7–10; Isaiah, Isa. 6; Jeremiah, Jer. 1:4–5; Ezekiel, Ezek. 2). Yahweh reveals, through his spokesmen, the hidden thread connecting events which are apparently utterly remote from one another; thus, in the time of Hosea the repentance of Israel, the unfaithful wife (Hos. 2:16–25), and in the time of the exile the return to Palestine (Isa. 40:3–5; Jer. 16:14–15; Mic. 7:14–15) are presented as leading to a renewal of the wonders of the Exodus, despite the centuries which intervene. The history of Israel is made up of recurring motifs, variations on a basic theme. In short, if the saving plan thus embraces time in its totality down to the final judgment,[17] the reason is that Yahweh is sovereign master of all becoming. The divine gaze reaches "from eternity to eternity" (Ecclus. 39:20, JB). Heaven and earth are to disappear but salvation will be eternal (Isa. 51–68), like God himself.

Privileged Points of Time

Human duration is punctuated by decisive moments at which the interplay of countless obscure determinisms seems to provide an especially favorable point of impact for our projects.[18] God's wisdom takes advantage of this human experience and singles out certain moments for his interventions whether of wrath or of grace: "Thus says the Lord: In a time of favor I answer you, on the day of salvation I help you" (Isa. 49:8; cf. 2 Cor. 6:2). At such moments major events occur through which God's plan moves forward into a new stage:

thus, for example, the call of Abraham, especially the coming forth from Egypt, and, later on, the entrance into Canaan. Such salvific events sum up and fulfill the past, while also opening up a new vista. The promise comes true, the covenant is honored and confirmed, and the "hand" of God accomplishes what his word had foretold. At such moments a new meaning is given to history, for salvation is coming in the shadow-filled light of faith and hope.

For the believer, the event is both history and mystery; its human reality and very real historical factuality conceal a religious depth. The event is *dabar*, or word of God. The "today" of salvation is this most precious of moments when God invites man to give him an answer: "Oh, that today you would hear his voice: 'Harden not your hearts as at Meribah, as in the day of Massah in the desert . . . ' " (Ps. 95:7–8; cf. Exod. 17:1–7), but, on the contrary, "Seek the Lord while he may be found, call him while he is near" (Isa. 55:6). Just as the man who is careful of his own interests applies himself to discerning, then grasping, the opportune moment, so the believer who is attentive to God knows how to recognize in the fleeting instant and the insignificant event a call of grace, a "visit" from God.[19] The Day of Yahweh, the Day of all days, will be, above all else, the day that puts an end to history, avenges Israel upon its enemies, and establishes justice forever (cf., e.g., Joel 2:1–11; Amos 5:18–20; Zeph. 1; cf. also Pss. 97–99).

These major events which mark the history of Israel are to be preserved in the memory of community and individual. Remembrance is one of the fundamental acts of religious fidelity. Through it, man makes present again to his own awareness what is constantly present to the eternal thought of God; the believer makes an effort, however feeble, to match through memory the unwearying eternity of the divine mind that guides the course of history. One of the chief concerns of Deuteronomy is this duty of remembering. The Israelite must always keep present in mind and heart the great historical moment of Egyptian slavery and the Exodus: "Recall," "remember," "do not forget" (cf. Deut. 4:9; 5:15; 7:18; 9:7; 16:12; 32:7–8; cf. Ps. 105:1–15 [=1 Chron. 16:8–22]). Each generation has the duty of passing on to the next, in unbroken oral tradition, the memory of Yahweh's great deeds (Ps. 44:2; 78:1–8). The pious believer thinks ceaselessly of the former times (Ps. 77:6–7; 143:5); infidelity consists in forgetfulness of God's interventions in history, forgetfulness of his "hand," and is a major fault that threatens to bring Israel to the supreme apostasy of idolatry (Ps. 78:42; Neh. 9:17–18; Jer. 2, esp. verse 32).

To keep its memories alive Israel follows the universal anthropological practice[20] of using monuments, that is, stones, altars, or names given to places where particular divine manifestations or interventions occurred.[21] The event has a kind of continuing reality in the form of the witnessing stone, mute of itself but eloquent to faith. But, in addition to these reference-points set up in space, Israel provides itself with a collection of markers scattered through time, inasmuch as periodic ritual reminders sustain the collective and individual memory. Each week the Sabbath commemorates not only the rest of God the Creator but also Israel's emergence from Egypt where hard labor had bowed her to the ground (Exod. 20:8–11; Deut. 5:15). Each year, the great moments celebrated in cosmic religions—feast of the beginning of the spring grain-harvest, of its completion in summer, and of the wine-harvest in autumn—acquire an historical meaning as well. Passover celebrates the Exodus, and the feast of Booths recalls the nomadic years in the desert (Exod. 12:1–28; 23:14–19; Lev. 23:5–44; cf. Isa. 61:2). Certain years as a whole also acquire a special religious value: the sabbatical year, the jubilee year (Lev. 25:1–22).

In the liturgical gathering the evocative power of the word makes the past event present; the individual believer and the people as a whole relive the event by hearing of it.[22] After the reading, prayer then commemorates in festive and symbolic fashion the deed of Yahweh and offers him thanks for it; such is the function of the historical psalms (Ps. 68, which is in the epic mode; Pss. 78; 105; 106; 107).[23] Thanks to such ritual, Israel constantly relives its whole history. The year reduces the national and religious past to its essential elements, so that the liturgical season is a more dense and concentrated kind of time than the historical time had been. The former doubtless unfolds within the latter, but its function is to express the essential meaning, inseparably national and religious, of the latter and thereby to give it a consecration. Israel is thus constantly penetrating ever more deeply, as the years pass, into the meaning of its election by God.

We must not make the mistake of thinking that the annually renewed liturgical cycle imprisons the believer in an inevitable eternal recurrence. It is precisely the peculiarity of biblical time, as contrasted with Greek or Far Eastern conceptions, that it progresses and moves towards a hidden consummation. Through the harmonics of history and the recurring ritual a secret linear movement is going on, for the infallible plan of God is on the way to fulfillment. Historical time and liturgical time are both open to a crowning act in the series of God's great deeds: the Day of Yahweh.

Since God is master of history as a whole no less than of the immensity of world-space, his praise must fill all of time as well as all of space. Such praise becomes a practical expression of that absolute supremacy over duration which we call the divine eternity. From the rising of the sun, therefore, to its setting (a temporal as well as a spatial measurement), the divine name must be praised: "Blessed be the name of the Lord both now and forever. From the rising to the setting of the sun is the name of the Lord to be praised" (Ps. 113:2–3). God's domination of history is itself a perpetual motive for religious wonder and thanksgiving (cf. Ps. 135:8–14; 136:10–26 [the great Hallel]; Dan. 2:21). Praise of God must go on from day to day and even through the nights (Ps. 19:3; 61:9; 68:20; 92:2–3; 96:2; 119:64; 145:2; Isa. 38:20); it must go from generation to generation. Praise is to be perpetual, just as God is eternal (cf., e.g., Tob. 3:11; 8:5, 15; Ps. 79: 13; 89:2; 104:31; 111:10; Dan. 3:26,52–90).[24]

II. THE NEW TESTAMENT

In the Incarnation the Eternal God Enters History

The New Testament writings express the divine eternity with the help of linguistic methods already found in the Old Testament, for the same experience of time is the substructure of the affirmations of faith.

The God who manifests himself to the seer of Patmos gives himself the highly meaningful names of "the Alpha and the Omega," "the Beginning and the End," "the First and the Last" (Rev. 1:8; 21:6; 22:13). Such formulas are an attempt to use the dialectical interplay of opposites to situate God beyond all beginnings and all endings, beyond all temporality and all history. On the other hand, the divine name once revealed to Moses is spelled out in terms of temporal succession: this is he "who is and who was and who is to come" (Rev. 1:4; cf. Exod. 3:14). The formula signifies both God's presence to all past, present, and future times, and his total freedom from duration; it signifies, in short, God's immanence to and transcendence over temporality. In this sense it can be said that God is in every moment of time and in none of them, just as he is "everywhere" but also "nowhere."[25]

God's eternity is really too basic an element of the Jewish faith for the New Testament to present any novelty on the point, apart from the few formulas just mentioned. What is new is the affirmation of the *eternity of Jesus* along with his divinity; more exactly, Jesus is God because as Word and Son he is eternal. Alluding to the opening words of Genesis, the beginning of the fourth Gospel situates the Word "in the beginning" with God, in an absolute pre-existence which is made sufficiently clear by the use of the imperfect tense: "In the beginning was the Word; the Word was in God's presence, and the Word was God. He was present to God in the beginning" (John 1:1–2). There is question here not of a primordial time like that of the mythic narratives but of an absolute anteriority of the Word in the order of being: "Through him all things came into being, and apart from him nothing came to be" (John 1:3); "through him the world was made" (John 1:10).[26] The Word is from the beginning (1 John 1:1); like God himself he is "the beginning" (1 John 2:13–14). Or, again, he is the beginning of God's works (Rev. 3:14); through him God made "the ages" (Heb. 1:2),[27] and "he sustains all things by his powerful word" (Heb. 1:3). Finally, some of the most solemn texts which proclaim the divine eternity in the Old Testament are applied to Christ by the writer of the Letter to the Hebrews.[28]

During his earthly life Jesus himself declares, in more or less explicit ways depending on circumstances, his own divine eternity. In saying, for example, that he is "from above" while other men are "from below" (cf. John 8:22–23), he is implicitly affirming his divinity and eternity. The idea of anteriority, customary in the Old Testament for expressing the divine eternity, is used in various circumstances by Jesus. For example, in his words to his unbelieving hearers after the discourse on the Bread of Life, he combines it with the spatial image "on high": "Does it shake your faith? What, then, if you were to see the Son of Man ascend to where he was before?" (John 6:61–62). Later, in his "priestly prayer," Jesus asks his Father for the glory which he had with him "before the world began" (John 17:5). Most importantly, however, Jesus on several occasions applies to himself the divine name revealed to Moses, the "I am" which connotes eternity. In particular, when the Jews reproach him for claiming to have "seen" Abraham and for daring to compare his brief life with the many centuries that had passed since Abraham, Jesus claims the Name for himself in such a way that, in contrast to man's fragile being, "I am" takes on an absolute meaning: "I solemnly declare it: before Abraham came to be, I am" (John 8:58). The being of Jesus, then, is, in some dimension of itself, transcendent and incommensurable with our human duration. Conscious as they were of being, like their ancestor, subject to change and death, Jesus' hearers so well understood the implication of his statement that they wanted to stone him as a blasphemer (John 8:59).[29]

On another occasion Jesus expresses his transcendence over becoming by claiming for his own words the divine privileges of immutability and infallibility: "The heavens and the earth will pass away, but my words will not pass" (Luke 21:33).[30] At the Last Supper (John 13:18–19), Jesus foretells his betrayal by Judas, so that, when the event has proved him right, his perfect knowledge and, with it, his divine Name or identity ("I am") may be recognized and his disciples' faith strengthened. After the resurrection, finally, Christ affirms his absolute mastery over time by promising his disciples that he will be with them all days to the end of the world (Matt. 28:20). The Letter to the Hebrews can, therefore, express, in a pregnant formula, in the common faith of the Church: "Jesus Christ is the same yesterday, today, and forever" (Heb. 13:8).[31] With the help of language drawn from the experience of time the New Testament is thus able to give unambiguous expression to the divine eternity.[32]

The *saving plan* of the eternal God unfolds in history in order that it may embrace man who is subject to time. After agelong preparation and expectation the Word is made flesh (John 1:14), takes for himself a human body that is subject to becoming, and thereby involves himself in duration. Without surrendering his eternity or impairing his transcendence, he "who abides before all time began to exist within time."[33] This unparalleled moment when the eternal God enters history is a mysterious one indeed, for it involves a double relationship: to the divine eternity and to human time.

The determination of seasons and moments belongs solely to God's mysterious power, and it is not for man to know them (Acts 1:7; cf. 17:26; Matt. 24:36; 1 Thess. 5:1–2). The gracious plan conceived "beforehand," that is, from all eternity, is carried out "in the fullness of time" (Eph. 1:10; cf. Tit. 1:2–3). In this "fullness of time" God sends his Son to be born of a woman and born under the Law (Gal. 4:4); and Jesus will later on say that "this is the time of fulfillment" (Mark 1:14–15; cf. Rom. 16:25–26; Heb. 1:1), that is, the duration of the time of expectation, as set by divine wisdom, has reached its end. The moment of the incarnation, as known and determined by God, has a "vertical" relation to eternity.

But this moment of moments is also part of the human time, and the evangelists are concerned to define Jesus' historical as well as his geographical "co-ordinates." Christ's bodiliness inserts him, first of all, into the living fabric of human generations. Without entering here into a discussion that would not serve our purposes, we may recall the importance which the evangelists give to the genealogy of Christ: Matthew puts it at the beginning of his work, Luke after the narrative of the baptism and on the eve of Christ's public ministry (Matt. 1:1–17; Luke 3:23–38).[34] One writer follows a descending order, the other an ascending, but both link Christ, implicitly or explicitly, with Adam, the head of the human race.[35] Matthew, however, stresses the legal membership of Jesus, via Joseph, in the chosen people as depositary of the promises that are fulfilled through his birth; Luke adopts a more universalist perspective.[36] Both nonetheless underline the virginal birth which makes Jesus the head of a new mankind in which the first creation is reshaped by God.[37] In summary: the Messiah is part of the unbroken line of generations, those of Israel and those of mankind as a whole. In Jesus, man with his vital duration—biological and spiritual, frail and doomed to death—is linked to the unebbing eternity of the living God.

The evangelists are also concerned to situate Jesus in the history of mankind and to date his appearance on earth in relation to contemporary events. Matthew puts the birth of Jesus in the reign of Herod, a while before the latter's death (2:1,19). Luke provides a number of links between Christ's history and general history: Zachary was carrying out his temple-service in the time of Herod (1:5); Jesus was born at the time of the census that had been ordered by Augustus Caesar and was being carried out when Quirinus was governor of Syria (2:1–3);[38] above all, he supplies numerous chronological details in formally dating the preaching of John the Baptist which was the direct prelude to the public ministry of Jesus (3:1–2). Mark situates Jesus by relation to the Precursor. All four authors relate the events of the public life sometimes to each other, sometimes (especially John) to the Jewish festal calendar. It is evident that the chronological procedures used do not correspond to ours, but this in no way invalidates the deliberate effort of the evangelists to fit Jesus into the unbroken chain of events which make up history.

Furthermore, Jesus is, like every other man, rooted in his own times, nourished by them, and indelibly marked by them: he is an Israelite born in the reigns of Herod and Augustus. The contemporary mentality, culture, and style of life and self-expression impregnate his whole being. Even his spiritual destiny is deeply marked by the political context. In the humiliated condition of his race Jesus must struggle ceaselessly against the most subtle and powerful temptation the Messiah could face: the temptation of a temporal messianism which would restore independence to the Jewish nation. He met that temptation as early as his stay in the desert (Matt. 4:1–11) and it was still there in his last moments on the cross (Matt. 27:39–42). Jesus Christ is thus fully of his own times, for the historian recognizes in him the mark and the temptation of a particular age.

In all these ways, then, the coming of the Word among men is fully a part of human history; it links time to eternity.

To be born is to be involved in becoming. In Jesus Christ God is no longer to be, as Creator, the master of all ages, nor even to "reserve" for himself certain days in the life of his people, such as the Sabbath, the Jewish feasts, or even "holy" years. Now he makes his own in a personal way the duration and vicissitudes proper to a human life. After the months of prenatal development (Matt. 1:18–25; Luke 1:26–2:5), the Word appears in a baby's body that must grow through adolescence (Luke 2:40,52) to full maturity (Luke 3:23); he has the specifically human experience of passing time, of the cosmic and biological rhythms that give context to man's works and days. He gradually acquires, like other children, the idea of objective time and discovers the value of subjective time. But the same growth that brings awareness of personal duration and, perhaps, the temptation to reserve that duration for himself, also allows him to reach an ever more perfect understanding of the unconditional demands of his mission. Christ belongs entirely to God and to men, and this requires the constantly renewed gift of his days and his whole life (cf., e.g., John 9:4; 10:15; Matt. 20:28). The consequence is a series of tensions within the life of Jesus—between his various duties and between himself and those who can rightfully ask for part of his time. Thus, as early as his twelfth year, the child slips away from his parents in order to "be busy with his Father's affairs" (Luke 2:49,JB). Before entering upon his public life Jesus devotes forty days to recollection, fasting, and prayer in the desert (Luke 4:1–13). During the years of his ministry he often passes the night in prayer to God (Mark 1:35; Luke 6:12), while ceaselessly spending his days, from morning to late evening, in receiving the healthy and the sick, the just and the sinners (Mark 1:32–34; 6:35); he grants Nicodemus a night-time interview (John 3) and preaches the Good News to the crowds for three days running (Mark 8:2); people dispute about where he is to go (Mark 1:36–39; cf. 2:1–12). In thus giving his time to others, the Master has no time to eat—to the point that his family thinks he has gone mad (Mark 3:20–21)—or even to receive his mother and closest relatives (Mark 3:31–35).

Temporality and Reality of the Man Jesus

For man inserted into duration there is no full-scale reality except in time; the individual and the event are real only if they are historical. In making his own the duration proper to a human life, Jesus therefore becomes objectively real for other men. He is not located in a mythic past but in historical duration and a network of generations, and is related to events and key persons. Some men saw him and gave testimony to the fact, in oral form initially and soon thereafter in writing. The living reality is also confirmed, before and after the resurrection, by a series of events: meetings, words, actions, and works which give endlessly detailed expression to the mysterious depths of the person. Through this body made up of events, as through his body of flesh, Jesus is made accessible to himself and his fellows, and says what he is. In the bitter discussions with his enemies which the fourth Gospel reports, he lays claim to the words and the works which express his identity, for both are inseparable from his very being.

Like it or not, then, we are in real danger of undermining the historical reality of Jesus if we try to remove from the sphere of history various of the events, actions, and words reported by the witnesses. The criticism of a Bultmann, with his cavalier attitude to the textual data (due either to a faulty method or to philosophical presuppositions), impoverishes the reality of Jesus' person. When the criticism takes an extreme form, the person threatens to become unreal, and the incarnation of the Son of God may be reduced to an illusion; here we are back in the docetism which drew opposition as early as the apostle John, and Christianity becomes the myth from which the scholar was supposedly rescuing it! If, on the contrary, we approach the texts with the critical openness and respect that science demands, we find that the person, actions, and words of Jesus form a coherent total event, imposing itself on scholar and man-in-the-street alike as an objective fact within time.

To the believer the Son's entrance into time makes God real in a new way. In the "event which is Jesus" the Eternal One becomes a historical partner of every man, past, present, and future.

The Consciousness of Jesus at the Center of Time

Jesus exists in time as a living center from which all the perspectival lines radiate outward: his present is the necessary reference-point for the movement of duration; for him, as for other men, a given point of time draws near, becomes real, and passes away. In his preaching he appeals to that grasp of temporal distance which he has in common with each of his hearers. Thus the experience of the grain's slow growth and of the coming harvest is presupposed by the parables of the weeds (Matt. 13:24–30, 36–43), of the mustard-seed (Matt. 13:31–32), and of the seed that grows of itself (Mark 4:26–29). Similarly, the time belonging to the yeast in the dough (Matt. 13:33) and to the netful of fish which is drawn from the water only after the return to the shore (Matt. 13:47–50) provides the occasion for instruction on the development of the kingdom. The four months that must still pass before the harvest (John 4:35), the tender fig-leaves which tell us that summer is near (Matt. 24:32), the color of the sky (Matt. 16:2–3), the clouds in the west and the wind in the south (Luke 12:54–56) as signs of tomorrow's weather: all these allusions, so familiar to Christ and his hearers, show that in him the eternal God is sharing our experience of lived time.

There is, however, also a wholly unique title by which Jesus is at the center of history. Like his contemporaries he doubtless relates himself to Israel's past and speaks of the "forefathers" and the "fathers" (e.g., Matt. 5:21, 33; 23:29). But his subjective necessity, shared by all others, is paralleled, in this privileged instance, by another necessity that is providential and unique. In God's eternal plan Jesus is the Christ—that is, the promised and awaited Messiah—who is to be the term of the Mosaic dispensation and the beginning of a new mankind. For this reason Jesus is "objectively" at the center of history, and the sense of his divine mission gives his consciousness of time an unparalleled depth. We must insist a little on this point.

In relation to the past, Christ is aware of putting an end to the old dispensation and of bringing to light its true meaning. Consequently he presents the new law as being creatively faithful to the old and transcending it: "Do not think that I have come to abolish the law and the prophets. . . . You have heard the commandment imposed on your forefathers. . . . What I say to you is . . . " (Matt. 5:17, 21, 22). In addition to thus bringing the law to completion, Jesus also brings to its culmination the prophetic movement in Israel. From afar off Abraham "saw the day" of Christ and rejoiced in it (John 8:56; cf. Heb. 11:8–13). But, more importantly, the Scriptures bear witness to Jesus (John 5:39), and he fulfills in his person the messianic prophecies. It is of him that Moses writes (John 5:45–47); it is his glory that Isaiah saw, and of him that Isaiah spoke (John 12:31). Jesus had therefore solemnly presented himself as the Messiah at the beginning of his public ministry in the synagogue of Nazareth (Luke 4:16–30); after the resurrection he will open the "hearts" of the disciples on the way to Emmaus so that they can read the Scriptures in a "Christian" way (Luke 24:25–27). Finally, Jesus brings to fulfillment all the prefigurative institutions of the old covenant: his risen humanity is the new temple that replaces the Temple at Jerusalem; he is the authentic passover lamb (e.g., John 1:29; 19:31–36; Rev. 5:6–14), the perfect high priest (Heb. 4:14—5:10), and the new and final Israel. In this way the whole religious past of mankind is moving toward Christ, calling for him, foretelling him and, finally, reaching fulfillment in his being and mission. Inversely, the human consciousness of Jesus draws that past to itself, sums it up, and gives it, retrospectively, its full meaning.

But the consciousness of Christ is also "prospective," embracing the whole future of mankind. He who fulfills the prophecies of Israel is himself a prophet or, more exactly, the supreme Prophet whom all the others simply prefigured (Deut. 18:15–20; John 1:17–18; Acts 3:22–23; cf. 7:37). Jesus is master of his own future: if he predicts his passion and resurrection, he also gives his life when he decides to do so, and can take it back with full freedom (John 10:17–18); he tells his disciples about the persecutions (Matt. 10:17–22; John 15:18—16:4) and slow increase of his Church; but he also affirms his mastery of this history by imposing on the disciples the duty of worldwide witnessing (Acts 1:8), by promising his daily assistance until the end of time (Matt. 28:19–20), and by foretelling that his glorious coming will put an end to time and give access to the kingdom (Matt. 24, *passim*; 25:31–46; John 14:1–3). Above all, however, unlike the ancient prophets who communicated "oracles of Yahweh" and unlike the scribes who passed on a teaching they had received, Jesus spoke with authority (Mark 1:22), for he is the Son, the sole Word of God, and in him prophetic revelation, manifold and fragmentary in the past, culminates and reaches fulfillment (Heb. 1:22). By his word—and, in truth, by his being itself—Jesus is sovereign interpreter of history: the whole of hermeneutics must find its beginning and end in him.

It is not enough, however, simply to say that the consciousness of Jesus, more than any other human consciousness, embraces the whole extent of past and future time. For Christ even less than for any other man, the consciousness of time is not reducible to a kind of ideal boundary of a mathematical kind situated between the retrospective and the prospective. In this privileged instance, on the contrary, the lived moment is of the utmost plenitude. If past and future turn towards Jesus to receive their definitive meaning, it is in the present of his consciousness that he embraces them both. The totality of human duration, together with the individuals who people it, is gathered up in his consciousness in order to be embraced in a single, ever actual, saving will. Situated by his body in a limited period of duration, Christ renders himself intentionally present to the immensity of all the ages. Here we can adapt the words of St. Thomas which we quoted earlier: by suffering at one moment in history, he delivered the whole of time by his passion.

Finally, if every human consciousness perceives duration as such from the vantage-point of that hidden source which it carries within itself,[39] the consciousness of Christ has access to the universality of time by a further, entirely special title. Being united to the person of the Word by the very act which gives him his existence, Jesus has an ineffably profound relationship to the Eternal God. More than any other consciousness, that of Christ has a mysterious apex at which it opens out upon eternity and at which, consequently, it can embrace all of history; it sums up time on the horizontal level of duration, because at each moment it is raised to the heights of eternity.[40]

"Now" and "Then": The Hour of Jesus

Conscious as he is of his mission and his unique historical role, Jesus is his own reference-point in time, and this by divine right. Constant reference to the Father's will purifies this attitude of any danger of contamination by egoism. At the same time, however, within his own individual human existence, Jesus has full experience of temporal distance: the ever-present "now" and a "then" that is somewhere off in the past or the future. He experiences the slow, inexorable passage of time that leads to a moment which had long been far off: his "hour"—that is, his passion, resurrection, and ascension. It is in relation to this climactic event that the other episodes of his life and the decisions which were both the freest and the most urgently demanded of him, fall into place and acquire their full meaning. This "hour" beyond all others is the central point of a destiny which itself controls all of history.

A person's "hour," as we noted elsewhere,[41] is the point of time at which his destiny, in its most personal form, can come to fulfillment thanks to a happy convergence of circumstances. Thus Christ's enemies have an hour which they have long desired, sought, and prepared for: the moment when they will bring about his death (Matt.

21:33–45; 26:1–5; John 5:18; 7:1, 19–20,25; 11:53; 18:31); then they will have revenge on someone whose authority rivaled theirs. Then, with the help of Judas, the occasion is contrived: the hour has come; "then" has become "now." With a word, Jesus tears the mask from their murderous intentions: "This is your hour—the triumph of darkness!" (Luke 22:53).

Yet in God's plan that same hour is also the hour of Jesus—that is, the hour of his final testing and glorification. Thus, according to whether it is viewed from the standpoint of the hatred of the murderers or that of the salvific intention of their victim, the same hour takes on opposite meanings. In short, God's purpose surrounds and outflanks the dark strategies of men, diverting them to his own ends.

At Cana, Jesus' hour had not yet come; yet at his mother's request he provides for the needs of his hosts in such a way that his glory begins to be manifested (John 2:1–11). Throughout his public life he sees his hour coming, calculates the distance that separates him from it, and orders his activity in the light of that mysterious term fixed by his Father. The hostile and impatient desire of his enemies and the unenlightened zeal of his disciples alike fail to hasten the moment. If the authorities want to arrest him, as at the feast of Booths (John 7:1,30; cf. Luke 4:28–30) or after the discourse in front of the temple treasury (John 8:20), they cannot do it, always for the peremptory reason that his hour has not yet come. If the disciples urge him to "display himself to the world at large," they draw this reproof: "It is not yet the right time for me, whereas the time is always right for you . . . . The time is not yet ripe for me" (John 7:3–8).

But this hour which has long been only a distant future, has finally drawn near, and Jesus approaches it in full awareness of its providential meaning: "The hour is on us when the Son of Man is to be handed over to the power of evil men" (Matt. 26:45). It is, however, also the hour when Christ is "to pass from this world to the Father" (John 13:1), the hour when the Son of Man is to be glorified (John 12:23), the hour of mutual glorification for Father and Son: "Father, the hour has come! Give glory to your Son that your Son may give glory to you" (John 17:1). Just as the cross is sign both of ultimate abasement and ultimate exaltation, so the same hour is the hour of darkness and the hour of glory.

This privileged moment that is about to become "now" presents to

Jesus' consciousness such a force of signification that all temporal distance is eliminated: the hour has come (John 16:5),[42] it is here (John 13:1). Before the consummation of the event, it already appears to Jesus as accomplished; its effects are obtained: more than any human subject, the Prophet of prophets is present to the future in intention. Thus, as the final Passover draws near, Jesus declares: "I came to this hour" (John 12:12); "Now has judgment come upon this world" (John 12:31). Later, to his disciples, he says: "Take courage! I have overcome the world" (John 16:33). In a prophetic anticipation of certitude, the fruits of the imminent passion seem already given in the present.

Paradoxically, this hour in which Jesus least belongs to himself he calls "his hour." According to Luke, it is then that Christ's purpose will be "accomplished" (Luke 13:32). The paschal mystery doubtless means an exaltation which will bring the mission and person of Jesus to supreme fulfillment. But that summit is reached only at the price of a total self-giving; the accomplishment is the accomplishment of a perfect sacrifice. Jesus' hour is therefore not his own in the all-too-human sense of a moment which is anticipated as satisfying personal or even egoistic interests. On the contrary, Jesus' hour is the hour in which he no longer belongs to himself. On the one hand, the Father determines the moment from all eternity; on the other, Jesus ceases forever to dispose of himself and freely hands himself over to death for the glory of the Father and man's salvation. The moment when Christ *is* most himself is the moment when he completes the total surrender of that dearest of *possessions*: his duration as a human being.

Subjective Duration and Measurement of Time

Given its appreciation of the temporal distance that still separates it from its hour, the consciousness of Jesus is torn between desire and fear, eagerness and apprehension. Christ experiences passing time: its course seems now too slow, now too quick, according as he envisages one or other aspect of the term to which he is moving. Thus, in a moment of spiritual distress noted by Luke, Christ reaches out to the ultimate event which is to crown his mission: "I have come to light a fire on the earth. How I wish the blaze were ignited!" (Luke 12:49; cf. 22:15). But immediately fear floods in at the thought of the debt of pain which must be paid: "I have a baptism to receive. What anguish I feel till it is over!" (Luke 12:50).[43] The same inner division occurs again, according to John's testimony, as the last Passover draws near: "My soul is troubled now, yet what should I say—Father, save me from this hour? But it was for this that I came to this hour. Father, glorify your name!" (John 12:27–28).

According to the Synoptic accounts, it is at Gethsemani that the imminence of the event produces the most agonizing division in the soul of Jesus: "He advanced a little and fell to the ground, praying that if it were possible this hour might pass him by. He kept saying: "*Abba* (O Father), you have the power to do all things. Take this cup away from me. But let it be as you would have it, not as I" (Mark 14:35–36). Once the hour has begun, Jesus is torn between eagerness to get through it (he says to Judas: "Be quick about what you are to do": John 13:27) and the anguish of soon leaving his own: "I am not to be with you much longer" (John 13:33). Like every human consciousness, that of Jesus unites with, or opposes to, the objectively measured flow of time the subjective (and contradictory) measure of desire and fear.

In another text, finally, the experience of temporal distance is found linked with the symbolism of a day's duration: "We must do the deeds of him who sent me while it is day. The night comes on when no one can work" (John 9:4). Night, which interrupts each's day occupations, is the daily experienced symbol of another night, the night of death, which leads to no new dawn for the dead person. Jesus lives his whole life symbolically in each of his days, and, inversely, his whole life is a single day between the morning of birth and the evening of death.[44]

The disciples of Christ will in their turn have experience of an "hour," sometimes painful, sometimes joyous. The Master's passion will be a time of tears and lamentation for them; but soon their sadness will be changed into joy. A woman about to bear a child suffers when her hour comes, but presently her joy is great because she has brought a man into the world (John 16:20–21). Even after the paschal events, the disciples will know an "hour" of anguish like that of Jesus, the hour of persecution and death: "Not only will they expel you from synagogues; a time will come when anyone who puts you to death will claim to be serving God!" (John 16:2). Christ is the master of that distant hour, which man's will to live tries to put off; as prophet, he rises above all temporal distance and instructs his disciples so that "when their hour comes" they may recall his words (John 16:4); then they will be preserved from being scandalized (John 16:1).

Divine Eternity and Human Time in Jesus Christ

Our human experience, it has been noted, shows that we can rise out of the flow of time and that in privileged circumstances we even have a sense of being open to the eternal.[45] Such data, inadequate though they are, allow us to draw near in some measure to the mystery of the temporality of Jesus. The latter is exceptional in that it is assumed by the person of the Word. Three particular moments in it deserve our attention here: the transfiguration, the agony, and the risen life.

The transfiguration, which we shall study later on as a change in the bodily appearance of Jesus,[46] is a revelation in splendor of the presence of the divine eternity within the present moment of a mortal life. The glory that spreads through Jesus's bodily humanity and radiates from it is the very glory of the Eternal One, incommunicable to anyone who is not God (1 Chron. 29:11–12; Isa. 42:8; 48:11). For a fleeting moment the divinity of Jesus is made manifest. In addition, the whole of mankind's religious history is brought to a focus, being summed up in Christ as master of time. All duration is, as it were, condensed into a single unified point. The past of Israel is there, in the persons of Moses and Elijah, and receives from its long-awaited, now-present Messiah its definitive fulfillment. The finite present moment in the life of Jesus is taken up, without being dissolved, into the infinite present moment of God and, from that vantage-point, dominates all the millennia of history. Finally, the eschatological future is heralded in this anticipation of the glory to come. In short, the Son of Man sums up and contains in himself the totality of time: he is of yesterday and today and for the ages (cf. Heb. 13:8).

The agony in Gethsemani presents a kind of extreme antithesis to the transfiguration, for here glory gives place to abasement and the radiance of divinity to the darkness and agony of death. Far from giving Jesus the guarantee of his word, the Father is silent, and to all appearances abandons him. The disciples, who on Thabor had been seized by dazzled wonder, now remain most cruelly indifferent. To the timeless moment of ecstasy has succeeded the interminable struggle, the repeated, desolate prayer of the man sinking in the quicksands of time.[47] Nevertheless, even then, the reference of the instant to eternity does not fail. For in fact the agony reaches such extremity only in virtue of the exceptional relationship by which the human consciousness of Jesus is united to God. The apparent abandonment has its meaning only in contrast with the union of the Son with the Father in the order of being itself. Listen to Jesus' prayer: "*Abba* (O Father), you have the power to do all things. Take this cup away from me," and to his heroic acceptance: "But let it be as you would have it, not as I" (Mark 14:36). Here the meaning of the trial, if not its depth, can be glimpsed: the Father seems to be rejecting the Son—worse still, to be repudiating by his silence the promises given at the baptism and the transfiguration. Indeed it is the relation of Jesus to the Father which, in joining time up with eternity, confers on the mysterious tragedy its unfathomable significance. The same tension is reflected in the episode of the fourth Gospel which comes closest to the Synoptic accounts of the agony: the anguish of the "hour" is so great only because of the necessity of glorifying the Father (John 12:27–28). Christ's "hour" is thus kept in constant relation to the Father. The "hour" is that privileged moment when, in the human consciousness of Christ, time and eternity are at once opposed, come together, and clash in an ineffable tension.[48]

The temporality of the Easter life will be of an absolutely new kind. Without doubt the Gospel of John presents the mortal life of Jesus as enveloped and filled to overflowing by the glory of the eternal Word. Even though this glory remains veiled and wholly interior, it is the infinite dimension of a presence, the secret of its mysterious depth. The pre-resurrection time experienced by Jesus is the fragile supporting structure where eternity at once penetrates and withholds itself. Between this mortal life and the risen life there is an intermediate period which has a twofold meaning. In man's eyes the time in the tomb is that of definitive absence; for every other human being this duration measures the progressive disappearance of the body. But in God's plan it is the time of the "descent into hell" in which Christ masters the depths of the created universe and subjects them to his own lordship. Finally, after this period comes "paschal time." Between this new existence and the former mortal life there is a continuity, and the narratives of the apparitions lay heavy stress on it, for without it there could be no question of a "resurrection."

But the relationship of Christ to time has changed. The Lord manifests himself in time, as in space, but he is not subject to it; he borrows from temporality the proof of real existence it affords, but he also escapes its limitations. On the one hand, then, we find the apparitions dated as well as localized: "Jesus rose from the dead early on the first day of the week. He first appeared to Mary Magdalene" (Mark 16:9; cf. John 20:1); "two of them that same day were making their way . . . " (Luke 24:13); "while they were still speaking about all this, he himself stood in their midst" (Luke 24:36); "on the evening of that first day of the week . . . . A week later" (John 20:19,26); "appearing to them over the course of forty days" (Acts 1:3).

These are indeed summary indications and far from satisfying our expectations of chronological precision, but they show the concern of the witnesses to situate the risen Christ within human time. On the other hand, however, if Jesus affirms his presence in time, he also shows himself the sovereign master of time. The conqueror of death indeed escapes from the time of the grave and returns to the world of men; they are not to seek the Living One among the dead (Luke 24:5). But the new presence of the Lord is no longer subject to the limitations of spatial and temporal continuity. Jesus shows himself unexpectedly: distance is nonexistent for him; he chooses particular points in time in order to insert himself into the thick of men's duration and lets himself be recognized in whatever fleeting moments he chooses. In this fashion the appearances, with their clarity and suddenness, give evidence of an habitual, even if mysterious, presence of Christ: even though he cannot be seen, he is always "here and now," near and active among us. Thus he can promise his disciples to remain with them "always, until the end of the world" (Matt. 28:20).

By withdrawing his humanity from the visible universe on the day of the ascension, Jesus makes it clear that since the resurrection he dwells in the Father's Glory, and shows that in him, as sole Mediator (1 Tim. 2:5), man's time is forever linked to the eternity of God. The paschal "this day" unites man's "today" to the "today" of eternity. God's transcendence over time, which had been so forcefully asserted in the old covenant, finds its definitive revelation in the risen Christ.

Christ Structures History and Gives It Its Meaning

As center of universal history, Jesus divides it into "before," "now," and "after." The time "before" Christ was the time of slow preparation. For the chosen people it was the time of the promise given to Abraham (Gen. 12–23; Rom. 4:1–25; 9:6–24; Gal. 3:6–9), of training under the Law (Gal. 3:24–25), of prefigurative events (1 Cor. 10:1–6; 11, *passim;* cf. Rom. 5:14; 15:4), and of prophecies (Heb. 1:1). On Israel's side it was a time of messianic faith and hope; in the light of the people's unfaithfulness, it was also the time of God's "forbearance" (Rom. 2:4; 3:26; 9:22; 1 Pet. 3:20). For the pagans it was a time of "ignorance" (Acts 17:30; 1 Pet. 1:14) and of enslavement to mute idols and the most degrading passions (1 Cor. 12:2);[49] the nations were then "without Christ" (Eph. 2:12) and exposed to God's wrath (Rom. 1:18; cf. 1 Pet. 2:10).

Finally, Jesus, Messiah and Son of God, is born into human history and gives time a meaning that even the liveliest messianic faith could not have glimpsed. We noted above the sense in which the Christ fulfills Israel's past. Let us show here how Jesus gives his own time and future history a new direction.

If the man of Nazareth is fully "of his own time," he is not therefore a simple product of race, environment, and historical moment; rather, he makes the time his own in order to modify it and give it a meaning. Not that the life of Christ deflected the contemporary course of events and left its mark on the age: the age is the age of Augustus, not of Jesus Christ. All the dreams of temporal messianism received, first from Jesus and then from the facts, a scathing rejection. The paradox of this extraordinary life is that of its empirical obscurity combined with its depth of spiritual meaning. Christ will have nothing to do with the affairs of Caesar, but he does give human existence a new direction, so that the thirty-odd years of his life are, among all the possible centers of time that might be chosen, the center that is richest in meaning: "If anyone is in Christ, he is a new creation. The old order has passed away; now all is new!" (2 Cor. 5:17).

Through the virginal conception of Jesus and his resurrection God indicates that in his incarnate Son he is reshaping the first creation. If Jesus is not subject to the two opposed conditions that bound every human life—namely, generation and death—it is because the new man, who is called to enter the kingdom, will no longer be subject to the necessity of begetting or to the fate of dying, for he will be immortal (Matt. 22:29–33; Luke 20:34–40).[50] Proof of this renewal of man can be seen in the numerous *conversions* that arise from the Master's call. At a simple sign some fishermen leave their nets: for them the time for catching fish has passed; *henceforth* they will catch men (Luke 5:10). We may recall, too, the startling conversions of the royal official who found faith along with all his household (John 4:46–54), the woman known to be a sinner (Luke 7:36–50), and Zacchaeus (Luke 19:1–10). The resistance of the rich young man when challenged to change his way of life is a negative confirmation (Matt. 19:16–30).

The Lord's death shakes the faith of his followers and deprives their life of the meaning and direction they had willingly embraced. But then the resurrection calls forth a new conversion. The presence of the living Lord, whether to the Twelve or to the holy women or to any other disciple, radically changes the meaning of recent events and of history as a whole. The time of depression and despair gives way to the time of new-found joy and faith. The disciples at Emmaus can be taken as symbolic here: once they have recognized the Master, they reverse their plans, give up their present journey, and return immediately to Jerusalem, filled with their former faith; the inner conversion gives rise to an about-face in space and time.

That is how it will be in every authentically Christian life. Jesus Christ is the one who radically changes the meaning of every existential project and gives human duration an unprecedented significance by opening man's eyes to the resurrection and the kingdom. The about-face is doubtless more evident in conversions of adults: from the first disciples and Saul of Tarsus to Augustine or Charles de Foucauld, conversion is a vital break; it cuts a life's span into a "before" and an "after" in relation to the decisive call. But the qualitative change in lived time is no less in the "born Christian" who has tried to live his Christian life; the rupture may be less spectacular, but it is there at every moment; it continues to deepen, like a living fissure, until it reaches the innermost depths of the personality.

The resurrection of Christ is thus the *event* beyond all others, an auspicious event if ever there was one, for it dominates and orders all others. The obscure facts lost in the night of time—the succession of geological eras, the slow and obscure advances of life, especially the coming of man and the manifestation of spirit, the rise of civilizations, the collapse of empires and the destruction of cultures, the multiplicity of personal destinies, and the multitudinous movement of history—all these are, as it were, gathered up and culminate in the supreme act by which God in Jesus Christ reconciles the world to himself (2 Cor. 5:19) and gives time its meaning by linking it to eternity.

Thus, for the Christian the event of salvation is the essential reference-point which allows him to judge the sudden reversals of human history and to discern their deepest meaning. Worldwide upheavals, hidden joys and sorrows, the death of the most obscure individual—all derive their meaning from their relation to the one saving event. Thus, too, Christ has become, for a large segment of mankind, the temporal reference-point which takes precendence over all others. I can situate myself in the stream of duration in relation to countless important or unimportant events of human history, but there is one event, a "once for all," that has a kind of unqualified value: the coming of the Word of God as mortal man (cf. John 1:14–18), his redemptive sacrifice (Heb. 7:27;9:12,26,28; 10:10,12,14; cf. Rom. 6:10; 1 Pet. 3:18), in short, his passage "among us" (Acts 1:21). The Christian's gaze turns instinctively to that unique moment, and each person in the Christianized world situates himself in relation to it. The foundation of Rome has yielded its place to another beginning: the beginning of a new human race in Jesus Christ, having primacy over all created things (Col. 1:15, NEB) and of many brothers (Rom. 8:29), the first to return from among the dead (Col. 1:18, NEB). In such and such a year "Before Christ," "In the year of our Lord . . .": I orientate myself within the immense span of the millennia by relating myself to that dawn of a new age.

As master of the world's future, Christ orders and structures it and gives it its character: it is no longer a time of sin alone but the *time of grace*, the time of the Church, as well. Henceforward, human duration is redeemed and sanctified. Each person now has the power and duty of recognizing in the passing moment "the favorable time," "the day of salvation" (2 Cor. 6:2). Through Christ as mediator between time and eternity, the today of men is linked to the eternal today of

God and to his ever-living salvific intention (cf. Heb. 3:7–14; 11, *passim*). The "signs of the times" are also to be accepted and interpreted in faith as heralding the salvation to come (cf. Matt. 16:1–4; Luke 20:25–28). Watchfulness becomes a basic attitude of Christian existence.[51]

Furthermore, Christ exercises his mastery over future time by endowing his Church with *institutions*. Whether it is a matter, for example, of Peter's primacy (Matt. 16:18–19) or of the power given the apostles to forgive sins (John 20:21–23), the intention of ruling the future finds expression even in grammatical details.[52] But among all the institutions one is supreme: that which actualizes within a given moment the unique act that sealed forever the convenant between God and man and saved mankind. Jesus entrusts the Eucharist to his disciples as a *memorial*: "Do this as a remembrance of me" (Luke 22:19), "every time . . . you proclaim the death of the Lord" (1 Cor. 11:25).[53] However, unlike a human monument, the Eucharist is not simply a commemorative rite; rather, the redemptive act becomes present at each point of time, just as it embraces and contains all creation. Finally, this memorial is also the prophetic heralding of the glorious return: in the Eucharist, Christ gives himself to men "until he comes" (1 Cor. 11:26). In the eucharistic action, the whole time of salvation is gathered up and brought into focus.

Liturgical Time

We have noted elsewhere the anthropological need of periodic returns and commemorative cycles.[54] Just as Israel had set up ritual feasts as fixed markers in the flow of time in order to sustain its fidelity to the covenant, the Christian people has a liturgical cycle to help it enter more deeply into the mystery of our salvation in Jesus Christ. In the basic temporal unit of the year, the whole religious history of humanity symbolically unfolds. From Advent, the time of agelong preparation, to the last Sunday after Pentecost, which anticipates the glorious return of Christ, all the stages of the redemptive mystery are celebrated—that is, symbolically relived, in a festive mode—by the assembled Christian people. There is no question here of evoking a prehistorical, mythical time or of simply commemorating, as Israel did, a past rich in instruction. Rather, the believer is summoned to live out, ritually, in the annual cycle, the mystery that mankind has lived historically for millennia. Just as each man makes room within the temporal unit of each day for the values he regards as most indispensable, so the Christian year gathers up within itself what faith considers to be the supreme reality: the stages of salvation. In liturgical time, religious history is condensed; the whole of the latter's duration comes to a point, as it were, and expresses to faith its essential meaning.

Furthermore, since Christ is yesterday, today, and for all ages (Heb. 13:8), the celebration in which he is high priest actualizes within the human present the saving mystery accomplished once and for all. The liturgical *today*, with its dense richness, gathers up into a passing moment the whole of duration and draws it into communion with the immutable present of the eternal salvific action. In the time, historical and eschatological, of the Church, Christian worship renders present and active the whole efficacy of Christ's mortal life and eternal offering.[55] The believer is present, in Jesus Christ, to the whole of human time and to the eternity of God himself: "the man who . . . has faith in me . . . *possesses* eternal life" (John 5:24). Christian life unites in an often painful but always real tension the mystery of time and the mystery of eternity.

The End of Time

Time receives its meaning from the term towards which it is moving, namely, the final encounter of man with God towards which Christ has re-orientated the whole of duration. In this respect the time of the Church is marked by a radical ambiguity. If Christian time, unlike that of the old dispensation, already represents a certain fulfillment, it is nonetheless an imperfect fulfillment. The time of the Church is a time of faith and not of clear vision, of signs and not of face-to-face meeting (1 Cor. 13:8–13), of hope and not of final possession (Heb. 11:1), of evangelization (Mark 16:15–20), of witnessing (Acts 1:8; cf. Luke 21:13), of testing and even persecution (Luke 21:12–18); it is not a time of rest. The end of ecclesial time and universal time will come with the Day of the Son of Man (Luke 17:22–24). If the day of

Yahweh preached by the prophets of Israel found a first realization in the coming of the Messiah-God, it will find its definitive realization only in the coming of the glorious Lord.

At that point the ambiguity of history as a time both of sin and of grace will finally be eliminated. The real meaning of each life, each action, each moment, will be made manifest. For proof we need only think of the prediction of the Last Judgment according to Matthew. When the sovereign judge reproaches some for having rejected him and congratulates others for having given him so much, all will ask the same question: "Lord, when . . . ?" (Matt. 25:31–46). And he will answer: "I assure you, as often as you did it for one of my least brothers, you did it for me" (Matt. 25:40). Time, then, will reveal its mystery. The least actions that filled the moments of human duration will manifest their true meaning, so different at times from the meaning that the individual thought he was giving them.

In ignorance of the day and the hour (Matt. 24:42; 25:13; Acts 1:7; 1 Thess. 5:1–11), the Church lives in watchful expectation and in hope that is intensely active yet wholly abandoned to the divine will (cf. 1 Cor. 1:7–9; 2 Cor. 6:2–10). By repeatedly crying to its Lord: "Come!" (Rev. 22:17,20), the Church sustains its certainty that the Son of Man, who is master of the Sabbath (Matt. 12:1–14, especially 8; John 5:1–18), can hasten the day when he will receive his own into the Sabbath of eternal rest (Heb. 3:7–4:11).

NOTES

1. Jean Mouroux, *The Mystery of Time: A Theological Inquiry*, trans. John Drury (New York: Desclée, 1964). Cf. also Oscar Cullmann, *Christ and Time: The Primitive Christian Conception of Time and History*, trans. Floyd V. Filson (Philadelphia: Westminster, 1950).

2. Cf. Mircea Eliade, *The Sacred and the Profane: The Nature of Religion*, trans. Willard R. Trask (New York: Harcourt, Brace, 1959), pp. 68–113; *Myth and Reality*, trans. Willard R. Trask (New York: Harper and Row, 1963), pp. 39–53.

3. Cf. Charles Hauret, *Beginnings: Genesis and Modern Science*, trans. and adapt. from 4th French ed. by E. P. Emmans, O.P. (Dubuque: Priory Press, 1955), p. 43. It is a universal idea in the world's religions that man must reproduce in daily life and in ritual the acts done at the beginning by the gods;

independently of any question of reciprocal influence, such as historians of religion discuss, we must recognize a general anthropological datum here; cf. Eliade, *Myth and Reality*, pp. 21–38; *The Myth of Eternal Return*, trans. Willard R. Trask (New York: Pantheon, 1954), pp. 21–48.

4. References are hardly needed, but we may at least remind the reader of Gen. 21:33; Ps. 29:10; Dan. 6:26; cf. 13:42. Recall, too, Aristotle's well-known "definition" in *Metaphysica*, XII, 7, 1072b,29: God is "a living being, eternal, most good" (trans. W. D. Ross, *The Works of Aristotle*, 8 [Oxford: Oxford University Press, 1928[2]]). On the divine eternity, cf. St. Thomas Aquinas, *Summa theologiae*, I, q. 10; on naming God from his attributes, cf. q. 13.

5. Cf. Ps. 74:16: "Yours is the day, and yours the night; you fashioned the moon and the sun"; Ps. 139:12: "For you darkness itself is not dark, and night shines as the day." Cf. Job 12:22; Dan. 2:22.

6. Isa. 40:12: Who but Yahweh has "weighed the mountains in scales and the hills in a balance"?

7. Inversely, when confronted with the manifestations of divine power, the eternal mountains "melt like wax" (Ps. 97:5), "skip like rams" (Ps. 114:6), and are "shattered" (Hab. 3:6); cf. Ecclus. 16:18–19.

8. Isa. 43:10: "Before me no god was formed, and after me there shall be none"; 43:12–13: "I am God, yes, from eternity I am he."

9. The speeches of Yahweh (chapters 38–41) simply develop this scathing reminder of the divine transcendence.

10. Whether or not Hezekiah's "Hymn of Thanksgiving" (Isa. 38:10–20) is a later addition, it is filled with a human authenticity that puts it on a level with Job's complaints.

11. Pseudo-Dionysius, *De divinis nominibus*, 10:2 (PG 3:397; cf. 495), shows that God may be represented as an old man or as a youth; the dialectic of opposites situates God in the transcendence of eternity. Origen has the same thing to say about Christ in *In Genesim homiliae*, 1 (PG 13:265).

12. Cf. *The Humanity of Man*, pp. 93, 100–01, 124–25.

13. The divine name revealed to Moses: "I am who am" (Exod. 3:14), does not seem originally to have conveyed to the Hebrews an absolute quality of existence but rather the continued active presence of God to his people. Later reflection will interpret the Name as indicating perfect existence and will find in it the idea of eternity.

14. Cf. Isa. 41:8–9: "You, Israel, my servant, Jacob, whom I have chosen, offspring of Abraham my friend." The promise once made to Abraham and the convenant concluded later on Sinai ground the believer's confidence when he prays; cf., e.g., Ps. 22:5; 44.

15. Cf. Isa. 45:4: Yahweh says to Cyrus: "For the sake of Jacob, my servant, of Israel my chosen one, I have called you by your name, giving you a title though you know me not."

16. In Isa. 41 the coming and the victories of Cyrus, which were to make possible the return from exile, find their significance in the saving plan of God and are expressly related to his eternity (cf. verse 4, quoted above). The same

connection between God's eternity and the prediction of events can be seen in Isa. 44:6–8; 48:12–16. On the transcendence of God's thoughts and ways, cf. Isa. 55:8–9; on the infallible effectiveness of his word, which conveys his will, cf. 55:10–11.

17. Cf. below, pp. 117–18. "The End of Time."

18. Cf. *The Humanity of Man*, p. 100.

19. Cf. below, Chapter 6, "The Visit of God."

20. Cf. *The Humanity of Man*, p. 132.

21. Thus Gen. 12:6: at the Oak of Moreh "Abram built an altar . . . to the Lord who had appeared to him"; Gen. 28:18: after the dream in which he saw Yahweh, Jacob "took the stone that he had put under his head, set it up as a memorial stone," and gave the place the name Bethel; Gen. 32:31: Jacob gives the name Peniel to the place where he had wrestled with God and seen his face; cf. Gen. 35:3–7. Josh. 4:1–9: after crossing the Jordan, Joshua has twelve memorial stones set up; Josh. 24:26–27: after the assembly at Shechem at which the people renewed the covenant and put a seal on their unity, Joshua sets up a large stone: "This stone shall be our witness, for it has heard all the words the Lord spoke to us. It shall be a witness against you, should you wish to deny your God." But since the practice of setting up memorial stones was already common in Canaan, the Law (e.g., Exod. 23:24) and the Prophets (e.g., Hos. 10:1; Mic. 5:12) will forbid it to Jews in order to obviate the danger of idolatry.

22. Cf. *The Humanity of Man*, p. 167.

23. Cf. the songs of the people after crossing the Red Sea, Exod. 15:1–21; of Moses, Deut. 32:1–45; of Deborah, Judg. 5; of Tobit, Tob. 13; of Judith, Jth. 9. All of these are used in the Christian liturgy.

24. Faith in God as master of time and events also finds expression in the petitionary prayer that God should hasten the time of salvation; e.g., Ecclus. 36:7; Ps. 80; etc.

25. Liturgical language uses the same method to express the divine eternity in the doxological formula "Glory be . . . ": "as it was in the beginning, is now, and ever shall be, world without end."

26. Cf. Col. 1:16–17: " All [things] were created through him, and for him. He is before all else that is. In him everything continues in being."

27. "The ages" is a measure of time, but here it designates measured creation as a whole, "the universe"; cf. Heb. 11:3.

28. E.g., Ps. 2:7 (Heb. 1:5): "You are my son; this day I have begotten you"; Christian tradition takes the words "this day" to mean the eternal and immutable "today" of God. Cf., further, Ps. 45:7–8, in Heb. 1:8; Ps. 102:26–28, in Heb. 1:11–12.

29. The same reaction from his hearers in John 10:32 when he says: "The Father and I are one" (30).

30. Cf. Ps. 119:89:"Your word, O Lord, endures forever; it is firm as the heavens"; Isa. 40:8; "The word of our God stands forever"; Isa. 55:10–11.

31. The Son of Man appears in Rev. 1:13–20 with "hair . . . as white as snow-white wool," a symbol of eternity (cf. Dan. 7:9), and declares: "I am the

First and the Last and the One who lives. Once I was dead, but now I live—forever and ever."

32. The language of tradition cannot but have recourse to the same tools as the biblical writers used, for example, the idea of anteriority. Recall the first antiphon for First Vespers of Epiphany: "Born before the morning star and before all the ages, the Lord our Savior has today appeared in our world"; the opening words are inspired by Ps. 110:3 (according to the Vulgate) and Ps. 2:7. Cf. the hymn for Christmas Vespers: "Jesus, redeemer of all mankind, whom the Father brought forth before the light came into being . . . . "

33. St. Leo the Great, *Sermo XXIII in Nativitate Domini*, 2:2 (PL 54:195).

34. On the "genesis" of Jesus Christ, cf. León-Dufour, *Etudes d'evangile* (Paris, Editions du Seuil, 1965), pp. 47–81.

35. The heading given the genealogy by Matthew (1:1): "A family record of Jesus Christ, son of David, son of Abraham," recalls Gen. 5:1: "This is a record of the descendants of Adam"; Luke 3:38 expressly names the common ancestor of mankind.

36. Matthew's intention is clear enough from the title given the genealogy, from the "summary" in 1:17, and from the second part of chapter 1 (18–25), which focuses, it would seem, on the legal paternity of Joseph. The two evangelists are evidently making free use for pedagogic purposes of the historical data.

37. Cf. Matt. 1:18–25. Luke draws a parallel between the annunciation to Zachary and the annunciation to Mary and between the unexpected conception of John the Baptist and the virginal conception of Jesus; both, though each in a different way, are effects of God's mercy and power. Note, too, that Luke calls Adam "son of God" (3:38) by reason of creation, and Jesus "son of God" by reason of his virginal conception (1:35b).

38. We cannot enter into the problems which this "census" sets for the historian.

39. Cf. *The Humanity of Man*, pp. 114–16.

40. Cf. Mouroux, *The Mystery of Time*, pp. 118–28.

41. Cf. *The Humanity of Man*, p. 100.

42. Other passages express the same experience of time: "An hour is coming, and is already here, when authentic worshippers . . . " (John 4:23; cf. 21); "I solemnly assure you, an hour is coming, has indeed come, when the dead . . . " (John 5:25).

43. The intensely human conflict of opposed feelings finds expression even in the details of expression. The initial "But" of verse 50 (omitted in English versions) is, according to Lagrange, *Evangile selon saint Luc*, "clearly adversative" (p. 373). More mysterious and striking, doubtless, is the opposition between the contrasted elements of fire (49) and water (50); cf. Ecclus. 15:16; 1 Kings 18:32–38.

44. In the prophets the "day" sometimes means a period of indefinite length in which God intervenes in history; cf., e.g., Isa. 2:17; 4:1. In John 14:20 "the day" refers to the time of the Church, after Christ's resurrection.

45. Cf. *The Humanity of Man*, pp. 115–16.

46. See below, Chapter 5, section 10, "The Transfiguration."

47. Cf. Mouroux, *The Mystery of Time*, pp. 138–39.

48. In Luke's narrative there is a mysterious moment when the relationship of time to eternity emerges in a striking way. To the repentant thief Jesus says: "This day you will be with me in paradise" (Luke 23:43). Is this the "today" of men? the "today" of God? or is the distinction of the two almost eliminated here?

49. On the spiritual condition of the pagans, cf. especially Rom. 1–2; cf. 1 Pet. 4:2–3.

50. It is noteworthy that the virginal conception and the resurrection are both affirmed, following the Gospel, in the Creeds—and that both are challenged in times of crisis.

51. Cf. below, Chapter 6, section 8. "The Visit on the Last Day."

52. The future tense used in these cases is both "institutive" and "prophetic"; the present tense expresses the "foundational" action.

53. The prophetic, anticipatory ritual of the Supper becomes, during the time of the Church, a memorial. Chapter 7, below, will go more deeply into this aspect of the Eucharistic mystery.

54. Cf. *The Humanity of Man*, p. 132.

55. On the permanent efficacy of the passion, cf. St. Thomas Aquinas, *Summa theologiae*, III, q. 22, a. 5, ad 2. On the efficacy of the mystery of worship, cf. the essay by Irénée-Hervé Dalmais in *The Church at Prayer: Introduction to the Liturgy*, ed. Aimé-Georges Martimart, trans. Austin Flannery, O.P., and Vincent Ryan, O.S.B. (New York: Desclée, 1968), pp. 190–211.

PART II

MEDIA OF REVELATION

In the prophets of Israel, God is already using all the human means of expression and communication in order to reveal to man the divine plan of salvation. In Jesus Christ, the Son takes to his own person all these ways of signifying God's intentions. A transcendent meaning is therefore constantly circulating from word to hand, to face, to gaze; it finds its many-sided expression within the unity established by a single presence. Here the inexhaustible interiority found in every human presence gives an inkling of infinite depths.

CHAPTER 3

THE WORD OF GOD

If man's word is but one element constituting his presence and cannot be separated from his gestures, neither can God's transcendent word be separated from the divine action in history. As the divine plan of salvation is gradually brought to fulfillment, the mystery of God's word is thereby gradually revealed, most notably on the day when the Word becomes flesh and enters personally into time: "In times past, God spoke in fragmentary and varied ways to our fathers through the prophets; in this, the final age, he has spoken to us through his Son" (Heb. 1:1–2); "The Word became flesh and made his dwelling among us" (John 1:14).

I. GOD'S SILENCE AND GOD'S WORD

The Silence of God

The God who speaks is, first of all, the God who is silent: his silence is prior, basic, essential to his mystery. Divine Wisdom exists eternally, before he sets his hand to any work (Prov. 8:22–31), and the Word is in God from all eternity, for he is God himself (John 1:1). The Father "predestined us through Jesus Christ to be his adopted sons" (Eph. 1:5), but this plan was not immediately revealed. Rather, it was "kept in silence for long ages" (Rom. 16:25, NEB), "God's wisdom: a mysterious, a hidden wisdom. God planned it before all ages for our glory. None of the rulers of this age knew the mystery" (1 Cor. 2:7–8). It is this wisdom of which it is said: "Eye has not seen, ear has not heard, nor has it so much as dawned on man what God has prepared for those who love him" (1 Cor. 2:9). In short, if man is the living being who speaks, God is, beyond all else, the one who keeps silent.

Sometimes this silence is a heavy burden for man—all the more so if his belief in God is firm. The moment, however, when this silence brings real anguish to heart and mind and becomes truly scandalous is before the spectacle of the just man being persecuted. Then, stripped of all earthly help, man turns to God and cries out to him, but he receives no answer; evil triumphs and heaven is silent: "From the dust the dying groan, and the souls of the wounded cry out, yet God does not treat it as unseemly" (Job 24:12). "I cry to you, but you do not answer me; you stand off and look at me" (Job 30:20). "Who can get me a hearing from God? I have had my say, from A to Z; now let Shaddai answer me" (Job 31:35, JB; cf. Pss. 55; 69; 73:2–6; Isa. 52:14–53:10; Jer. 12:1–5).

Silence and Speech of the Universe

In some respects the universe, too, seems mute. In his hours of depression man is confronted with the cold indifference of things, which form an impassive setting for our ever-changing lot: "One generation passes and another comes, but the world forever stays. The sun rises and the sun goes down; then it presses on to the place where it rises. Blowing now toward the south, then toward the north, the wind turns again and again, resuming its rounds" (Eccles. 1:4–6). Still worse: a bitter irony seems to emanate from the natural world when the annual renewal of the earth in springtime mocks the old man in his decline: "The almond tree is in flower, the grasshopper is heavy with food and the caper bush bears its fruit, while man goes to his everlasting home" (Ecclus. 12:5, JB).

But this seeming silence does not mean that the universe bears no meaning. If you know how to understand its language, it gives witness to God: "The heavens declare the glory of God, and the firmament proclaims his handiwork" (Ps. 19:2).[1] In their regular recurrence the natural cycles perpetuate this witness and form a kind of *cosmic tradition*: "Day pours out the word to day, and night to night imparts knowledge" (Ps. 19:3). This witness given by the universe is not articulated in words but it is inescapable and "universal" in its reach; it comes to man's ear in every place: "No sound that anyone can hear; yet their voices goes out through all the earth, and their message to the ends of the world" (Ps. 19:3–4, JB).

Consequently the pagans who have failed to acknowledge the true God, creator of the universe, are much to be condemned. The Wisdom of Solomon is forceful on the point: "All men were by nature foolish who were in ignorance of God, and who from the good things seen did not succeed in knowing him who is, and from studying the works did not discern the artisan" (Wisd. 13:1; cf. Job 36:22–33), "for from the greatness and the beauty of created things their original author, by analogy, is seen" (Wisd. 13:5).[2] The apostle Paul repeats the same condemnation of idolatrous pagans:

> In fact, whatever can be known about God is clear to them; he himself made it so. Since the creation of the world, invisible realities, God's eternal power and divinity, have become visible, recognized through the things he has made. Therefore these men are inexcusable. They certainly had knowledge of God, yet they did not glorify him as God or give him thanks (Rom. 1:19–21).

During his first missionary journey with Barnabas, about ten years earlier (45–49), Paul had proclaimed the same doctrine to the pagans of Lystra: if God in the past has allowed the Gentiles to go their own way, "yet in bestowing his benefits, he has not hidden himself completely, without a clue. From the heavens he sends down rain and rich harvests; your spirits he fills with food and delight" (Acts 14:16–17).[3]

These assured statements, especially that of Acts, had received explicit advance confirmation from a pagan of genius, for Plato had collected the testimonies of the natural world and interpreted them in straightforward fashion. Clinias in the *Laws* finds it easy to assert beyond any doubt the existence of the divinity. The proof is: "to begin with, . . . the earth, and sun, and planets, and everything! And the wonderful and beautiful order of the seasons with its distinctions of years and months!"[4]

Thus through his fundamental situation man is confronted by the universe as a sign, and he is constantly engaged in asking questions of it. Like every other dialogue, this one involves the often painful alternations of accord and incomprehension, silence and word—or, rather, of *eloquent silence* and *mute silence.*

The World's Silence and God's Word

As a man, I sometimes see myself as caught between the agonizing silence of things and the still more agonizing silence of God. The universe, visible but indifferent, threatens to crush me. God, invisible and mute as well, gives rise to a deep-seated fear, for he eludes me and is already judging—perhaps condemning—me. Thus I conceive the mad desire to enter into a seemingly impossible dialogue with divinity itself. Others have had the same dream: the existence of the Pythian oracle at Delphi, the Cumaean Sibyl, and numerous mystery religions are proof of it. It is out of this primordial eternal silence that the revelation of the true God will one day enter history.

When the divine word at last resounds, the silence of mystery still envelops it, as it were contains it, giving it all its wonder and its power to excite. The message of salvation would not have been so arresting in the ears of men if the one who spoke were not the once silent God. As it is, this word—in the true sense of the phrase, unheard-of—fills the whole space which the agelong silence of the world presents to it: there it resonates, awakening endless echoes.[5] The word, revelatory of God's will, breaks the silence in favor of Israel over all other peoples (cf. Ps. 147:19–20; Isa. 42:14).[6]

In Jesus Christ, however, since he is the personal Word of God made flesh, "that divine secret kept in silence for long ages" is "now disclosed . . . made known to all nations" (Rom. 16:25–26, NEB), "manifested in the flesh, . . . seen by the angels, preached among the Gentiles, believed in throughout the world" (1 Tim. 3:16). The voice of preachers of the Good News "has sounded over the whole earth, and their words to the limits of the world" (Rom. 10:18).[7]

The Desert's Silence and God's Word

If it is to be heard by man, God's word must be received into the heart's silence as a mysterious space which it seeks to fill. Since the silence of things prepares the way for interior silence, God often calls his partner in dialogue into the *desert*. There, far from the noise of the world, the two partners are directed wholly to each other, and can no longer avoid the confrontation.

Thus it was at the edge of the desert, on the slopes of Mount Horeb, that Moses heard God's first words, issuing from the bush (Exod. 3:1–4:18).[8] Above all, it was in the same desert, after being delivered from Egyptian slavery by Yahweh's power, that the Hebrews went to meet their God and heard his voice during the awesome theophany of Mount Sinai (Exod. 19:16–19). It was in a lonely face-to-face meeting on the mountaintop that Moses conversed with Yahweh and received the words of the Decalogue (Exod. 19:20–20:21). Then Israel accepted God's word and gave its own promise of fidelity (Exod. 24). The covenant was concluded and the two parties were joined into oneness, through this unique exchange of words. Because God had spoken, the barren solitude had become the birthplace of the chosen people, and Israel is forever the people to whom God spoke. During the forty long years of its wilderness journeying, Israel lived not on bread alone but on everything that came from Yahweh's mouth (Deut. 8:3).

For the religious consciousness of Israel the silent desert continued to be the privileged place for the dialogue of God and his people. The prophet Elijah remembered this when, harried by persecutors and concerned to safeguard the covenant, he made a pilgrimage into the desert to God's mountain, Horeb (1 Kings 19). In the time of Hosea (around 750), when Israel, the faithless wife, is ready to return to Yahweh, her first husband, Yahweh says he "will lead her into the desert" where they first fell in love, and "speak to her heart." In that silent solitude, God's word will recover all its power to enthrall. Then the faithless wife will forget even the names of the Baals and will be married once again to Yahweh in tenderness, love, and fidelity (Hos. 2:9–22).

The close connection between the desert silence and God's word is maintained in the new dispensation. At the very beginning of the latter, the word of God is addressed to John, son of Zachary, in the desert (Luke 3:2). Thither the Forerunner draws the crowds in order to preach repentance and the imminent coming of the kingdom of heaven to them (Matt. 3:1–12; Luke 3:1–18). In the desert silence

Jesus is baptized and God's voice puts a seal on his mission; there he prepares himself, through fasting and in the struggle with Satan, for preaching the Good News (Matt. 3:13–4:17). On the mountain, which is a parallel to Sinai, he promulgates the new law (Matt. 5–7), and in the desert he welcomes the crowds and nourishes them with his teaching (Mark 6:30–44 and parallels; John 6). One of the parables supplies the reason behind the importance of the desert: the seed of the word cannot thrive in a heart in which "worldly anxiety and the lure of money choke it off. Such a one produces no yield" (Matt. 13:7, 22). Those who are completely taken up with this world's business are unable to accept the invitation to the banquet of the kingdom (Luke 14:15–24).

The Rhythm of Silence and Word

The dialogue between God and man is thus, in both covenants, a tissue of words and silences, each meaningful and revelatory. Even when God breaks his silence to disconcert the temerity of Job (Job 38–42) or, at the Judgment, to reproach his sinful people (Ps. 50:21), Israel always regards prophecy as a special favor from God (cf., e.g., Hos. 12:10–11; Amos 8:11–12).[9] Guilty generations therefore find themselves denied the blessing of a prophet's words.

In the dark days of the high priest Eli, for example, "a revelation of the Lord was uncommon and vision infrequent" (1 Sam. 3:1); when God's word did break this threatening silence, it was to herald punishment (1 Sam. 3:4–14). Before the siege of Jerusalem, Yahweh withdraws his word from the mouth of the prophet Ezekiel in order to punish his faithless people: "He said to me: Go shut yourself up in your house . . . I will make your tongue stick to your palate so that you will be dumb and unable to rebuke them for being a rebellious house" (Ezek. 3:24–26; cf. Isa. 29:10). Again: "There shall be disaster after disaster, rumor after rumor. Prophetic vision shall fade; instruction shall be lacking to the priest, and counsel to the elders" (Ezek. 7:26).[10] And in fact we find that Daughter Zion's "prophets have not received any vision from the Lord" (Lam. 2:9; cf. Dan. 3:38). Later, after the sack of Jerusalem by Antiochus Epiphanes in 169, the psalmist bewails God's silence: "Deeds on our behalf we do not see; there is no prophet now, and no one of us knows how long" (Ps.

74:9).[11] In the time of Judas Maccabaeus the silence of God has been of long standing, and the cessation of prophecy was regarded as having occurred at a distant decisive moment (1 Macc. 9:27). But men still hoped for the renewal of inspiration: they hid the defiled altar stones "until a prophet should come and decide what to do with them" (1 Macc. 4:46), and Simon is recognized as leader and high priest "until a true prophet arises" (1 Macc. 14:41).[12]

In the dramatic dialogue between Israel and her God the silence of the prophets was a sign and, in that sense, a word. It was a punishment for past sins, especially deliberate deafness, and a preparation for future words; it created in men's hearts the limitless space of desire and hope, where the message of salvation might find acceptance.

In Jesus Christ, the Word made flesh, God's word is forever given to men, and prophetism finds its unsurpassable fullness (Heb. 1:1).[13] But the mysterious alternation of silence and word does not therefore cease. The newborn child in the crib is an "in-fant": one who cannot speak (Latin *in-fans*). He gives hints of a more than human wisdom during his vist to the teachers in the Temple (Luke 2:46–47), but then he remains hidden for thirty years in the toil-filled silence of Nazareth. Yet in his very silence there is a word and a lesson in humility. During his public ministry, long hours of prayer alternate with preaching. Jesus used deliberate silences sometimes to condemn bad faith and intrigue, sometimes to rebuff false witness and accusations against him.[14] Finally, the approaching silence of death and, later, the silence that follows upon the ascension give priceless value to the "last words" that precede the twofold departure.

If we look a bit further, we see that the alternation of word and silence affirms God's transcendence. Just as God is both everywhere and nowhere in space and exists in every instant yet is beyond temporality, so he escapes the categories of both word and silence. The Silent One beyond all others is also subsistent Word, the Wholly Other whom no category, whether abstract or anthropological, can enclose or grasp: present in each moment of our human alternatives, yet infinitely beyond them.

With Christ's ascension to his glory, the dialogue between God and man, far from being broken off, reaches its perfection. On the one hand, in giving us his Son, his eternal Word, the Father says everything at once: in Jesus Christ we have been filled with the treasures of speech and knowledge (1 Cor. 1:5), for in him "every treasure of wisdom and knowledge is hidden" (Col. 2:3).[15] On the other hand, the risen Christ, present at God's right hand, now intercedes for us (Rom. 8:34; Heb. 7:25; 9:24; 1 John 2:1). These two movements—of revelation of God to man and of intercession for man before God—are forever fulfilled in the *very being* of Jesus Christ, for he *is*, to the believer, both the definitive "Yes" of God to his own promises and the "Amen" of man to God's glory (2 Cor. 1:20, 21). The silence of God—or, rather, a breaking off of the dialogue begun between himself and man—is no longer to be feared. For in Jesus Christ, who is word given by God to man and by man to God, the two partners are but one and ceaselessly accept each other. The nuptial "Yes" has been spoken once and for all and finds constant expression in the Church. The glorified Christ is the indestructible, living, subsistent dialogue between God and mankind.[16]

II. EFFICACY OF GOD'S WORD

God's Word: Beginning and Act

"In the beginning, when God created heaven and earth . . . he said . . . " (Gen. 1:1–2); "By the word of the Lord the heavens were made; by the breath of his mouth all their host" (Ps. 33:6). God's word is first; it is unqualified initiative, found at the beginning of everything, or better, it creates the beginning itself. Beings who do not exist come irresistibly into existence when God calls them: "He spoke, and it was made; he commanded, and it stood forth" (Ps. 33:9); "You spoke, and they were made; you sent forth your spirit, and they were created; no one can resist your word" (Jth. 16:14).

Thus, at God's *order*, a totally new *order*, a cosmos, makes its appearance. In giving existence to beings, the divine word imposes on them a law which is naught else but that word itself: "At [his] command they were created; he has fixed them in their place for ever, by an unalterable statute" (Ps. 148:5–6, JB). The word of God is thus the powerful and fruitful source that brings into being, contains, and rules all the marvels of creation, marvels of infinite greatness and infinite smallness, and all the variations of power and beauty scattered throughout nature; it embraces all beings and firmly establishes them.[17]

The universe, thus born from God's word and subsisting only by it, also bears its imprint, mark, and traces. We see why the universe can be *eloquent* for man, why "the heavens declare the glory of God" (Ps. 19:2). It is because they are the echo of that divine word or, better, that word "realized," that is, translated into things (Latin: *res*), without the infinite transcendence of their creator being affected in the slightest. The mute work speaks and tells of the workman who made it.

But God addresses a further word to himself, and that word, an "initiating" word as always, is perhaps even more astounding and significant: "Let us make man" (Gen. 1:26). Here the divine word inaugurates a wholly new kind of order, that of mankind: it sets in motion the destinies of countless self-responsible beings and the varied history of civilizations; it gives birth to the mysterious universe of consciousnesses. "Let us make man in our image, after our likeness" (*ibid*.).[18] In creating man in his image and breathing into his nostrils a breath of life (Gen. 2:7), God creates a being who is able to hear and respond to him, to "understand" with ear and mind the blessing that brings fruitfulness (Gen. 1:28–30) as well as the commandment with regard to the forbidden fruit (Gen. 2:16–17). The divine word creates human speech and human hearing: "Who gives one man speech and makes another deaf and dumb? . . . . Is it not I, the Lord?" (Exod. 4:11), says God to a Moses who is dismayed by his own lack of eloquence.

As a man, I am the interlocutor, the *responsible* partner whom God has provided for himself: I can *respond* to him in genuine dialogue. Even if my human word is created and therefore "second" and always "received," it commits me and I can genuinely give it. God creates my word and knows it even before it is on my tongue (Ps. 139:4), yet he requires and waits for the "Yes" of his creature at every stage in his plan of salvation: the "Yes" of the people at the making of the old covenant (Exod. 24:3), its "Amen" at the renewal of the covenant in the time of Ezra (Neh. 8:6), the "Be it done" of Mary at the dawn of the new dispensation (Luke 1:26–38), and, above all, the "Amen" which mankind, in Jesus Christ, says to God's glory (2 Cor. 1:20–21).

The light which the revelation of Jesus Christ throws back on the earlier revelation illumines new depths in God's creative work. From all eternity the Word is in God; he is himself God and effects the creation of everything: "In the beginning was the Word; the Word was in God's presence, and the Word was God. He was present to God in the beginning. Through him all things came into being, and apart from him nothing came to be. Whatever came to be in him, found life" (John 1:1–4). If nothing can begin to be except through this Word, God's only Son, neither can anything subsist without him, for "he sustains all things by his powerful word" (Heb. 1:3). Since, moreover, in God's eternal plan "the Word became flesh and made his dwelling among us" (John 1:14), it follows that God's great word: "Let us make man" contained in germ, along with the rest of human history, the man Jesus Christ, who was made flesh in the fullness of time (Gal. 4:4). In him who is eternal and transcendent as God and created as man, all that is effected by God's creative word is gathered up into unity and recapitulated: "He is the image of the Invisible God, the first-born of all creatures. In him everything in heaven and on earth was created . . . all were created through him, and for him. He is before all else that is" (Col. 1:15–17; cf. Eph. 1:3–14).[19]

The first call to salvation that God had addressed to sinful man, his first redemptive word, likewise involved Jesus Christ in a hidden way. Adam has fled from God's face and hidden "among the trees of the garden" (Gen. 3:8). God's word is straightway addressed to him and finds him in his guilty solitude: "Where are you?" (Gen. 3:9). This question is both beginning and act: it expresses God's concern, his "love for man" ("philanthropy": cf. Tit. 3:4), the care he still has for his fallen creature; and it contains germinally the whole plan for salvation and its unfolding across the millennia of history. The merciful love that echoes in the question is the radical source of all the situations in which God the Savior and man confront each other: "the very fact of his calling a person," says St. Ambrose, "is a testimony of salvation to him who comes, because the Lord calls those for whom he feels pity."[20]

But of all the marvelous deeds of God in favor of sinful man which are implicit in this first call—"Adam, where are you?"—the preeminent one is the Savior himself: he who will come "to search out and save what was lost" (Luke 19:10; cf. John 3:15–16) and go seeking the strayed sheep (Luke 15:4–7; cf. John 10:7–18). Even before this first dialogue between God and man is finished, a mysterious victory over the serpent's offspring is promised to the offspring of the woman; the first redemptive call culminates in the first heralding of restoration (Gen. 3:14–15).

When the fullness of time begins, another call, promised and awaited from the beginning, resounds in the history of mankind: "The beginning of the Good News about Jesus Christ," says Mark (1:1). We might also translate it as "Good News of the beginning" or "new beginning," because news is always first and initiatory, and the message which the world is going to receive in the gospel is the beginning of a new order. In Jesus Christ, God "takes in hand again," reshapes, re-says all created things, in accordance with the eternal word in which he says the world to himself, and despite the rejections that sin involved. The evangelical word is an act in which God commits himself and gives man and the universe a new beginning.[21] The Christian God is the God who *re-creates* by *re-saying*: "He wills to bring us to birth with a word spoken in truth so that we may be a kind of first fruits of his creatures" (James 1:18). Christian man is *re-generated* by God's word: "Your rebirth has come, not from a destructible but from an indestructible seed, through the living and enduring word of God" (1 Pet. 1:23) and awaits the heavenly completion of universal renewal: "The One who sat on the throne said to me, 'See, I make all things new! ' " (Rev. 21:5; cf. Rom. 8:19–23).

The Prevenient Word

The creative word of God is wholly prevenient, a totally gratuitous initiative; by its unlimited power it gives existence to the beings it addresses. My words can reach only a man who already exists, but by his word God sets me before him in existence, out of the nothingness proper to me.

If the words of revelation presuppose this creative prevenance, they are also in their turn completely unnecessitated. No one can force God to break his silence; man, however powerful or virtuous, cannot claim or merit God's speaking to him. God freely decides to speak and launches his word upon the eddying currents of history, and man can only receive God's call as a gracious gift. God is the first to speak.

Thus, as soon as sinful man is first addressed—"Adam, where are you?"—he receives the salutary effects of this prevenient gift, for the deathly solitude created by his sin is removed. The creature emerges a second time from the abyss; he can now hope. Man still exists but now exists by a new title in relation to the God who calls him to repentance.

Throughout history the prevenance of the divine word finds clear expression in the person of God's spokesmen. To make himself understood by men God uses human language; he provides himself with the intelligent cooperation of some of his servants, commissions them to speak in his name, and sends them to their brothers. The narratives of prophetic vocations in the Bible are significant here. In them we often find the same pattern: divine call, protest from the one chosen, reassurance by God, sending. The prevenance of the word is thus first exercised towards the future prophet: the call surprises Moses in his solitude (Exod. 3:1–14), Samuel in his childish simplicity (1 Sam. 3:1–18). The vision of the Holy One terrifies Isaiah because he is aware of his own unworthiness (Isa. 6:8). It is a prevenance in which force and a skillful strategy are strangely mingled. Amos, for example, compares God's calling to the terrible roar of a lion: "The lion roars—who will not be afraid! The Lord God speaks—who will not prophesy!" (Amos 3:8). Ezekiel obeys the call, even though, he says, "my heart, as I went, overflowed with bitterness and anger" (2:14–15, JB). Jeremiah, on the other hand, says: "You duped me, Lord, and I let myself be duped" (20:7).

When Moses and Jeremiah protest that they are wholly lacking in eloquence, God promises them help, reassures them, and gives them proof that will accredit them with their people (Exod. 3:11–17; Jer. 1:4–8). Better still: not only does he promise to teach Moses what he is to say (Exod. 4:10–12) but, in a deeply meaningful gesture, he puts his own words on the lips of Jeremiah (Jer. 1:9)[22] and tells him: "You will be my mouthpiece" (Jer. 15:19; cf. 5:12–13; Luke 1:70; Acts 3:18, 21). He orders Ezekiel to eat the scroll that carries the prophetic message (Ezek. 2:8–3:3). Of himself man is dumb when he must speak of God. The only one who can utter God is God himself and the man who puts aside his own words and receives and transmits those of the Wholly Other. In proclaiming: "Thus says the Lord!" the messenger asserts the commission he has received, his renunciation of his own words, and his intention to be faithful to God.

Armed with divine authority, the prophet now goes to his fellow men, meeting them on their journeys, asking them riddles, provoking them, challenging them in their interior situation before God (cf. 2 Sam. 12:1–4; 1 Kings 11:29–40; etc.). He intends to fulfill the expectations of receptive men (for the Word looks for a welcome) but also to hunt out the deafness that is due to bad faith. To this end, God's spokesman[23] tries to win attention by varied means: he raises his voice and even cries out (Isa. 40:6,9; 58:1; Jer. 2:2; Ezek. 21:17; Mic. 6:9), but he also engages in unusual gestures and actions, prescribed by God, which will strike the imagination of his hearers with their symbolism: Isaiah's nudity (Isa. 20), the suggestive names he gives his children (Isa. 7:3; 8:1–4, 18), Jeremish's celibacy (16:2),[24] Ezekiel's dumb silence as he lies on the ground (4:1–8),[25] Hosea's return to his unfaithful wife (Hos. 1:2–8). The prophet thus heralds the word with his whole being; his whole life is a word and a sign, a witness.

When his time comes, the Forerunner, in whom prophetism reaches its transcendent climax (Matt. 11:9–15), is met in the desert by God's word (Luke 3:1–2) and proclaims the imminence of the kingdom to the crowds (Matt. 3:1–6), unmasking the hidden rejections and the pretended self-assurances of guilty men (Matt. 3:7–12).

But the supreme embodiment of the prevenance of God's word is Jesus Christ himself, the Word made flesh. The unparalleled graciousness involved in the incarnation cannot really be described. God in person comes to man, carries his initiative of love to the point of himself becoming a man. The Word made flesh pitches his tent among us and meets us at every stage of our life, from birth to death (John 1:14).

Foreseeing his own return to the Father, Jesus chooses a few men and sends them to preach (Mark 3:13–14). Just before his ascension he commissions them to go in the power of the Spirit and preach the Good News to every creature (Mark 16:15–16), to bear witness to him even to the ends of the earth (Acts 1:8). Once they have been transformed by the Spirit, the Twelve are unable to keep the word to themselves; they carry it indeed, but they are also carried by it (Acts 4:20), for it is never chained (cf. 2 Tim. 2:9), but must "make progress and be hailed by many others" (2 Thess. 3:1).[26] The dynamism inherent in the message forces its bearers out to meet other men in an irresistible movement of prevenance. *Word*, *mission*, and *prevenance* are inseparable, for the divine power, the "intentionality," of the word, infallibly engenders the thrust outward to others. The action of the apostle and his often tragic confrontation with his fellow men is an answer to and a visible translation of the prevenient power of God's word.

All Christian preaching has for its inner drive this movement of divine prevenance; it does not wait for the hearer to come, but goes out to meet him, crossing all the geographical, psychological, and social distances. It seeks encounter, nearness, even intimcy with every man. It publicly proclaims, before all peoples (Latin: *prae-dicere*, to say in front of), the divine offer of salvation.

God's Word and God's Presence

God's word goes before him and heralds him. The prophet walks on ahead of God to meet men and to prepare the way for Yahweh (cf. Isa. 40:3–5). Every herald of the old and new covenants, simply by the power of his word, prepares for God's coming and presence and deserves the name of forerunner. It is highly significant that Zachary says of his son John: "You . . . shall be called prophet of the Most High; *for* you shall go before the Lord to prepare straight paths before him" (Luke 1:76; cf. 1:17).

But Christ goes even further, proclaiming John "a prophet indeed, and something more!" because he is the great Forerunner of whom Malachy spoke: "It is about this man that Scripture says, 'I send my messenger ahead of you to prepare your way before you' " (Matt. 11:7–15; 17:10–13; cf. Mal. 3:1,23–24). John, in turn, points to Christ as the one who is coming after him (Matt. 3:11; John 1:15) and for whose presence he prepares by his preaching.

Jesus Christ also prepares for his own coming in various places by having others preach his word: "The Lord appointed a further seventy-two and sent them in pairs before him to every town and place he intended to visit" (Luke 10:1). Gregory the Great remarks: "Rightly does the Lord send them ahead of him to all the towns and places he himself was to visit. For in fact the Lord does follow upon his preachers; preaching comes first, then the Lord comes to our interior dwelling after the words of exhortation have preceded him."[27]

We may even say that the word gives men an anticipated presence of God. If my word is in a measure myself, since it expresses and communicates me, then the word of salvation is the Savior himself, making him personally present to its hearers. This is why, in welcoming or refusing the word authentically transmitted by the apostolic ministry, men are welcoming or rejecting Jesus Christ and the Father.[28]

This presence is realized first of all in the initial proclamation of salvation, the kerygma. However, the word as proclaimed in the liturgical assembly makes Christ present to believers in a specific fashion: "He is present in His word, since it is He Himself who speaks when the holy Scriptures are read in the church."[29] This type of presence is certainly different from the Eucharistic presence, to which it proximately or remotely refers, but it is nonetheless a real presence under the quasi-sacramental sign which the word is. It is an active presence in which Christ exerts his saving power, and a here-and-now presence which touches the Christian assembly in the "today" of its existence.[30]

The Revelatory Word

The mystery of the human word, with its subtle and volatile character, is a marvelous instrument for the mystery of God, for through the human word the divine mystery can announce itself without disclosing itself, diffuse its radiance without surrendering itself. Speaking at man's level, God yet remains in himself invisible and as impalpable and elusive as the word he uses. Between the light given and the splendors still hidden there is no proportion. If God speaks rather like a man, he does so to say that he is wholly different from man: "As high as the heavens are above the earth, so high are my ways above your ways and my thoughts above your thoughts" (Isa. 55:8–9). The radical anthropomorphism of a revelation expressed in human language is thus wholly at the service of God's transcendence. This is eminently true of the sublime revelation of God's name to Moses: "I am who am" (Exod. 3:14).

If a human word can be used for such confidences, the reason is that the word is then being controlled not by man's spirit but by the Spirit who "scrutinizes all matters, even the deep things of God" (1 Cor. 2:10). "Prophecy has never been put forward by man's willing it. It is rather that men impelled by the Holy Spirit have spoken under God's influence" (2 Pet. 1:21; cf. 1 Pet. 1:11). Isaiah (61:1), Ezekiel (2:12, 14), and Joel (3:1–2) all bear witness to that fact. Above all, the Spirit visibly descends on Jesus, the Word made flesh, the definitive Revelation of God, on the day of his baptism (Matt. 3:16); it is the Spirit who sends him "to bring glad tidings to the poor" (Luke 4:18). Christ's words are "spirit and life" (John 6:63), because in him God's Word and God's Spirit are inseparable. Jesus Christ is on that account the perfect Revealer of the Father: "No one has ever seen God. It is God the only Son, ever at the Father's side, who has revealed him" (John 1:18).

The Master in turn promises the Spirit to his disciples to give them understanding of the teaching received (John 14:26; 16:13), to prompt them with answers to their persecutors (Matt. 10:20), and to inspire them with courage for bearing witness even to the ends of the earth (Acts 1:8). On Pentecost the Spirit in fact descends on the Twelve in the form of fiery tongues (organs of speech), and the apostles immediately begin to preach fearlessly (Acts 2:3–21). The Acts of the Apostles in their entirety deal with the Spirit's activity in the testimony of men (cf. especially Acts 4:8, 31; 6:10; 10:44–48). Finally, Paul teaches that every profession of faith in Jesus as Lord (1 Cor. 12:3) and every word of wisdom or knowledge are gifts of that same Spirit (1 Cor. 12:8). The Christian soldier must arm himself with "the sword of the spirit, the word of God" (Eph. 6:17).[31]

Spokesmen, Presence, Revelation

If God avails himself of spokesmen to proclaim his intentions, it is because man could not sustain the experience of the divine transcendence. He who speaks with awesome claps of thunder and flashes of lightning on Horeb could not take fragile man as a partner in dialogue. Not alone the sight of his face but his word itself would bring death. Hence the Hebrews plead with Moses: "You speak to us, and we will listen; but let not God speak to us, or we shall die" (Exod. 20:19). Here we find the profound justification for prophetism: the superabundance of the divine glory which one cannot come close to without dying is filtered through the man. At the same time, the ineffable mystery of God is withheld, sheltered from any manifestation that would degrade it.

But there is another consideration that deserves our attention here. In Moses and the prophets who succeed him, the mediation of a man gives God's word its full power to arouse men (Deut. 18:15–19). From this point of view, God could find no better way of reaching men than through a man (presupposing always, of course, the interior action of the Spirit). The voice God makes use of to speak to men is not detachable, indeed, from the rest of the personality; it is, on the contrary, a datum of a whole human presence. The spokesman is simultaneously audible, visible, and tangible; he stands there (Jer. 1:17) as partner in a dialogue which cannot be avoided. Through him God's word and presence confront an individual, to his joy or his condemnation. Thus, in the person of Nathan it is God himself who addresses David and forces him to admit his guilt (2 Sam. 12:1–13). It is God again, always God, who tells Hezekiah, through the mouth of Isaiah, of the fatal character of his illness and then of his imminent cure (Isa. 38). The invisible Yahweh borrows from the man he chooses his visibility and the words and gestures which constitute his presence.

In Jesus Christ, God is not content to send an emissary chosen from among men; instead, the Word personally makes his own an authentic manhood. Just as in each man the phenomenality expresses the subject, so everything in Jesus expresses God: his teaching, of course, directly communicates the Father's word (John 3:34; 6:16; 8:28; 12:49–50; 14:24; 17:8,14); but, beyond this, his body and flesh are a word (John 1:14), as are his presence, gestures, deeds (John 5:36; 10:22–38; 14:10–12),[32] silences, joys, sufferings, resurrection, and ascension. It is by his very life and existence that Jesus signifies God.

The emissary of Christ (2 Cor. 5:20) therefore does not refer his hearer to the invisible God of the old covenant, but to God incarnate. For the believer of today, the humanity of the emissary represents —that is, renders present—and signifies the humanity of the God-Man. Thus is manifested the reciprocity that links every human being to Jesus Christ. God-made-man becomes for each person the interlocutor here present. There is no danger of his remaining an abstract idea or even a figure lost in the distant mists of history. He is manifested by a living being and becomes himself a living being for me; he is signified by a person and becomes someone for me.

God's Word as Promotive Power

We have already made the point that the simple fact of God's addressing sinful man is an act of restoration, for here fallen man is promoted to the rank of God's interlocutor (Gen. 3:9). Still more is there an ennobling of the great confidants and heralds of God, such as Moses: God converses with him "face to face, as a man speaks with his friend" (Exod. 33:11, JB); God speaks to him "face to face . . . , plainly and not in riddles," and not in vision or dream (Num. 12:8). So great a dignity comes to Moses from this fact that God severely reproaches those who dare murmur against his intimate confidant (Num. 12:1–10). For that matter, every prophet, since he is addressed by God and commissioned to speak his words, enjoys a position of dignity in Israel: God forbids any mistreatment of him (Ps. 105:15), and Jesus will weep over Jerusalem that puts prophets to death (Luke 13:34).

The whole Israelite people, moreover, is set apart and privileged among all peoples because of the word God addresses to it: "He has proclaimed his word to Jacob, his statutes and his ordinances to Israel. He has not done thus for any other nation; his ordinances he has not made known to them" (Ps. 147:19–30; cf. Rom. 9:4). At a later date Christ affirms—incidentally but nonetheless clearly—this same "elevating" power of the word. During a discussion of his divine sonship with the Jews, he quotes Psalm 82:6, in which the function of judges is declared to be divine; he then widens the scope of the text in order to make his own point: "If it calls those men gods to whom God's word was addressed—and Scripture cannot lose its force . . . " (John 10:34–35).[33] Those who receive divine revelation are thus divinized after a fashion; through faith and prayer they become partners in dialogue of the living God.

With Jesus Christ himself the dialogue concerning salvation reaches its climax of intimacy. By being engaged in it the disciples pass from the rank of servants to that of friends: "I no longer speak of you as slaves, for a slave does not know what his master is about. Instead, I call you friends, since I have made known to you all that I heard from my Father" (John 15:15). The disciples are already "cleansed" by their Master's words to them (John 15:3) and filled with his joy (John 15:11; 16:21–22; 17:13). The Good News, received in the dialogue of faith and prayer, brings a "healing" and "elevating" grace; it promotes God's partner in dialogue to a new existential status.

The divine word also exercises its promotive power on Jesus, but in a special way. The Father's address could not confer upon the Son a dignity that was not already his by nature; still less could it "raise him up" as it does sinful man. Here, rather, God speaks in order to unveil the eminent dignity of Jesus of Nazareth and the divine character of his mission.

Scripture had, of course, already borne constant witness to the Messiah, and Jesus appeals to this testimony, which is the testimony of God.[34] In addition, the works done in him by the Father (John 5:19–23,30,36; 10:22–39; 14:10–11) and the doctrine which is not his own but that of the one who sent him (John 7:16) provide converging testimonies. Above all, several times during his mortal life Jesus receives a solemn testimonial from the Father. On the day of his baptism, while the Spirit is manifesting himself visibly and resting upon Jesus, God acknowledges his beloved Son, in whom he is pleased (Matt. 3:16–17). At the transfiguration, God's word is added to those of Moses and Elijah (the whole former covenant) in proclaiming the divine sonship of Jesus and authenticating his teaching (Matt. 17:1–8). Shortly before the passion, at a moment when anxious fear of the imminent "hour" seizes the soul of Christ, the Father's voice is heard again, promising to complete his glorification (John 12:27–29). Finally, since every saving event is a word of God (Hebrew *dabar*:word and event), the resurrection and ascension constitute the most solemn recognition that could be given to Jesus, for in these events he is declared "Son of God in power" (Rom. 1:4), exalted, honored with the Name which is above every name, and established forever as Lord to the glory of God the Father (Phil. 2:9–11).

Penetrating Power of God's Word

Inaccessible though divine wisdom is (Job 28), the words of the Law brought it near and made it familiar despite its mystery. The Law for its part is not found in the unapproachable heights of heaven or beyond the seas: "No, the Word is very near to you, it is in your mouth and in your heart for your observance" (Deut. 30:14, JB). Paul applies this text to the new Law and understands it of "the word of faith which we preach" (Rom. 10:8). The slow and long-continued repetition of the word gradually inscribes the Law within the heart of the devout man, so that it comes spontaneously from heart to lip: "The mouth of the just man murmurs wisdom, and his tongue speaks what is right; with the Law of his God in his heart . . . " (Ps. 37:30–31, JB; cf. Ps. 19:15; 49:4).

If the words of the old Law were to remain written in the heart of the faithful (Deut. 6:6–9), the Good News heralded by Jeremiah will likewise be "within them," written not any longer on stone tablets but "upon their hearts" (Jer. 31:33; cf. 2 Cor. 3:3).[35] Christ will teach, in the parable of the sower, that "the message about God's reign" is sown in the hearts of men and bears fruit there according to their dispositions (Matt. 13:3–23),[36] and Paul understands that "the word of faith" must give rise to "faith in the heart" and "confession on the lips" (Rom. 10:8–10).[37]

God's word, however, does not take the form only of a spoken or written word. Every event is a word of God and must therefore be kept in the heart. The Virgin Mary keeps in her heart and meditates on the events of Jesus' infancy, for they are genuine words of God (Luke 2:19, 51).

Whether consoling or reproachful, God's word reaches into the innermost depths of the human person who receives it. The prophetic word is therefore likened to a sharp-edged sword and a polished arrow (Isa. 49:2). Penetrating like a knife, it lays bare our most secret intentions, brings to light the hidden lairs of unacknowledged pride and egoism, and compels us to judge and even to condemn ourselves: "Indeed, God's word is living and effective, sharper than any two-edged sword. It penetrates and divides soul and spirit, joints and marrow; it judges the reflections and thoughts of the heart" (Heb. 4:12). This is why Saint Paul recommends to the Christian soldier "the sword of the spirit, the word of God" (Eph. 6:17).

At other times the word of God brings divine comfort to men in the depths of their being. That was the aim of Deutero-Isaiah: "Comfort, give comfort to my people, says your God. Speak tenderly to

Jerusalem, and proclaim to her that her service is at an end, her guilt expiated" (Isa. 40:1–2). And in Hosea God says: "I will allure her . . . and speak to her heart" (Hos. 2:16).[38] The psalmist, in turn, bases his dearest hopes on the word of God: "I trust in the Lord; my soul trusts in his word" (Ps. 130:5; cf. Ps. 19:8–12), and prays God to be mindful of him: "Remember your word to your servant since you have given me hope. My comfort in my affliction is that your promise gives me life" (Ps. 119:49–50 and *passim*).[39]

There is thus an intimate connection between God's *word* and man's *heart*: the innermost center of personality, where everyday choices as well as the radical decisions of life are made, is the place where the word must be received and kept.

God's Word as Man's Food

The word is not inactive in us (1 Thess. 2:13). It abides in man's interior in order to stimulate the long-term effort at assimilation which we call meditation and, as a food, to give life to the believer.

The nutritive character of the word is often taught in Scripture. Deuteronomy roundly declares that "not by bread alone does man live, but by every word that comes forth from the mouth of God" (Deut. 8:3; cf. Acts 7:38), a text which Christ will repeat during his temptations in the desert (Matt. 4:4). The psalmist draws delight from the words of the promise: "How sweet to my palate are your promises, sweeter than honey to my mouth!" (Ps. 119:103; cf. Ps. 19:11),[40] and therefore he seeks to find ever greater nourishment in them: "I gasp with open mouth, in yearning for your commands" (Ps. 119:131). Amidst trials, contempt, and opposition, Jeremiah reminds God how eagerly he had received his word: "When I found your words, I devoured them; they became my joy and the happiness of my heart" (Jer. 15:16).

In a vision and a gesture of startling symbolism God gives Ezekiel to understand that the divine word must be his food:

> "Open your mouth and eat what I shall give you." It was then I saw a hand stretched out to me, in which was a written scroll which he unrolled before me. It was covered with writing front and back . . . . He said to me: "Son of man, eat what is before

> you; eat this scroll, then go, speak to the house of Israel." So I opened my mouth and he gave me the scroll to eat. "Son of man," he then said to me, "feed your belly and fill your stomach with this scroll I am giving you." I ate it, and it was as sweet as honey in my mouth (Ezek. 2:8–3:3).

Later, the seer of Patmos will receive the same order from God's messenger (Rev. 10:8–11).

The Book of Wisdom makes the word of God superior to any earthly food: "Lord, . . . it is not the various kinds of fruit that nourish man, but it is your word that preserves those who believe you!" (Wisd. 16:26). It is, consequently, a terrible divine punishment—a terrible hunger, said Amos—to be starved for God's word and not be able to find it: "Yes, days are coming, says the Lord God, when I will send famine upon the land: not a famine of bread, or thirst for water, but for hearing the word of the Lord. Then shall they wander from sea to sea and rove from the north to the east in search of the word of the Lord, but they shall not find it" (Amos 8:11–12).

The nutritive character of God's word takes on a wholly unlooked-for dimension of reality in Jesus Christ. In order to reach man more surely, the eternal Word of God was made flesh (John 1:14). Jesus is the Word of life (1 John 1:1; cf. John 1:4). The connection between Christ's word and man's nourishment is indicated in Mark when the Master multiplies the loaves in the setting of his teaching activity (Mark 6:30–34).[41] John presents the discourse on the bread of life as spoken in the same circumstances; Jesus there offers himself as the bread of life to anyone disposed to believe in him (John 6:34), and proclaims that his words are spirit and life (John 6:63). Paul, in his turn, will exhort the faithful to cling to the "word of life" (Phil. 2:16).

But then the Word made flesh becomes bread in a new sense. The authentic manna, the bread which in the fullest sense is descended from heaven, the bread which truly gives life, is the flesh of Jesus, given for the life of the world (John 6:51–58).[42] The incarnate Word presents himself as food. The anthropomorphism of Word-food ceases to be a figurative manner of speaking because it is consummated in reality. The believer is nourished not only by the teaching but by the flesh itself of the incarnate Word. The "two tables" are inseparable and will give vital strength to Christians at the Eucharistic gathering.[43]

The Effective Word

In itself, God's word is all-powerful. It created the universe, for at its call beings rose irresistibly out of nothingness. Its rule over these beings is sure and unfailing: "Just as from the heavens the rain and snow come down and do not return there till they have watered the earth, making it fertile and fruitful, giving seed to him who sows and bread to him who eats, so shall my word be that goes forth from my mouth. It shall not return to me void, but shall do my will, achieving the end for which I sent it" (Isa. 55:10–11). The psalmist likes to describe this mastery of God's word over the forces of nature: "He sends forth his command to the earth; swiftly runs his word! He spreads snow like wool; frost he strews like ashes. He scatters his hail like crumbs; before his cold the waters freeze. He sends his word and melts them" (Ps. 147:15–18).[44]

He who at the beginning exerted his rule over the abyss of waters (Gen. 1:2–13; Job 38:8–11; Ecclus. 39:17) and at his will imposed silence on the sea (Ps. 65:8; 89:10; 107:29), will one day, through the omnipotence of his Word-made-flesh, calm the turbulence of wind and water on Lake Genesareth (Matt. 8:23–27).

The word of God also shows its power in the *history* of men: it contains this history in a sense within itself, declares and interprets it. Without eliminating the free play of human action, God's word reveals his intentions for past, present, and future, and thus it has an eminently *prophetic* import. In particular, God tells what the future will be—sometimes clearly, sometimes obscurely—before he brings it to pass. *The word precedes the intervention of God's hand in history.* At the appointed time the divine hand, in which history is "held," infallibly carries out the promises of his word, and in return illumines the depths of their meaning.[45]

The word of God is represented therefore as the unfailing instrument of his plans. In order to punish the faithlessness of Israel and its scorn of the prophetic word, God tells Jeremiah he will "make my words in your mouth, a fire, and this people is the wood that it shall devour!" (Jer. 5:14).[46] And again: "Is not my word like fire, says the Lord, like a hammer shattering rocks?" (Jer. 23:29). Elsewhere it is the image of the sword that expresses the destructive power of the divine word, for example at the exodus from Egypt: "Your all-powerful word from heaven's royal throne bounded, a fierce warrior, into the doomed land, bearing the sharp sword of your inexorable decree. And as he alighted, he filled every place with death" (Wisd. 18:15–16). The Servant of Yahweh says that God made his mouth a sharp sword (Isa. 49:2, JB), and the Apocalypse will say that from the mouth of the Son of Man, who is sovereign judge of the nations, "a sharp two-edged sword came" (Rev. 1:16), "a sharp sword for striking down the nations" (Rev. 19:15; cf. 2 Thess. 2:8).

Because of its infallible prophetic effectiveness, whether in blessing or cursing,[47] the divine word is something quite different from a purely conceptual, abstract statement; rather, it is an event, a concrete, living fact (Hebrew *dabar*: word and event), fraught with human and divine meaning. Inversely, events are also words: God utters himself and reveals himself in them.[48] This is the case with Israelite institutions. These came into being at Sinai out of God's word and reveal his will for the people; but, at the same time, being as it were *permanent events* they make God's word an integral part of social life, incarnating it after a fashion, giving it flesh in facts.

The event-word beyond all others, the one which Israel was, in God's plan, heralding and preparing, is the incarnation of the Son. Here the personal, subsistent Word is written down and acquires a visible "embodiment" in history. The Word becomes flesh (John 1:14; cf. Heb. 1:1–2) and, solely by virtue of his human and divine reality, a system of relationships that reason cannot grasp is established between man and God. Every promise is kept, fulfilled, and transcended. Through the Good News, God saves man and adopts him as his son in Jesus Christ.

The all-powerful effectiveness of God's word is thus sovereignly manifested in the Word made flesh. Simply with a word Jesus cures the centurion's son (Matt. 8:5–13; cf. Wisd. 16:12; Ps. 107:20) and drives out unclean spirits (Matt. 8:16–17; Mark 1:23–28; 5:8; etc.; the preaching of the kingdom is closely linked with the expulsion of demons [cf. Mark 1:39; 3:14–15]). Simply with a word he cures the paralytic (Matt. 9:6), calms the storm (Matt. 8:26), and forgives sins (Matt. 9:2). This all-powerful and life-giving word seeks man out even in death: the command of Jesus brings back to life the daughter of Jairus (Matt. 9:18–26), the son of the widow of Naim (Luke 7:11–16), and Lazarus (John 11:43–44); at the call of the Son of Man the dead will come forth from their tombs on the last day (John 5:28–29).

Indeed, his words are "spirit and life" (John 6:63). Unlike heaven and earth they will not pass away (Matt. 24:35); they are already giving eternal life (John 6:68).

Just as Jesus showed himself "a prophet powerful in word and deed" (Luke 24:19), so the apostles in their preaching show the power of God's word. The gospel comes "as power and as the Holy Spirit and as utter conviction" (1 Thess. 1:5, JB). But if the apostolic word is supported, as Christ promised (Mark 16:17–18), by miracles that accredit it (Acts 2:4–12; 3:1–10; 5:1–12, 19, 21; 9:36–42; etc.), these are not simply "signs" of its invisible effectiveness in the secrecy of consciences. When received by the ear and welcomed into the heart not as a merely human word but as God's word, the preaching of the gospel is active in the believer (1 Thess. 2:13; cf. Rom. 1:16); it transforms him, re-creates him in accordance with God's saving intentions. When meditated on in faith and repeated by the lips in prayer, it becomes part of his being, takes on flesh in him, as it were, and transforms and reshapes him. Far better than the word in the old Law, it keeps a man "faultless in his way" (Ps. 119:9; John 15:3) and brings him strength, joy, assurance, consolation, and life (Ps. 19:8–12; 119: 42, 50, etc.; Rom. 15:4; 1 Cor. 14:3; etc.). In short, since word and hand are inseparable, we may say that *God puts his hand to man's making, once again, through his all-powerful word* or, again, that God's word in Jesus Christ exercises an *interpretative power*, giving a radically new meaning to the universe and to man.

There is question here of nothing less than a new act of generation (1 Cor. 4:15). As an "indestructible seed," God's living and eternal word begets us a second time (1 Pet. 1:23); when implanted in us, it can save our souls (James 1:21). The preaching of the gospel, which is an authentic worship of God, makes of the nations "a pleasing sacrifice, consecrated by the Holy Spirit" (Rom. 1:9; 15:15–16; cf. 1 Tim. 4:5). As brought to birth by the word of truth, we are the *first fruits of the new creation* (James 1:18; cf. Gen. 1).[49]

The Name of God

For biblical man, the name is the word in which the person himself finds expression, and knowledge of the name gives power over the one who hears it. God, however, is so transcendent that his Name is inaccessible to man. Thus, God is known in the earlier ages only as the God of the fathers, the one who intervened in their lives, "the God of Abraham, the God of Isaac, the God of Jacob" (Exod. 3:6, 13).[50] His Name is as mysterious as his very self; he is, in himself, unknowable and incommunicable.

It is therefore an act of utmost condescension when God agrees to give his name in answer to Moses' request: "I am who am" (Exod. 3:14–15). Of all the words of revelation, the Name is the most precious, for it represents the supreme act of trust on God's part and sets up between God and man a kind of communication beyond the power of reason to conceive. It is also the revelation which carries to its ultimate consequences the ambiguity inherent in every manifestation of God. For, on the one hand, the mystery of Yahweh's inner being continues to be preserved by the tautology and, on the other hand, God positively affirms his transcendence: he exists, in a totally unqualified way. The whole activity of salvation will bring to light his attributes.[51]

In this sublime act of trust God gives man a hold over him, as it were, inasmuch as he makes it possible henceforth to call him, invoking him by name, and such an appeal must be, in itself, irresistible to God. To his creature the Creator offers help, indeed almost puts his omnipotence at man's disposal: "Our help is in the name of the Lord, who made heaven and earth" (Ps. 124:8). This Name, as a substitute for God, will receive the same veneration as God himself and will not be pronounced by the devout Jew.[52]

With the incarnation of the Son, revelation reaches its climax (Heb. 1:1–2). More than the name of any other person chosen by God, the name of the Messiah to be born expresses his unique role in the divine plan. Furthermore, in the Messiah, God himself is revealing himself, no longer simply as he who is, but as he who saves: "Jesus" means "Yahweh saves," and in fact it is he who "will save his people from their sins" (Matt. 1:21; cf. Acts 4:12). On the other hand, since he is aware of his own equality with God (cf. Phil. 2:6–11), Jesus claims for himself the ineffable name given in Exodus (John 8:24, 27, 58 [cf. 10:30–33]; 13:13,19; 18:5–8); in this way both the continuity and the progress between the two phases of revelation are brought out clearly.

In exalting Jesus to his right hand after the resurrection (Acts 2:32–36), the Father openly recognizes his right to "the Name which is above every name"; he makes Jesus "Lord" and sharer in his own glory (Acts 2:32–36; Phil. 2:9–11; cf. Eph. 1:21).[53] It is in virtue of the divine power of this Name that the apostles exercise control over illness (Mark 16:18; Acts 3:6, 16; 4:7, 10, 12, 17, 30; 9:34; etc.) and even over demons (Mark 9:38; 16:17; Acts 16:18; 19:12–13; etc.).[54]

Clearly, then, God's glory and universal presence demand that his Name shall be praised throughout the world (Exod. 9:16; cf. Rom. 9:17; Ps. 48:11). Jesus Christ came to reveal that Name to men (John 17:3–6, 26), and bids his disciples pray that it be hallowed. He himself prays for its glorification and offers himself in order to secure this by his sacrifice (John 12:28). He sends forth his apostles in order that "in his name, penance for the remission of sins . . . be preached to all the nations" (Luke 24:47; cf. Acts 4:17; 5:28,40; 10:43). Such will be the mission of Paul especially (Acts 9:15–16; cf. 15:26). Thus the savior's Name will be glorified in Christians and they in him (2 Thess. 1:12; cf. John 14:13–14).[55] On the last day they will receive a mysterious new name which will express their own renewal (Rev. 2:17) and they will bear forever the Name of Christ and the Name of the Father (Rev. 3:12; 14:1; cf. 3:5).

The Unitive Power of God's Word

The unfinished city of Babel is forever the symbol of the confusion of tongues, inflicted as punishment for the sin of arrogance (Gen. 11:1–9). Mankind is fragmented, incapable of bringing any common undertaking to completion, reduced to impotence. When God undertakes to save man, therefore, he tries to restore the broken unity and to gather a people by the power of his word. At the foot of Sinai the Hebrews became God's people because together they listened to the same voice, the voice of Yahweh heard in the spectacular display of thunder and lightning; they agreed to be "called together" and united by God's address to them (Exod. 19–24). Israel is henceforth the privileged people of God because it listened to God's word and spoke it back to him solemnly in faith. The covenant is made: God and his people are now one in virtue of the freely exchanged word of the Law (Exod. 24:34). After the Exile, therefore, when the deported people return to their own country, it is through a solemn reading of the Law that they are reborn. They become once more the people of

God—that is, the community which listens to the unique call and responds to it (Neh. 8). It is easy to see why such a covenant, made in the desert by an exchange of words, should be represented by the prophets as a marriage between God and his people (Isa. 1:21; Jer. 3:1–12; Ezek. 16:23; cf. Isa. 50:1; 54:6–7; 62:4–5).

When the time is ripe, Jesus Christ, Word of God made flesh, sows "the word of the kingdom" (Matt. 13:19, JB), the word which at once tells of the kingdom of God and brings it into existence. Crowds from all parts of Palestine gather to hear the word of the new Law (Luke 6:17b–18; cf. 4:42; Mark 2:13; 3:7–10; 6:32–33; 7:14–23; 8:1–9). All those who hear Christ's voice assemble in a unique flock around a unique shepherd (John 10:16). But there is much more to be said: Jesus Christ himself, the eternal Word incarnate, *is* the Word of the new Law given by God to man, received by man, and spoken back to God in the adherence of faith. It is in Christ's being itself, then, that the new and eternal covenant is sealed. God and man are henceforth one in the living Word that they exchange. Jesus is at once God's "Yes" to his promises and man's "Amen" to the offer of salvation (2 Cor. 1:20).

On the day of Pentecost the miracle of tongues heals the division of mankind produced at Babel. In the divine omnipotence the Spirit transcends the limitations of the letter. The *word* of salvation breaks the resistances inherent in the *vocables*, and the message triumphs over the ponderous opacity of the verbal structure that is its vehicle. On hearing the one and only word of salvation, men gather and are reunited over and above all linguistic divisions: they hear the one truly universal language: the language of the love that saves. On this day the Church is born of the Spirit and the word that calls it together, brings it into being as the "ecclesial body"—that is, the "congregation" or "convocation."[56] From the first moment until the end of time, the Christian people is constituted at once by the act of "convoking" the assembly by preaching the message and by the assembly which "is convoked" by the reception of the message in faith. But God's call, which is the basis of Christian unity, does not destroy the differences between individuals by molding them into a formless mass; on the contrary, it differentiates and multiplies the gifts given to individuals for their own good and the good of all (1 Cor. 12:4–20; Eph. 4:1–16). Unity here is a living, organic thing; it is the call which the faithful hear that brings them together "as members of the one body" (Col.

3:15). In the same way, men of every tongue will some day be gathered together before the throne of the Lamb (Rev. 7:9–12).

The Spoken and the Written Word of God.

Because it is itself living (Heb. 4:12), the word of the living God must be heralded to living men by the mouth of a living man: thus the here-and-now actuality of the call to salvation manifests itself.

But there is another aspect of the mystery of God's word which must be revealed: its *definitive, irrevocable* character. "Though the grass withers and the flower wilts, the word of our God stands forever" (Isa. 40:8; cf. Ps. 119:89). And Christ in his turn says: "The heavens and the earth will pass away, but my words will not pass" (Matt. 24:35).

It is thanks to writing that the infallibility of God's plan is made manifest. What God wills, what he says, he does not retract; and here is his word, fixed in stone or on parchment for all the coming generations to see: what is written is written (cf. John 19:22). Moreover, we see the decisive force of the argument "It is written," to which the Bible and Christ himself so often recur. Once set down by the inspired writer, God's word is irrevocable, and no one can add to or subtract from it (Rev. 22:18–19); writing consecrates it forever, gives it the force of law and a hold on the future. When the future becomes the present, men journey backward in faith: they refer to what was written yesterday in order to decipher today's event and to grasp its meaning in God's plan. Thus written word and event-word fuse into a single *dabar* or effective word of God (cf. Luke 24:25–27,32,44–47). The image of the eternal book (cherished by the author of Revelation), as well as the necessary anteriority of Scripture in relation to all the reading made of it, bring out the absolute transcendence of God's eternal plan.

There is another consideration. Since the man to be saved is situated in duration, God's word must provide itself with the means of its transmission through history. This is already provided in oral tradition, which faithfully repeats, from generation to generation, the story of God's great deeds for Israel:

> What we have heard and know, and what our fathers have declared to us, we will not hide from their sons; we will declare to

> the generation to come the glorious deeds of the Lord and his strength and the wonders that he wrought . . . . He . . . established . . . that what he commanded our fathers they should make known to their sons . . . so that they too may rise and declare to their sons that they should put their hope in God, and not forget the deeds of God but keep his commands (Ps. 78:3–7; cf. Ps. 145:4).

Yet, however faithful the transmission and however tenacious the memory, the inevitable risk of forgetfulness remains. The word of God needs the material support of writing. The message of salvation, intended for all generations, must be held down with a material weight if it is not to be dispersed to the four winds of history. Thus at times God orders his heralds to commit his words to writing (cf. Isa. 51:6–8).

Under the new covenant, the message of salvation intended for all nations until the end of time (Matt. 28:18–20) and to the ends of the earth (Acts 1:8) calls more than any other for the means of becoming perennial and universal. Proclaimed first in the living voice of Christ and the apostles, the Good News is soon written down in permanent form. This account of the event coming from eyewitnesses will arouse and strengthen the faith of believers (John 20:30–31; cf. Luke 1:1–4; 1 John 1f.). In the course of the ages, the diffusion of the Book and the translation of Scripture into every language will do their part in bringing about the realization of the universality of the message which was manifested with so much splendor on the day of Pentecost.

Because it is both definitive and transmissible the written word is the *necessary foundation and norm* of every institution. Moses, indeed God himself, had fixed forever in writing the words of the old dispensation. The hardness of the material deliberately chosen —stone—gave strong emphasis to the permanence of the covenant's provisions (Exod. 24:4,12; 32:15–16; 34:28; Deut. 27:8; cf. Job 19:23–24). In 622, during the reign of Josiah, the rediscovery of the book of the Law leads to a solemn renewal of the covenant (2 Chron. 34:14; 35:18). Finally, after the Exile, the solemn reading of the Law restores life to Israel's institutions. Thus it is evident that the religious institution is a *speaking* institution: it heralds God, as the universe does, it too born of the eternal Word.

The new covenant foretold by Jeremiah will also be written: no longer, however, on tablets of stone which are external to man but in the very hearts of the faithful, where it will be the effective inner law governing their conduct (Jer. 31:33 [cf. Heb. 8:8–13; 10:16]; cf. Prov. 7:3; Rom. 2:15; 2 Cor. 3:3). Or, better still, although the Good News must be consigned to writing, the true law of the new covenant is the Spirit of Christ which dwells in men's hearts (Gal. 5:13, 26; Rom. 8:14–18; cf. Rom. 5:5).

Preserved by the institutional Church which it nourishes, the written word gives to the believer a certain *presence of God*. The Book speaks to his eyes and to his faith; it is the support of a dialogue which is always fresh and mysterious. Not only does the Book enable me to cross over the temporal and geographical distances that separate me from the human author (prophet, sage, or apostle), but above and beyond all distance interior to history, I traverse the infinite distance that separates me from the intentions of God. On the vertex of the instant I enter into dialogue with the Eternal One "who is and who was and who is to come" (Rev. 1:4). For the Book "was written . . . to be a lesson for us who are living at the end of the ages" (1 Cor. 10:11,JB), so that "we might derive hope from the lessons of patience and the words of encouragement in the Scriptures" (Rom. 15:4). Yet Christianity is not a religion of a dead book: written down, the word remains always a living word; unalterable, it must be forever proclaimed anew, as on the day when God spoke it for the first time. The Book guarantees to the public proclamation its irrevocable fidelity; the proclamation gives the message its always contemporary actuality. The constant passage from silent meditation to communal proclamation constitutes the rhythm of the Church's life and manifests what is unique about God's plan: its absolute transcendence and its presence within history.

If all writing is composed of matter and meaning, of body and soul in the image of the human being of the author, the same holds true for the Book. Under the exterior presented by the letter, God reveals to me his inner intentions. But the vital tension through which body and soul are united is projected onto Scripture: letter and spirit give themselves to each other in order to constitute the word of God; to separate them, in fact or in thought, would be to destroy the word itself. Taken alone, the letter would be no more than the bloodless exterior, the envelope emptied of its contents, the vocable from which the word—the meaning it constituted—had, so to speak, leaked out. Literalism is materialism: it can manifest itself in a positivist hermeneutics wherein the Christian message would be dissolved in the cultural themes adopted for the purposes of the study; it can likewise show itself in philological analysis where the dissection of the words lets their original meaning excape.[57] But it can also be expressed in moral formalism—that is, the servile observance of rites in which the intention is misconceived or even wholly betrayed. Christ ceaselessly inveighed against this aberration, denouncing the blindness which led Pharisees and scribes to deny the very Moses to whom they were appealing (Matt. 15:1–20; 21:33–46; 23:13–36; John 5:37–47; 7:14–24; 8:9,40; 10:22–39). Word of God made flesh by the power of the Spirit, Jesus Christ is himself the fulfillment and interpretation of the Scriptures (cf. e.g., John 5:45–47; 8:56; 12:16,41;19:24, 36–37), the beginning and the end, the Alpha and Omega of the Book as he is of God's plan (Rev. 1:8).

God's Word and Truth

God's word is revealed to men within a dispensation of promise and covenant. It is not, then, at first as the expression of an absolute knowledge, infallible and infinite, that this word reveals its truth. God is not a master of knowledge who is engaged in solving the riddles of the universe; he is the Savior who involves himself with mankind. His word is *act;* it is "true" because it is *faithful*.

From the moment of the Fall, God is ever more closely bound to man, first by the mysterious promise of victory for the offspring of the woman, then by the successive covenants with Noah, Abraham, and Moses. As compared with his people's word, so changeable, so often faithless, God's word is immutable and infallible; his promise will not pass away (Ps. 119:89; cf. Isa. 40:8). The psalmist likes to repeat that God's word is tested (Ps. 119:140, cf. 162; Ps. 19:8), has no alloy of deceit in it (Ps. 18:31), is seven times purified like unadulterated silver. Yahweh will not fail to give salvation to the wretched; to those who thirst for it (Ps. 12:7; cf. Isa. 45:23–25). The devout Jew praises at length Yahweh's fidelity to the oaths he gave to David, his chosen one

(Pss. 89, 132), and constantly recalls to him his promise, which is the source of man's courage and hope (Ps. 119, *passim*).

Being promise and covenant, Yahweh's word is by that very fact *prophetic;* that is, by recalling the past and interpreting the meaning of the present, it also reveals the future. According to the Greek conception, the truth of speech, of the human *logos*, consists chiefly in saying what really was or what really is; but the "truth" of God's word consists primarily in its relationship to what will be. Yahweh's oracle anticipates the future, exerts mastery over it, and reveals its shape. More particularly, *God's word states today what his hand will do tomorrow for his people.* The same word that in the beginning shaped the world to be created becomes, in the course of history, the prophetic shaper of the world to be saved. The truth of God's word is therefore manifested progressively to the eye of the believer, in the measure that yesterday's future becomes today's present. *God is faithful*: that is the revelation which each day brings. "Upright is the word of the Lord, and all his works are trustworthy" (Ps. 33:4); "Yours is a mighty arm; strong is your hand, exalted your right hand. Justice and judgment are the foundation of your throne; kindness and truth go before you" (Ps. 89:14).[58] In short, *God's hand does today what his word promised yesterday*. His works effect what his love plans; history is the long gesture of divine fidelity.

The most striking manifestation of the fidelity of the God who does not lie is the proclamation of the gospel at the appointed time (cf. Titus 1:2–3), that is, the coming of the Son in the flesh or, more simply, the Son himself. For in the Son, God is united to man in an embrace of love, of supreme "philanthropy" (Titus 3:4), in order to save him forever. Before the birth of Jesus, Mary, his mother, and Zachary, father of the Forerunner, sing their praise of God's fidelity to his ancient promises (Luke 1:46–55,67–79). John the evangelist celebrates it in his turn: "grace and truth have come through Jesus Christ" (John 1:17,JB), "full of grace and truth" (1:14).[59] Christ is God's "Yes" to his promises and man's "Amen" to God's glory (2 Cor. 1:20); Jesus is always living and present before God to intercede for us. The dialogue of man with God, which Job thought so heartbreakingly impossible, is therefore forever pursued, in an atmosphere of loving confidence, in Jesus Christ (Heb. 4:14–16; Eph. 3:12).

Christ is truth in a further sense which is proper to him alone. Being himself God, he brings man the truth about God in a decisive and definitive way (cf. Heb. 1:1). His words are all true. The devil is the father of lies, but Jesus speaks the truth (John 8:44–46); indeed, he was born and came into the world for the purpose of bearing witness to the truth (John 18:37). According to Ignatius of Antioch's magnificent formulation, Christ is "he on whose lips there are no lies, through whom the Father has spoken truthfully."[60] But we must make the point more emphatically: Jesus *is* the Truth, as he is the Way and the Life. For, by infallibly revealing the Father, he leads man to eternal life (John 14:5–7); his message is the "word of truth" (Eph. 1:13; Col. 1:5). After the ascension the Spirit of truth will recall Christ's words to his disciples and guide them to all truth (John 16:13; 14:26).

In the Church, then, the preacher of the gospel is a missionary of truth, and his action must be marked by a constant effort to renounce his own word and to be the faithful spokesman of his principal. The Old Testament already shows awareness of this basic requirement in its debate over true and false prophetism. The unfailing complaint against the false prophets is that they proclaim a man's word as coming from God, and do it only too often in order to please the mighty or the crowd (Deut. 18:20; 1 Kings 22; Jer. 14:13–16; 23; 28; Ezek. 13). The asceticism and the greatness of God's herald, in the new as in the old dispensation, consists, therefore, in constantly dying to his own word, in not using the message for his own purposes (whether as weapon in a partisan conflict or as an occasion for speculations of an entirely human wisdom), but in letting himself be possessed by the word in order to communicate it with total fidelity (cf. 1 Cor. 1:17–2:16; 2 Cor. 4:2; 1 Thess. 2:4–7).[61]

God's Word and Man's Faith

If another man's word to me solicits my belief, God's word to me asks for my faith. The word of God is also the "word of faith" (Rom. 10:8). In this pregnant formula, "word of faith," a number of relationships are focused. To begin with, the word addressed to me is offered as *motive* for and *object* of my acceptance. To believe is never an empty and purely formal act; we do not believe in nothing or believe that we believe: we "believe in the word" (John 4:50; Mark 1:15). We must therefore avoid opposing, in a simplistic and equivocal way, belief and faith.

While being the object of the faith that is coming into existence, the word is also its *source*; that is, it gives rise to the very acceptance of itself. As prevenient grace, God's word carries within itself the grace of the beginning of faith: "Faith comes from what is preached, and what is preached comes from the word of Christ"(Rom. 10:17, JB; cf. Acts 4:4; Gal. 3:2)[62]

Anticipated, therefore, by the apostle who is sent (Rom. 10:14–15), and perhaps attracted by such exterior signs as miracles (Mark 16:17; Acts, *passim*; Rom. 15:18–19) and the testimony of believers (Acts 1:8), a man accepts the message "not as the word of man, but as it truly is, the word of God" (1 Thess. 2:13). Finally, the word will constantly nourish this faith, the growth of which will cease only with the end of our life on earth (Eph. 4:13; cf. Col. 1:10). Like the word that engenders it, faith is, therefore, God's gift (Eph. 2:8; cf. Rom. 12:3); Christ is both its author and perfecter (Heb. 12:2).

If we ask why the message of the kingdom (Matt. 13:19) can be received only by faith, we must recall that the message is essentially a *word of love*. Pagan philosophies and religions offer a powerful divinity which is at best sovereign Thought or perfect Being, but is indifferent to mortals. Christian revelation, on the contrary, affirms the most improbable (even if the most desirable) of truths, and one that no human mind could conceive: "God is love"(1 John 4:8,16; cf. Acts 20:24). Better still: "God so loved the world that he gave his only Son, that whoever believes in him may not die but may have eternal life" (John 3:16–17). From all eternity man is embraced by God's love in Jesus Christ: "Love, then, consists in this: not that we have loved God, but that he has loved us" (1 John 4:10); "he first loved us" (4:19). The infinite, absolute reality of such a love, translated into the gift of the Son and the Spirit, can in no way be demonstrated; it is, and can only be, an object of faith: "We have come . . . to believe in the love God has for us" (1 John 4:16). The "word of his grace" (Acts 20:32,JB) is a "word of faith."

Among all the words of love, the word that offers salvation is the most generous, the most wholly gratuitous, and the one that most imperatively calls for belief. For it was not through any merit on our part that God saved us (for, on the contrary, we "deserved God's wrath" and "were dead in sin" [Eph. 2:3]), but "because of his great love for us" (Eph. 2:4; cf. 5b,8) and "because of his mercy" (Titus 3:5). To accept such an incomprehensible offer it is necessary to believe. The "word of salvation" (cf. Acts 13:26; James 1:21) can only be a "word of faith."

Among all the possible offers of salvation, the one that most requires faith is the one which from the standpoint of reason is the most painful for the savior and the most disproportionate to the result sought. Now the means of salvation employed by God—namely, the cross of Jesus Christ—challenges, indeed overturns—all the mind's standards. That what seems to be the total failure of God should in reality be his definitive victory over evil and the saving of man is "a stumbling block to Jews, and an absurdity to Gentiles" (1 Cor. 1:23). "It pleased God to save those who believe through the absurdity of the preaching of the gospel" (1 Cor. 1:21). To accept such a proclamation requires of man a complete renunciation of the certainties of reason and total entrusting of himself to the word of God. The "word of the cross" (cf. 1 Cor. 1:18) is eminently a "word of faith."

If the hearer rebels against the word and deliberately refuses the commitment of faith, it is God himself and Christ that he is rejecting, for God has given himself wholly in the message of saving love and is present in it always and at every moment. By the inner logic of his rejection man can reach the point of willing the death of Jesus Christ: "The fact is, you are trying to kill me, a man who has told you the truth which I have heard from God" (John 8:40, cf. v. 37). The deeper tragedy of culpable disbelief is that it makes the liberating truth ever more opaque and scandalous to a man and leads him to ever greater interior blindness: "I speak the truth, and for that very reason you do not believe me" (John 8:45,JB). Such a man accepts the dictatorship of Satan and will die in his sin (John 8:44–47, 21–24; cf. 1 Pet. 2:7–8). After Jesus' return to the Father, his representatives will run up against the same disbelief: "If you find that the world hates you, know it has hated me before you . . . . They will harry you as they harried me" (John 15:18,20). Despite the human limitations and defects of his spokesmen, God nonetheless continues to be mysteriously present in those who "re-present" him, and the welcome they receive will really be given to Christ and the Father: "He who hears you, hears me. He who rejects you, rejects me. And he who rejects me, rejects him who sent me" (Luke 10:16; cf. 1 Thess. 2:13).

Conversely, to believe in the word is to accept its full saving effectiveness. The gospel "is the power of God leading everyone who believes in it to salvation" (Rom. 1:16); the word of the cross "to us who are experiencing salvation . . . is the power of God" (1 Cor. 1:18). To believe in the word is to welcome God into oneself, to receive Christ that he may dwell in our hearts through faith (Eph. 3:17). But what is at stake here is not a mere intellectual adherence: to believe in the word is also to keep it and live it; it is to act in the truth (John 3:21, literally "to do the truth"; cf. James 1:22–25). By so living a man is a member of Jesus' family (Luke 8:21) and "blest" (Luke 11:28). God's love reaches its full perfection in the believer, who lives in communion with him (1 John 2:5) and already possesses eternal life (John 5:24).

Word, Witness, Christian Tradition

The word of salvation, intended for all nations, is the Good News beyond any other. Therefore it cannot be kept to himself by anyone who has received it, for the power of God which is present in it seeks irresistibly to spread abroad. It grows like a living seed (Matt. 13:3–9,18–32,36–43; Acts 6:7; 12:24; 13:49; 19:20; 1 Thess. 1:8; cf. Rom. 1:8); it spreads; it must run and be glorified (2 Thess. 3:1) even to the ends of the earth (Acts 1:8; cf. Matt. 28:19–20).

The reason for this is that the news is not simply a piece of knowledge, but involves the whole of man's existence. The spokesmen of salvation will therefore not be mere bringers of information; they must be witnesses, that is, messengers who stake their own lives on the word they proclaim. The prophets of Israel and John the Baptist are witnesses to Christ. But he whom they herald, Jesus Christ, is witness in a complete and unqualified way. His birth and coming into the world have no purpose but to bear witness to the truth (John 18:37). His testimony has its source in an ineffable knowledge of God, for he alone has seen the Father (John 1:18; Matt. 11:27). He bore witness, as we have pointed out, by his very being; his words, actions, and sufferings, and, finally, his martyr's profession before

Pontius Pilate (1 Tim. 6:13), are simply a detailing of that basic attestation. In their turn, Jesus' disciples must proclaim from the housetops what they have heard in private (Matt. 10:27) and carry their witness to the ends of the world, and at times to the ultimate in self-giving: martyrdom (Luke 21:12–19; cf. Acts 6).

Within the institutional Church, which is a community of witnessing, each Christian generation and each individual Christian enters through faith into communion with the apostolic witnessing (1 Cor. 15:1–11; 2 Tim 2:2) and, beyond that, with the testimony which the consciousness of Jesus was constantly rendering to God. But the word produces its full fruits in a man only if it is repeated to himself, deepened, interiorized, and then communicated to others that their joy may be complete (1 John 1:1–4). In this way the active "tradition"—that is, handing on of the message—gradually shapes a living milieu, or tradition in the objective sense of the term, in which the word constantly bears fruit and is rejuvenated by the breath of the Spirit. It was in this context that the Gospels came to be written in the first days of the Church as the condensation and firm support of the living tradition.[63]

NOTES

1. According to Ps. 29 the storm tells of Yahweh's awesome power; cf. Exod. 13:21–22; 19:16–19; Job 37:1–13; Ps. 50:3.

2. The rest of chapter 13 levels a harsh accusation of guilt against idolatry.

3. In so acting, God was proving faithful to his covenant with Noah: no second flood would destroy the ordered regularity of nature (Gen. 9:8–17). On the revelation of God in nature, cf. Antoine Chavasse, *Eglise et apostolat*, 3rd ed. (Paris: Casterman, 1957), pp. 34–35.

4. Plato, *Laws,* X, 886a, 2–5, trans. A. E. Taylor (1934), in *Plato: The Collected Dialogues*, ed. Edith Hamilton and Huntington Cairns (New York: Pantheon, 1961), p. 1441.

5. According to a constant tradition, the divine words are addressed to the whole universe; cf., e.g., Isa. 1:2; Mic. 1:2.

6. Cf. also Wisd. 18:14–16: when God and his word intervene triumphantly in history, they emerge from an eternal silence.

7. Paul is here applying to preachers the text of Ps. 19:5; cf. Eph. 1:9–12.

8. On the "desert," cf. *The Humanity of Man*, p. 47, and above, p. 55.

9. Infidelity to God's word dries up the spring of prophecy; spiritual

deafness and spiritual dumbness go together (Luke 1:18–20). Docile listening to the word, on the contrary, unlooses tongues and frees the prophetic spirit (Luke 1:38, 46–55, 64–79).

10. Cf. Jer. 18:18: those who plot against the prophet's life try to reassure themselves by claiming that this threefold misfortune (silence of priest, wise man, and prophet) will not occur.

11. The date of composition of this psalm is disputed: some think the sack of the Temple to which it refers took place in 587. Calès thought that the psalm might have been composed in the Chaldean period and rewritten under the Maccabees: cf. Jean Calès, S.J., *Le livre des Psaumes* (Paris: Beauchesne, 1936[6]), Vol. 2, p. 18.

12. These hopes were based especially on Deut. 18:18–19.

13. Origen, *Commentary on Matthew*, 14:14 (PG 13:1221), shows how Christ alone wholly fulfills the words of Scripture.

14. Cf. Matt. 21:23–27: discussion of Jesus' authority; John 8:1–11: discussion of the woman caught in adultery; Mark 14:61: questioning of Jesus before the high priest; John 19:9: questioning of Jesus before Pilate.

15. John of the Cross has the Father say: "I said everything to you when I said to you: 'Jesus Christ.' "

16. What was said in *The Humanity of Man*, pp. 139–44, "Silence and Word," shows that the public proclamation of God's word in the liturgical assembly requires the vital rhythm of silence and word to be carefully respected. A continuous or wordy commentary *kills* the word. The congregation can interiorize the call of God only in a silence that is not mere emptiness but the very *fullness* of the message. Only then will the congregation be able to say a profounder "Amen" in blessings and responses, responsorial psalmody, etc. On the Jewish *berakoth* (blessings) and Christian prayer, cf. Louis Bouyer, *Eucharist: Theology and Spirituality of the Eucharistic Prayer*, trans. Charles Underhill Quinn (Notre Dame, Ind.: University of Notre Dame Press, 1968), Chapters 3–5.

17. Cf. St. Augustine, *Confessions*, Book XI, 5:7–8:10.

18. Cf. Isa. 41:4: it is Yahweh "who has called forth the generations from the beginning."

19. Cf. also St. Thomas Aquinas, *Summa theologiae*, I, q. 24, a. 3, and Origen, *Homilies on Genesis*, 1 (PG 12:145): " 'In the beginning God created heaven and earth.' What is the 'beginning' of everything but our Lord Jesus Christ, Savior of all, first-born of every creature? In this beginning, that is, in his Word, God made heaven and earth." This commentary, free though it is, stresses the unqualified "initiatory" role of him who is the Word of God. Cf. also Origen, *Commentary on John*, 1:32 (PG 14:56).

20. St Ambrose, *Paradise*, 14:70, trans. John J. Savage, Fathers of the Church 42 (New York: Fathers of the Church, Inc., 1961), p. 348.

21. The whole Gospel would have to be quoted here; we will mention only the Beatitudes (Matt. 5:1–11) and the discourse that follows on them.

22. The same gesture is made to Daniel (10:15–19). Compare the purification of Isaiah's lips (6:6).

23. "Prophet" (Greek: *pro* + *phemi*) means one who speaks in place of another, an interpreter; the idea of predicting the future is secondary. Cf. Exod. 7:1–2: Aaron will be Moses' "prophet."

24. Jeremiah also performs some symbolic actions: 19:1–13; 27:1–22; 32:1–44.

25. In Ezek. 24:15–23, God forbids the prophet to mourn for his wife.

26. We have here one of the bases for a theology of mission.

27. Gregory the Great, *Homilies on the Gospels*, Book I, no. 17 (PL 76:1139).

28. Cf. below, this chapter, "God's Word and Man's Faith." Cf. St. Augustine, *Homilies on the Gospel according to John*, 30:1, trans. C. M. (Oxford: Parker, 1848–49), I, 442: "Let us hear the Gospel even as we would hear the Lord himself present."

29. Vatican Council II, *Constitution on the Sacred Liturgy*, chapter 1, number 7, in Walter M. Abbott, ed., *The Documents of Vatican II* (New York: Guild-America-Association Press, 1966), p. 141.

30. Cf. St. Augustine, *Sermo* 85:1,1 (PL 38: 520): "The Gospel is Christ's mouth. He sits in heaven but does not cease to speak on earth." Cf. A.-M. Roguet, "La presence active du Christ dans la Parole de Dieu," *Maison-Dieu* 82 (2nd quarter, 1965), 8–28.

31. Cf. Clement of Alexandria, *The Teacher*, II:2 (PG 8:409): the Spirit is the power inherent in the Word, as the blood is in the body.

32. Cf. St. Augustine, *Homilies on the Gospel according to John*, 24:2, trans. C. M., vol. I, p. 373: "Since Christ is the Word of God, every deed of that Word is to us a word."

33. Jesus argues as follows: If Scripture calls judges gods, since judgment comes from God (cf. Ps. 58:1), much less is it a blasphemy when "he whom the Father has consecrated and sent into the world" says that he is God's Son.

34. On the scriptural witness: John 1:45; 2:22; 12:16; 19:28, 36–37; 20:9; Luke 4:21. On Jesus' appeal to this testimony: Luke 24: 25–27; 32:44–47; John 5:39, 45–47; 8:37–39.

35. Ps. 95:7–8 warns against the hardening of the heart which prevents a man from hearing God's voice; cf. also Ps. 105:28.

36. The disciple must make his home in Christ's word (John 8:31; cf. 8:37) and keep it (John 8:55; 12:47; 14:21, 23; 15:10, 20; 17:6). The word must dwell in the disciple (John 15:7). On the notion of mutual inclusion, cf. above, pp. 47–49.

37. Cf. Matt. 12:34: "The mouth speaks whatever fills the heart."

38. Cf. Isa. 8:16–20 (JB): the prophet seals a revelation in the *heart* of his disciples.

39. Cf. Origen, *On Exodus* (PG 12:269B): God's word is the soul's physician.

40. Cf. Also the theme of the banquet set by Wisdom: Prov. 9:1–6; Ecclus. 24:19–27.

41. Cf. below, Chapter 7, sections 6, 7, and 8, "Meal and Revelation," "The Proclamation of the Messianic Feast," and "The Multiplication of Loaves."

42. Cf. below, Chapter 7, section 9, "Institution of the Eucharistic Meal."

43. Yves M.-J. Congar, "The Two Forms of the Bread of Life in the Gospel and Tradition," in *A Gospel Priesthood*, trans. P. J. Hepburne-Scott (New York: Herder and Herder, 1967), pp. 13–38. Cf. St. Augustine, *Sermo* 56:7,10 (PL 38:381): "The daily bread which the children seek is God's word which is distributed to us daily. It is our daily bread, but it is the spirit, not the flesh, that lives by it . . . . Our daily food is God's word which is always being distributed to the churches"; *Sermo* 57:7, 7 (PL 38:389): "What I preach to you is a daily bread; the readings you hear each day in church are a daily bread; the hymns you hear and sing are a daily bread."

44. In verse 19 the psalmist passes from the word as ruling power to the Law as revelatory word. Cf. also the composition of Ps. 19 where God's revelation in nature and his revelation in the Law form a balanced diptych.

45. The whole history of Israel could be called on for testimony. Cf., e.g., 2 Kings 10:10; Ps. 105:19; Ecclus. 39:18; Jer. 44:24–30.

46. Cf. also the account of the prophet's call in 1:9–10. Cf. Hos. 6:5: "I smote them through the prophets, I slew them by the words of my mouth"; cf. Hos. 12:11.

47. Cf. Xavier Léon-Dufour, ed., *Dictionary of Biblical Theology*, trans. P. Joseph Cahill, *et al.* (New York: Desclée, 1967), articles "Blessing" and "Curse."

48. Cf. Georges Auzou, *The Word of God: Approaches to the Mystery of the Sacred Scriptures*, trans. Josefa Thornton (St. Louis: B. Herder, 1960), pp. 160–61.

49. We may note that Newman challenges the Lutheran doctrine of forensic justification in the name of the sovereign efficacy of God's word; cf. *Lectures on the Doctrine of Justification* (London: Longmans, Green, 1924), lectures 3–4 (pp. 62–103).

50. The Creator God, on the contrary calls all creatures by their name and in this way gives them existence (Gen. 1: Ps. 147:4; Isa. 40:26; cf. Bar. 3:33–35). Cf. A.-M. Besnard, *Le mystère du Nom* (Paris: Editions du Cerf, 1962).

51. The various interpretations offered of the Exodus text are not mutually exclusive and can, in our opinion, be accepted simultaneously. Pseudo-Dionysius, *De divinis nominibus*, I:6, 7 (PG 3:596–97), shows that God is both nameless and many-named; this position affirms transcendence by means of a dialectic of opposites. Cf. St. Thomas Aquinas, *Summa theologiae*, I, q. 13 *passim*.

52. The "Name" signifies God's presence in Deut. 12:5, 11; 1 Kings 8:29. Cf. John 3:18: to believe "in the name of the only Son" is to believe in Jesus.

53. The Name, taken without qualification, belongs to Jesus in Acts 5:41; 3 John 7.

54. On the name of Jesus as remedy for all ills, cf. St. Bernard, *Sermons on the Song of Songs*, 15 (PL 185:843).

55. On the invocation of the name of Jesus in the Eastern and Western church traditions, cf. A Monk of the Eastern Church, *The Prayer of Jesus: Its*

Genesis, Development, and Practice in the Byzantine-Slavic Tradition, trans. A Monk of the Western Church (New York: Desclée, 1967).

56. [The word "church" is derived from the Greek *kyriakon*, i.e., "Lord's (house)." The French *église*, Spanish *iglesia*, and Italian *chiesa*, and the English adjectives ecclesial and ecclesiastical, are derived from the Latin *ecclesia*, Greek *ekklesia*, i.e. "the group called forth, or apart, and gathered together." (Tr.)]

57. Cf. *The Humanity of Man*, pp. 169–174, "Word and Vocable."

58. The unshakeable fidelity of God finds expression in the image of Yahweh as the Rock of Israel, e.g., Deut. 32:4; Ps. 92:16. Pascal formulates the point concisely in *Pensées*, Fr. 654 (Turnell, Fr. 535, p. 263): "In God the word does not differ from the meaning because he is true; nor the word from the effect because he is powerful; nor the means from the effect because he is wise."

59. Cf. Matt. 7:24–27: whoever puts the words of Jesus into practice builds his house on a rock. "Word—rock" is far from being an empty rhetorical formula.

60. Ignatius of Antioch, *To the Romans*, 8:2, in *The Epistles of St. Clement of Rome and St. Ignatius of Antioch*, trans. James A. Kleist, S.J., Ancient Christian Writers 1 (Westminster, Md.:Newman, 1946), p. 84.

61. Cf. *The Humanity of Man*, p. 176.

62. Cf. St. Thomas Aquinas, *Summa theologiae*, II-II, q. 6, a.1.

63. Cf. Yves M.-J. Congar, *Tradition and Traditions: An Historical and a Theological Essay*, trans. Michael Naseby and Thomas Rainborough (New York: Macmillan, 1967); Henri de Lubac, *The Sources of Revelation*, trans. Luke O'Neill (New York: Herder and Herder, 1968).

CHAPTER 4

THE HAND OF GOD

The Bible often speaks of God's "arm," "hand," "right hand," and "finger." The anthropomorphism is obvious, yet it transmits a simple and firm religious doctrine. In man a work is the result both of the word that formulates the project and of the hand that executes it. In like fashion the Bible, while attributing God's works to his omnipotent word, often also represents them as issuing from his hand.

I. GOD'S HAND AND THE WORLD

Creation as Absolute Prevenance by God's Hand

The creation of the universe is the absolutely first initiative, and in it every beginning has its origins. It marks the sovereign prevenance of the divine hand. Yahweh himself proclaims this: "My hand laid the foundations of the earth; my right hand spread out the heavens" (Isa. 48:13).[1] "The heavens are my throne, the earth is my footstool . . . . My hand made all these things when all of them came to be, says the Lord" (Isa. 66:1–2). "It was I who made the earth, and man and beast on the face of the earth, by my great power, with my outstretched arm" (Jer. 27:5). This traditional teaching receives extensive and beautiful expression, too lengthy to be reproduced here, in the book of Job (cf., e.g., 36:22–37:24; 38–41). It is also one of the favorite themes of the psalmist: "Of old you established the earth, and the heavens are the work of your hands" (Ps. 102:26); "His is the sea, for he has made it, and the dry land, which his hands have formed" (Ps. 95:5).

Man's trust in God's power has its sure foundation here: "Ah, Lord God, you have made heaven and earth by your great might, with your outstretched arm; nothing is impossible to you" (Jer. 32:17).[2] Should man forget that God is the Creator, the animals can remind him: "Ask the beasts to teach you, and the birds of the air to tell you, or the reptiles of the earth to instruct you, and the fish of the sea to inform you. Which of all these does not know that the hand of God has done this?" (Job 12:7–9). The Second Book of Maccabees (completed around 124 B.C.) will go a step further and say that the Creator made heaven, earth, and all that is in them "out of what did not exist" (2 Macc. 7:28,JB). Thus the creative hand bridged the infinite distance between the sovereign God and the nothingness of creatures. God's right hand touches the universe in the abyss of nonexistence and draws it out into the daylight of existence.

Contact of the Hand of God, Worker and Artist

If man's hand is an organ of his relations with the world, God's hand establishes a strictly indissoluble relationship between this world and the Creator. For, while man's hand comes into contact with a world that is "already there" and "given" from the very start, God's hand brings into existence a universe which of itself has no existence. In a creative gesture God sets his hand to a world still to be born, gives himself to it, and gives it wholly to himself. In this initial contact an absolute omnipotence is at work: the universe springs into being under the irrestible Hand and remains totally dependent on it. Because of this prevenient contact the world is completely relative to God, while God is in no way relative to the world.[3]

The divine hand, therefore, unlike the human hand, risks no harm from its contact with the world. Instead, it is the latter that is moved as soon as God's hand touches it: "He . . . touches the mountains, and they smoke!" (Ps. 104:32; cf. Ps. 144:5). Still more terrible will be the contact of condemnation: "I melt the earth with my touch, so that all who dwell on it mourn, while it all rises up like the Nile, and settles back like the river of Egypt" (Amos 9:5).

The contact of the creative hand is so powerful that it produces its effect directly. Man's hand must often use a tool to bridge the gap between his will and his power, but God's hand effects by its own power his whole creative plan, just as his word immediately effects what it says. Yahweh stresses the point in speaking to Job (38–41), while the Book of Wisdom will praise God as maker and master, author, provider, and father of all things (13:1–14:3, *passim).*

The operative hand of God is eminently that of an *artist.* The *tohu-bohu* (the primeval empty waste) is replaced by a hierarchically ordered universe which is as God wants it to be: "God saw how good it was" (Gen. 1:1–25, *passim).* The psalmist therefore cannot but admire it: "You make me glad, O Lord, by your deeds, at the works of your hand I rejoice. How great are your works, O Lord! How very deep are your thoughts!" The theme is developed at length in Psalm 104, which praises in detail the wonders of creation. But the Book of Wisdom goes a step further. Some men stop at the surface of created things: "out of joy in their beauty they thought them gods" (Wisd. 13:3); they forget the Maker of things and idolize his works "because the things seen are fair" (13:7). They must learn how to see aright and to interpret correctly the great splendors of creation, "for the original source of beauty fashioned them" (13:3).

The Hand of God, Symbol of His Sovereign Mastery

Man's hand reaches out to things in order to lay hold on them; the hand is the organ of laborious conquest and of possession. God's creative hand, on the contrary, gives things their very existence; it contains them, maintains them, retains them as his undisputed "possession." We have already seen how forcefully God asserts this state of things (cf. also Jer. 27:5).

The consequences are clear: "Mine are all the animals of the forests, beasts by the thousands on my mountains. I know all the birds of the air, and whatever stirs in the plains, belongs to me" (Ps. 50:10–11). The psalmist confesses this ownership enthusiastically: "Yours are the heavens, and yours is the earth; the world and its fullness you have founded; north and south you created; Tabor and Hermon rejoice at your name. Yours is a mighty arm; strong is your hand, exalted your right hand" (Ps. 89:12–14; cf. Ps. 24:1–2; 95:5). Later on, Paul will preach the same doctrine on the Hill of Mars at Athens: "The God who made the world and all that is in it, the Lord of heaven and earth, does not dwell in sanctuaries made by human hands; nor does he receive man's service as if he were in need of it. Rather it is he who gives to all life and breath and everything else" (Acts 17:24–25).

In short, man's weak hand cannot really give anything to the all-powerful hand of God which creates all things (including man's hand), contains them all, and possesses them all.

The Hand, Wisdom and Freedom of God

If a man's hand is guided by his practical knowledge and his intelligence, the works of God's hand spring from a sovereign wisdom: "The Lord by wisdom founded the earth, established the heavens by understanding; by his knowledge the depths break open, and the clouds drop down dew" (Prov. 3:19–20); "who is a better craftsman than [Wisdom]?" (Wisd. 8:3).

This Wisdom was present and helped God the creator in the way a craftsman is present at each stage in the carrying out of a plan (Prov. 8:22–31; cf. Wisd. 9:9; 13:1–5). The psalmist is filled with wonder as he gives expression to the same thought: "How manifold are your works, O Lord! In wisdom you have wrought them all—the earth is full of your creatures" (Ps. 104:24). Thus we meet again the acknowledgment of God's great deeds in the course of man's history: "The works of his hands are faithful and just" (Ps. 111:7).

God's wisdom, thus manifested in the endless variety of his works, is inseparable from his freedom. He multiplies beings as though he were at play (cf., e.g., Job 38–41).[4] His sovereign freedom is also shown in the rest he takes after the work of the six days (Gen. 2:2–3).[5]

God's creative work is, finally, the fruit of God's sovereignly free and freely given love; the Great Hallel celebrates the goodness of the Creator:

> Who alone does great wonders,
> for his mercy endures forever;
> Who made the heavens in wisdom,
> for his mercy endures forever;

Who spread out the earth upon the waters,
 for his mercy endures forever;
Who made the great lights,
 for his mercy endures forever;
The sun to rule over the day,
 for his mercy endures forever;
The moon and the stars to rule over the night,
 for his mercy endures forever (Ps. 136:4–6).

When the climactic moment of biblical revelation has come, the New Testament will penetrate more deeply into this mystery. Jesus Christ, "the beloved Son" of God, is the one in whom, by whom, and for whom all things have been created (John 1:1–9; Col. 1:14–20; Eph. 1:4–6).

II. GOD'S HAND AND MAN

Before the immensity and splendor of the created universe, man may at first sight seem a wretched and insignificant little thing. The psalmist says as much to God: "When I behold your heavens, the work of your fingers, the moon and the stars which you set in place—what is man that you should be mindful of him; or the son of man that you should care for him?" (Ps. 8:4–5). Before and after Pascal, Christian thought has often reflected on this theme. Man is a negligible quantity in the sense that he is negligible in the quantitative sphere.[6] Yet relations between God's hand and man's hand are so close, in such important ways (especially in Jesus Christ), that both the grandeur of man and the infinity of God are revealed in an incomparable fashion.

The Prevenient Hand of God Creates Man

Among all God's works man takes first place as the masterpiece of the divine hand. The second account of creation shows God kneading the clay in order to shape a human body from it: "The Lord God formed man out of the clay of the ground and blew into his nostrils the breath of life, and so man became a living being. Then the Lord God planted a garden in Eden, in the east, and he placed there the man whom he had formed" (Gen. 2:7–8). This privileged being, then, no less than other creatures, remains dependent in his origins; he continues to be in God's hand like clay in the artisan's: "Like clay in the hands of a potter, to be molded according to his pleasure, so are men in the hands of their creator" (Ecclus. 33:13).[7]

It would be perverse of man, then, not to admit this dependence but to set himself up in judgment on God's works: "Your perversity is as though the potter were taken to be the clay: as though what is made should say of its maker, 'He made me not!' or the vessel should say of the potter, 'He does not understand' " (Isa. 29:16; cf. 45:11–12; Jer. 18:6; Rom. 9:20–21).

To be the work of God's hands also gives man a claim on God's mercy. The believer reminds the Creator of this in times of distress: "Yet, O Lord, you are our father; we are the clay and you the potter: we are all the work of your hands" (Isa. 64:7). The prayer of Job is still more striking, and even poignant:

> None can deliver me out of your hand! Your hands have formed me and fashioned me; will you then turn and destroy me? Oh, remember that you fashioned me from clay! Will you then bring me down to dust again? Did you not pour me out as milk, and thicken me like cheese? With skin and flesh you clothed me, with bones and sinews knit me together. Grace and favor you granted me, and your providence has preserved my spirit (Job 10:7–13).

God, then, *put his hand to man*, as yet nonexistent, in order to bring him into existence; his gesture was one of total prevenance of spontaneous, free, creative love. Michelangelo's fresco on the Sistine ceiling is a marvelous evocation of this mysterious first contact: God's hand creates man's hand (cf. 2 Macc. 7:10–11), summons it, draws it to itself as collaborator in a history that is unfathomably mysterious and embraces eternity as well as time. The same Hand that created nature now draws man out of nothingness to constitute the beginning of history.

As organ of welcome, God's hand receives new-made man into the world of living things and, so to speak, installs him there: "The Lord God planted a garden in Eden, in the east, and he placed there the man whom he had formed" (Gen. 2:8); "The Lord God then took the man and settled him in the garden of Eden, to cultivate and care for it" (2:15); "The Lord God formed out of the ground various wild animals and various birds of the air, and he brought them to man to see what he would call them; whatever the man called each of them would be its name" (2:19).

After creating man, God, who is master of his creatures, "hands things over" to man, as it were, by delegating to him power over the numerous beings of the visible world; the restriction as to the tree of the knowledge of good and evil is intended as a sign of basic dependence. Man then takes possession of his domain by way of the privileged word which effects appropriation: the name (Gen. 2:20).[8] After the deluge, the lower realms of creation are once again entrusted to man's hands (Gen. 9:2). The psalmist thanks God for this eminent dignity given to man: "You have made him little less than the angels, and crowned him with glory and honor. You have given him rule over the works of your hands" (Ps. 8:6–7a).[9]

When he thus fashioned with his own hand the body of the first man, the Creator was also fashioning in advance the humanity of the "second Adam": did he not love the latter even before the world was made? (John 17:24). God was to entrust the universe to Jesus Christ, even more than to his ancestor according to the flesh, as to Lord of all creation: "The Father loves the Son and has given everything over to him" (John 3:35). This is why the "sheep" who hear his voice cannot be snatched from his hand, that is, from his saving power: "I give them eternal life, and they shall never perish. No one shall snatch them out of my hand" (John 10:28).

It is with full awareness of this universal power over creation that Christ approaches his "hour," the hour in which his sacrifice will complete the mystery of salvation. "Fully aware that . . . the Father . . . had handed everything over to him" (John 13:3; cf. 17:2–3; Matt. 11:27), Jesus nonetheless takes the part of a servant and washes his disciples' feet. Then, after reaching the extremes of humiliation by way of his death on the cross, Christ is raised up by the Father to a universal lordship (Phil. 2:6–11). The Son of Man in the Apocalypse holds in his right hand seven stars, which symbolize the seven churches of which he is the supreme Judge (Rev. 1:16).

God's Hand, Organ of His Power over Man

All things are in God's hand; this hand is everywhere present, and man cannot escape it: "No one can escape his hand" (Tob. 13:2; cf. 2 Chron. 20:6; Wisd. 11:21; 16:15); "In his hand is the soul of every living thing, and the life breath of all mankind" (Job 12:10).[10] God's grasp is powerful and unremitting. Like Rodin's Adam on the first day, I too remain enclosed in God's hand: "Behind me and before, you hem me in and rest your hand on me" (Ps. 139:5). However far away I try to flee, to east or west, God's hand is there: "If I take the wings of the dawn, if I settle at the farthest limits of the sea, even there your hand shall guide me and your right hand hold me fast" (Ps. 139:9–10).

Everywhere present and endowed with total power over man, God's hand is the *instrument of his justice;* it is raised against all who oppose his will. This hand of justice struck Pharaoh and his army at the crossing of the Red Sea; Moses and the people sang of it with overflowing joy: "Your right hand, O Lord, magnificient in power, your right hand, O Lord, has shattered the enemy. . . . When you stretched out your right hand, the earth swallowed them. . . . Terror and dread fell upon them. By the might of your arm they were frozen like stone, while your people, O Lord, passed over, while the people you had made your own passed over" (Exod. 15:6,12,16; cf. Wisd. 16:16). Deuteronomy, in turn, will have for one of its leitmotifs the fact that God freed his people "with his strong hand and outstretched arm" (Deut. 4:34;5:15; 7:19; 26:8; cf. Exod. 6:6, etc.).

Later on, pious Jews at the beginning of the second century before Christ will ask God to raise his hand once more against their pagan enemies: "Raise your hand against the heathen, that they may realize your power. . . . Give new signs and work new wonders; show forth the splendor of your right hand and arm" (Ecclus. 36:2,5; cf. Ps. 89:11b). But often the wicked do not realize it: "O Lord, your hand is uplifted, but they behold it not" (Isa. 26:11). Nonetheless the divine judgment against Assyria will be infallibly carried out: "This is the plan proposed for the whole earth, and this the hand outstretched over all the nations. The Lord of hosts has planned; who can thwart him? His hand is stretched out; who can turn it back?" (Isa. 14:26–27). Through Ezekiel God will later swear: "Very well, the Lord Yahweh says this: I raise my hand and I swear that the nations round you shall have their own insults to bear" (Ezek. 36:7,JB). The divine arm is, in fact, always "long enough," the divine hand strong enough, to reach its adversaries: "Your hand will unmask all your enemies, your right hand all who hate you" (Ps. 21:7,JB). Such, for example, are the Egyptians, whose terror (a prelude to their conversion) Isaiah foretells: "On that day the Egyptians shall be like women, trembling with fear, because of the Lord of hosts shaking his fist at them" (Isa. 19:16). Such, too, is Assyria: "The Lord will make his glorious voice heard, and let it be seen how this arm descends in raging fury and flame of consuming fire, in driving storm and hail" (Isa. 30:30).

But God does not reserve his blows for the pagans alone; he raises his hand against the faithless sons of Israel as well: "Whatever they undertook, the Lord turned into disaster for them" (Judg. 2:15; cf. Ps. 106:26–27). In a poem on the Lord's revenge on the Northern Kingdom, Isaiah uses the image of the raised arm with tragic intensity: "The Lord raises their foes against them and stirs up their enemies to action. . . . For all this, his wrath is not turned back, and his hand is still outstretched!" (Isa. 9:10–11; cf. 5:24–25). The latter of these two verses constitutes the refrain of the poem; its periodic repetition gives extraordinary force to the divine threat it expresses.

In the time of Jeremiah, guilty Jerusalem feels the heavy weight of God's hand upon it during the siege of 598: "You have disowned me, says the Lord, turned your back upon me; and so I stretched out my hand to destroy you, I was weary of sparing you" (Jer. 15:6). A few years later, in the siege of 588, God directs to his own people the same language he had used to express his intervention against the guilty Egyptians at the time of the Exodus: "I myself will fight against you with outstretched hand and mighty arm, in anger, and wrath, and great rage!" (Jer. 21:5). At another period, the ever-present divine hand that dispenses justice was raised even against the chosen one of God, King David, in punishment for his sin of pride in making a census of the people (2 Sam. 24:14–17; 1 Chron. 21:13–17).

Elsewhere the hand of God symbolizes the sinner's remorse rather than his punishment. The guilty man is tormented by anxiety until he confesses his sin, and he recognizes in his experience God's heavy hand: "As long as I would not speak, my bones wasted away with my groaning all the day, for day and night your hand was heavy upon me" (Ps. 32:4–5). But God's hand is stretched out even over the just man in order to test him (Job 1:11; 2:5). Unfortunate Job asserts this to his visitors: "Pity me, pity me, O you my friends, for the hand of God has struck me!" (Job 19:21). Therefore he utters the poignant prayer: "Withdraw your hand far from me, and let not the terror of you frighten me" (Job 13:21).

We are able, then, to understand the warning given centuries later by the writer of the letter to the Hebrews to those who might scorn the new covenant of salvation in Jesus Christ: "It is a fearful thing to fall into the hands of the living God" (Heb. 10:31). But we must also immediately add: this fearsome God became man out of love for men; he abandoned himself as a child into the hands of men, and in the end delivered himself into the hands of sinners (Matt. 17:22; 26:45).

God's Hand and Man's Praying Hand

The divine hand that terrifies man constantly draws him to itself as well; to it man turns in hope, raising his voice and his own hand in prayer for salvation: "Aloud to God, I cry; aloud to God, to hear me; on the day of my distress I seek the Lord. By night my hands are stretched out without flagging" (Ps. 77:1–2; cf. 88:10); "Let my prayer come like incense before you; the lifting up of my hands, like the evening sacrifice" (Ps. 141:2; cf. 141:8; 134:2).[11] In thus opening wide his upraised arms and his hands, the whole man becomes a desire, an appeal, a prayer.

Does his unhappy state continue? Then a man may fear that God's hand, which once was ready to help his faithful ones, has now turned away in forgetfulness: "I say: 'This is my sorrow, that the right hand of the Most High is changed.' I remember the deeds of the Lord; yes, I remember your wonders of old. And I meditate on your works; your exploits I ponder. . . . Among the people you have made known your power. With your strong arm you redeemed your people, the sons of Jacob and Joseph" (Ps. 77:11–13, 15–16). God's hand is, after all, man's sole hope when distress becomes overmastering: "Rise, O Lord! O God, lift up your hand! Forget not the afflicted! . . . You do see, for you behold misery and sorrow, taking them in your hands. . . . Break the strength of the wicked and the evildoer" (Ps. 10:12–15). Again, at the moment when man feels lost and about to drown in a sea of misfortune, he prays: "Reach out your hand from on high—Deliver me and rescue me from many waters, from the hands of aliens, whose mouths swear false promises, while their right hands are raised in perjury" (Ps. 144:7–8).

When rescue is not forthcoming, the believing soul is tempted to doubt: Is God powerless? Is his arm too short to save, to reach down to man in the depths of his distress? God had already reproached

Moses for such a lack of faith: "The Lord answered Moses: Is this beyond the Lord's reach? You shall see now whether or not what I have promised you takes place' " (Num. 11:23). God mutters the same reproach to his people through the mouth of Second Isaiah: "Is my hand too short to ranson? Have I not the strength to deliver?" (Isa. 50:2).

The appeal to God is at times expressed with trustful impatience: "Awake, awake, put on strength, O arm of the Lord! Awake as in the days of old, in ages long ago!" (Isa. 51:9; cf. 33:2). Finally, in a gesture of complete trust, the psalmist surrenders to the divine hand: "Into your hands I commend my spirit; you will redeem me, O Lord, O faithful God" (Ps. 31:6). On the cross Christ will make this prayer his own, with hands outstretched in a supreme gesture of appeal and self-surrender (Luke 23:46).[12]

God's Hand, Organ of Gift and Protection

To the appeal of man's voice and hand God's hand always responds. To begin with, since no living thing ever escapes its radical creaturely indigence, it can continue to exist only by God's power: its constantly recurring hunger—in its extreme form, fatal—is a sign of this tenuous hold on existence. To all these hungry creatures, men and animals, whose whole being is a thrust towards him, God ceaselessly gives food: "They all look to you to give them food in due time. When you give it to them, they gather it, when you open your hand, they are filled with good things" (Ps. 104:27–28; cf. Job 36:31; Acts 14:17). Christ therefore teaches his disciples to ask each day for daily bread (Matt. 6:11) which the heavenly Father gives to every living being. Each being depends on the creative and sustaining hand of God (Matt. 6:25–34).[13] If God is present to man's outstretched hand, he is also the one who stirred him to stretch it out in prayer.

But famine is not the only threat to man; countless other dangers beset him, and his own hands cannot ward them off. He therefore turns spontaneously to the all-powerful hand of God (acknowledged clearly or obscurely) to asks for *protection*. From among all the peoples of the earth Israel has been set aside ever since the creation of the world and protected by God's hand; God reminds her of this: "I hid you in the shadow of my hand, when I spread out the heavens and laid the earth's foundations and said to Zion: 'you are my people' " (Isa. 51:16, JB).[14] Israel was vividly aware of this: "He is our God, and we are the people he shepherds, the flock he guides" (Ps. 95:7).

Elsewhere, in another image, the divine protecting hand is not that of a shepherd but of a toiling vinedresser: "Take care of this vine, and protect what your right hand has planted" (Ps. 80:16). Again, through the mediation of Hosea, God recalls to his faithless people the tender watchfulness he once showed them: "It was I who taught Ephraim to walk, who took them in my arms" (Hos. 11:3; cf. Isa. 40:11). The believer, on his side, is aware of walking hand-in-hand with God who leads him (Ps. 73:23). All the just are assured that whatever befalls them their God sustains them: "He shall shelter them with his right hand, and protect them with his arm" (Wisd. 5:16); "The souls of the just are in the hand of God, and no torment shall touch them" (Wisd. 3:1; cf. Deut. 33:3).

God's Hand, Organ of Salvation Offered

If God's hand, sometimes avenging, sometimes protecting, intervenes in history, it does so in order to execute a tremendous plan. He who put his hand to the creation of world and man, also puts his hand to history and introduces into it a mysterious finality: *salvation*. Thus he bends the course of events so as to carry out his gracious purpose.[15]

The whole history of Israel is marked by Yahweh's powerful interventions. They are foretold by the prophetic word and effected by the might of God's hand: *the hand of God keeps the promises his word has made*. This is eminently the case with the Exodus, which was both a deliverance from slavery in Egypt and a consecration of God's people (Exod. 6:6–7; Ps. 114:1–2). It had been foretold to Moses by God himself (Exod. 3:7–12; 6:6–8) and then carried out in brilliant fashion "with his strong hand and outstretched arm." Then the rescued people sang the praises of God's arm which, following a constant law of his plan (cf. Isa. 51:4–5), "judged" some and saved others (Exod. 15:6, 12, 16).

The Book of Wisdom echoes this canticle of the rescued when it sings the praises of God's wisdom and God's arm: "She [Wisdom] took them across the Red Sea . . . and they sang, O Lord, your holy name and praised in unison your conquering hand" (Wisd.

10:18–20).[16] So too, in Israelite tradition, thanksgiving for victory will take the form of a hymn to the arm or "right hand" of God: "The right hand of the Lord has struck with power: the right hand of the Lord is exalted; the right hand of the Lord has struck with power" (Ps. 118:15–16).

As a result, the confidence of Israel and likewise its duty of fidelity to God and his law are grounded in the memory of the saving interventions that God effected "with his strong hand and outstretched arm" (cf. also Ps. 136:10–22; Jer. 32:21). The function of ancestral tradition is to transmit to future generations both the remembrance of the deeds of God's arm and the precepts of the Law: "O God, our ears have heard, our fathers have declared to us, the deeds you did in their days, in days of old. . . . For not with their own sword did they conquer the land, nor did their own arm make them victorious. But it was your arm and your right hand and the light of your countenance, in your love for them" (Ps. 44:2–4; cf. 77:16; 78:3–7; 89:11).

Yahweh's arm has its strength within itself; it is powerful enough to save (cf. Isa. 40:10; 59:16; 63:5; Ps. 98:1). But Israel often forgets God's hand (Ps. 78:42); its constant temptation is to rely on human help, especially on pagan allies. One theme of prophetic preaching is the denunciation of the uselessness and treacherousness of such support: "This Egypt, the staff on which you rely, is in fact a broken reed which pierces the hand of anyone who leans on it" (Isa. 36:6; cf. Jer. 17:5; Job 40:9,14; contrast 2 Chron. 32:8–20). Therefore God intends to strip Israel of all these false supports. In the future the chosen people will owe its salvation to Yahweh's arm alone; the return of the exiles, for example, will be his doing: "On that day, the Lord shall again take it in hand to reclaim the remnant of his people" (Isa. 11:11; cf. 51:5); "The Lord shall dry up the tongue of the Sea of Egypt, and wave his hand over the Euphrates . . . so that it can be crossed in sandals" (Isa. 11:15).

Let God, then, answer the trusting prayer of his faithful ones: "Yahweh, have pity on us, we hope in you. Be our strong arm each morning, our salvation in time of distress" (Isa. 33:2,JB). The same prayer will be uttered in the period of Seleucid overlordship: "Give new signs and work new wonders; show forth the splendor of your right hand and arm" (Ecclus. 36:5).

Like the community as a whole, the individual believer is aware that he owes salvation to God's hand as organ of the unfailing divine fidelity: "Though I walk amid distress . . . you raise your hand, your right hand saves me. . . . Your kindness, O Lord, endures forever; forsake not the work of your hands" (Ps. 138:7–8).

In short, if God's hand is the instrument at times of his anger (cf. Heb. 10:31), at times of his saving action, it is the good or bad dispositions of men that determine his action: "The favoring hand of our God is upon all who seek him, but his mighty wrath is against all who forsake him" (Ezra 8:22).

The history of salvation under the old covenant is thus represented by the interplay of two hands, God's and man's, which seek each other out, join, separate, and join again. But whereas the hand of the saving God always anticipates man and is always faithfully held out, man's hand often sins through refusal and the rejection of a freely given salvation for which man himself had prayed. By man's doing the covenant is often broken.

In the working out of Israel's destiny, the destiny of all mankind is involved, for Israel is to be the first fruits of God's saving action; it is to be a prophetic people and recipient of the promise of salvation. If the divine intention to bestow universal salvation is to be accomplished, God must once again reach out his hand to the hand of lost man and establish a permanent and unbreakable covenant.

The intended salvation has in fact come, for God has taken the initiative. She who is to be mother of the Savior proclaims God's action when she is touched by the Spirit who makes men prophesy: "He has shown might with his arm. . . . He has upheld Israel his servant, ever mindful of his mercy" (Luke 1:51,54). Simeon, in taking the infant Jesus into his arms, is welcoming the Messiah into the bodily and spiritual space that is created by faith and hope (Luke 2:28). Through Mary's "Be it done" and the acceptance by Simeon and Anna, all of faithful Israel welcomes and receives the Savior.

But the salvation bestowed is infinitely greater than the salvation hoped for. In Jesus Christ, man and God, not only do the divine and human hands become forever joined, but lost man and the saving God are united to form but a single being. The prevenient hand of God lays hold of man with such a mighty love that the two now constitute one living being, Jesus Christ. By the very act that makes him exist

Jesus reconciles and forever reunites the two extremes, divine and human, in the single person of the Son of God. The new covenant of salvation is forever established and sealed; "Jesus" means "God saves." By reason of the redemptive incarnation salvation is now Someone. It is salvation both offered and accepted: offered to the world by Christ as God; accepted by him as man in the name of mankind of which he is the head.

The Saving Hand of God Uses Man's Hand

The hand of God which created the universe without material or tool could save mankind though its own sheer power. Instead, God wishes to give man a part to play in the work of salvation as the freely cooperating instrument of his plan. In a gesture of election, God's hand rests on the man of his choice, [17] transmits to him divine power, helps him, and accomplishes "by his hand" the action of salvation. The salvific initiative always belongs to God, and the execution of the plan is ultimately the work of omnipotence; of itself the creature can accomplish nothing. Yet the hand of the man who is chosen and "used" by the "right hand" of God expresses in a splendid way the here-and-now active presence of the All-Powerful One in history.

Noah and Abraham collaborated in the work of salvation, but it is the narrative of Exodus that makes the hands of God's chosen ones (Moses and Aaron) the instrument of the divine will. God will lay his own hand on Egypt and the Egyptians (Exod. 7:4–5), but the hand and the staff of Moses and Aaron will inflict the terrible plagues.[18] Here, the hand keeps the fearful promises expressed in words (Exod. 9:6). In this way the power of God's hand is manifested (Exod. 9:16).

When Israel saw the Egyptians in pursuit as it emerged from Egypt, "the Lord said to Moses . . . 'Lift up your staff and, with hand outstretched over the sea, split the sea in two, that the Israelites may pass through it on dry land' " (Exod. 14:15–16). The divine power is then exercised *through the gesture* of God's servant: "Then Moses stretched out his hand over the sea, and the Lord swept the sea with a strong east wind through the night" (Exod. 14:21). Consequently the victory song of Moses and the sons of Israel attributes the whole glorious deed to God's hand: "When you stretched out your right hand, the earth swallowed them!" (Exod. 15:12). The psalmist would later say: "You led your people like a flock under the care of Moses and Aaron" (Ps. 77:21).[19]

Throughout its history Israel will be saved (or punished) by the hand of certain men whom the divine hand raises up and uses: for example, Joshua and the Judges. King David, the "anointed one" of the Lord, will be in a special way the instrument of God's purposes. Between God's hand and the king's hand there exists a kind of living continuity: "I have found David, my servant; with my holy oil I have anointed him, that my hand may be always with him, and that my arm may make him strong. . . . I will set his hand upon the sea, his right hand upon the rivers" (Ps. 89:21–22,26). Some of the prophets suffer under the weight of the hand that chose them: "My heart, as I went, overflowed with bitterness and anger, and the hand of Yahweh lay heavy on me" (Ezek. 3:14,JB). Similarly, the hand of the mysterious messenger makes known to Daniel God's awesome choice of him to receive the revelation of events that are written in the Book of Truth: "I felt a hand touching me, setting my knees and my hands trembling. He said: 'Daniel, you are a man specially chosen . . .' " (Dan. 10:10). In his care to use only weak instruments so that his own intervention may be the more evident (cf. Deut. 32:29–31; Judg. 7; 2 Cor. 4:7), God will even make use of a woman's hand, that of Judith (Jth. 9:10). This fact will glorify her in the eyes of all the people (Jth. 15:10).

God chooses and makes use even of pagans (though they do not realize it) in carrying out his purposes of chastisement or grace. Assyria, probably in the person of Sennacherib, is "my rod in anger, my staff in wrath" against Israel (Isa. 10:5–27; cf. 8:5–8). Into the hands of Nebuchadnezzar God puts the nations and even the beast of the field (Jer. 27:4–8; 28:12–14). Babylon is a terrible destructive hammer in Yahweh's hands (Jer. 51:20–23; cf. 50:23). Finally, Cyrus, whom God raises up, calls by name, and leads from victory to victory, is his "anointed one" and is entrusted with the task of rescuing the oppressed and bringing the exiles home (Isa. 41:1–7, 25; 45:1–6, 9–13).

All these men whose hands God uses are prophetic figures, living signs, of the supreme liberator promised to Israel: the Messiah.

After having on many occasions borrowed the voice of the prophets to speak to his people, in the fullness of time God speaks to them in the voice of his Son (Heb. 1:1–2). Thus, to the chosen men whose hands of flesh God borrowed for the accomplishment of his plans succeeds the incarnate Son himself, whose hand is the very hand of God. In its works, beginning with the creation and under the old dispensation, the hand of God was made flesh: invisible in itself, it became visible in our nature. Incapable in itself of being grasped, it offers itself now to our grasp in Jesus Christ. Reciprocal and symmetrical with all human hands, the hand of God-made-man is held out until the end of time to man in distress. It is the one and only hand by which salvation comes to all.

By this very fact, in Jesus Christ the "hand of God" ceases to be a metaphor: *the anthropomorphism is done away with as a figure of speech, for it has become a living reality*. The teaching of the Old Testament is at once transcended and fulfilled. God has taken upon himself the form *(morphé)* of man *(anthropos)*; (cf. Phil. 2:7). The manhood of the Son puts to flight all the dangers of anthropomorphism by bringing it to consummation. Now the true God takes on flesh, a human face and voice and hand, without ceasing to be God. To put it better: God's own hand, which Christ is,[20] acquires human experience of the world and of daily toil. But this hand has more to do than collaborate in "progress," however legitimate that may be. Its work is to signify and accomplish the ever active will of God for man's salvation.

The laying of hands on children may be a simple act of blessing (Matt. 19:13–15),[21] but on many occasions Jesus effects healings by the touch of his hand in order to proclaim the coming of the messianic kingdom (Matt. 11:2–6; cf. Luke 4:17–19). Here are some telling episodes: "A leper came forward and did him homage, saying to him, 'Sir, if you will to do so, you can cure me.' Jesus stretched out his hand and touched him and said, 'I do will it. Be cured.' Immediately the man's leprosy disappeared" (Matt. 8:2–3). The woman who was badly stooped: "When Jesus saw her, he called her to him and said, 'Woman, you are free of your infirmity.' He laid his hand on her, and immediately she stood up straight and began thanking God" (Luke 13:12–13). As Jesus passed through the district of the Ten Cities, a deaf mute was brought to him: "Some people . . . begged him to lay his hands on him. Jesus took him off by himself away from the crowd. He put his fingers into the man's ears and, spitting, touched his tongue; then he looked up to heaven and emitted a groan. He said to him, '*Ephphatha!*' (that is, 'Be opened'). At once the man's ears were opened; he was freed from the impediment and began to speak plainly" (Mark 7:32–35). Christ's hand also opens to the light the eyes of the man born blind:"Jesus spat on the ground, made mud with his saliva, and smeared the man's eyes with the mud. Then he told him, 'Go wash in the pool of Siloam.' . . . So the man went off and washed and came back able to see" (John 9:6–7).[22] On other occasions, the initiative of manual contact does not come from Jesus; instead, sick people spontaneously touch him in order to be healed.[23]

Jesus even expels impure spirits "by the finger of God"—a manifest sign of the kingdom's coming: "If it is by the finger of God that I cast out devils, then the reign of God is upon you" (Luke 11:20).[24]

There are other works of power, no less significant. Christ's hand raises up the disciples who lie prostrate before his glory at the transfiguration (for no one can see God and live; Matt. 17:7);[25] and catches Peter to draw him out of the mortal depths of the waters that are threatening to engulf him (Matt. 14:28–32). But, above all, this same hand seeks out man in the abyss of death in order to recall him to life:

> One of the officials of the synagogue, a man named Jairus, came near. Seeing Jesus, he fell at his feet and made this earnest appeal: 'My little daughter is critically ill. Please come and lay your hands on her so that she may get well and live.' . . . People from the official's house arrived saying, 'Your daughter is dead . . . ' Taking her hand he said to her, '*Talitha, koum*,' which means, 'Little girl, get up.' The girl, a child of twelve, stood up immediately and began to walk around" (Mark 5:22–23,35,41–42).[26]

So, too, in the case of the son of the widow at Naim: "Then he stepped forward and touched the litter; at this, the bearers halted. He said, 'Young man, I bid you get up.' The dead man sat up and began to speak" (Luke 7:14–15).

Finally, the words of Jesus in the Temple at the feast of the Dedication indicate clearly that his hand is the hand of God himself. The sheep entrusted to Jesus' hand remain in some sense in that of the Father: "I give them eternal life, and they shall never perish. No one shall snatch them out of my hand. My Father is greater than all, in what he has given me, and there is no snatching out of his hand. The

Father and I are one" (John 10:28–30). The conclusion, along with the parallelism of the verses, makes it clear that the hand of Jesus and the hand of the Father are one.[27]

But we must be careful to realize that the hand of Jesus, like the hand of any other man, cannot be considered in isolation, detached from the living totality of his person. The hand is an element in the complete human presence and receives its whole meaning from the latter; it acts and has meaning only in connection with the comprehensive attitude, the gaze, and the word, all of which enunciate, explicate, and confirm the intention. The person of the Son permeates all the components of his human presence; the latter are themselves inseparable one from another, although the emphasis is differently distributed between them in the various narratives. Thus, according to Mark and Luke, Jesus links his word to a gesture at the raising of Jairus' daughter; Matthew mentions only the gesture of his hand. At other times, the circumstances or Jesus' intention will determine whether or not word is to predominate over gesture. By raising Lazarus solely by the power of his word (John 11:43–44), Jesus is illustrating and confirming his earlier teaching concerning the power of the Son of Man: "An hour is coming in which all those in their tombs shall hear his voice and come forth" (John 5:28).

On the other hand, if the objective and universally accepted meaning of the manual gesture is indispensable for an understanding of the saving events, it is not enough. For the event becomes charged with a new meaning in the cultural context in which it occurs. To grasp the full literal sense of the biblical accounts, we must know the moral significance that leprosy, deafness, muteness, and blindness had in the minds of Jesus' contemporaries; we must know that the "raising up" of a sick or dead person points to the resurrection which the Messiah brings to both body and soul.[28] The hand of Jesus is eloquent, even as his word is active.

On the day of the ascension the humanity of Jesus leaves the visible world. The hand of God the Savior seems to draw back from the world, and the salvation that has been signified seems forever compromised. But Christ has passed on to his apostles the mission he has himself received from his Father (John 20:21); he pours his Spirit out upon them on Pentecost. From now on the apostles lend the invisible

Christ their own visibility, and the "humanity" of the Church mediates to the world the humanity of its Head. By the hands (the ministry) of the Twelve the saving power and love of God continue to exert their influence. God's hand remains *active* and *signified* in human history.

The cure of the cripple in the Temple (Acts 3:4–26)[29] and the raising of the Christian woman, Tabitha, at Joppa (Acts 9:36–42) clearly manifest the real situation. For, after having called upon the name of Jesus or having knelt in prayer, Peter extends his hand and grasps the hand of the crippled man (Acts 3:6–7) or the dead woman (Acts 9:40–41) and restores the person to health or life.[30] It is the power of Jesus Christ that is being exerted in the gesture of the apostle (Acts 4:5–12). God's hand continues to effect salvation by taking the initiative in regard to the hand of lost man: the divine hand "raises man up," "sets him on his feet."[31]

The prayer of the apostles and disciples under persecution shows clearly that the initiative belongs to God and that man only offers his "service": "Now, O Lord, look at the threats they are leveling against us. Grant to your servants, even as they speak your words, complete assurance by stretching forth your hand in cures and signs and wonders to be worked in the name of Jesus, your holy Servant" (Acts 4:29–30). Events show that not only is the Spirit poured out but God is present and active: "Through the hands of the apostles many signs and wonders occurred among the people" (Acts 5:12);[32] "The hand of the Lord was with them and a great number of them believed and were converted to the Lord" (Acts 11:21). Thus it is the saving power and love of God and the very hand of Jesus Christ that make, through the hands of the apostles, the gestures of salvation.

In the *sacramental economy* the benefits of the redemptive incarnation are spelled out in detail and applied to men. The minister acts, as did the apostles, "in the name" of Jesus Christ, that is, with his authority and according to his intention to save; he acts "in the person of Christ," as classical theology puts it, using juridical language. The visible minister lends the invisible Savior his humanity, his voice, his gestures, that energy of human presence which carries the minister towards others. By such a mediation the recipient of the sacrament effectively encounters God the Savior. Thus, by the hand of the minister which is placed on the catechumen's head, God adopts a new child in Jesus. The fingers that touch the ears of an infant are reproducing the gesture of Christ when he touched the ears of the deaf mute. The catechumen is thereby disposed to hear the word of God and to praise him.[33]

This co-ordination of man's "ministry" *(ministerium)* or "service" *(servitus)* and God's sovereign "power" *(potestas)* [34] is reflected in the notion of *opus operatum* that was worked out in medieval theology. In this concept, the roles of God and minister in the sacramental act are precisely defined, and the sacramental act is carefully distinguished from its opposite, the magical act. In a magical rite, man's hand takes the initiative in an action that is supposedly able to bring the hidden forces of nature under man's control. In the sacramental act, the whole initiative in salvation belongs to God. The minister supplies a go-between in the form of his own human self, so that through the gestures and words of a man a transcendent power may be signified and may pass to effect salvation. If the dispositions of the believer do not put any obstacle in the way, God's action exerts its omnipotent effectiveness.

Let us note, finally, the necessary concurrence of gesture and word in the sacramental rite. In human action, the movement of word and hand together sketch out, as it were, the contours of the effect to be produced. The hand states the intention and brings it to pass; the word declares the intention and makes it a reality. Gesture and word together form a single, indivisible action that produces the result. The same is true of sacramental action. Without the gesture the word could not manifest God's "handling" and reshaping of man; as a simple proposition, it could leave the hearer with the impression that God is not "keeping his word" and bringing to pass what he has promised. Conversely, the rite without the word would lose its meaning; the divine intention of salvation, which the rite brings into play, remains obscure, and the sacramental gesture would be in danger of degenerating into ritualism or magic or a silly mannerism. It is clear, then, how certain "Christian" populations could be "sacramentalized" without being evangelized. The deeper meaning of the rite is that God's hand is here and now making real, for this individual man, the salvation which his word has promised.

God's Hand and Revelation

If man's works express his intentions, his abilities, and even his ideals, the attributes of the Creator are likewise reflected in the universe, for there God manifests his glory through the combined power of his word and his hand. Man need therefore simply look at the great work which creation is, and he will acknowledge its author (Wisd. 13).[35] Listen to the invitation issued by Sirach: "Behold the rainbow! Then bless its Maker, for majestic indeed is its splendor; it spans the heavens with its glory, this bow bent by the mighty hand of God" (Ecclus. 43:11–12).

Since the works of the creative hand allow men to recognize their author, they also help to name him. For Melchizedech, king and pagan priest (Gen. 14:19), for Abraham (Gen. 14:22), for Israel and the Christian (Ps. 115:15; 121:2; 124:8; 134:3; 146:6; Acts 14:15; 17:24; Rev. 14:7), the One who makes himself known through creation is forever the God "who made heaven and earth." In thus rising from the work to the maker, human knowledge is following an order which is the opposite of that followed in the making of the world. Though such knowledge cannot reach or express the inner being of God, it does know God, indirectly but genuinely, as the One on whom all other beings depend,[36] the One who holds everything in his hand.

Not only does the universe bear witness to the Creator; God's interventions in history also reveals his perfections. The psalmist proclaims as much: "The works of his hands are faithful and just; sure are all his precepts, reliable forever and ever, wrought in truth and equity" (Ps. 111:7–8). The believer is therefore concerned to meditate on events in which the hand of God is mysteriously at work: "Great are the works of the Lord, exquisite in all their delights" (Ps. 111:2); "I remember the days of old; I meditate on all your doings, the works of your hands I ponder" (Ps. 143:5).

The events of the departure from Egypt, which forever shaped the religious awareness of Israel, were authentic "epiphanies" of God and preludes to the majestic theophany of Horeb. God had told Moses of his intention of revealing himself even to the pagans: "So that the Egyptians may learn that I am the Lord, as I stretch out my hand against Egypt and lead the Israelites out of their midst" (Exod. 7:5). Consequently, when the gnats descended on the country, "the magicians said to Pharaoh, 'This is the finger of God' " (Exod. 8:15). In other words, the event was signed: "God."

Deuteronomy will carefully remind the people of all this: "Did any god venture to go and take a nation for himself . . . by testings, by signs and wonders, by war, with his strong hand and outstretched arm, and by great terrors, all of which the Lord, your God, did for you in Egypt before your very eyes?" (Deut.4:34); "Call to mind what the Lord, your God, did to Pharaoh and to all Egypt: the great testings which your own eyes have seen, the signs and wonders, his strong hand outstretched arm with which the Lord, your God, brought you out" (Deut. 7:18–19; cf. 26:8).

In telling of the crossing of the Red Sea and later of the Jordan, the Book of Joshua highlights God's intention to reveal himself: "in order that all the peoples of the earth may learn that the hand of the Lord is mighty, and that you may fear the Lord, your God, forever" (Josh. 4:24). And the psalmist expresses thanks for the revelation: "You are the God who works wonders; among the peoples you have made known your power. With your strong arm you redeemed your people, the sons of Jacob and Joseph" (Ps. 77:15–16).

Let us recall, finally, that the tablets of the Law, which were regarded as written by the very finger of God and were certainly the work of his hand in a special way, revealed his will to Israel forever (Exod. 24:12; 31:18; 32:15–16; Deut. 9:10; Ps. 19, *passim* and 147:15–20).[37]

The sense of God manifesting himself in events which are the work of his hands is so strong in Israel that Isaiah presents future divine interventions as real theophanies. Sometimes, as in the promised New Exodus, God even seems to save Israel precisely in order to manifest himself: "that all may see and know, observe and understand, that the hand of the Lord has done this" (Isa. 41:20; cf. 30:30). God raises up Cyrus and makes him take to arms "so that toward the rising and the setting of the sun men may know that there is none besides me"(Isa. 45:6). In a bold anthropomorphism the prophet even represents God as "pulling up his sleeves" and using his arm in order to give evidence of his surpassing power and of the promised salvation: "The Lord comforts his people, he redeems Jerusalem. The Lord has bared his holy arm in the sight of all the nations: all the ends of the earth will behold the salvation of our God" (Isa. 52:9–10).

Sirach addresses the following prayer to God:

> Raise your hand against the heathen, that they may realize your power. As you have used us to show them your holiness, so now use them to show us your glory. Thus they will know, as we know, that there is no God but you. Give new signs and work new wonders; show forth the splendor of your right hand and arm (Ecclus. 36:2–5).

God reveals himself, then, in the works of his hand; he manifests in them his power, his holiness, his intention of saving. In regard to this last, God's hand manifests his *fidelity* by keeping the promises he has made.

The supreme manifestation of God's hand in history is, however, Jesus Christ, and consequently it is in him that revelation, too, reaches its highest point. Everything in him is word and manifestation of God: discourses, actions, even silences. More especially, the fleshly hand of Jesus, the visible hand of the invisible God, does "works" which are all divine "signs" (John 2:11).[38] The Father does them with the Son and in him (John 5:17–19,36; 10:37–38; 14:10–11). But, contrary to the suggestions of Satan and even of his own disciples (Matt. 4:1–11; John 7:3–5), Christ does not act to win glory from men (John 5:41,44); he seeks only the glory that comes from God and returns to God (John 1:14; 7:18; 8:54; 11:4,40; 12:28; 13:31–32; 14:13; 16:14; 17:1,4–5,10,22–24). The works of Christ's hand are revelatory signs much more than they are benefactions. For the "work" heals or raises up only this individual, whereas the sign reaches every man and reveals salvation to him.[39] As "signs," his miracles confirm his preaching (e.g. Matt. 9:1–8; John 10:25, 37–38; 11:15,42–48; 20:30–31; cf. 5:36 and Mark 16:17); they are a further stimulus to those whom his words have not brought to faith (John 14:11; cf. 3:2),[40] while they also convict of sin those who reject them (John 15:24; cf. 16:8–9).

God's hand, like his word, is mysterious: it is revelatory only to the pure of heart. When Isaiah foretold the Servant of Yahweh, he felt forced to say: "Who would believe what we have heard? To whom has the arm of the Lord been revealed?" (Isa. 53:1). Later on, John would see this prophecy fulfilled in the refusal of some to believe (John 12:37–40). When faith is lacking, men constantly demand new signs and are never content (John 2:18; 6:26; 11:47; Matt. 12:38–39; 16:1–4; Luke 16:27–31). An upright conscience, on the contrary, welcomes the signs that are given, believes in them, finds nourishment in them, and asks for no others (Luke 2:12; cf. 1:34–37; John 2:11,23; 4:48–54; 7:31; cf. 9:16, 33).

The believer living in the Church must probe history unceasingly in order to discover God's finger in it. But if he is to do this successfully, he must be possessed by the Word. We mentioned earlier the abuse called ritualism in which the gesture loses its meaning because its close connection with the word is lost. To this deviation in the cultic sphere there corresponds, in man's reflection on everyday life, a *monism of facts.* To be satisfied with facts and with their empirical observation or scientific study (statistics, sociology, etc.) is to cut oneself off from any Christian judgment on them and to condemn oneself to a conformist empiricism wholly lacking in moral and evangelical values. Only a constant study of God's word, of "doctrine" at all its levels of development, makes it possible to decipher events and orientate action. To faith, the fact is only *indicative:* only God's word is *normative.*

The texts of the Roman Missal, until its recent revision, celebrated the divine hand in a special way during the season of the Epiphany, or "manifestation." The "right hand" of God, which is invoked in the collects and praised in the offertory songs, effected in Jesus Christ the "works" which are related in the corresponding sections of the gospel.[41] Finally, in the whole sacramental ministry and in the whole apostolate of the Church, the hand of minister or apostle manifests the saving power and love of Christ who is at work today in man's history.

NOTES

1. Cf. *The Humanity of Man*, pp. 192–93, "The Hand as Organ of Anticipation."

2. Cf. Ps. 124:8: "Our help is in the name of the Lord, who made heaven and earth."

3. Cf. St. Thomas Aquinas, *Summa theologiae*, I, q 13, a. 7. Aristotle, *De generatione et corruptione*, I.6 323,a25–33, had already claimed that a contact

between the two could not be reciprocal; the unmoved first mover (which is not a creator) touches the sublunary world but is not touched by it in return, reciprocity being found only between beings of the same order.

4. Cf. *The Humanity of Man*, pp. 210–11, "The Hand as Organ of My Freedom."

5. Cf. Exod. 20:11: "On the seventh day he rested." There is a natural connection between rest and freedom. The exodus is a coming forth from the house of slavery, a liberation, and an entering into the land of rest (Deut. 5:15; Ps. 95:11).

6. Cf. Pascal, *Pensées*, Fr. 347–48 (Turnell, Fr. 391, p. 221).

7. This doctrine may be illustrated by Rodin's sculpture, *The Hand of God*, in which man is still held and cradled in the divine hand as a child is cradled in its mother's womb.

8. On the "name," cf. *The Humanity of Man*, pp. 164–66.

9. Verse 7b uses another image to convey man's royal power over earthly things: "putting all things under his feet." This image completes and confirms the preceding one. Cf. Ecclus. 17:1–3.

10. Cf. *The Humanity of Man*, pp. 212–14, "The Hand as Organ of Contact and Power."

11. In connection with the following discussion, cf. *The Humanity of Man*, pp. 214–18, the hand as organ of request and prayer, of giving, of hoped-for salvation, and of salvation offered.

12. The text is used as a response at Compline in the Roman Breviary and in the prayers for the dying. The Christian prays with upraised hands in union with the suffering Christ; cf. Tertullian, *De oratione*, 14 (PL 1:1273); St. Augustine, *Enarrationes in Psalmos*, 62:13 (PL 36:755).

13. It would be blind simplism to think that progress has made recourse to God in prayer useless. The discoveries made by resourceful men are possible only because God is creator both of natural forces and of intelligence. Progress in no way weakens the radical dependence of man on God.

14. In Isa. 49:2 the Servant of Yahweh uses the same terms to express his own calling by God: "He . . . concealed me in the shadow of his arm."

15. The Bible teaches both God's infallible mastery of history (Isa. 48:3) and the responsibility of man who at times is hardened against God (Isa. 48:4), at times faithful. Cf. Ecclus. 16:11–20.

16. The text is used in the Roman Missal for the Introit of Easter Thursday; cf. Acts 13:17.

17. Thus God touches the mouth of Jeremiah in order to transmit his words to him (Jer. 1:9; cf. Isa. 6:6–7); God protects his Servant by hiding him "in the shadow of his arm" (Isa. 49:2); the psalmist prays that God's help may be "with the man of your right hand" (Ps. 80:18); finally, this divine hand will be "upon" John the Baptist (Luke 1:66). For the linked interventions of word and hand, cf. Ezek. 1:3.

18. Without going into a study of the various documents used in the narrative, we refer the reader to Exod. 7:17 and 19–20; 8:1–2 and 12–13; 9:2–3 and 22–23; 10:12–13; and 21–22.

19. These simple texts are of great importance for understanding the economy of salvation and especially of the Christian sacraments.

20. Cf. St. Augustine, *Sermo* 291:2 (PL 38:1317); "Christ is God's hand, the Son of God is God's hand, the Word of God is God's hand." Cf. also *Tractatus in Joannem*, 48:7 (PL 35:1744); *Enarrationes in Psalmos*, Ps. 118, Serm. 32 (PL 37:1595); Ps. 143:14 (PL 37:1865).

21. Elsewhere a touch of the hand communicates the Holy Spirit (Acts 8:17; 9:17–18; 19:6) or a particular charism (1 Tim. 4:14; 2 Tim. 1:6; 5:22).

22. Other examples of healing touch: Matt. 8:14–15; 20:29–34; Luke 6:19. Cf. Matt. 19:13–15; Mark 10:13.

23. Cf. Matt. 9:20–22: the woman with a flow of blood, who is healed by touching the edge of Christ's robe; Mark 6:53–56: various illnesses cured by touch.

24. Cf. also the cure of the epileptic demoniac in Mark 9:14–29; verse 27: "Jesus took him by the hand and helped him to his feet."

25. Cf. below, Chapter 5, section 1, "To Be God Is to Be Invisible."

26. In the gesture of his hand Christ declares himself mediator of salvation. Commenting on this mediation (in connection with Gal. 3:19–20), St. Augustine, *Sermo* 156:5,5 (PL 38:852), writes: "If you were not prostrated, you would need no mediator; but since you are prostrated and cannot rise up, God has sent a mediator and thus stretched out his arm to you as it were." Cf. St. Gregory of Nyssa, *Oratio catechetica*, 32 (PG 45:80B).

27. From among numerous texts we may quote St. Jerome, *Commentary on Isaiah*, 18:65,2 (PL 24:655; *Corpus Christianorum*, 73A:744–45): "We may take the outstretched hands as symbolic of the generosity of the giver who will refuse nothing he is asked. . . . Outstretched hands also signify the mercy of a father who rejoices at taking his children to his heart again."

28. Cf. Xavier Léon-Dufour, *Etudes d'evangile* (Paris: Editons du Seuil, 1965), pp. 125–32.

29. In Acts 3:12, note Peter's protest against the interpretation of bystanders who attributed the cure to the power or holiness of the two apostles ("as if we had made this man walk by some power or holiness of our own"); verse 16 stresses the fact that the name of Jesus, as object of faith, has cured the cripple.

30. Cf. below, Chapter 5, section 17, "The Visibility of the Envoy."

31. Cf. above, Chapter 1, section 14, "The Up-Righting of Man in Jesus Christ."

32. On the transmission of the Spirit through the laying on of hands, cf. the texts cited above, note 21. Many sick people sought at the least, some kind of contact, however indirect and tenuous it might be: the touch of Peter's *shadow* as he passed by in the streets of Jerusalem (Acts 5:15). Cf. *The Humanity of Man*, pp. 241–42 on the shadow.

33. Cf. Ps. 51:17: "O Lord, open my lips, and my mouth shall proclaim your praise."

34. Cf. St. Augustine, *Tractatus in Joannem*, 5:18 (PL 35:1424). We may note, with St. Thomas Aquinas, that Christ as God is the source of grace and

that as man he can be called the"Minister" of God, though in a unique way, since his manhood is an instrument which is united to the very divinity itself: "Christ as God is the effective source of grace; as man he serves God in the infusion of grace" *(De veritate*, q. 27, a. 3, ad 2). Other servants or ministers act not by their own power but by the power of another *(De veritate*, q.27, a. 4, ad 2).

35. On what follows, cf. *The Humanity of Man*, pp. 218–21, "The Revelatory Hand."

36. Cf. St. Thomas Aquinas, *Summa theologiae*, I, q. 12, a. 12.

37. Cf. Chapter 3, above, note 44.

38. For the synonymity, cf. John 6:30.

39. In John 14:10 note the suggestive parallelism between words *(rhemata)* and works *(erga)*. Cf. St. Augustine, *Sermons on the Gospel of John*, 44:1(PL 35:1713): "The marvelous things our Lord Jesus Christ did are both works and words: works because they are deeds, words because they are signs. Cf. *Serm*. 98:3 (PL 38:592–93).

40. Cf. John 11:42, the prayer of Jesus before raising Lazarus: "that they may believe that you sent me."

41. Cf., e.g., the collect and offertory song (Ps. 117:16–17) for the Third Sunday after Epiphany, repeated on the Fourth, Fifth, and Sixth Sundays; and the collects for Wednesday of Lenten Ember Week and the Third Sunday of Lent.

CHAPTER 5

THE FACE OF GOD

Man's word is active and his hand is eloquent, but each receives its necessary complement from the gaze and the whole face. By its position the face dominates the body like a summit, thus bringing to its height the body's whole power of expression. A man must consent to show his face if his presence to others is to be effective and real. If, then, God takes the initiative in speaking to man and even in extending a helping hand to him, the revelation of his being and his saving presence will be complete only if he offers his face to the gaze of his human partner in dialogue.

I. THE OLD TESTAMENT

To Be God Is to Be Invisible

The desire to see God is as old as the religious sentiment, indeed as old as man himself. To pierce the veil of the invisible, to look into the beyond, to contemplate face-to-face the God who is unknown yet felt to be there—the yearning torments those who, far from being absorbed by the spectacle of our world, are made restless by it. Yet a visible God would be a God cut down to man's size, a caricature of the true God, an empty shadow and an idol.

Xenophanes observed that man makes God in his own image, yielding to anthropomorphism: "The Ethiopians say that their gods are snub-nosed and black; the Thracians that theirs are blue-eyed and redheaded";[1] and, even more bitingly: "If cattle and horses and lions had hands and could paint and produce reproductions, as man can, the horses would paint the gods to look like horses, and the cattle would paint them to look like cattle; in short, they would turn the gods into bodily beings like those of each animal species."[2] To this foolish desire reason opposes a quite contrary certitude: "There is but one God; he is sovereign master of Gods and men, and resembles mortals neither in body nor in thought."[3] If God is to be God, he is the Most High, the Wholly Other, the Transcendent; he is beyond man's power to grasp him with word or hand or gaze. The God who is silent, ineffable, and intangible, is also invisible.

The religious man cannot but experience real anguish here. Even the face-to-face encounter with other men troubles me at times, for the other sees me more clearly than I see myself; but at least I can see these others. God, the omnipotent, is also the all-seeing, and he sees me infinitely more clearly than any human being can—to his eyes I am totally transparent; but I cannot in turn catch even a glimpse of him! I fear this penetrating gaze which I cannot return. Moreover, as a religious man I suffer from God's apparent absence from the world. Men around me measure reality by what is visible; what they see is all that matters, and the invisible is equated with the nonexistent. My God, therefore—invisible, yet alone totally real—is likely to be thought of as the great Absence, as absolute nothingness. If then I introduce an image of God into our visible world, I do it so that he may affirm his presence in the universe and take his place among men. If I represent God, it is to *make him exist* this side of death where lonely mankind toils. In short, I am tired of seeking God without seeing him; I want to feel that in prayer my words, hands, and eyes are encountering Someone. Hence I give a sensible support to my appeals, my gropings, my longings, so that they may not be lost in the void of earth and heavens. But my efforts are inexorably condemned from the very beginning. Here any image is a betrayal. God is so great and my representation of him so deficient that the latter can only be a lie. To make God visible, accessible to my eyes, is necessarily to deny and annihilate him. In short, God is the one I most desire to contemplate and the one who most stubbornly eludes my gaze.

Biblical man suffered all the more from this invisibility of the distant God because in the beginning Creator and creature had lived in an astounding intimacy. The account in Genesis shows God breathing the breath of life into Adam's nostrils: God's word calls Adam into existence; God's hand forms him. Man comes to birth in some way mysteriously face-to-face with God (Gen. 2:7). This creative encounter of the two faces, the human and the divine—one would almost be tempted to say, this kiss bestowed by God on man, his masterwork—is prolonged in the familiarity of the original innocence. But sin disrupts the grace of this face-to-face relationship. The guilty couple conceal themselves, hide from God's gaze in the midst of the trees of the garden (Gen. 3:8–9); they are soon driven out of Eden, deprived of the Creator's presence and his intimacy. Cain in his turn, aware of the curse upon him, flees from God's gaze: "I must avoid your presence and become a restless wanderer on the earth" (Gen. 4:14).

God doubtless did converse with the patriarchs. He speaks to Abraham in a vision (Gen. 15:1), concludes a covenant with him under the symbolism of fire (Gen. 15:17–21), and appears to him to tell him of his future posterity (Gen. 17:1); but the patriarch falls face to the ground and cannot look on God face-to-face (Gen. 17:3). Jacob, in turn, after the dream in which God makes known his promise to him, is awestruck: "In solemn wonder he cried out: 'How awesome is this shrine! This is nothing else but an abode of God, and that is the gateway to heaven!' " (Gen. 28:16). Greater still is his religious fear when he has won his wrestling match with a mysterious adversary: "Jacob named the place Peniel, 'Because I have seen God face to face,' he said, 'yet my life has been spared' " (Gen. 32:31).[4] As creature and sinner, man is aware that he cannot face God and still live. Biblical tradition will remain convinced to the end that seeing God means death. As an animal cannot sustain the gaze of man, his master, so man in turn cannot endure the gaze of his God.[5]

At the Exodus and during the events at Mt. Sinai, the immense power of the invisible God is manifested. At an earlier point, when Moses curiously approaches the burning bush ("I must go over to look at this remarkable sight"), he is stopped by Yahweh's voice: " 'Come no nearer!' . . . . Moses hid his face, for he was afraid to look at God" (Exod. 3:3–6). How paradoxical: at the very moment when God, through a simple sign, lifts a little the veil over his mystery, man is forced to hide his own face because the face-to-face meeting would be too much for him! Yahweh agrees to reveal his name, but the one chosen to hear it cannot gaze on God (Exod. 3:13–14).

At the great theophany on Mt. Sinai, Moses must order the people, at Yahweh's express bidding, to stay far away from the mountain and not even to touch the foot of it, under pain of death (Exod. 19:20–25). God manifests himself in cloud, fire, smoke, and the trembling of the mountain; these are all phenomena which indicate his holy and awesome presence but leave him still mysterious (Exod. 19:18–20). Moreover, Moses has hardly reached the top of the mountain when God sends him back to the Israelites: "Go down and warn the people not to break through toward the Lord in order to see him; otherwise many of them will be struck down. The priests, too, who approach the Lord must sanctify themselves; else he will vent his anger upon them" (Exod. 19:21–22); "The people remained at a distance, while Moses approached the cloud where God was" (Exod. 20:21; cf. 24:1–2).

This strictly enforced spatial separation brought home to the Israelites the infinite spiritual distance that separates creature from Creator, the sinner from the Holy One. The transcendence of the true God is thus manifested in a way accessible to the senses.

It is doubtless true that the seventy elders of the people climb the mountain and share in some measure in Moses' privilege: "They beheld the God of Israel. Under his feet there appeared to be sapphire tilework. . . . After gazing on God, they could still eat and drink" (Exod. 24:9–11). But the vision and the intimacy are only imperfect in kind. Truly to encounter God, Moses must leave the elders, climb further up, and enter alone into the cloud that covers the mountaintop. And even there the divine presence is manifested to him in a *sign*, for the glory of the Lord "was seen as a consuming fire on the mountaintop" (Exod. 24:12–18).

All these cosmic phenomena surrounding the theophany at Mt. Sinai are signs from God to his people; their ambiguity is the same as that of the revelation of which they are the instruments. For they affirm the transcendence of God before the eyes of the body and the spirit, yet veil his awesome face: they manifest the Presence yet withhold it, show the Glory yet keep it in reserve. The signs of himself which God gives are both the continual support and the abiding test of faith: they are offered to the vision of the believer like points of rest, stages on his journey, and sure ways of access to a sublime reality whose paradox is always to conceal itself.

The prohibition of carven images follows upon and confirms the revelation of Yahweh as the invisible God. The Decalogue prescribes: "You shall not have other gods besides me. You shall not carve idols for yourselves in the shape of anything in the sky above or on the earth below or in the waters beneath the earth; you shall not bow down before them or worship them. For I, the Lord, your God, am a jealous God" (Exod. 20:3–5; cf. 20:23).

The transcendent God cannot be likened to any created reality; he is the Wholly Other. The image would do violence to the sublime grandeur of the model; it could not but be a caricature. Moreover, a sensible representation of God would be in danger of leading astray the believer surrounded by idol-worshipping peoples; it might lose its value as a sign, fix the gaze of the believer on itself and substitute itself, in its materiality of stone or wood, for the One whom alone it was intended to evoke. Finally, since it could be endlessly reproduced, it would lead Israel to the denial of the one God: polytheism and idolatry go together. The prohibition of images and the oneness of the place of worship both tend to preserve monotheism. Deuteronomy will therefore place great emphasis on these prescriptions, making reference to the theophany of Horeb:

> Then the Lord spoke to you from the midst of the fire. You heard the sound of the words, but saw no form; there was only a voice. . . . You saw no form at all on the day the Lord spoke to you at Horeb from the midst of the fire. Be strictly on your guard, therefore, not to degrade yourselves by fashioning an idol to represent any figure, whether it be in the form of a man or a woman, of any animal on the earth or of any bird that flies in the sky, of anything that crawls on the ground or of any fish in the waters under the earth (Deut. 4:12, 15–18).[6]

Great, therefore, is Moses' indignation when he comes down from the mountain and sees the Israelites prostrate before the golden calf (Exod. 32). The people were weary of waiting for their leader and disappointed at not seeing their God; they wanted to give a face to the Yahweh who had led them out of Egypt! Pride may also have been at work: Yahweh is not inferior to the visible gods of the pagans nor Israel to the surrounding peoples. Therefore they gave their liberating God the shape of a bull, so often used in eastern cultures to represent the godhead. They doubtless were not prostrating themselves before a pagan god; it was Yahweh they wanted to signify, make visible, and honor. But by their very act they profaned the mystery of God and reduced him to the level of his creatures and to the ranks of the powerless gods. It is no longer the true God, transcendent and faceless, but the work of its own hands, an idol, that Israel adores. Yahweh's anger is stirred and Moses appeases him only with difficulty. The golden calf is reduced to powder, the covenant broken, the tablets of the law smashed. The lawgiver has to climb the mountain a second time so that Yahweh may renew the covenant (Exod. 34). From now on Yahweh will manifest his mysterious presence to his people through the sign of the cloud at the entrance of the Tent of Meeting (Exod. 33:9–10; 40:34–38).

Though the familiarity of Moses and his God was very great, God nonetheless remains invisible to his chosen one. In an act of unparalleled condescension God did indeed reveal his Name to Moses, and it is said that within the Tent of Meeting "The Lord used to speak to Moses face to face, as one man speaks to another" (Exod. 33:11; cf. Ecclus. 45:5).[7] But the meaning of this last is that God showed Moses exceptional favor; the phrasing brings out the intimacy of their conversation and of God's presence. Revelation will not be complete, however, as long as Yahweh has not shown his face. Moses longs for a greater knowledge of God, the desire torments him. This ardent champion of the invisible God, his avenger in face of a faithless people, the man who veiled his face before the burning bush lest his gaze should fall on Yahweh—this man burns within himself with the desire to see his God and confesses it in an urgent entreaty: "Show me your glory, I beg you" (Exod. 33:18, JB).[8] Yahweh agrees to reveal himself in a special way: "I will make all my beauty pass before you, and in your presence I will pronounce my name, 'Lord'; I who show favors to whom I will, I who grant mercy to whom I will" (Exod. 33:19). God's face, however, must remain invisible: "But my face you cannot see, for no man sees me and still lives" (33:20). Then, with the utmost delicacy, " 'Here,' continued the Lord, 'is a place near me where you shall station yourself on the rock. When my glory passes I will set you in the hollow of the rock and will cover you with my hand until I have passed by. Then I will remove my hand, so that you may see my back; but my face is not to be seen' " (33:21–23).

This sublime and touching anthropomorphism marks the culmination of God's revelation to Moses. The gracious divine favor makes itself strongly felt; the prophet enjoys a privileged intimacy with Yahweh. But God forever holds the mystery of his being in reserve. Moreover, the anthropomorphism here clothes a symbolic meaning of extraordinary importance. That God hides Moses in the crevice of the rock, puts his hand over the opening, and passes by, allowing only his back to be seen—surely, one is tempted to say, these images are simplistic, even childish. Yet, close though they are to the thoughts of the least cultivated of men, these representations in no way derogate from the divine majesty. Quite the contrary: the intention, the point, of the account is to give the greatest possible emphasis to the absolute invisibility of God. In an unexpected turning of the tables, *the anthropomorphism has for its sole purpose a vigorous assertion of transcendence.* The biblical use of anthropomorphism expresses conjointly the divine will to communicate with man and the ineffability of the mystery.

Nevertheless the confrontation of Moses with God did not fail to be specially favored. When the lawgiver comes down from the mountain,

> he did not know that the skin of his face had become radiant while he conversed with the Lord. When Aaron, then, and the other Israelites saw Moses and noticed how radiant the skin of his face had become, they were afraid to come near him . . . . Moses called them . . . . When he finished speaking with them, he put a veil over his face. Whenever Moses entered the presence of the Lord to converse with him, he removed the veil until he came out again. Then the Israelites would see that the skin of Moses' face was radiant; so he would again put the veil over his face until he went in to converse with the Lord (Exod. 34:29–35).[9]

In this sublime meeting, the face-to-face encounter exercised its power of producing likeness. The light of the divine countenance is reflected on the face of Moses, transfiguring it and imparting some slight resemblance to the divine. If every face-to-face encounter transforms a man unawares, there is all the more reason that no one can draw near to God without being touched by the splendor of the divine glory.

The events of the Exodus contain the whole drama of Israel's consciousness in face of the mystery of the invisible God. During its subsequent history the chosen people will live with this inner division: torn between the fear of a face-to-face encounter in which the two partners, divine and human, would confront each other in their dreadful inequality and the unsuppressible desire that the One who sees all would at last consent to be seen. If to see God is to die, not to see him is to languish.

Fear of Seeing God

Every time God manifests himself in an event, material nature trembles and shudders. A theophany shakes the cosmos; thus does the cosmos pay homage to its maker. This is what happened at the Exodus, as we have already pointed out. The psalmist, later on, will adopt the epic style in describing nature's reaction: "O God, when you went forth at the head of your people, when you marched through the wilderness, the earth quaked; it rained from heaven at the presence of God, at the presence of God, the God of Israel, the One of Sinai" (Ps. 68:7). And again:

> The sea beheld and fled;
>   Jordan turned back.
> The mountains skipped like rams,
>   the hills like the lambs of the flock . . . .
> Before the face of the Lord, tremble, O earth,
>   before the face of the God of Jacob,
> who turned the rock into pools of water,
>   the flint into flowing springs (Ps. 114:3–4,7–8).[10]

At an even later point, when the exiled believer asks God to intervene for his people, he will evoke the turmoil of nature in analogous imagery:

> Oh, that you would rend the heavens and come down,
>   with the mountains quaking before you,
> as when brushwood is set ablaze,
>   or fire makes the water boil!

> Thus your name would be made known to your enemies
> and the nations would tremble before you,
> While you wrought awesome deeds we could not hope for,
> such as they had not heard of from of old
> (Isa. 63:19–64:3; cf. Jth. 17:15; Mic. 1:2–4).

The wise man offers his own strong testimony: "Behold, the heavens, the heaven of heavens, the earth and the abyss tremble at his visitation; the roots of the mountains, the earth's foundations, at his mere glance, quiver and quake" (Ecclus. 16:16–17; cf. 43:18–19; Rev. 20:11). Thus men have maintained an inner certainty that to see God is to die. Gideon (Judg. 6:22–23) and Elijah (1 Kings 19:13) alike are frightened by the nearness of God.

Even apart from moments of theophany in which God makes himself visible through signs of his presence, *the omnipotent is the all-seeing*. His gaze, which at the beginning rested with satisfaction on the works of his hands (Gen. 1:1–31),[11] allows nothing to escape it. Even the most secret actions of man are always as it were displayed before God's eyes. The Invisible One is the Seer beyond compare: "The works of all mankind are present to him; not a thing escapes his eye. His gaze spans all the ages; to him there is nothing unexpected" (Ecclus. 39:19–20; cf. Gen. 16:14). A man is a fool, then, if he thinks he can hide his conduct from God's eyes:

> The man who dishonors his marriage bed and says to himself, "Who can see me? Darkness surrounds me, walls hide me; no one sees me; why should I fear to sin?" Of the Most High he is not mindful, fearing only the eyes of men; he does not understand that the eyes of the Lord, ten thousand times brighter than the sun, observe every step a man takes and peer into hidden corners. He who knows all things before they exist still knows them all after they are made (Ecclus. 23:18–20; cf. 16:17–23; 2 Macc. 9:5; 12:22; 15:2; Job 35:13–14; Ps. 90:4).

The psalmist is keenly aware that man cannot evade God's face and his gaze any more than he can evade his hand: "O Lord, you have probed me and you know me; you know when I sit and when I stand; you understand my thoughts from afar. My journeys and my rest you scrutinize, with all my ways you are familiar" (Ps. 139:1–3; cf. 33:13–15). After all, is this not the God who created our senses and endowed his creatures with sight? "Shall he who shaped the ear not hear? or he who formed the eye not see?" (Ps. 94:9). Later on, Christ would teach that the heavenly Father "sees in secret" (Matt. 6:4,6), and the writer of the Letter to the Hebrews would say: "Nothing is concealed from him; all lies bare and exposed to the eyes of him to whom we must render an account" (Heb. 4:13). Unlike man, who is the prisoner of appearances and is inclined to judge others by their face or looks or "air," God knows even our intentions: he "knows the hearts of all men" (1 Kings 8:39; Ps. 7:10; Isa. 11:3; Jer. 11:20; 17:10; 20:12; Rev. 2:23).

This penetrating power of the divine gaze can torment the believer to the point of anguish. Conscious of his weakness and his sins he fears to encounter the face of God. To see the Holy One is necessarily to appear before him, meet his gaze, be judged and evaluated; how could such a judgment not be a condemnation? After the Fall, Adam and Eve hide themselves; the gaze of God penetrates them, turns them in upon themselves, makes them aware of their sin (Gen. 3:8). After Cain, Jacob, Moses, and Gideon (Judg. 6:22–24), it is Isaiah's turn to face the majesty of the thrice holy God in his Temple: "Woe is me, I am doomed! For I am a man of unclean lips; yet my eyes have seen the King, the Lord of hosts!" (Isa. 6:5). One of the seraphim must purify the prophet's lips and thus wipe away his sins.

It is Job in the depths of his wretchedness who most poignantly expresses the terror of being constantly pierced and scrutinized by the divine gaze: "What is man, that you make much of him, or pay him any heed? You observe him with each new day and try him at every moment! How long will it be before you look away from me, and let me alone long enough to swallow my spittle? Though I have sinned, what can I do to you, O watcher of men?" (Job 7:17–20; cf. 10:4); " . . . biding your time, I know, to mark if I should sin and to let no fault of mine go uncensured . . . . Turn your eyes away, leave me a little joy, before I go to the place of no return" (Job 10:13–14, 20–21,JB).

Ezra's prayer rightly expresses the sentiments of the repentant sinner. Here we no longer have the convulsive terror of Job before a judge too lacking in generosity, but a lively awareness of unworthiness and a fear of even raising one's eyes to the Holy One: "My God, I am too ashamed and confounded to raise my face to you, O my

God . . . . Here we are before you in our sins. Because of all this, we can no longer stand in your presence" (Ezra 9:6,15). This attitude—humble, contrite, and loving—will be that of the publican in the Gospel and will win his justification (Luke 18:13–14).

Sinners, on the other hand, will disappear when on the last day the face of Yahweh will rise like a star: "My enemies are turned back, overthrown and destroyed before you . . . . Rise, O Lord, let not man prevail; let the nations be judged in your presence" (Ps. 9:4,20). This last day is given the splendid name of "day of your face" (literal translation of Ps. 21:10).[12]

In its religious outlook, then, Israel experienced at a very deep level one of the essential components of the religious sentiment: reverential fear.[13] God's face causes man to recoil, gives rise in him to a movement of self-defense or flight. As a creature and sinner, how could any son of Adam endure the presence of the Holy One?

Desire of Seeing God

The fear of seeing God's face would not cause the religious man such great suffering were it not, paradoxically, closely related to its opposite: the longing to see God. The Israelite is torn by this inner tension, which at times reaches the point of anguish. He whom man most dreads to see is at the same time the One he aspires most of all to contemplate.

To be admitted into the presence of one of the great men of this world, to obtain an interview, is a mark of high favor to an individual or a group. In allowing a subordinate to appear before him and speak in his presence, the man of power is allowing the other to exist before him. In letting himself be seen, he is communicating to some extent his very being and its riches. Thus "the whole world sought audience with Solomon, to hear from him the wisdom which God had put into his heart" (1 Kings 10:24). If the royal face is lit by a smile, the petitioner is consoled and benefited: "In the light of the king's countenance is life, and his favor is like a rain cloud in spring" (Prov. 16:15), "his favor, like dew on the grass" (19:12).[14]

All the more reason, then, for the devout Israelite to see the benevolence of the divine face as the source of all good and the surest pledge of happiness. It was the gaze of the Creator that filled the world with blessings on the first day: "The Lord looked upon the earth, and filled it with his blessings" (Ecclus. 16:27; cf. Deut. 26:15). Hence living things that are hungry fix their eyes on the hand of God who provides nourishment: "The eyes of all look hopefully to you, and you give them their food in due season; you open your hand and satisfy the desire of every living thing" (Ps. 145:15–16). Consequently too, the formula for blessing entrusted to Aaron and his sons calls down upon men the light of God's face: "The Lord bless you and keep you! The Lord let his face shine upon you, and be gracious to you! The Lord look upon you kindly and give you peace!" (Num. 6:24–26).[15]

The constant effort of the believer, then, is "to seek the face of God," his benevolent and helpful presence. In addition to the voiced appeal, the suppliant arms and outstretched hands, the eyes of man are raised as if to compel the lowering of God's gaze to him. The whole being of the believer is concentrated in this movement of the pupils. The gesture brings about the believer's presence to God, presents his whole-hearted gift of himself and the plea of his poverty. In personal trials a man's prayer finds expression in a look: Sarah says, "And now, O Lord, to you I turn my face and raise my eyes" (Tob. 3:12; cf. 1 Sam. 21:1), and the psalmist: "To you I lift up my soul, O Lord, my God. . . . My eyes are ever toward the Lord . . . . Look toward me, and have pity on me" (Ps. 25:1–2,15–16); "O my strength! for you I watch" (Ps. 69:10). This "vis-à-vis" is a source of happiness and joy, and the just man's face reflects the light that is in the face of God: "Look to him that you may be radiant with joy, and your faces may not blush with shame" (Ps. 34:6).[16]

In time of pressing need and especially at the solemnities that mark the seasons of Israel's religious life, the believer seeks Yahweh's face, not simply by calling to him or raising hands or eyes to him, but with his whole being. Body and soul alike are caught up in the movement of the eyes, and the petitioner goes on pilgrimage. From the most distant parts, even from the far-off lands of the Diaspora, Israel sets out, braving the strains and dangers of the way. Men thus "ascend" in order to see the face of God in his sanctuary and to ask the aid of his hand: "I lift up my eyes to the mountains; whence shall help come to me?" (Ps. 121:1); "To you I lift up my eyes who are enthroned in heaven. Behold, as the eyes of servants are on the hands of their masters, as the eyes of a maid are on the hands of her mistress, so are our eyes on the Lord, our God, till he have pity on us" (Ps. 123:1–2).[17]

The levite, exiled far from the Temple, recalls these solemn liturgies and yearns to see the face of God again: "As the hind longs for the running waters, so my soul longs for you, O God. Athirst is my soul for God, the living God. When shall I go and behold the face of my God?" (Ps. 42:2–3).[18]

Such an encounter, which is both awe-inspiring and highly personal, brings the believer security and the "salvation of his face" (Ps. 42:6,12, literal translation; cf. 2 Chron. 16:9). But the journey to the sanctuary would have no value if it were not the sign of a sincere and sustained effort to live according to God's will: "Who can ascend the mountain of the Lord? or who may stand in his holy place? He whose hands are sinless, whose heart is clean, who desires not what is vain nor swears deceitfully to his neighbor. . . . Such is the race that seeks for him, that seeks the face of the God of Jacob" (Ps. 24:3–6; cf. Ps. 15).

Let God, then, not hide from his questing servant: "My heart has said of you, 'Seek his face.' Yahweh, I do seek your face, hide not your face from me" (Ps. 27:8–9, JB; cf. 40:17; 69:7). And let the servant, for his part, faithfully remember God and persevere in his moral effort: "Look to the Lord in his strength; seek to serve him constantly. Recall the wondrous deeds that he has wrought, his portents, and the judgments he has uttered" (Ps. 105:4–5 [=1 Chron. 16:10–11]).

Outside the great solemn festivals, each day's awakening brings the believer the grace of a fresh encounter, a new face-to-face meeting with God: "I in justice shall behold your face; on waking, I shall be content in your presence" (Ps. 17:15). In the evening, when daylight fails, the believer turns confidently to the light of God's face: "Let the light of your countenance shine upon me!" (Ps. 4:7).[19]

The "Eclipses" of God's Face

Encounter with God is supreme happiness. If the Israelite is in distress, then, it is because God's favor has been withdrawn from him and God is hiding his face: "When you hid your face I was terrified"

(Ps. 30:3; cf. 119:132), exclaims the psalmist, and Job asks God: "Why do you hide your face and consider me your enemy?" (Job 13:24; cf. Ps. 88:15; 102:3).

This seeming indifference of God before the suffering of his faithful ones emboldens the wicked man who persists in evil: "He says in his heart, 'God has forgotten; he hides his face, he never sees' " (Ps. 10:11; cf. 13:2). But Job, though crushed by adversity, still hopes to see with his own eyes Yahweh taking up his cause and rendering him justice: "This I know: that my Avenger lives, and he, the last, will take his stand on earth. After my awaking, he will set me close to him, and from my flesh I shall look on God. He whom I shall see will take my part: these eyes will gaze on him and find him not aloof" (Job 19:25–27, JB).[20]

Ever since the day when the Spirit of God hovered over the waters (Gen. 1:2) and God communicated his own life-breath to the first man (Gen. 2:7), the divine face has been the source of all life: if it turns away, living things return to nothingness; if it turns back again to creatures, they are rejuvenated: "If you hide your face, they are dismayed; if you take away their breath, they perish and return to their dust. When you send forth your spirit, they are created, and you renew the face of the earth" (Ps. 104:29–30). To die is to be deprived of this life-giving face-to-face relationship and to be no longer able to enjoy God's marvelous presence. The mortally ill king Hezekiah exclaimed in sorrow: "I shall see the Lord no more in the land of the living" (Isa. 38:11; cf. Ps. 27:4,13), and the psalmist prays: "Hasten to answer me, O Lord, for my spirit fails me. Hide not your face from me, lest I become like those who go down into the pit" (Ps. 143:7).[21]

If every blessing comes to the believer from the benevolent face of Yahweh, the same is true for the chosen people during their long history. It was the favorable gaze of God's face, along with the strength of his arm, that settled the ancestors in the Promised Land: "Not with their own sword did they conquer the land, nor did their own arm make them victorious, but it was your arm and your right hand and the light of your countenance, in your love for them" (Ps. 44:4). Conversely, in times of national infidelity, Yahweh turns away from Israel: "I will show them my back, not my face" (Jer. 18:17; cf. Exod. 33:18–23). To that same face the people turn in order to beg for rescue: "If your face shine upon us, then we shall be safe" (Ps.

80:4,8,20).[22] This "dawning" will mean the defeat of the nation's foes: "One look of reproof from you and they will be doomed" (Ps. 80:17, JB). Sometimes the petition takes on an even more urgent tone: "Awake! Why are you asleep, O Lord? Arise! Cast us not off forever! Why do you hide your face, forgetting our woe and our oppression?" (Ps. 44:24–25; cf. 69:18; 89:47; Isa. 8:17).

In more specific terms, Israel often appeals to the divine *gaze*. Let Yahweh deign to cast his eyes on his faithful ones, and by that very act they will receive assurance of salvation. Consequently, the exiles pray: "O Lord, look down from your holy dwelling and take thought of us; turn, O Lord, your ear to hear us. Look directly at us, and behold" (Bar. 2:16; cf. Isa. 63:15; Ps. 84:10; Ecclus. 36:1).[23] The Book of Lamentations echoes them: "Remember, O Lord, what has befallen us, look, and see our disgrace" (Lam. 5:1). But if God has turned his face away in order to punish his people, he will turn it back to them and save them: "In an outburst of wrath, for a moment I hid my face from you; but with enduring love I take pity on you, says the Lord, your redeemer" (Isa. 54:8; cf. Hos. 14:9).

The Most High God does not refuse to look pityingly on the weak and the poor, and the latter are thereby *raised up*, *promoted* to a wholly new dignity:

> High above all nations is the Lord;
> above the heavens is his glory.
> Who is like the Lord, our God, who is enthroned on high
> and looks upon the heavens and the earth below?
> He raises up the lowly from the dust,
> from the dunghill he lifts up the poor
> to seat them with princes,
> with the princes of his own people
> (Ps. 113:4–8; cf. 10:14; 102:18,20–21).

The gracious gaze of God is, in fact, directed to the humble, the "poor of Yahweh," in preference to the proud: "The Lord is exalted, yet the lowly he sees, and the proud he knows from afar" (Ps. 138:6). He himself declares it through Isaiah: "My eyes are drawn to the man of humbled and contrite spirit, who trembles at my word" (Isa. 66:2,JB; cf. 57:15). On the threshold of the new covenant the Virgin Mary, called to become mother of the Messiah, will rejoice in God her

Savior, "for he has looked upon his servant in her lowliness" (Luke 1:48) and thus raised her to high dignity.

This benevolent gaze of God is always the source of his liberating interventions in history. The divine gaze sought out the children of Israel in their distress, in order to save them from Egyptian slavery (Exod. 2:25; 3:7–10). Later on, during the exile, this same God who had turned his face away in punishment, just as he had silenced the prophetic word and withdrawn his hand, would turn his face again to the house of Israel and pour out his spirit upon it: "They transgressed against me, and I hid my face from them. . . . No longer will I hide my face from them, for I have poured out my spirit upon the house of Israel" (Ezek. 39:23,29).[24]

In the last analysis, it is the interior dispositions of man which determine whether the expression on God's face is to be hostile or gracious towards him: "The face of Yahweh frowns on evil men, to wipe their memory from the earth; the eyes of Yahweh are turned towards the virtuous, his ears to their cry" (Ps. 34:16–17, JB).[25] Especially does the turning of the heart, or man's "conversion," move God also to turn, to "convert" himself towards the repentant sinner: "When you turn back to him with all your heart . . . . then he will turn back to you, and no longer hide his face from you" (Tob. 13:6). The Book of Isaiah will therefore describe the liberation of Jerusalem as the recovery of a face-to-face relationship between Yahweh and his people, as an ineffable and blissful exchange of looks: "Listen! Your watchmen raise their voices, they shout for joy together, for they see Yahweh face to face, as he returns to Zion" (Isa. 52:8, JB).

The Temptation of Images

The God of Israel is a "hidden God" (cf. Isa. 45:15). Therefore, as we have already observed, the believer is tempted to draw him out of the shadows and give him a face and a gaze. But images, which soon come to be revered for their own sake, are only appearance without substance, emptiness, nothingness; when they are multiplied, they become a betrayal of the one God.

Prophetic preaching and sapiential teaching were constantly struggling against this temptation to idolatry and denouncing this pitfall which threatened to destroy Israel's fidelity to the one God of the covenant.[26] Thus the Book of Isaiah insists that the Most High is beyond any possible representation of him: "To whom can you liken God? With what equal can you confront him?" (Isa. 40:18); "To whom can you liken me as an equal? says the Holy One" (Isa. 40:25; cf. Acts 17:29).

Isaiah goes on to heap ridicule on the powerlessness of idols, which are, after all, the work of man's hands (cf. 40:19–20; 41:6–7; 44:9–20; cf. Ps. 115:4–7 and 135:15–18). But Jeremiah's satire on the false gods is especially biting: "With nails and hammers they are fastened, that they may not totter. Like a scarecrow in a cucumber field are they, they cannot speak; they must be carried about, for they cannot walk. Fear them not, they can do no harm, neither is it in their power to do good" (Jer. 10:4b–5; cf. 10:1–16; 2:11; Hos. 8:4–7). The Book of Wisdom in its elaborate critique of idolatry uses a series of antitheses to bring out the foolishness of the man who has gone astray into idolatry: "When he prays about his goods or marriage or children, he is not ashamed to address the thing without a soul, and for vigor he invokes the powerless; and for life he entreats the dead; and for aid he beseeches the wholly incompetent, and about travel, something that cannot even walk. And for profit in business and success with his hands he asks facility of a thing with hands completely inert" (Wisd. 13:17–19).[27]

The *non sequiturs* of idolatry are to be explained by idolatry itself. By his fixed gaze man hands himself over to the wretched object he contemplates (Ezek. 20:24; cf. Ps. 119:37; Isa. 57:8), loses himself in it, and becomes like it. *The face-to-face meeting exercises, here as elsewhere, a transformative action.* Idols draw their worshippers to themselves: "Their makers shall be like them, everyone that trusts in them" (Ps. 115:8). The blind idol robs man of his clearsightedness; the senseless idol reduces its worshipper to senselessness: "The whole lot of them are brutish and stupid: the teaching given by these Nothings is void of sense" (Jer. 10:8, JB) and "Vanity they [your fathers] pursued, vanity they became" (Jer. 2:5, JB; cf. 2 Kings 17:15; Rom. 1:21–22). In fact, then, in seeking to provide himself with a visible God, man lost God and lost himself; he sank into the opaque nothingness of a material thing.

On the last day Yahweh will finally manifest himself openly; the assembled nations will see his glory (Isa. 66:18) and flesh will bow down before his face (Isa. 66:23). Through the power of this final theophany the idols will crumble, their falsehoods will be shown in broad daylight, and their disconcerted worshippers will be forced to acknowledge their emptiness: "Great is the Lord and highly to be praised; awesome is he, beyond all gods. For all the gods of the nations are things of naught" (Ps. 96:4–5); "All who worship graven things are put to shame, who glory in the things of naught; all gods are prostrate before him" (Ps. 97:7; cf. Isa. 2:6–22; 45:16).

On the other hand, the whole of nature, which other texts show as stricken with fear before the face of Yahweh, will tremble with joy on the day of the final theophany: "Let the heavens be glad and the earth rejoice; let the sea and what fills it resound; let the plains be joyful and all that is in them! Then shall the trees of the forest exult before the Lord, for he comes; for he comes to rule the earth" (Ps. 96:11–13). But it is, above all, the faithful people that will rejoice before the face of its God, Savior and sovereign Judge: "Light dawns for the just; and gladness, for the upright of heart. Be glad in the Lord, you just, and give thanks to his holy name" (Ps. 97:11–12); "Sing praise to the Lord with the harp . . . . Sing joyfully before the King, the Lord . . . . Before the Lord, for he comes, for he comes to rule the earth; he will rule the world with justice and the peoples with equity" (Ps. 98:5–9).[28]

This supreme moment, when God will finally show his face openly and the peoples will appear before the sovereign judge, will be the "Day" beyond all days, a day of punishment for some and deliverance for others, but for all "the day of God's face" (cf. Ps. 21:10, JB).

If the religious history of Israel is in truth a complicated dialogue of God with his people, and if it can be represented as the dramatic interplay of two hands—God's and man's—seeking each other out, clasping, separating and grasping each other anew, it can also be symbolically expressed as the drama of two faces which ceaselessly call to each other, confront each other, and hide from each other. The Face of God, source of life and salvation, refuses to let itself be seen unveiled and deliberately turns away before the infidelities of the chosen people. It remains the supreme object of desire even as it fills the believer, a creature and a sinner, with fear. This division within the religious consciousness is given clear expression in Psalm 51, the *Miserere*. The same man who prays, "Turn away your face from my sins, and blot out all my guilt" (Ps. 51:11; cf. Ps. 90:8; 130:3) is in haste to beg: "Cast me not out from your presence, and your holy spirit take not from me" (Ps. 51:13).[29] According to the very measure of his faith and his love, the faithful servant of the true God is a man torn by conflict.[30]

Will God forever leave his own a prey to such a painful dilemma? Will he remain, until the Day of his Face, the One who attracts and repels irresistibly? The God whose countenance is at once the unique source of happiness and of the threat of death?

II . THE NEW TESTAMENT

Without profaning his mystery or lessening his transcendence, the Most High God responds to man's desire, to the attraction of his gaze, just as he responds to the call of his voice and the groping of his hand: "The Word became flesh . . . and we have seen his glory" (John 1:14).

The Incarnation, Epiphany of God

Assuredly, God in his divinity and his incommunicable attributes is hidden from our fleshly eyes: "No one has ever seen God" (John 1:18). The king of ages remains invisible (1 Tim. 1:17); he dwells in inaccessible light, and no man has seen him or will see him (1 Tim. 5:16). The believer himself, in the light of faith, can see him only as in a mirror, in a confused and imperfect manner (1 Cor. 13:12; 2 Cor. 5:7). But in Jesus Christ, God assumes and makes fully his own a human nature—and with this nature a visible body; with this body, a face; with this face, eyes; and with these eyes, a gaze. Henceforth man can see the human face, meet the human gaze, of God.

Perhaps it is not wholly impossible to make some approach to the mystery of the divine intention. On the one hand, man, more than any other visible creature, reflects the image and likeness of the Creator (Gen. 1:26–27). Could not a visible manhood, therefore, best serve God's will to reveal himself despite his infinite transcendence? On the other hand, could not a man best show God to men—in the reciprocity of dialogue, of hand, of look, of presence? The best icon of God will always be man.[31]

In Jesus Christ, Son of God and Son of man, God shows himself to mankind with a real face and says: " Here I am!" Not content to have revealed his name to the chosen people, to have challenged them by the voice of the prophets, to have intervened in history by the hand of Moses, of the kings of Israel, and of foreign oppressors and liberators, God now *appears.* By the very fact of a visible body which has been made his own God is henceforth manifested; he comes under the senses of anyone who is prepared to recognize him, gives himself to that person in an *act* of appearing which is inseparable from his being, at once human and divine.

Understanding and faith will never exhaust the consequences of this epiphany, so marvelous and yet so humble. But let us note that in manifesting himself corporally to the world *God affirms his own existence.* If a man by his nature seeks to appear before his fellow men in order to affirm his own reality and if his "existence for others" is connected with his manifestation of himself, then God too takes a body and a face to show that he exists. Through the presence, life, and human activity of Jesus of Nazareth the sovereign and unconditioned existence, life, and activity of God are affirmed to us. The human means of expression have become means of revelation. The "Here I am!" which this human face expresses has become the vehicle of the "I am" which God pronounces concerning himself (Exod. 3:14; John 8:24,28,58; 13:19).[32]

The spontaneous objection of unbelief—God does not exist because no one has ever seen him—is shaken in its foundations. Henceforth God, now manifested in Jesus Christ, possesses full existence for the man who is disposed to believe—not for his mind alone but for his body as well, for his incarnated spirit as such. Here is God freely entering into reciprocity with every man until mankind and history shall have reached completion, a reciprocity belonging to a complete manhood in which every person can see his own image. Henceforth God is a reality set before man through a body, and that symmetrical and reciprocal with his own body; thus God becomes, in a sense, unavoidable. Whoever sees Jesus Christ or hears him spoken of will have to make a choice in his regard. God has acquired citizenship in the world of men by "setting up his tent among us."

This epiphany of God in a human body and with a human face is primary in the sense that it is identical with the birth of Christ itself:

for Christ as for every other man, *to be born* is *to put in an appearance*. The eastern liturgies have a strong sense of this and therefore celebrate the Birth of Christ as the Epiphany of the Incarnate God.[33] This visible manifestation is also, quite naturally, the primary theme of the apostolic preaching; Christ's disciples are those who have seen the Word made flesh and recognized God present in him: "The Word became flesh . . . and we have seen his glory" (John 1:14).

The manhood that God takes to himself in Jesus Christ is not a ghost, an apparition, a diminished reality. Against this temptation to docetism, which made itself felt from the very beginning, the apostle John struggles energetically; his testimony, so often repeated in his Gospel and the epistles is that Jesus Christ "came in the flesh" (John 1:14; 1 John 4:2–3; 2 John 7). Since the body of Jesus is fully real, the "features" and "face" of God are no longer, as in the Old Testament, metaphors calling to mind the being or presence of the invisible God. Here again, *anthropomorphism is eliminated as a stylistic procedure, for it has become a living reality;* it is no longer a pitfall for faith, but its support. Christ's face is truly the human face of God.

The Epiphany of Christ as Act of Witnessing

Like every human face, the face of Christ bears witness. Before witnessing to himself through word and action, Jesus already gives witness through his visible reality as this has appeared in the world. He utters himself, proclaims himself, in his appearing. If the Word could become flesh without derogating from itself, the reason is that the flesh by its nature is a word. This particular humanity is eloquent, it has a meaning which it utters; it is an act of attestation, a continuous, living deposition. The face of Jesus Christ bears witness to God before man and history.

Inevitably, then, this extraordinary witness has always been questioned and challenged. Contemporaries sought to get beyond the empirical identity of Jesus of Nazareth to a deeper identity which many felt to be there. The witness borne by appearance itself operates at two levels in Jesus. On the one hand there is the level of ordinary experience and legal identity: Jesus is the carpenter's son and a descendant of David (Luke 3:23; Mark 6:2–3). But there are other data which force men to penetrate further: "the appealing discourse which came from his lips" (Luke 4:22) and the "signs" that he worked (John 2:11; 3:2; cf. Mark 6:2–3) are an integral part of his self-manifestation and point to a higher, hidden identity. Therefore men observed him intently: when he spoke in public at the synagogue in Nazareth, his fellow-townsmen "had their eyes fixed on him" (Luke 4:20).[34] The Pharisees spy upon him in their eagerness to discover some violation of law or tradition (Luke 14:1). The "Greeks" who came to Jerusalem for the final Passover want "to see Jesus" (John 12:20–21). The debate concerning the real identity of this man who had appeared in first-century Palestine runs through the whole gospel and is one of its main lines of emphasis. To some he is John the Baptist, to others Elijah, Jeremiah, or one of the prophets (Matt. 16:13–14). To Nicodemus, a man of upright and enlightened conscience, Jesus is "a teacher come from God" (John 3:2). In the eyes of the crowd he might be the "Son of David" (Matt. 10:27; 12:23; 20:31), and it is under this messianic title that he is acclaimed when he enters Jerusalem (Matt. 21:9). To those who refuse to believe, he is a tool of the prince of demons (John 10:32) and a blasphemer (John 10:33). To Peter, spokesman for the Twelve and receptive to the light that comes from the Father (Matt. 16:16–17), to Martha (John 11:27), and to many others, Jesus is the Christ, the Son of the living God. He himself claims before Caiphas to be Messiah and Lord (Matt. 26:63–64) and before Pilate to be King of the Jews (John 18:33–37); this latter title, written on the placard on Golgotha, will forever identify this crucified man to history (John 19:19–22). But the debate is not thereby ended, for "the man Jesus Christ" who passed through our visible world at a particular point of space and time will be the object of endless questioning as long as men exist.

Jesus himself has, in fact, put into a few words the whole mysterious power of attestation which his epiphany contains. To the unbelieving Jews he declares: "Whoever puts faith in me believes not so much in me as in him who sent me" (John 12:44). He repeats and develops this striking declaration in his conversation with Thomas and Philip:

> "If you really knew me, you would know my Father also. From this point on you know him, you have seen him." "Lord," Philip said to him, "show us the Father and that will be enough for us."

> "Philip," Jesus replied, "after I have been with you all this time, you still do not know me? Whoever has seen me has seen the Father. How can you say, 'Show us the Father'? Do you not believe that I am in the Father and the Father is in me? . . . . Believe me that I am in the Father and the Father is in me, or else, believe because of the works I do" (John 14:7–11).

Christ here affirms his mysterious identity as the Son who lives in perfect communion of being with God. The meaning of his bodily epiphany is thus very forcefully expressed: to see Jesus is also to see the Father. Through the visibility of the man, God makes his appearance. This fundamental act of bodily epiphany is then confirmed, spelled out in detail, and interpreted by attestations in word and work.[35] But the latter, like all attestation, call upon men's belief, or, in our terms, their faith. Only he who consents to believe interprets correctly the data of his own senses. Only the believer sees the Father in the Son.

The attestation made by the *visible* humanity of Christ is taken up by those who have *seen* it with their own eyes. The witness of the apostles has its origins in the spontaneous experience of their senses and in the meaning which faith discovers there. The "eyewitnesses" become "ministers of the word" (Luke 1:2). After Pentecost the Twelve will offer no other proof of their right to speak than that they had seen and heard Jesus of Nazareth and had "eaten and drunk" with him after his resurrection (Acts 10:39–42; cf. 1:3,8,21–22; 2:32; 3:15; 4:33; 5:32).[36] Even Paul experienced the visible presence of Christ (1 Cor. 15:8; Acts 26:15–16).[37] In Jesus Christ "the mystery of our faith" was manifested in the flesh (1 Tim. 3:16), the gracious favor of God, his goodness and love for men (his "philanthropy") have made their appearance (Tit. 2:11; 3:4; 2 Tim. 1:9–10). The apostle John conveys with incomparable power the reality of this bodily epiphany and its impact in men's perceptual experience. In Jesus Christ, God offered himself to all of man's senses and submitted to their prolonged, attentive examination. Men did more than experience him, they were able to test him: "This is what we proclaim to you: what was from the beginning, what we have heard, what we have seen with our eyes, what we have looked upon and our hands have felt and examined—we speak of the word of life. (This life became visible; we have seen and bear witness to it, and we proclaim to you the eternal life that was present to the Father and became visible to us)" (1 John 1:1–3).[38]

Thus the apostolic testimony prolongs the testimony which the consciousness and the divine, audible, tangible presence of Jesus render to the eternal Word and eternal Life.

The Epiphany of Christ as Revelation of God

In Jesus Christ the human means of expression become God's means of revelation. It is important to insist here on the dialectic of veiling and unveiling which reaches its perfection in the humanity of Christ. Since he is both divine and human, Jesus has the right to let the splendor of the divine glory shine forth in his body; he is, after all, "the reflection of the Father's glory" and "the exact representation of the Father's being" (Heb. 1:3). But, apart from the fleeting moments of his transfiguration before three privileged disciples, Jesus "did not deem equality with God something to be grasped at"; he "emptied" himself by descending to the level of our common human condition (Phil. 2:6–7). Here, then, God is both unveiled and veiled, manifested but still hidden, self-declared yet not forced upon us with a constraining evidence that would suppress the freedom of the act of faith. The humanity of Christ expresses God while preserving his mystery. Revelation here reaches its climax.

We should not conclude, however, that the manhood of Jesus is a mask or caricature behind which God hides his true self. Just as it is not a ghost, a shadow, or a fleeting phantom, so the body of Christ is not an illusory appearance. Plato long ago taught that any falsehood—and, much more, any dissimulation—would be unworthy of the divinity.[39] Above all, the visible appearance of Jesus is not that of a human person who would be manipulated like a double and make a second along with the divine person. On the contrary, the manhood assumed is immediately united to the Word; it subsists only in and through him. Jesus is "someone" only by reason of the person of the Son. In virtue of this "hypostatic" union the visible humanity strictly belongs to God himself, without reservation, detour, or artifice. The bodily epiphany is God's epiphany. The human is not falsified nor the divine mystery betrayed. We may go further and say that the face of Jesus Christ, more than any other face, brings to its perfection the act of sincerity which is inherent in every human face and which in this instance is identical with the act of God revealing. The "Here I am!" of man coincides with the "I am" of God. The appearances are true and Jesus is the Truth, for he is in the Father as the Father is in him (John 14:6,10).[40]

This privileged manhood is thus an authentic sign of God; or, better, the most faithful, available, and meaningful sign of God that can ever be given to the world.[41] Reciprocal with each human being until the end of history, this sign anticipates him, moves him, challenges him. Jesus does not bring to men a rational proof of God's existence but *an affirmation of it in signs:* there must be a God, for he manifests himself to us in bodily form;[42] he must be present to men in the loving gift of himself, for he offers himself to our gaze in the anticipative openness of a face.

Yet there is in this sign a deliberate element of obscurity. Every suspicion of "exhibition" is excluded. If we may so put it, Jesus always refused the limelight, always refused to be the "star" of the moment. Despite the permanent temptation of temporal messianism, he constantly rejected the easy success he might have by bewitching the crowd. At his birth, the evident helplessness of a newborn child is offered as the distinctive sign of the awaited Messiah (Luke 2:12). As he begins his public life, Jesus rejects the flattering suggestions of the Tempter (Matt. 4:1–11) and, soon after, the enthusiams of the crowds (John 6:15)[43] and even the inopportune zeal of his disciples.[44] The messianic entrance into Jerusalem is marked by deliberate humility (Matt. 21:1–11). Finally, the passion will convince those close to the Master that there will be no earthly messianism. For a few hours, the Incarnate Son of God will, as it were, be in the spotlight of shame, "placarded" before the eyes of all (Gal. 3:1). If he had given in to the crowd's hunger for wonders, Jesus would have betrayed the mission given him by the Father (cf. Matt. 20:22; 26:39–42; John 4:34; 5:30; 6:38; 18:11; etc.); he would have ceased to be the authentic Revealer; the man would have become the idol of the mob, been sought out for the temporal advantages he could give and the wonders he could work in the realm of the senses, and would have lost all his import as a sign; reduced to a simple bodily image and emptied of his transcendent meaning, he would in fact have become a "nothing," a figure without depth, a stumbling block for men seeking salvation. When, on the contrary, Christ, the New Israel, wins the victory—in the desert and throughout his life—over that temptation of the image which had so often betrayed the chosen people, he defends in his own person the transcendence of the one true God. The glory which men give is incompatible with the glory which comes from God (John 5:44; 7:18; 8:50,54; 12:43).

The incarnate Word reveals himself, then, only in the shadowy light of an ordinary life and in the ambiguity of signs. The humanity of Jesus shows the ambivalence—or, better, the lack of evidence—characteristic of every human presence. The inner state of a man, his uprightness or duplicity, his constancy or inconstancy—in short, his deeper moral identity—is never given as a clear and indisputable fact. If, then, in giving myself to any human being, I must trust what his face tells me and what his actions and words reveal to me of him, how much more is such an act of free self-surrender required in accepting Jesus as Savior of the world! God's revelation in bodily form can only be accepted in faith. If men are to give the correct answer to Jesus' question: "And you, . . . who do you say that I am?" (Matt. 16:15), they need a light that comes from the Father and is freely accepted. In the judgment he makes, the believer is interpreting the supreme sign which God gives of himself. The gaze of faith ratifies and, as it were, accepts responsibility for the loving gaze which the Father directs to men (John 17:24), for the eternal decree which constitutes the Man-God sole Head of all redeemed creatures (Eph. 1:5–14; Col. 1:15–20; 2:9).

The ambiguity inherent in the sign is thus surmounted but not eliminated; it remains present within the act of faith and the life of faith. On the one hand, the sign calls for faith, arouses it, creates it, and thereafter nourishes it. But on the other hand, this same sign, since it is lacking in the cogency of evidence, constantly puts faith to the test, exposes it to questioning and to the fluctuations of doubt. *Sign that supports, sign that tests:* the life of faith receives its rhythm from this profound dialectic, a kind of vital pulsation that always stimulates it towards new advances. The meaning of the principal sign—the manhood of Jesus—is spelled out in a multiplicity of secondary signs: words, everyday actions, and miracles (which are signs more than they are prodigies) (John 2:11, 18; 4:48; 6:26; 9:16; 11:47; 20:30; cf. Mark 16:17). From the sign given at Bethlehem ("an infant wrapped in swaddling clothes . . . and lying in a manger" [Luke 2:12,16]) to the "sign of Jonas" (Matt. 12:38–40) offered on the morning of the resurrection, the whole bodily epiphany of the Man-God is a call, a support, and a test for the believer. Having thus become a "sign that is opposed" (Luke 2:34), the Nazarene will never cease to create a division among men. It is necessary either to accept or reject the face that God gives himself in Jesus Christ.

Many have seen and have not believed. Others have seen but have believed only after doubting. The belated faith of Thomas is sufficient proof of the living reality of the risen Christ and of the freedom of adherence to him (John 20:24–29). But if man can see Jesus and not believe, once he believes he can see God and not die. The age-old terror of the believer confronted by the divinity is at last dispelled by Jesus Christ. For, in accepting the reciprocity of a human face-to-face meeting, God offers himself to his creature as partner in a dialogue that leads to salvation. It is really God who is seen by the bodily gaze and the gaze of the mind and of faith.[45] Conversely, the human gaze of Jesus Christ is truly the gaze of God himself. The interior light of faith, which is God's gift, allows the believer to recognize God's glory in this meeting of gazes: "For God, who said, 'Let light shine out of darkness,' has shone in our hearts, that we in turn might make known the glory of God shining on the face of Christ" (2 Cor. 4:6).

Idolatry, therefore no longer lies in wait for the believer who wants to look upon an image of his God, for in adoring the humanity of Christ, which is immediately united to the person of the Word, it is that person himself, it is God, to whom our worship is directed.[46] Here the image is not separate from the original; there is no duality of existence between them; the image subsists only in the divine person (Col. 1:15; Heb. 1:1–3).[47] The prayer of Moses, unanswered in former times, now finds its fulfillment. To the moving appeal of the lawgiver, "Show me your glory, I beg you" (Exod. 33:18), comes the response, in the new dispensation, of the apostle John's dazed testimony: "The Word became flesh . . . and we have seen his glory" (John 1:14).

The Epiphany of Christ as Interpretation of Man

If every human individual takes to himself the being of the species and gives it a new expression in a new face, the Man-God in his turn confers on humanity a totally original and unprecedented meaning, one that is strictly supernatural. For his contemporaries, whether disciples or foes, the face of Jesus of Nazareth was the vehicle of a message: his epiphany signified, at the same time, the end of certain religious forms and the coming of a new type of believer of whose piety the Beatitudes are the perfect expression.

The Pauline theme of the new man penetrates more deeply into the gospel message by setting over against the first Adam, who brought sin and death to humanity and tarnished the image of God in man, the last Adam, Christ Jesus. In the second Adam man is re-created and recovers his original integrity (Rom. 5:12–21);[48] "If anyone is in Christ, he is a new creation; the old being has disappeared and a new being is born" (2 Cor. 5:17, translation by the author).

Immersed by baptism into the death of Christ and liberated from sin and the Mosaic law, the Christian is summoned to rise with Christ Jesus to a new life (Rom. 6:4–14), to "put Christ on" more and more (Rom. 13:14; Gal. 3:27; Eph. 4:24), to live by the power of the Spirit as an adoptive child of God (Rom. 8:14–17), and to bear the fruits of holiness for eternal life (Rom. 8:5–13; Gal. 5:19–25). In Jesus Christ there was revealed "that new man created in God's image, whose justice and holiness are born of truth" (Eph. 4:24) and in whom all the barriers that divide men are destroyed (Col. 3:10–11; Gal. 3:27–28; Eph. 2:14–18).

In this way Christ reinterprets man, gives him a new meaning, and prophetically manifests the face of a future mankind as God intends it. Every man who hears the proclamation of salvation is called to rediscover himself and to understand himself in a new way in Christ. "We not only do not know God except through Jesus Christ, but we only know ourselves through Jesus Christ. We only know life and death through Jesus Christ. Except in Jesus Christ, we do not know the meaning of our life or our death, or God or ourselves."[49] The Christian mystery is an *interpretation of man* no less than it is a revelation of God.

In thus making his appearance among men the incarnate Son also reveals various individual men to themselves, as he encounters them during his earthly life.

Like every human gaze, that of Christ is an effective act of presence; it overcomes all distance and effects an encounter. The same gaze which in some circumstances makes Jesus present to God his Father also makes him present to men in an unparalleled act of knowing. According to the evangelists, Jesus enjoyed a privilege which in the Old Testament is reserved to God: for, unlike other men, Christ, when he gazed at men, went beyond appearances and read their hearts, thus penetrating to their innermost hidden attitudes. From a distance he knew Nathaniel and the purity of his conscience (John 1:47–48); after his discourse on the Bread of Life he was "fully aware" of the hostility that his teaching had engendered in some of his hearers (John 6:61). Moreover, "Jesus knew from the start . . . the ones who refused to believe, and the one who would hand him over" (John 6:64, cf. 71; 13:11,27–28; cf. Mark 3:5); he knows that a feeling of rivalry is causing turmoil in his disciples' hearts (Luke 9:46–48), or that they would like to ask him questions (John 16:19,30), and he anticipates these questions. The secrets of men are open to him: he knows the merit of the widow's gift of her mite (Mark 12:41) and proves to the Samaritan woman that he knows her turbulent past (John 4:16–19; cf. Luke 7:47–49).[50] If he knows all his hearers and therefore does not trust himself to them, it is because "he needed no one to give him testimony about human nature. He was well aware of what was in man's heart" (John 2:25). After the resurrection, a repentant Peter acknowledges this perfect knowledge of Christ's and appeals to it for proof of his own sincere love (John 21:17).

The gaze of Christ, then, familiar as he is with the secrets of men's hearts, is especially meaningful; it sometimes expresses reproach, sometimes an appeal, which his word will often make explicit. When faced with the hardening of the Pharisees against him, Jesus looks at them with anger (Mark 3:5). More often he picks out, from among the many people following him about, an individual of good will who is ready to serve the kingdom, and he invites such a man to follow him: Levi in his tax booth, whom he straightway calls and wins over (Mark 2:14; Matt. 9:9), Simon and Andrew (Mark 4:18–20; John 1:42), James and John (Matt. 4:21–22), the rich young man (Mark 10:21, cf. verses 23, 27). The same gaze seeks Peter out after his denial and calls him to conversion: a wordless gaze, to be sure, but one that draws its meaning from Christ's earlier words: "Before the cock crows . . . " (Luke 22:61).[51] Although he has acquired bodily eyes and sees henceforth as men do, God in Jesus Christ does not cease to read the secrets of men's consciences (cf. Job 10:4).

Christ's gaze, then, not only sees a man as he is; it also sees him as he could become. Beyond the present self it sees an ideal self, and discerns the potential of generosity that is latent in the depths of human freedom. By this very fact the prevenient gaze of Christ brings with it a choice, a call, a heightening of dignity; it expresses God's will for man. But what is involved here is not an irresistible ontological decree, an act of predestination that would be destructive of freedom. If Christ can by a gaze exercise power over evil spirits and illness (Luke 9:38), he does not impose his will on man's freedom in the same fashion; in the latter situation he invites and proposes but leaves him "subject to his own free choice" (Ecclus. 15:14). The episode of the rich young man makes this clear.

Finally, it is not only man but history and all creation that receives a new meaning from the gaze of Jesus upon them. Just as, in Christ, God's creative Word "speaks" the world again and his hand "refashions" it, so his gaze "revises" it, correcting the havoc wrought by sin and raising all things to a new level of meaning.

The Transfiguration

The transfiguration is an entirely special episode, without parallel except in the resurrection itself. Before the eyes of three privileged disciples—Peter, James, and John—the humanity of Jesus is "transfigured:" "His face became as dazzling as the sun, his clothes as radiant as light" (Matt. 17:2). Despite the change in the Master's face, the disciples are in no doubt of his identity, as Peter's exclamation shows (Matt. 17:4). The prodigy takes place within the context of the close relationships binding Jesus and his disciples, but it dominates the course of those relationships. The "high mountain" in the wilderness, the dazzling vision, the Father's voice, the luminous cloud, the terror of the witnesses—all are features that evoke the events at Sinai and receive from the latter the greatest part of their religious intelligibility. The *epiphany* here is, in reality, a *theophany*. In it Jesus manifests his divinity: the glory which belongs to him as only Son, which is ordinarily veiled, breaks out at last and spreads throughout his humanity; his physical appearance becomes transparent, revealing his real identity. The disciples have the evidence of their senses that in their daily dealings with the Master, it is God himself at whose side they walk, God himself whose intimacy they share. The confession of the disciples at Caesarea receives its "experimental" confirmation (Matt. 16:16).

The personages of Moses and Elijah do not—if one should dare to put it that way—play the role of theatrical extras, intended to give balance to the composition of the tableau by their harmonious symmetry. The lawgiver and the prophet bring Christ the witness of the old dispensation, recognize him as the one whom the regime of figures and shadows foretold, and before whom the old order must now disappear (1 Cor. 10:6, 11; Heb. 10:1; cf. Heb. 1:2, etc.).[52] But Moses is also present as a man of faith and a friend of God (Exod. 33:11), eager to contemplate his glory. The poignant prayer he addressed to God in former times, "Show me your glory, I beg you" (Exod. 33:18), which had necessarily remained unanswered then, now receives its overwhelming response. God manifests his glory to his servant in the humanity of Jesus. Only in Jesus, the perfect Revealer of the Father, are the eyes of the creature given access to the face of God. Elijah, too, who had only sensed the presence of God on the mountain in the murmuring of a light breeze (1 Kings 19:12–13), shared with Moses the vision of the divine glory "on the face of Christ" (2 Cor. 4:6).

But if it illuminates retrospectively the revelation of the past, the scene at the transfiguration also foretells the future: Christ appears to his own in the condition wherein he will manifest himself on the last day. The writer of the second epistle of Peter is convinced of this as he offers the testimony of the apostles: "It was not any cleverly invented myths that we were repeating when we brought you the knowledge of the power and the coming of our Lord Jesus Christ; we had seen his majesty for ourselves" (2 Pet. 1:16, JB). This theophany, more than any other, has a radically eschatological bearing. Christ is here anticipating for his privileged disciples—and for those who will believe in him on the disciples' word (cf. John 17:20)—the glorious manifestation of his "Day" (1 Cor. 1:8; 3:13).

Thus the witness of which the human face of Jesus is the bearer, the affirmation which his perceptible presence, his words and actions transmit, are converted here into a light given to the senses, to the spirit, and to faith. The "I am" of God radiates in this living manhood. The dilemma of being and appearing, which affects Jesus as it does every man and is productive of confusion in the eyes of others, is finally resolved. Jesus appears for what he is : the Son of God, "the reflection of the Father's glory, the exact representation of the Father's being" (Heb. 1:3). This transfiguration is not a ludicrous or degrading metamorphosis like those which the mythologies conjured up (Peter assures us of this) or a deceptive substitution of persons or an alienation of human nature.[53] The light shining from Jesus' face is no longer, as it was in the case of Moses, a luminous reflection received from the face-to-face meeting with God (Exod. 34:29–30; 2 Cor. 3:7,13); it belongs wholly to Jesus himself. The true being of the Son of God transfigures his human appearance, raising it, without destroying it, to a glorious supernatural condition. For a few fleeting moments the appearance of Christ is changed into his "theandric" reality.

The Disfiguration

The transfiguration occurs, in the accounts of Matthew and Mark, between a formal prediction of the passion and an allusion to the latter (Matt. 16:21–23, and 17:9; Mark 8:31–33, and 9:9–10). The anticipation of glory bridged the abysses of suffering in which the disciples' faith was in danger of foundering. Yet the Book of Isaiah had already described the mysterious humiliations of the Servant of Yahweh, even providing details with regard to the debasing of his physical appearance, his "disfiguration" under the blows received without resistance: "I gave my back to those who beat me, my cheeks to those who plucked my beard; my face I did not shield from buffets and spitting" (Isa. 50:6).

But the Servant "faces" his adversaries—"faces up" to them in the truest sense of the expression—thanks to the support he receives from his God: "The Lord God is my help, therefore I am not disgraced; I have set my face like flint, knowing that I shall not be put to shame" (Isa. 50:7).[54]

The humiliations which the Servant suffers bring him as low as man can be brought: "There was in him no stately bearing to make us look at him, nor appearance that would attract us to him. He was spurned and avoided by men, a man of suffering, accustomed to infirmity, one of those from whom men hide their faces, spurned, and we held him in no esteem" (Isa. 53:2–3).[55]

It is not against the light of an unendurable glory that men veil their faces here, but before an intolerable excess of degradation, like that of the leper.

The early generations of Christians recognized in the passion of Christ, outraged and despised (cf. passion narratives, especially Matt. 26:67–68), the fulfillment of the prophecies concerning the suffering servant (Acts 3:13; 8:32–33). In his proclamation of the abasement of the Son of God, St. Paul avails himself of an early Christian hymn: renouncing the glory which was his by reason of his divine state, he made his own the state of a creature, and "was known to be of human estate, and it was thus that he humbled himself, obediently accepting even death, death on a cross!" (Phil. 2:8).

The sorrowful epiphany of the Son of God does not constitute an alienation of his divine nature or an unthinkable substitution of personality. In his humiliations as in his glorious transfiguration, he remains the Son, and it is precisely this divine identity which confers on his diverse states all their worth. Christ freely surrenders not only the glory of being God but also the glory of being man; he appears "disfigured" ("de-featured"), deprived of that natural beauty which belongs by right to every human being, yet sufficiently recognizable for one to see how far he has fallen. Both his divine and human realities are betrayed by his appearance. Jesus submits to being taken for what he is not, presents himself to the gaze of others as "a worm, not a man; the scorn of men, despised by the people" (Ps. 22:7; cf. Isa. 52:14). He brings upon himself a judgment of scorn and condemnation, for he is regarded as a wrongdoer, "smitten by God and afflicted" (Isa. 53:4). The gaze of men, who see only outward appearances, passes a degrading judgment with regard to his identity; hence the sarcasm: "If you are God's Son!" (Matt. 27:40; cf. Ps. 22:8–9).

This epiphany, mysterious beyond all others and repellent to reason, unquestionably contains inexhaustible depths of meaning for faith. The Crucified is essentially a *sign*, revealing at once God's horror of sin and his passionate love for the sinner. But God is not here manifesting only his presence to all human suffering, even the most excessive—his loving "immanence" to the mystery of suffering. For this same disfigured humanity which reveals God as present to fallen man also reveals him as transcending every created value. By the paradoxical path of negation and total renunciation, the being of God affirms itself as lacking any measure in common with this visible appearance which nonetheless is privileged to reflect the image and likeness of its creator. "Annihilating himself" in Jesus, God shows that the image is nothing in comparison with the model. Thus the disappearance in agony of Christ's manhood subtracts nothing from the being of God, just as his appearance in our common human condition and then in the glory of the transfiguration could neither debase nor enhance the divine majesty.

Here we recognize once again the dialectic of opposites. Presence in the heights and in the depths, mastery of the past as of the future, word and silence, dazzling intervention or seeming impotence in history—in all this, as we have said, God affirms his transcendence. Similarly, by the opposite means of transfiguration and disfiguration God reveals himself as the Wholly Other: he situates himself above and beyond all appearances, whether noble or ignoble, and declares himself inaccessible to any judgment of created eyes or created spirits. In Jesus, who is now exalted and now humiliated, the transcendence of "the Lord of glory" is clearly manifested (1 Cor. 2:8).[56]

The Gaze of Faith

If a man's gaze can express his total gift of himself, it is understandable that the movement of faith should pass over into the movement of the gaze. Making use of the attraction which any object that is held up has for the human eye,[57] Moses, at God's order, had raised up in the wilderness a healing sign for the Israelites, whose numbers had been decimated by serpent bites: whoever had been bitten and turned his gaze to the bronze serpent was cured (Num. 21:4–9). The Book of Wisdom gives an admirable commentary on the incident: this saving sign reminded the faithful of the law of God, and anyone who turned to it was saved, not by the material object itself but by God, the savior of all (Wisd. 16:6–7). Thus, while the gaze fixed on an idol delivers man up to total subjection to the idol, the "conversion" of the eyes to God expresses and effects a conversion of the heart to him (cf. Isa. 17:7–8; Ps. 119:37).[58]

Christ therefore, in predicting his own redemptive crucifixion, presents himself as the saving sign which had been prefigured in the bronze serpent: "Just as Moses lifted up the serpent in the desert, so must the Son of Man be lifted up, that all who believe may have eternal life in him" (John 3:14–15). The turning of the believer's gaze is not formally expressed in this text, but the reference to the bronze serpent clearly implies it. Christ makes it quite evident in the discourse on the bread of life: "Indeed, this is the will of my Father, that everyone who looks upon the Son and believes in him shall have eternal life. Him I will raise up on the last day" (John 6:40).

"To see" Christ, like "to come" to Christ, means "to believe" in him.[59] The movement of the gaze, like that of his steps, carries a man to Jesus in a spiritual act and movement of total surrender. The "pro-cess" of faith and the turning of the heart become real in the turning movement of the body and gaze, as they do in the raising of the hands and arms, in an attentive listening, and in the voice raised in appeal. Thus the apostle John sees in Christ's being raised up on the cross a supreme fulfillment. To him who has predicted: "When you lift up the Son of Man, you will come to realize that I AM" (John 8:28), the eyes of witnesses turn: "The centurion . . . declared, 'Clearly this man was the Son of God!' " (Mark 15:39; cf. Matt. 27:54; Luke 23:47). The prophecy of Zechariah is thus fulfilled: "They shall look on him whom they have thrust through" (Zech. 12:10; John 19:37).

Faith is a gaze directed to the sign which God gives of himself in Jesus Christ, a gaze that discovers and welcomes the salvific meaning of the sign.

The Paschal Epiphany

On the evening of Good Friday, Jesus' mission seemed to have ended in the bitterest of failures. The epiphany of the Messiah, having increased in clarity through the vicissitudes of his obscure role as a workman and then his public life, is now engulfed in death. Here he is, buried, one of those who have "disappeared" and who inexorably withhold themselves from our senses—he who had "appeared" to the hearing, the touch, the sight of men. The stone at the door of the tomb and the seals put on it remain as the pitiful signs of his passage through our sensible world.

The disappearance of the Master destroys his disciples' courage. This visible manhood had been the support of their hope: having ceased to see, they are tempted to cease to believe (cf. Luke 24:19–21).

Yet the holy women go to the tomb expecting the sight of it to speak to them of the dead man; they will put their questions to the monument, call upon the witness of mute matter; their eyes cannot accept no longer seeing, and press their search in spite of it (Matt. 28:1). But the sight of the stone rolled aside, the messenger who proclaims the resurrection, and the place where the body had been laid and which had confined it, casts them into new anxiety. They remain torn between fear and joy as long as the Master has not presented himself to their gaze.

Peter and the disciple whom Jesus loved have an analogous experience. The emptiness of the sepulchre, the winding-sheet on the ground, the cloth which had covered the head rolled up in a place apart—all bear witness that the body had rested there; they give its measure, even if they do not preserve its shape, and serve to underline its absence. Yet of itself this negative and indirect witness is not enough—were it not for the more watchful faith of Peter's companion. A theft of the body is not inconceivable (John 20:3–10).[60]

This negative testimony of things is soon complemented in a positive and irrefutable way: he who had twice "disappeared," first from the society of the living and then from the abode of the dead, has "appeared" in a variety of circumstances and to very diverse witnesses. Here the epiphany regains its full power to convince through evidence that is direct and unequivocal. The Master is living, for men have seen him; he is alive, he has conquered death, because he has shown himself. The "argument" of the empty tomb, questionable in itself, is complemented and acquires its full meaning from that of the apparitions.[61]

It is these events which establish or revive the faith of the dejected disciples, whether on the road to Emmaus or gathered at Jerusalem. Jesus is all at once standing in their midst (Luke 24:36–45),[62] and this sudden appearance, like the earlier one on the lake (Matt. 14:26), stuns them; they believe they are seeing a "spirit." Then the Master reassures them with his voice, offers them his hands and feet to examine, to feel of. He is indeed flesh and bone, he is indeed "himself." It is a sense experience that is likewise "critical," the mutual verification of senses and witness ruling out any illusion. Better still: Jesus asks for something to eat. With a joy that remained hesitant they give him a piece of grilled fish, and he eats it before their eyes (Luke 24:41–43).[63] The belated faith of Thomas and his examination of the wounds of the

Crucified corroborate the fact of the paschal epiphanies and the interpretation given them by the disciples' faith: they have *seen* and *believed* (John 20:8,24–29). Finally, during the forty days of his new presence among his own, Jesus multiplies the sensible proofs of his resurrection: he shares the meals of the disciples and even prepares one with his own hands on the lake shore (John 21:1–14; cf. Acts 1:4). All danger of illusion is removed and all docetism has judgment passed on it.

The essential argument of the disciples, therefore, is always the same: he who had "disappeared" has "appeared" again. So say the holy women to the disciples (Matt. 28:8; Luke 24:9–11; John 20:18), the disciples among themselves (Luke 24:34–35)[64] and especially to Thomas (John 20:25), the Twelve to the crowds on Pentecost, and finally Paul himself, the last ("as one born out of the normal course") to be favored with an appearance of the Master (1 Cor. 15:1–11).[65]

In short, since the decisive proof of the existence of a living man is his "epiphany," his perceptible manifestation to the senses of others, the paschal epiphany of Christ—the fact that he caused himself to be seen by numerous clear-minded and critical witnesses chosen by God (Acts 10:40–42)—provides a solid basis for the faith of the Church. Generations of Christians believe without seeing because others *saw*, *believed*, and *witnessed* (cf. John 20:29–31; 1 John 1:1–3; Luke 1:1–3; 1 Cor. 15:1–8; etc.).[66]

The Disappearance into Glory: the Ascension

On ascension day the paschal epiphany of Christ, having been detailed with a multiplicity of proofs over a period of forty days, comes to an end abruptly. After a final meal taken with his disciples—the sign above all others of his living human reality—Jesus raises himself up while they are looking at him, and a cloud hides him from their eyes (Acts 1:9). The disciples remain standing there confusedly, for they are not sure that the disappearance is final: the Master's humanity, companioned and reciprocal with theirs, is now stealing away from familiar intercourse with them. The mutuality of sensible presence is ruptured. The Eleven have the sensation of losing for a second time the one who, contrary to all expectations, had reappeared on the morning of the resurrection (cf. John 20:9). But two messengers draw the disciples out of their dazed condition, announcing to them the final reappearance of the parousia. Then the disciples begin to understand the significance of the event. The elevation above the earth expresses the fact that Jesus possesses a superterrestrial, superhuman identity, that he is sovereign over the whole extent of the creation. The cloud, evocative of the theophanies—those of Sinai and the transfiguration in particular (Exod. 14:21–22; 19:16; 24:16–18; Matt. 17:5; 24:30; cf. Dan. 7:13)—and the disappearance itself finally show that the Master has passed over to the side of the holy God. This new disappearance is not a descent into the invisibility of nothingness and death, but an ascent to the inaccessible God whom man cannot see. Thus, in concealing himself from their sight, Jesus completes the revelation given in the transfiguration and the resurrection. The glory and the divine power which are fully his by right draw him to the side of the invisible One. The disappearance brings the cycle of epiphanies to a close, but like each of them it again reveals the divinity. Paradoxically, when Christ escapes from the sight of men, his equality with God is manifested and asserted. Peter proclaims it to the crowds at Pentecost. Having raised Jesus from the dead, God has seated him at his right hand as "Lord and Christ"—that is, one in full possession of the divine prerogatives.[67] The disappearance of Jesus completes —that is, brings to an end and perfects—the earlier manifestations and prepares for the supreme manifestation on the last day.[68]

The Epiphany of the Church

Yet the disappearance of Jesus seems to terminate the dispensation—begun at the dawn of history—wherein salvation is always represented by signs. The humanity of the Word, the most intimate and most eloquent sign of salvation that could have been given to man, the one which brought to fulfillment the old order of shadows and prefigurations, has suddenly withdrawn from the world. Doubtless the Eleven had not at once perceived the full significance of this critical instant. But the words of the messengers now awaken in them the memory of the Master's instructions, and especially the echo of his final order to them: "You are to be my witnesses" (Acts 1:8). On the morning of Pentecost, Jesus takes possession of the apostles, of that power of presence and of signification which constitutes their permanent community. Through them the call to salvation becomes audible in as many languages as there are linguistic groups capable of hearing it (Act. 2:4–12). It even becomes visible and tangible in these men of flesh and bone whose boldness compels attention. In Peter's own words, the gift of the spirit is a fact accessible to the senses: through its effects it manifests itself to the eyes and to the hearing of the crowd. [69]

Thus the Church is born as an audible, tangible, visible reality; it presents itself to men's senses and attracts their attentive scrutiny, sometimes hostile and sometimes welcoming. To be born is to appear; the nascent Church manifests itself in a multiform epiphany by the power of the Spirit. The visible Church thus continues the mission of signifying which had been exercised by the humanity of Jesus; the Church receives from this humanity its reason for existence, its meaning and measure, and lends the Lord, now invisible at the Father's right hand, its own visibility. In this way the dispensation marked by a salvation proclaimed through signs continues on until the final, glorious appearance of Christ. He who says: "I am the light of the world" (John 8:12) also says to his followers: "You are the light of the world . . . . Your light must shine before men so that they may see goodness in your acts and give praise to your heavenly Father" (Matt. 5:14–16; cf. 1 Pet. 2:12). If there is question of works, "It is the Father who lives in me, accomplishing his works," says Jesus, and he adds: "The man who has faith in me will do the works I do" (John 14:10–12). There is the same continuity in the ministry of the word: "What I tell you in the darkness, speak in the light. What you hear in private, proclaim from the housetops" (Matt. 10:27); "Go, therefore, and make disciples of all the nations . . . . Teach them to carry out everything I have commanded you" (Matt. 28:19–20). The mission of the visible Church is thus continuous with the mission of the Word made flesh and consists of signifying salvation through sensible means to men endowed with senses. It consists of giving a kind of face to Christ and God. The human means of *expression*, which for Jesus were means of *revelation*, become for the Church and for each Christian the means of *bearing witness.*

The Face-to-Face Relationship of Faith

During the time of witnessing which extends from the Lord's disappearance to his appearance in glory, the face-to-face relationship of disciple and Master continues mysteriously in faith. Assuredly the knowledge of God and his Christ which comes by faith is lamentably deficient: "Now we see indistinctly, as in a mirror" (1 Cor. 13:12), and the life of faith brings painful "nights" which every believer experiences in some degree. The splendor and the suffering of the believer's existence both come from his loving Christ without seeing him (1 Pet. 1:8). Yet the Master had made the strange announcement: "In a short time the world will no longer see me; but you will see me, because I live and you will live" (John 14:19, JB).

In the encounter of faith, despite the frustration of the senses, the believer does in some way "see" his Lord and knows him, through a kind of reciprocity which exists between one living being and another, "with the enlightened eyes of the mind" (Eph. 1:18).[70]

This face-to-face relationship is no less real for being mysterious. It consists in a personal encounter in which the Christian, like Moses of old in his dialogue with God, receives a reflection of the Lord's glory. The face of the believer, which is already by its creation reciprocal with the face of Jesus Christ and in the latter's presents itself in faith like a mirror to reflect the splendor of "the glory of God shining on the face of Christ" (2 Cor. 4:6). There is no need at all for a protective veil: it is with uncovered face that the believer receives and reflects the glory of the Son. And so, since every face-to-face meeting in love, admiration, and adoration has power to transform, the glorified Christ mysteriously transfigures his disciple, producing in the man of faith a likeness to himself: "All of us, gazing on the Lord's glory with unveiled faces, are being transformed from glory to glory into his very image by the Lord who is the Spirit" (2 Cor. 3:18).[71]

The Church therefore keeps its eyes fixed on Jesus, the Head who brings faith to perfection (Heb. 12:2). This wordless face-to-face of *contemplation* is the hidden spring that gives life and strength to Christian witnessing.

The Epiphany of Glory

The manifestation of Christ in the flesh—the epiphany of grace—prepared the way for his manifestation in glory (Tit. 2:11–13). The Lord must manifest himself visibly to all creatures; his humanity must allow his divinity to shine through and reveal its splendor as it did on the day of the tranfiguration. The dilemma of being and appearing in Jesus Christ is surmounted by faith, but painfully and in obscurity; it will at the end be removed in the full light of day. The deeper identity of Jesus will be made manifest: "They will see the Son of Man coming on the clouds of heaven with power and great glory" (Matt. 24:30).[72]

The power inherent in the supreme manifestation of God will, according to the Old Testament, reduce the deceptive appearances of idols to their true nothingness.[73] Paul adds that "the lawless one" must reveal himself first. Then the coming of the Lord will mean a supreme confrontation of the two manifestations, the ultimate and tragic face-to-face encounter of the "son of perdition" and the Son of God. But the very splendor of Christ's coming will crush the Enemy: "Thereupon the lawless one will be revealed, and the Lord Jesus will destroy him with the breath of his mouth and annihilate him by manifesting his own presence" (2 Thess. 2:8). In this way the enterprise begun with the first coming of Christ will be completed, for "it was to destroy the devil's works that the Son of God revealed himself" (1 John 3:8; cf. 3:5). Then, too, there will be punishment for all those "who do not acknowledge God nor heed the good news of our Lord Jesus Christ" (2 Thess. 1:8).[74] Their punishment, and their ruin, will be to exist "apart from the presence of the Lord and the glory of his might" (2 Thess. 1:9).

On the other hand, the agelong desire of those who "have looked for his appearance with eager longing" (2 Tim. 4:8) will be satisfied. Their "blessed hope" will be fulfilled by "the Appearing of the glory of our great God and saviour Christ Jesus" (Tit. 2:13, JB). On that day of "revelation" (apocalypse; cf. Luke 17:30; 1 Cor. 1:7; 2 Thess. 1:7; 1 Pet. 1:5,7,13; 4:13), of "appearing" (epiphany; cf. 1 Tim. 6:14; 2 Tim. 4:8; Tit. 2:13), and of "presence" (parousia; cf. 1 Cor. 15:13; 2 Thess. 2:1),[75] Christ will make himself visible a second time to those who wait for him, and he will give them salvation (Heb. 9:28). This revelation of Christ's glory will bring Christians overflowing joy (1 Pet. 4:13). As they stand before the throne and the Lamb (Rev. 7:9,15), God's chosen ones "shall see him face to face and bear his name on their foreheads" (Rev. 22:4–5).

As long, therefore, as we live in the today of faith, "we see indistinctly, as in a mirror," but when he comes, "we shall see face to face. My knowledge is imperfect now; then I shall know even as I am known" (1 Cor. 13:12). By that very fact the Christian's transformation into the image of his Lord will be completed. While we walk by faith, the mystery of our adoptive sonship remains hidden: "We are God's children now; what we shall later be has not yet come to light" (1 John 3:2). But when the final revelation of God and his Christ comes, the transformative power of the face-to-face relationship will complete our likeness to God and Christ: "We know that when it comes to light we shall be like him, for we shall see him as he is" (1 John 3:2).

Man, who was created in the image of God (Gen. 1:27) but disfigured by sin, is called to be restored in this likeness through Jesus Christ. The Father has predestined us "to share the image of his Son" (Rom. 8:29). It is on the last day that we shall definitively put on "the man from heaven" (1 Cor. 15:49), and this by the power inherent in the glorious appearance of Christ: "Your life is hidden now with Christ in God. When Christ our life appears, then you shall appear with him in glory" (Col. 3:3–4). This supreme manifestation, in which Christ will reveal himself and will reveal man to himself, will transform even the body of the Christian; the body will be rescued from all its wretchedness and will be perfected in its likeness to its Head: "We eagerly await the coming of our Savior, the Lord Jesus Christ. He will give a new form to this lowly body of ours and remake it according to the pattern of his glorified body" (Phil. 3:20–21).

Stephen, the first martyr, provided the Church with the first example of this glorious transformation. At the moment of dying for his witness to Jesus Christ, at the moment when the gaze of faith was about to change into the vision of glory, God seems to have granted his servant an anticipation of the final face-to-face meeting that awaited him: "Stephen . . . filled with the Holy Spirit, looked to the sky above and saw the glory of God and Jesus standing at God's right hand. 'Look!' he exclaimed, 'I see an opening in the sky, and the Son of Man standing at God's right hand' " (Acts 7:55–56). And the transformative power of the vision was already raising the man's appearance to a new and supernatural state: "The members of the Sanhedrin who sat there stared at him intently. Throughout, Stephen's face seemed like that of an angel" (Acts 6:15).

It is for this transforming vision that the gaze of the whole Church is undergoing preparation in the contemplation of faith.[76]

The Visibility of the Envoy

Created as he is in the image and likeness of the Creator, every man bears on his face some reflection of the divine splendor.[77] In the Church, heir to both the visibility and the mission of Jesus Christ, every Christian is sent as a witness and revealer of his Lord. However, those who receive an official mission to proclaim Christ's word and to perform saving actions in his name represent him—that is, are signs of his presence—through special credentials. Through these men—visible, audible, and tangible—who have been constituted ministers of salvation, the faithful can encounter the invisible Savior at work in this place in the world, in this moment of history. The presence of this mortal being here given signifies the presence of the glorified and living Christ who searches men out to save them. In this regard, the account of the cure of the cripple in the Temple, as reported in Acts, is particularly instructive:

> When he saw Peter and John on their way in, he begged them for an alms. Peter fixed his gaze on the man; so did John. "Look at us!" Peter said. The cripple gave them his whole attention, hoping to get something. Then Peter said: "I have neither silver nor gold, but what I have I give you! In the name of Jesus Christ the Nazorean, walk!" Then Peter took him by the right hand and pulled him up. Immediately the beggar's feet and ankles became strong; he jumped up, stood for a moment, then began to walk around. He went into the Temple with them—walking, jumping about, and praising God (Acts 3:3–8).[78]

All the elements of the encounter with Jesus Christ in the person of his envoys are brought together and detailed here: the intense exchange of looks that translates, on one side, the pressing need of the unfortunate man and, on the other, the solicitude of the two apostles in the presence of his suffering; the invocation of the name of Jesus whereby he is proclaimed the true author of the words, the gestures, and the healing which are to follow; the mysterious presence of Christ—apparently absent and invisible but in fact "re-presented" thanks to the apostles, his conscious and free instruments; the word that utters the inconceivable command: "Walk!"; the gesture of Peter's hand which, grasping the hand of the invalid, raises him up and completes the cure. Everything in the apostles' behavior signifies the salvation offered to man by Jesus Christ.

After the death of the last apostle, the whole Church continues to signify the presence of Christ in history. The Church's ministers continue the same ministry of bearing witness by performing sacramental gestures, governing the Christian community, and, especially, by preaching the Word. Such preaching is, of course, not simply to be identified with the Word of God itself. Unlike the prophets and apostles the preachers of today, though aided by Christ, do not have the charism of inspiration. Nonetheless, in setting forth the gospel the shepherds do manifest the prevenient love of God the Savior.

The new visibility that Jesus Christ has through the ministers of his sacraments is of a unique kind, and all false interpretations of it must be avoided. First of all, however great the power of the grace with which God helps his ministers, the human appearance of the latter undergoes no *metamorphosis.*[79] Peter remains Peter; his exterior and his personal identity are unchanged; people recognize him and can put a name to him. In his concern to bring salvation immediately within the comprehension of each individual, God sends Peter as he is to other men as they are. Nor is the personal appearance of the minister to be thought of as a *mask* behind which Christ is present; any mystification of this kind would be beneath the dignity of God. The envoy, moreover, presents himself and speaks and acts, not in his own name but in the name of Christ, and it is in the name of Christ that the believer receives him. Nonetheless the minister must take care that his presence and action are not a *caricature* of God's action; he must deliberately enter through faith into Christ's intentions and make his words, gestures, and attitudes authentically *significative* of the coming salvation. We can see here the urgency of a proper education in the expressive functions: voice, gestures, attitudes, gaze, bearing, "presence."

Is the minister's role reducible to that of a simple *supernumerary*? Not at all. The latter is passive, whereas the minister of Christ, though subordinate to the action of the Lord, is active. The supernumerary is simply a human element in a setting; the minister signifies and carries out the divine intention to save. It is true, of course, that the personal identity of the minister, like that of the supernumerary, is of no significance. Whether Paul, Apollos, Cephas, or someone else performs the outward action (1 Cor. 1:11–16), it is Christ who does the baptizing. Man offers his "ministry," his "service." The "power" belongs to the Lord alone.[80] Yet the minister, unlike the supernumerary, plays an active part in the sacramental gesture with his whole bodily and spiritual being. For the same reason, the ministerial action is not a *mimicry* that would "reproduce" Christ's gestures of institution. Mimicry is only an inefficacious imitation belonging to the realm of play. A sacrament, on the contrary, effects here and now what it signifies.

Neither is the minister an abstract, fleeting *silhouette*, still less an evanescent *shadow*. The Christ who is present in the glory of the Father is not a pure spirit or a phantom-like, insubstantial reality capable of assuming a new appearance in his ministers after the fashion of a ghost or a reincarnated soul. His humanity is no less fully real for being glorified, and it must be represented before living men by other men of flesh and blood. The latter may be sinful, mortal men, but they provide their energy of living presence in order authentically to signify Jesus Christ.

Can the ministers of salvation be considered to be simple *doubles* of the one who commissions them? By no means. Christ does not rob his emissary of his visible appearance, as do the gods of pagan mythology. Any mystification of that kind, even if it were metaphysically conceivable, would be repugnant to divine wisdom, for the minister is a *free* instrument. Finally, the minister is not chosen for his function because of some physical resemblance to the historical Christ, as are the stand-ins used by dictators at times. The minister of word or sacrament is a sign of Christ by his visible presence, his gestures, and his words; these manifest and execute in a way perceptible to the senses the intentions of God the Savior. All that is needed for the reciprocity proper to the saving encounter is the specific human likeness and corporeity shared by Christ, his minister, and the man being called to salvation.

In the sacramental act the ministerial function is not reducible to a simple *embassy*, analogous to that of a diplomat accredited to a foreign government. In the *actual* exercise of his functions, an ambassador acts by himself, to the exclusion of any causality which his own distant government might conceivably exercise *at that moment* through its representative. The sacramental minister, on the contrary, is not an intermediary; he exercises an instrumental causality that is *here and now* subordinate to the causality of the sole Mediator, Jesus Christ. The ministerial act is wholly relative to and dependent on the act of God, and is the execution and manifestation of the latter.[81]

The believer is not being deluded, then, when he seeks in the sacrament not this or that human being but an encounter with Christ who alone saves; the face, the visible appearance, and the presence of the minister are simply half-way houses in the vision of faith.[82]

This is, of course, not to say that all obscurity is thereby dissipated; we are dealing, after all, with a manifestation through signs. If the presence of the envoy makes Christ present to me in a certain fashion, this latter presence is not reached either by the indirect means of a rational demonstration or by a phantasmagoric apparition. The minister does not demonstrate God to me but shows him to me through the exercise of his official function and in a veiled way; he does not prove God but signifies him, offering himself to our senses as a pledge that God is here present and active as savior in human history. Consequently the person, words, and gestures of the minister are always deeply ambiguous. The man I see and hear is not really the person with whom I am engaged in dialogue; the latter is neither visible nor audible. He who speaks to me speaks to me in the name of another, as substitute for him and in his place. He is and yet is not simply himself; the being which is his own now points beyond itself to a transcendent reality. The ambiguity inherent in every sign is carried to the extreme where a man is himself the sign, and it cannot but disturb me to some extent. My attention wanders back and forth between the phenomenality of the individual I see and the salvific meaning of which he is the vehicle. And even when this salvific meaning is to the fore in my mind, the limitations, the abrasive qualities, and even the failings of the man before me may well cloud my vision and produce a feeling of disillusionment. The human sign *supports* and nourishes my faith, but it also *tests* it. The knowledge of which I enjoy a foretaste is wrapped in obscurity; it leads me to hope for a full manifestation—an "apocalypse"—which will be the immediate presence, the definitive "parousia," of Christ.

Besides, make no mistake about this: the ambiguity of his situation is something the minister of God himself is the first to feel. There are times when he finds himself questioning his own position and questioning God with regard to his strange state of life. As envoy of the Other par excellence, he has become to some extent alienated from himself and others. In the words he speaks and in the gestures and actions he performs, he recognizes himself and does not recognize himself. The message he brings to others touches him too, judges and condemns him in his turn. His mission is even for himself the object of faith and a mystery. This is not the morbid experience of a doubleness in the personality; it is the lucidly experienced testing of an extraordinary vocation, sometimes painful and sometimes exalting, which makes a man live two existences in one—or rather, which gives to the unique mystery of personal existence an unparalleled dimension of meaning. The "I" of the man becomes in a sense less than nature, owing to his interior detachment, but greater than nature through the power of God which takes hold of it and "handles" it. Egotism is constantly called to disappear to give place to the power of God. The poignant "confessions" of a Jeremiah, the confidences of a Paul, give insight into this strangest and most profound of all intimacies: that of the "man of God" (cf. Jer. 20:7–18; 2 Cor. 10–13).

The Mediation of the Icon

In its effort to sustain its vision of faith, the Church not only utilizes the support of human signs; it also has recourse to the material icon. Eastern Christians, whose cult of "the holy images" developed over more than a thousand years, acquired very profound spiritual intuitions in this area. During the crisis of the eighth century, the grievance constantly expressed by the iconoclasts was that any representation of the invisible God would lead to idolatry. What iconoclasm involved was a rejection of the decisive advance in revelation accomplished in Jesus Christ and a desire to lead the Christian back to the exclusive worship of the invisible God of the old covenant. John Damascene, therefore, while rejecting any and all representations of the invisible God, justifies the representation of Christ by the fact of the incarnation.[83] The icon, as a theandric image, thus preserves the benefits of Christ's manifestation in the flesh and extends them during the period from the ascension to the parousia. The veneration of the images of the saints is justified in an analogous way.[84]

The image is, in fact, only a sign; it has no stability or power in itself. Entirely relative to the reality represented, and as it were absorbed by it, the icon is a support for the eye and a point of rest for the vision of faith. Cultic veneration transcends the representation to reach the model,[85] rests on the visible sign in order to encounter the invisible reality.

As a consequence, the icon does not attempt to produce any material resemblance—impossible in any case—to the reality portrayed. The holy image is not a photograph—a copy conforming to the model seized in an instant—nor is it even a portrait which would seek to express the balance of qualities in the face that would constitute a norm over the years of its mortal duration. Since it is symbolic, the icon avoids the dangers of naturalism and expressionism, so pernicious in the sphere of sacred art; it brings into representational art a kind of truth which is absolutely new and specific. Stripping the image of man of temporal vicissitudes, of the weight of the physical, and even of the opacity which the flesh in itself always retains, iconography seeks to disclose a face belonging to eternity. The artist surmounts the limitless distance that separates the here-below from the beyond, the mobile present of history from the changeless present of the afterlife. The humanity of the Lord or of the saints then appears as God wills and sees it from before the creation of the world. Beyond the unformed face of childhood, the prophetic face of youth, completed little by little in maturity, old age, and death, there is here revealed the transfigured face which time can touch no longer: an eternal archetype, it is in its origin, in the thought of God, as in its term, beyond the fulfillments belonging to mortal being. Here it seems as if a confluence of the Platonic concept of ideal forms and the Christian faith serves to define a new kind of truth: *eschatological truth.*[86]

When the image of Christ and of the saints is so conceived and executed, this world below is even now open upon eternity. The role of the symbol is in fact to liberate man from the captivity of the senses and the limits of his earthly horizons in order to render the beyond present to him.[87] Thanks to the icon, the glorious realities of the kingdom of God become near at hand and familiar, already given to the vision of the eye and that of faith and hope. The image takes its place in the dispensation of signs which the Church is and helps the believer to "realize" that the kingdom of God is in our midst (Luke 17:21).[88] The transcendent takes its place within the immanence of the world and of history. Conversely, our terrestrial and temporal horizon, newly interpreted, is opened out and enlarged to disclose the vista of future glory.

Thus the dilemma of idol and image that tormented the religious consciousness of Israel is definitively resolved. The idol is wholly material, the icon is spiritualized; the idol satisfies the understanding, the icon constrains the understanding to purify itself; the idol imposes itself by its solidity, the icon tends to exhaust its own materiality; the idol is opaque, the icon is full of light; the idol fixes the religious vision on itself, the icon projects it towards a higher reality; the idol is of the world, the icon is in the world without belonging to it; the idol draws the worshipper to the surface of his own being, the icon calls him to descend further into the depths of his being. A man-made thing, the idol speaks of man to man; closes him in on himself and confines him to immanence. The symbol of a reality revealed by God, the icon leads the believer to renounce himself, sweeps him beyond himself, opens him to the transcendent. The idol is but a vain appearance, empty and full of deceit. The icon unveils in Jesus Christ glorified or in redeemed man their most essential reality, their plenitude, their eternal truth. The idol subjects the divinity to an interpretation which is "reductive" and debasing. The icon exercises an interpretive function which is "restorative" and heightens transcendence.

In short, the dialectic of idol and icon sums up and illustrates the key moments in universal religious history. Paganism is the reign of error, in which the image satisfies the avidity of the eyes but leads the spirit of the believer astray. Under the Mosaic covenant, the idol is denounced and unmasked; man is undeceived; the true God reveals himself but remains, alas, invisible. In Jesus Christ this *true* God, become *visible*, grants the appeal made by both the eyes and the faith of man.

NOTES

1. Xenophanes, in Diels-Kranz, *Die Fragmente der Vorsokratiker*, 5th ed. (Berlin, 1934–38), Vol. 1, ch. 21 (ch. 11[4]) B, Frag. 16.
2. Xenophanes, *ibid.*, Frag. 15.
3. Xenophanes, *ibid.*, Frag. 23.
4. Etymologically, "Peniel" means "face of God."

5. Cf. *The Humanity of Man*, pp. 255–56, "Gazing at Animals."

6. The ensuing verses are a warning against worship of the stars. It is to be noted that Islam has rejected even the representation of the human face.

7. Originally every prophet was called "the seer" (1 Sam. 9:9).

8. Cf. *The Humanity of Man*, pp. 143–46, "Face and Identity."

9. Christian tradition has long been familiar with the question of the "vision" of God which Moses enjoyed; cf., e.g., St. Augustine, *De trinitate*, II, 15–17 (PL 42:861–66); St. Thomas Aquinas, *Summa theologiae*, I, q. 12, a. 11; cf. II-II, q. 175, aa. 3–6.

10. The eschatological manifestation of the sovereign Judge will also make all the cosmic powers tremble (Ps. 96:9–13; 97:1–6; 98:3,7–9).

11. The account of creation is marked by this leitmotif: "God saw how good it was."

12. The eschatological context justifies us in thinking that the time in question is that of divine judgment.

13. Cf. Rudolf Otto, *The Idea of the Holy*, trans. John W. Harvey (New York: Oxford University Press, 1923, 1950).

14. Cf. *The Humanity of Man*, pp. 262 and note 35 and 272–76, "The Enriching Gaze."

15. God's face is the object of man's desire; conversely, the exiled people is as precious to God as the apple of his eye (Ezek. 2:12; cf. Deut. 32:10; Ps. 17:8).

16. Cf. Ps. 16:11: "fullness of joys in our presence [=before your face]"; Ps. 21:7: the messianic king finds happiness and joy "near the face" of Yahweh.

17. This psalm, undoubtedly post-exilic, does not allude to "going up" but it is nonetheless classified as a pilgrimage song.

18. Cf. Ps. 63:2–3 (JB): "God, you are my God, I am seeking you . . . . I long to gaze on you in the sanctuary, and to see your power and your glory."

19. This psalm is read in Compline for Sunday.

20. This solemn text (note the introduction to it in verses 23–24) paves the way for the explicit revelation of bodily resurrection.

21. Cf. Ps. 13:4: "Give light to my eyes that I may not sleep in death." Compare our experience of the death of others, *The Humanity of Man*, pp. 258–59.

22. The Latin liturgy uses this text as a response during the Advent season. Cf. Ps. 25:15: "My eyes are ever toward the Lord, for he will free my feet from the snare."

23. Solomon at the dedication of the Temple had asked: "May your eyes watch night and day over this temple" (1 Kings 8:29).

24. Cf. Ps. 102:17: "When the Lord has rebuilt Zion and appeared in his glory."

25. Cf. St. Bernard, *Sermons on the Song of Songs*, 57:2 (PL 183:1050–51): "God's gaze is, in itself unchanged, but it differs in its effects, for it varies with the merits of those on whom it falls, striking fear into some and bringing others consolation and security." Cf. *Serm.* 74:11 (PL 183:1144).

26. Idolatry is often condemned as prostitution on the part of Israel, the faithless spouse of Yahweh; cf. Isa. 57:6–13; and especially Hos. 1–3. On the idolatrous gaze, cf. *The Humanity of Man*, pp. 253–54 and 263.

27. Cf. also chapters 13–15, where the wise man judges worship of the stars and cosmic powers to be less culpable than worship of man-made idols.

28. The eschatological context justifies us in taking the expression to refer to the face of Yahweh rather than the face of the king; if the psalm is regarded as messianic in its bearing, it is to be applied to Jesus Christ.

29. Note again the connection between the spirit and the face of God.

30. The Christian liturgy expresses both of these components of religious consciousness. Thus the Roman Missal, in the Introit for the Common for the Dedication of a Church, juxtaposes Jacob's frightened exclamation: "How awesome is this shrine! This is nothing else but an abode of God, and that is the gateway to heaven!" (Gen. 28:17), and the ardent cry of the psalmist: "How lovely is your dwelling place, O Lord of hosts! My soul yearns and pines for the courts of the Lord" (Ps. 84:2–3).

31. Cf. Paul Evdokimov, *L'Orthodoxie* (Neuchâtel-Paris: Delachaux et Niestlé, 1965), p. 218. For what follows, cf. *The Humanity of Man*, pp. 225–47, "To Be Visible and Seen."

32. Cf. St. Jerome, *In Matthaeum*, 1:9 (PL 26:57): "The majestic radiance of the hidden divinity, which was reflected even in his human face, had power to draw immediately those who saw it." St. Augustine, *Letter* 140:3,7 (PL 33:140): "He became a man whom men could see, so that, healed by faith, they might afterwards see what they could not see" (trans. Sister Wilfrid Parsons: St. Augustine, *Letters*, vol. 3, Fathers of the Church 20 [New York: Fathers of the Church, Inc., 1953], p. 62).

33. The place which the cultural heritage of the East gives to the dialectic of the visible and invisible (in Platonism, for example) doubtless explains in part the attraction that Eastern Christians feel for the mysteries of light, in which God manifests himself (Epiphany, Transfiguration). But the Roman liturgy, too, in its celebration of the Epiphany on January 6, offers highly meaningful, though virtually untranslatable, formulas; cf., e.g., the Preface: "For your only-begotten Son restored our human nature by the new light of his immortality"; and, even more, the *Communicantes* prayer in the Canon: "Celebrating the most sacred day on which your only-begotten Son, coeternal with you in your glory, visibly appeared in the reality of our mortal flesh."

34. Note the strong intentionality expressed in the participle *atenizontes* (participle "gazing intently at," "fixing the eyes on").

35. Cf. Edmond Barbotin, *Le témoignage spirituel*, pp. 107–11.

36. Cf. Joseph Schmitt, *Jésus ressuscité dans la prédiction apostolique* (Paris: Gabalda, 1949).

37. Cf. Acts 26:15–16: "I am . . . Jesus . . . . I have appeared to you to designate you as my servant and as a witness to what you have seen of me and what you will see of me."

38. The translation in verse 1 has been changed slightly; to translate

epselaphesan simply as "having touched" (instead of "having felt and examined") is to weaken the force of the text. Cf. St. Ignatius of Antioch, *Letter to Polycarp*, 3:2.

39. Plato, *The Republic*, II, 381b–383a.

40. Alluding to the meeting of Jesus and his disciples, Mark 16:12 writes: "He was revealed to them completely changed in appearance." Luke 24:16 says that the disciples' eyes "were restrained from recognizing him." It is a constant fact that after the resurrection the disciples do not immediately recognize Jesus; it takes a word or gesture from him. This is not to say that Christ borrowed a deceptive appearance in order to mislead the disciples. Rather, the new conditions of Jesus' risen life and the disciples' conviction that he was dead and gone forever prevented them for a time from identifying him.

41. The manifestation of God in Jesus Christ is the most perfect of manifestations and the one which every other manifestation either prepares the way for or prolongs. More specifically, any further manifestation of God to men must be related to and judged by this unique epiphany. A supposed private revelation that is incompatible with the manifestation of God in Jesus is null and void for the believer and the Church.

42. Cf. Col. 2:9: "In Christ the fullness of deity resides in bodily form."

43. Jesus imposes silence concerning his miracles (Mark 1:44; 5:43; 7:36; 8:26) and prevents the demons from revealing his identity (Mark 1:25, 34; 3:12).

44. Recall the harsh reprimand to Peter (Matt. 16:23) in the very words used at the temptation (Mark 8:30; 9:9; John 7:3).

45. Cf. *The Humanity of Man*, pp. 279–81, "The Face of the Mediator."

46. Cf. St. Thomas Aquinas, *Summa theologiae*, III, q. 25, a. 2.

47. Cf. St. Thomas Aquinas, *op. cit.*, III, q. 2, a. 6.

48. Cf. Peter Lengsfeld, *Adam et le Christ* (Paris: Aubier, 1970).

49. Pascal, *Pensées*, Fr. 548 (Turnell, Fr. 602, p. 287).

50. Cf. below, pp. 282–84.

51. The gaze is given quite a different meaning in John 19:25–27: seeing, near the cross, Mary and the disciple whom he loved, Jesus entrusts them to each other as adoptive mother and son.

52. Cf. St. Augustine, *Sermo* 79 (PL 38:493): "Elijah and Moses were conversing with him, for the grace brought by the gospel receives testimony from the law and the prophets."

53. Cf. St. Jerome, *Commentary on Matthew*, 3:17 (PL 26:126): "Do not think that Jesus lost his earlier form or features or his genuinely corporeal nature, and acquired a spiritual or ethereal body . . . ; his substance is not lost, but its hidden glory is manifested." Cf. St. Thomas Aquinas, *Summa Theologiae*, III, q. 45, aa. 1 and 2.

54. Cf. Ezek. 3:8–9: Yahweh encourages his prophet: "I will make your face as hard as theirs and your brow as stubborn as theirs, like diamond, harder than flint."

55. Ps. 22, which is messianic in the typical if not in the literal sense,

describes in realistic detail the sufferings of the persecuted just man whose tribulations make a universal liberation possible.

56. We touch here on the foundations of a negative theology.

57. Cf. Matt. 5:14–15: "You are the light of the world. A city on a hill cannot be hidden. Men do not light a lamp and then put it under a bushel basket. They set it on a stand where it gives light to all in the house."

58. Cf. *The Humanity of Man*, p. 279, on the gaze as oblative.

59. "See": cf. also John 5:37–38; 12:45; 14:9; 19:36–37. "Come": cf. John 6:35,37,44–45,68; 14:16; Matt. 11:28; 16:24.

60. Theft of the body was the "official version" of the high priests, the soldiers being suborned with money (Matt. 28:11–15).

61. The preaching of the apostles regards the appearances as of basic importance; cf. Schmitt, *Jésus resuscité dans la prédiction apostolique.*

62. We do not here intend to study in detail all the apparitions of the Risen Christ or their chronology, but simply to offer some examples that will bring out the meaning of these sensible manifestations.

63. Some mss. add: "a piece of honeycomb." Another realistic detail that is added: "taking the remnants, he gave them to them." Cf. below, Chapter 7, "The Paschal Meals." Jesus had promised his followers the joy of this "seeing him again" (John 16:22).

64. Note the force of the adverb *ontos* ("truly," "really"; translated in NAB as "It is true!"), which excludes any subjectivist interpretation.

65. This passage stresses the firmness of the testimonies passed on by tradition, as well as the number of the witnesses and the variety of their circumstances; note also that in this text as in many others the passive verb "was seen" emphasizes the objectivity of the apparition.

66. Cf. Jean Daniélou, *La Résurrection* (Paris: Editions du Seuil, 1969), pp. 39–55.

67. The name "Lord" is proper to God. In Chapter 1, above, pp. 65–66 we studied the "sitting at the right hand" as a concrete and consecrated expression for equality.

68. Cf. St. Ignatius of Antioch, *Letter to the Romans*, 3:3: Christ manifests himself more perfectly now that he has returned to the bosom of the Father.

69. Cf. Acts 2:33: "He first received the promised Holy Spirit from the Father, then poured this Spirit out on us. This is what you now see and hear."

70. According to St. Bernard, *Sermons for the Feast of the Epiphany*, II: 4 (PL 183:149), faith has the eyes of the lynx: "Brothers, I ask you to examine and see how penetrating is the glance of faith. Consider attentively what lyncean eyes it has" (*St. Bernard's Sermons for the Seasons and Principal Feasts of the Year*, trans. a Priest of Mount Melleray [1921–25; reprinted: Westminister, Md.: Newman Press, 1950], II, p. 19). Cf. *Sermons for the Feast of the Ascension*, V:15 (PL 183:322): "They [the apostles] were taught by their faith, now endowed with the faculty of vision, if I may express it so" (*op. cit.*, II, p. 284). On the face-to-face relationship, cf. *The Humanity of Man*, pp. 267–69.

71. St. Thomas Aquinas, *Commentary on II Corinthians*, 3:3 (ed. Vivés, *Opera*, XXI, p. 82), comments on this text by applying his own theory of

knowledge: "Since all knowledge proceeds through an assimilation of the knower to the known, those who see must somehow be transformed into God. If they see perfectly, they are perfectly transformed, as the blessed in heaven are through the union that brings the beatific enjoyment of God; if they see imperfectly, they are imperfectly transformed, as men are on earth though faith." On the use of the veil in the Church, cf. 1 Cor. 11; Tertullian, *De virginibus velandis* (PL 11:935–62); and the studies referred to in *The Humanity of Man*, p. 284, note 38.

72. Note the traditional elements of a theophany.

73. Cf. above, this chapter, "The Temptation of Images."

74. The reference is to pagans and unbelieving Jews.

75. Parousia, in the strict sense, means the official visit of a sovereign.

76. The Christian expectation of the face-to-face encounter with God may be compared with a myth current among the Bantus (Fangs) of South Cameroun. In the beginning men lived in friendship with God. Before going off on a journey from them, God forbade men to bury anyone at all until he should return. His absence was prolonged and men violated the prohibition. When he did return, God was angry; he tore up the tree of eternal youth and withdrew to the west. Ever since, the Bantus of the area have buried their dead with their faces to the west, in expectation that God would finally return and they would again see him face to face. The practice, shared by some Pygmy tribes of the region, testifies to an authentic eschatological hope.

77. For St. Thomas Aquinas it is only by reason of his spirit (*mens*) that man bears the "image" of the Creator, while the body shows a simple "trace" (*vestigium*) of him (*Summa theologiae*, I, q. 3, a. 1, ad 2; q. 93, a. 2; a. 3, ad 2; a. 4, ad 1; aa. 6–7). This kind of exclusivism flows from the Augustinian tradition and is based on an identification of the image and trace with the rational (*op. cit.*, I, q. 33, aa. 2 and 6); it is difficult to harmonize this position with another firmly held Thomist doctrine, the substantial union of soul and body, and what we have here is an example of a tendency towards a kind of Platonic dualism. It is undoubtedly as an intelligent and free being that man is God's image. But ought not this privileged affinity permeate the corporeal being too, since the latter is animated by the *mens*?—Cf. Robert Jevelot, *Image et ressemblance au douzième siècle de saint Anselme à Alain de Lille* (Paris: Letouzey, 1967), I, p. 177.

78. Cf. what was said in Chapters 3 and 4, above, on the minister or servant of God. Cf. Antoine Chavasse, *Eglise et apostolat.* 3rd ed. (Paris: Casterman, 1957), pp. 106–7.

79. Cf. *The Humanity of Man*, pp. 232–33 and 279–81, "The Face of the Mediator."

80. Cf. above, pp. 186–87.

81. Cf. St. Ambrose, *De sacramentis,* 4:4,14 (PL 16:440).

82. Cf. St. Ambrose, *Defense of the Prophet David*, XII: 58 (PL 14:875): "You have shown yourself to me face to face, O Christ; I find you in your sacraments."

83. St. John of Damascus, *First Apology*, 4 (PG 94:1236): "I dare to present the invisible God not as he is in his invisibility but as he is in the visibility he took on for our sake by sharing our flesh and blood. I do not present the invisible divinity but the visible flesh of God. If it is impossible to show the soul, how much more God, who gave the soul its invisibility?" Cf. *op. cit.*, col. 1245.

84. Cf. Paul Evdokimov, *L'Orthodoxie*, pp. 216–38: "Initiation into the world of the icons." In the Christian art of the West, Fra Angelico seems best to have grasped and painted the mystery of the icon.

85. Cf. St. John of Damascus, *De fide orthodoxa*, IV:16 (PG 94:1160); St. Basil the Great, *De Spiritu Sancto*, 18:45 (PG 32:149); *Second Council of Nicaea* (787), sess. 7 (Denz. 600-1 [302]); *Council of Trent* (1563), sess. 25, Decree on Images (*TCT*, pp. 214–15); St. Thomas Aquinas, *Summa theologiae*, II, q. 25, a. 3; q. 8, a. 3, ad 3; II-II, q. 81, a. 3, ad. 3; etc.—Such behavior is the exact opposite of sympathetic magic (cf. *The Humanity of Man*, p. 207), yet the veneration of images is based on the same basic fact as such magic is: the intentionality of signs.

86. Cf. C. Virgil Gheorghiu, *The Twenty-Fifth Hour*, trans. Rita Eldon (Chicago: Regnery, 1950), pp. 6–12.

87. Cf. *The Humanity of Man*, pp. 35–36.

88. A completely "secular" society, that is, one in which God is in no way signified, is on the way to atheism.

PART III

TWO ENCOUNTERS BETWEEN GOD AND MAN

In braving the event and listening to the prophet, the believing Israelite was welcoming God's saving revelation. But it is above all in Jesus Christ that God offers himself to man as the partner in an encounter.

Among the many forms that interpersonal behavior takes, the visit and the meal occupy a privileged place in daily experience as well as in the Bible. Thus the man Jesus approaches the man to be saved in a place, a time, a mode of conduct, and a set of relationships which are all peculiarly rich in meaning. The divine will to share with men is made vividly plain.

CHAPTER 6

THE VISIT OF GOD

During the progress of the redemptive dispensation, God takes the initiative with regard to his creatures by making wholly unmerited advances to them. These "visits" have their point of entry where man is most "himself": in his creaturely nothingness, in the privacy of his distress or his hope, in the midst of his daily rounds and even in his home.[1]

I. THE OLD TESTAMENT

We have already considered the texts on the role of God's word, hand, gaze, and even his face in the work of creation. Taking all these elements and also the logic of anthropological language into account, the reader of the Bible would be justified in regarding the creation as the first "visit" of God to his work. Since this visit is a first and a total act of prevenance and the source of everything that follows, it is not made to already existing human partners but gives the latter to themselves and to God by bringing them into existence.

It is important to note, however, that the biblical vocabulary does not call creation a "visit"; the term usually has other meanings and is used in the perspectives of the history of salvation. But sometimes the verb "to visit" (Hebrew, *paqad)* does express God's concern for his creatures simply as creatures.

For example, material nature receives the beneficent "visit" of God each spring. The marvelous effects of this renewed act of creation are described at length by the psalmist as he thanks God for them. Like an omnipotent husbandman, the Creator traverses the countryside, prepares the earth and waters it with life-giving rain, blesses the seed and even the overflowing gladness of the harvest: "You have visited the land and watered it; greatly have you enriched it. God's watercourses are filled; you have prepared the grain. Thus have you prepared the land: drenching its furrows, breaking up its clods, softening it with showers, blessing its yield. You have crowned the year with your bounty" (Ps. 65:10–12).[2]

As for man, whose minuteness in the midst of the star-studded universe bewilders thought, it is God who by his benevolent will (*paqad;* Vulgate *visitare)* has made him king over this world and over the lower orders of being (Ps. 8:4–9). But it is in other contexts that the word "visit" acquires its full meaning.

Absence and Visit of God

Genesis delights in describing the state of original justice as one of familiarity between man and his creator. Through a totally unmerited favor on God's part, the garden of Eden is a place which man enjoys along with God and in which he is blessed by a continual divine presence that is the source of all his happiness (Gen. 2:4b–25). Sin puts an end to this relationship of trustful friendship and mutual presence. A guilty Adam and Eve run away, putting distance between themselves and God; they hide, remaining in a state of terrified watchfulness. Soon, as they recognize Yahweh's footstep, the man and woman try to hide from their visitor's gaze: "When they heard the sound of the Lord God moving about in the garden at the breezy time of the day, the man and his wife hid themselves from the Lord God among the trees of the garden" (Gen. 3:8).

This withdrawal of the guilty pair is an illustration of the new distance that will henceforth separate man from God: the distance of sin. But the prevenient call of Yahweh bridges the distance: "Where are you?" (Gen. 3:9).[3] Wretched though he is, man is sought out by God's word, his gaze, his presence. This first "visit" ends with the sentence of punishment, as the first pair are ejected from the garden of Eden and the cherubim are stationed to seal off the path to the tree of life (Gen. 3:16–24). The break seems definitive. God has apparently become the *Absent One*, and man's real punishment is this very absence which weakens him and fills him with anguish. Yet, over and above the call to sinful man that reveals God's anxious concern, the predicted defeat of the serpent and the obscure promise of a salvation leave room for hope. But since God has now become the Absent One, he will henceforth manifest himself to man only fleetingly and by way of exception, in the form of the *visit*.[4] In addition, since God remains invisible, he will visit man through *signs*.

God's Visit as Punishment and Favor

According to the Bible, mankind's religious history is marked by visits from God, sometimes in acts of chastisement, sometimes in acts of mercy. At times, even, the same event may have both meanings when viewed from different angles. The divine intention, proximate or remote, is always to offer man some form of salvation. Every especially significant event, then, can and should be regarded as a *visit* of God, even if the texts do not always use the word itself.[5]

Thus the Flood, for example, and the subsequent covenant between God and Noah constitute one of these decisive divine interventions, and represent both punishment and freely given salvation (Gen. 6:5–9:17). In a similar fashion the calling of Abraham and the promise made him are a visit of God. The word is expressly used in the Hebrew text in regard to the unhoped-for fatherhood bestowed on the patriarch: "The Lord took note of [lit.: "visited"] Sarah as he had said he would; he did for her as he had promised. Sarah became pregnant and bore Abraham a son in his old age, at the set time that God had stated" (Gen. 21:1–2).

But the major event out of which the history of God's people proceeds, namely, the Exodus, deserves in a special way to be called a divine "visit." The patriarch Joseph, as he was dying, had already predicted that liberation from Egyptian slavery would come from such a divine action: " 'I am about to die. God will surely take care of [lit.: "visit"] you and lead you out of this land to the land that he promised on oath to Abraham, Isaac and Jacob.' Then, putting the sons of Israel under oath, he continued, 'When God thus takes care of [visits] you, you must bring my bones up with you from this place' " (Gen. 50:24–25).

The call of Moses and the divine manifestation that accompanies it begin the liberating process. Yahweh "has seen" the wretchedness of his people, lent his ear to their outcry, recognized their distress, and resolved to rescue them (Exod.3:7–8). When he comes thus to meet his own people (Exod. 3:18), Yahweh manifests himself first of all to Moses in the burning bush (Exod. 3:1–3) and gives him a mission to Pharaoh and the children of Israel (3:10–22). In view of the latter, God entrusts Moses with the unique word in which his own divine mystery is expressed: the Name, and then with the message of emancipation: "I have visited you and seen all that the Egyptians are doing to you. And so I have resolved to bring you up out of Egypt where you are oppressed, into the land of the Canaanites" (3:16–17,JB).

Against the foreseeable resistance of the king of Egypt, Yahweh "will stretch out his hand" (3:19–20). All the elements of a visit of God within history emerge clearly here: the divine gaze directed to the situation of his people, the resolution to save them, the call to a chosen person, the decisive intervention by the divine word and hand.

We must emphasize the decisive change that this visit produced in the condition of the Hebrews. From slavery they pass over to freedom, from abasement to a wholly new dignity. By an exclusive privilege Israel becomes the chosen people of Yahweh: "When Israel came forth from Egypt, the house of Jacob from a people of alien tongue, Judah became his sanctuary, Israel his domain" (Ps. 114:1–2).[6] By this infinitely powerful visitation Israel is set on its feet, raised from its prostration, and promoted to a new and higher level of existence. Moses recognizes in the events the divine visit that Joseph had foreseen and so he takes with him the patriarch's bones, in order to carry out the oath sworn by his brethren (Exod. 13:19).

The saving visit of God is, however, received in different ways. Some open their hearts to the Word and "passage" of Yahweh, but others reject them, close their hearts, and harden themselves. This diversity of spiritual attitudes determines the meaning that God's visit is to have for each person: favor to some, punishment to others. For Israel the divine intervention is rescue and salvation; and after the event, faith and hope fulfilled are changed into thanksgiving (Exod. 15:1–18). Pharaoh, however, hardens his heart and refuses to listen to God's word as brought by Moses and Aaron. The soberly dramatic account of the plagues of Egypt echoes with the statement of this fact (Exod. 7:13,22; 8:11,15; etc.). Even when, under the impact of the tenth plague, the king lets the Hebrews go, he soon repents of his action and takes off in pursuit of them (Exod. 12:31–36; 14:5–9). The drowning of the Egyptian army in the waters of the Red Sea is the penalty for the sovereign's hardening of his heart (Exod. 14:27–31; cf. 15:1–18; Ps. 78:43–51; 105:23–39; 135:8–9; Wisd. 16–18, *passim).*

During the wandering in the wilderness Israel itself descends to murmuring, as it forgets the saving visitation of Yahweh. At the foot of Sinai, at the time of the episode of the golden calf (Exod. 32:11–35)[7] and on many other occasions (Num. 11; 12; 14; 16), only the intercession of Moses turns God from punishing the people. The psalmist reflects at length on the inconstancy and ingratitude of Israel that changes visits of grace into visits of anger: "How often they rebelled against him in the desert and grieved him in the wilderness! Again and again they tempted God and provoked the Holy One of Israel. They remembered not his hand nor the day he delivered them from the foe" (Ps. 78:40–42).

The prophetic event of the Exodus epitomizes the whole spiritual history of Israel. Israel will never cease to be the object of the divine initiative in the form of beneficent interventions which will constitute the fabric of "sacred" history. The latter is woven of events that follow a pattern: infidelity on the part of the people, divine visit of punishment, pleas to God and conversion, rescuing visit. It would be beyond the scope of our book to analyze this history here, but the earlier chapters have provided enough material for reflection. The hope for salvation is an appeal for God's visit, his word, his hand, his face, and his gaze.

The period of Judges is an excellent illustration of the alternation of visits of punishment and visits of favor. Nor are the Books of Kings lacking in incidents that emphasize the fluctuations with regard to fidelity and infidelity on the part of sovereigns and people and the providential import of the events that ensue.

More than any other events, schism and its consequences were a visitation of chastisement. Hence the psalmist's prayer is an appeal for a divine hearing, for a turning of the divine face towards his people, for a sudden "change of heart" on God's part, for the divine gaze and hand—in short, for a saving visitation of God: "O Shepherd of Israel, hearken. . . . If your face shine upon us, then we shall be safe. . . . Once again, O Lord of hosts, look down from heaven, and see; take care of [visit] this vine, and protect what your right hand has planted. . . . May your help be with the man of your right hand" (Ps. 80:1,4,15–16,18).

Even the supreme test of exile arises from God's intention to save his people. A poem of Isaiah celebrates the return from exile as a new visit by Yahweh (although the word as such does not occur). Through God's liberating action Israel's enemies are punished, Israel experiences a resurgence of vitality, and there is a recurrence of the wonders of the first Exodus: "Be strong, fear not! Here is your God, he comes with vindication; with divine recompense he comes to save you. Then will the eyes of the blind be opened, the ears of the deaf be cleared; then will the lame leap like a stag, then the tongue of the dumb will sing. Streams will burst forth in the desert, and rivers in the steppe" (Isa. 35:4–6).

At a later period, as is seen from the Book of Judith, faith is still being expressed in traditional categories. In time of trial, priests and ministers "cried to the Lord with all their strength to look with favor on [to visit] the whole house of Israel" (Jth. 4:15).

The pagan nations too will be visited by God, just as they will not elude his word, his hand, and his gaze. The benevolent visit of Yahweh to his people often has as its counterpart a visit of punishment to the oppressor nations, as in the model-event of the Exodus. The oracles uttered by Jeremiah against the pagan nations are especially significant. Read, for example, the oracle on Moab which is devasted by various scourges in the year of God's visitation (Jer. 48:44), or Egypt and its mercenaries: "They too turn and flee together, stand not their ground, when the day of their ruin comes upon them, the time of their punishment" (Jer. 46:21; cf. verse 25). Or the oracle on Babylon: "A stray sheep was Israel that lions pursued. . . . Now Nebuchadnezzar of Babylon gnaws her bones. Therefore, thus says the Lord of hosts, the God of Israel: 'I will punish [visit] the king of Babylon and his land, as once I punished the king of Assyria; but I will bring back Israel to her fold' " (Jer. 50:17,19; cf. verse 27). Elsewhere the prophet sums up his accusations in an epithet and repeats the threat: "I am against you, man of insolence, says the Lord God of hosts; for your day has come, the time for me to punish you" (Jer. 50:31). In the process, the idols will not escape: "The days are coming when I will punish [visit] the idols of Babylon; her whole land will be put to shame" (Jer. 51:47).

Later on, Zechariah predicts a visit of God in which the foreign princes will be treated as despotic shepherds and as "he-goats," while Israel remains "the flock" and will be honored: "My anger burns against the shepherds, and I mean to punish the he-goats. Yes, Yahweh (Sabaoth) will take care of his flock (the House of Judah), he will make it his proud steed (in battle)" (Zech. 10:3,JB).

Obviously, then, the afflicted man of faith will ask God to "visit" the pagans! (Ps. 59:6).

While God's visit is concerned primarily with the salvation of the people as a whole, the individual believer is at times visited in his personal life. Sometimes a simple dream will be recognized to be a sign-event and a visit from God (Gen. 20:3; Ecclus. 34:6).[8] Sometimes Yahweh visits a man in hidden places of his conscience and scrutinizes with his gaze the depths of the man's being: "Though you test my heart, searching it in the night, though you try me with fire, you shall find no malice in me" (Ps. 17:3). Thus Job, terrified in the night by dreams and visions which God sends him is aware, to the point of anguish, of the weight of God's gaze which inspects him, each morning "visits" him, and even scrutinizes him at every moment (Job 7:12–21).

The psalmist is confident that God will visit his people and is hopeful that he personally will share the blessings of that coming: "Remember me, O Lord, as you favor your people; visit me with your saving help, that I may see the prosperity of your chosen ones" (Ps. 106:4–5). Thus, with the passage of time, there is an ever deeper sense of the believer's personal relationship to his God. The divine interventions are awaited in vigilant faith, even more than dawn by the night sentry (Ps. 130:5–7; cf. Lam. 3:26).

Parallel to this is a strengthening of the two components of the religious sentiment of which we spoke earlier. Like the word, the hand, and the face of God, his visit is at once longed for and dreaded. Throughout the biblical tradition, the idea of chastisement is closely linked to the term "visit," as it is to the term "Day."[9] But the hope of salvation is not thereby dimmed; on the contrary, it increases in certainty as the history of the chosen people advances. God is the One who will come again, who takes leave of his people after each visit with the words: "Until we meet again!" He is faithful and always returns. This multiplicity of divine visits, made again and again over the course of the centuries, only serves to emphasize the usual absence of God. Thus, through promises which fall due and are kept, even in a way beyond expectation (those especially of the Exodus, the exile, and the return[10]), the hope grows of a final visit, imminent and yet far off: "the Day of the Face of Yahweh" (Ps. 21:10), which will bring eschatological judgment and eschatological salvation.

II. THE NEW TESTAMENT

To prepare for the visit that will bring history to an end, God's loving-kindness takes, in Jesus Christ, an initiative that reason cannot conceive: "the Word became flesh and made his dwelling among us, and we have seen his glory" (John 1:14).

Under the old dispensation, God's visits to his people had their external manifestation in a chosen person or an event—in either case, a means fraught with uncertainty. Under the new covenant, the encounter takes place in Christ. God in person comes close to his people, within the world and history, within the narrow limits of a life: become Emmanuel, he does not confine himself to looking at Job; now he takes to himself Job's suffering flesh, indeed becomes Job. What no human visit can effect is here accomplished: in a marvelous change, God puts himself existentially "in the place" of his creature.

The visit is totally gratuitous on God's part; out of love alone he shares man's existence by "coming" to him.[11] Now from the standpoint of man Jesus sees life as man sees it: rich in promise but limited by death. He enters deliberately into the network of social relationships: in a way no other visitor will ever equal, he makes his own the past, present, and future of his race and of mankind—indeed, the whole human condition. This unique visit is brought to its completion not by a physical presence, invaluable as this might be, but by the gift best fitted to maintaining presence in being: the gift of the body and blood once surrendered and sacrificed, and the gift of the Spirit (John 14:17). Finally, by the limitless power of this salvific visit man is advanced to a wholly new dignity, for the Son raises anyone who receives him to his own likeness and to the status of adoptive son of God.

This divine-human visit, unique in its plan, is carried out in a series of steps which it is important to analyze.

The Beginnings

The decisive visit in which the old and new dispensations are joined is preceded by a series of events which directly prepare for it. God's secret advances to Zachary (Luke 1:5–25) and Mary (Luke 1:26–38) are a prelude to the coming manifestations of the Precursor and the Messiah. The Virgin, chosen to become mother of Jesus, receives him into the intimacy of her faith and of her corporal being itself.[12] These chosen believers know that the promised and awaited Messiah is already here.

Although the "visitation" of Elizabeth by Mary is only an unobtrusive episode, it deserves our sustained attention. Mary's action, while remaining entirely natural, takes on a special meaning from the role of each of these persons in God's plan. The Virgin places herself in the movement of prevenient intentionality of the Savior she is carrying within her. As for Elizabeth, her welcoming of Mary and her faith in the coming Messiah merit for her an instant outpouring of the Spirit; she recognizes Mary as mother of the Messiah and marvels at the divine initiative of love that touches her as well: "Who am I that the mother of my Lord should come to me?" (Luke 1:43).

Mary in turn, under the inspiration of the Spirit, proclaims the goodness of God in her regard and the merciful fidelity to Israel which has prompted the messianic visit now in process of realization: "He has upheld Israel his servant, ever mindful of his mercy" (Luke 1:54). Sharing for some three months the same "here" and "now," the two women live, in the community of faith, the today of God's plan (Luke 1:56).[13]

At the birth of John, his father, Zachary, likewise discovers, by the light of the Holy Spirit, the providential meaning of the event: "Blessed be the Lord the God of Israel because he has visited and ransomed his people" (Luke 1:68). The rest of the canticle unfolds the content of the opening exclamation of thanksgiving. The birth of the

Precursor is the sign of the Messiah's coming, his visit of liberation, his faithful and merciful fulfillment of the prophetic oracles and the oath sworn to Abraham. The child's mission will be to prepare the way for the Lord in men's hearts: "All this is the work of the kindness of our God; he, the dayspring, shall visit us in his mercy" (Luke 1:78). Thus the canticle of Zachary is structured by the grateful acknowledgment of the longed-for visit with which it opens and closes.

That visit itself takes place at first in secret. Following a pattern visible in the Old Testament, the divine intervention is first announced to a few chosen individuals (the shepherds, the magi) before being proclaimed to the people at large. But even at the beginning, the visitor sent by God is a sign that is opposed (Luke 2:34), for some receive the Messiah with faith, but Herod attempts to destroy him (Matt. 2:1–18). Then the cloak of the hidden years is spread over Jesus until the day when he manifests himself to Israel.

The Visit Declared and Accepted

In each situation of his public life, the presence of Jesus with its global intentionality reveals the movement of salvific initiative. God comes to visit man through the design in Christ's human consciousness. This design is particularized in word, gesture, and gaze. It would be fruitful to read all the accounts of the public life within this perspective. The earlier chapters of this book will have provided some elements for reflection along this line. For the moment it is enough to emphasize the benefits of the visit when it is accepted.

In the synagogue of Nazareth, Jesus proclaims the saving purpose of his visit by applying to himself a messianic prophecy of Isaiah (Luke 4:16–21). The fact is that the fulfillment passes quite out of range of the foretelling, for Christ's divinity gives his every action a transcendent significance. All the more evidently, of course, are the benefits deriving from all the visits made and received between men transcended, though they provide a way of approach to the understanding of faith.

In addition to a friendly presence, a visit communicates a word: a message of joy or encouragement or consolation. Christ comes to men in order to proclaim the Good News, and becomes an itinerant visitor. He travels through Galilee and preaches in its synagogues

(Mark 1:14–15,35–39), especially that of Capernaum (John 6:59), and through the region around Lake Tiberias (e.g., Mark 4:1–2). He even preaches in the Temple (John 8:20) and in Samaria (John 4:1–42). His visits to homes (Martha and Mary [Luke 10:38], Simon the leper [Mark 14:3–9]) provide occasions for teaching. In all these encounters Jesus brings to men in their varied situations and needs the Word that enlightens, nourishes, and renews the meaning of life.

These visits are accompanied by gestures and "works" which undoubtedly ease the lot of some individuals but are nonetheless intended primarily as "signs" of the salvation being offered to all. In addition to the miracle at Cana (John 2:1–11), to which we must return, we would call attention especially to the cures Jesus effects. At Capernaum he cures the servant of a centurion who considers himself unworthy of a visit by Jesus to his home (Matt. 8:5–13)[14]; in the synagogue of the same city he liberates a possessed man (Mark 1:23–28; cf. 1:32–34); in another synagogue he cures a man with a withered hand (Mark 3:1–6) or straightens the woman whose disease caused her to stoop (Luke 13:10–13). There are also numerous cures during the journeys to Gennesaret (Mark 6:53–55), in the region of Tyre and Sidon (Mark 7:23–30), in Decapolis (Mark 7:31–37), at Bethsaida (Mark 8:22–26), at Jericho (Mark 10:46), or on the occasion of the visits to homes (the mother-in-law of Peter [Mark 1:29–31] or the man suffering from dropsy, at the home of a leading Pharisee [Luke 14:1–6]). In these situations Jesus shows himself to be the visitor who comes from God to seek out man where he is most himself, in the intimacy of his daily life and his suffering, in order to cure him, raise him up, and restore him fully to his own humanness, to other men, and to God.

The visit to Zacchaeus merits special attention (Luke 19:1–10) for it involves a spiritual conversion instead of a cure of any kind. The wish to see Jesus, which leads the man to climb the sycamore tree, is perhaps more than a simple urge of curiosity. At least we can see that Zacchaeus responds eagerly to the request for hospitality. The visit is doubtless one that increases Zacchaeus' dignity, for he is flattered to receive the Master into his house. But it is also, and more importantly, a visit of conversion. The mere presence of Jesus is a call, and Zacchaeus welcomes Christ into the intimacy of his conscience no less than of his house; he even makes the resolution to share his goods in ways that go beyond the strict requirements of restitution. Finally, it is a visit of salvation, as explicitly said and reinforced by the solemn declaration of Jesus that he "has come to search out and save what was lost" (Luke 19:10).

The power of the divine visit breaks through in the three accounts of persons being brought back to life. We shall consider them in an order useful to our exposition, though Luke presents the first two in a sequence opposite to ours.

At Jairus' request Jesus goes to the home of the family where the little girl has just died (Luke 8:40–42 and 49–50). In this domestic setting in which the child must have been born and grown up, where things and people had been witness to her laughter and play, Jesus' visit takes on a special character of a sharing in the sufferings of others. The child had died only a short time before, and Jesus, defying the ridicule of bystanders, says: "She is asleep" (Luke 8:52). Then comes the gesture of the Master's hand as he grasps the thin little hand of the girl; his command, impossible to resist: "get up," and the inconceivable act of setting her on her feet again (8:54–55). Here the power of restoration that belongs to every consoling visit brings about, by God's power, a return to life.

The young man of Naim has plunged much deeper into death, for he is on the road to the cemetery. A word of consolation to the mother: "Do not cry"; a touch of the hand to the litter; the word of command: "Young man, I bid you get up"—and the dead man sits up and begins to speak (Luke 7:11–15). Beyond the episode itself, it is the whole mission of Jesus that is clarified here. The believing crowd (whose astonished thanksgiving Luke is always alert to note, cf. 5:26; 13:17; 18:43; 19:37–38) glorifies God with the words: "A great prophet has risen among us" and "God has visited his people" (Luke 7:16). The clairvoyance of well-disposed hearts recognizes in Jesus' mission an authentic visit of God the rescuer and savior. Only the *rising up* of someone sent by God (v. 16, *egerthe)* can, by the effect of a mysterious reciprocity, command and effect the *resurrection* of man (v. 14, *egertheti)*.

The sign given at Bethany is a still greater breakthrough of the divine power. When Jesus reaches the home of Mary and Martha, Lazarus has been dead for four days; he is engulfed in the abode of the dead and has even begun to undergo corruption (John 11:39). It is when his friend has reached this extreme point of nothingness that the Master comes to visit him. To console the two sisters, the Visitor tests their faith in the resurrection and strengthens it. Martha recognizes in Jesus the Christ, the Son, he who was to come, the Visitor from God whom the world was awaiting (11:19–27). Sharing the common sorrow, Jesus goes off to the tomb. It is a visit of respect and friendship: though Lazarus is dead he is still worthy of being sought out; he continues to exist for Jesus, as for those close to him, in the order of relationships established by knowledge and love. But Christ does not stop at this entirely human action. To establish the credibility of his mission and his declaration that he is a visitor from God (11:41–42), Jesus calls to Lazarus, and Lazarus gets up out of his tomb. This sign gives rise to faith in numerous witnesses. But what is of importance for our purpose here is to note that the Master fulfills the hidden desire involved in every visit made to the dead. This action of Jesus is more prophetic than any other, for he is pointing forward to the ultimate visit in which God will raise up a new mankind from the dead (Ezek. 37:1–14; cf. Rev. 21:1–8).[15]

In each of these instances, since Jesus exercises his mission by visiting and bearing witness, man is left his full freedom to welcome or reject. When confronted with a divine emissary who comes in the subordinate role of a petitioner, the hearts of men reveal their innermost dispositions. In one and the same movement, a man opens—or closes—to Christ both the spiritual space of his faith and the bodily or domestic space. The Virgin welcomes Jesus into her womb, Simeon receives him in his arms (Luke 2:28), many believers open the door of their homes to him. The Master proclaims that such welcomes have a deeper meaning: "Whoever welcomes me welcomes, not me, but him who sent me" (Mark 9:37; cf. John 13:20, and 12:44). John notes, in addition, the increment of interior life which is the fruit of the visit's acceptance: "Any who did accept him he empowered to become children of God. These are they who believe in his name" (John 1:12).

This mystery of the visit accepted in faith finds its most forceful expression on the day of Jesus' solemn entrance into Jerusalem (Luke 19:28–38). The modest trappings intentionally adopted by the Master; the spontaneous reaction of the crowd with their acclamations to "the son of David" and to him "who comes . . . in the name of the Lord"; finally, the entrance into the Temple, which Mark records

(Mark 11:11)—all these elements give the event a most evident messianic meaning. The simple and upright of heart give solemn recognition to the fact that in Jesus God has visited his people.

The Visit Refused

Some people saw and heard, but did not believe: "To his own he came, yet his own did not accept him" (John 1:11); "The light came into the world, but men loved darkness rather than the light" (John 3:19).

Jesus was born outside the inn and forced into exile by Herod's persecution; all through his public life he meets with hostility from his fellow countrymen. Without reiterating the facts analyzed in earlier chapters, let us note here the importance of certain episodes that are especially rich in meaning.

Luke places at the beginning of the public ministry the solemn and decisive scene of the visit to the synagogue of Nazareth (Luke 4:16–30). When asked to do the reading, the young prophet applies to himself the messianic text from the Book of Isaiah: "The spirit of the Lord is upon me" (Isa. 61:1). In so doing, he was presenting himself as the awaited visitor and loudly claiming for himself the title and mission which were the objects of Israel's age-old faith. Then, aware of the hidden rejection in the hearts of some listeners, Jesus unmasks the unbelief of his fellow townsmen and even of Israel, and praises the good will shown by some Gentiles who were well known to Israelite history. This is too much for the Nazarenes: rejecting this controversial message, they drag the visitor, whom they know only too well, to the brow of the hill, with the intention of hurling him down. The ejection from the city serves as a powerful sign of the hostility of closed wills.

When he is received at table by a Pharisee and is reproached by his host for not observing the ritual ablutions, Jesus forcefully denounces the hypocrisy and the legalism of the Pharisees and their hostility to God's messengers, the prophets and apostles (Luke 11:37–54).

The parable of the homicidal vineyard workers, which Matthew alone records, repeats the same teaching but goes a step further by applying it to Jesus' own mission (Matt 21:33–46). After many servants (the prophets) have been sent to the workers by their master and slain by them, the son himself now comes to visit in person. Far from welcoming such a special visitor, they lay hands on him, eject him from the vineyard, and kill him. The high priests and Pharisees have no trouble in seeing that their own refusal is being condemned, but they only harden themselves in their murderous hatred.

On the eve of his passion Jesus therefore mourns for Jerusalem which has refused the message of messianic peace; war and distruction await her, for she has failed to recognize the moment when she was being visited (Luke 19:41–44). The idea of the visit (*episkope*) is inseparable from the idea of the time *(kairos)* or, more accurately, of the favorable moment determined by God. The time chosen by him is the time for the visit, just as, conversely, the visit is a sign that such a time is at hand (cf. Luke 12:54–56; 2 Cor. 6:2 = Isa. 49:8).[16] The task of a watchful faith is to recognize this unique mystery. Once the visit that is gracious beyond all others has been made to Jerusalem and refused, it will turn against her and become a visit of chastisement. A few days later the visitor from God is led to the gate, banished from the city enclosure, and hurled into the abyss of death.

The Paschal Visits

Though he had to all appearances been reduced to nothingness, Jesus continued to exist for some through their faith, hope, and love. The holy women cannot bring their minds to accept the absence of the deceased. As soon as the law allows it, they come at dawn on the first day of the week to see, or rather to "visit," the tomb (Matt. 28:1),[17] with the intention of embalming the body. He who had visited the dead Lazarus and restored him to his relations now lets himself be visited in his tomb. But lo! The Master comes, still living, to meet his friends; he presents himself to the eyes, the hands, the faith of those who seek him. No longer the visitor but instead the one visited, Jesus gives to the faithful the assurance that a visit to the dead is never fruitless, for it anticipates the definitive encounter of the last day.

The Risen One, who has surrendered himself in response to the call of a few women visitors, becomes a visitor in turn. As he promises, he rises up on many occasions before the eyes of his disciples, out of the fathomless depths of absence which constitute death. Thus the Eleven and their companions are torn by a conflict between fear and joy (cf. e.g., Luke 24:37,41). The unhoped-for visit immediately produces an extraordinary renewal of their vitality. The time of depression yields to an experience of the uttermost intensity—that of hesitation before a reality of surpassing beauty, and then a wordless, overflowing joy. The eternity into which Christ has entered invades the human moment and makes it blessed. Soon these repeated visits have healed doubt and restored faith. It becomes manifest that the absent one of yesterday is always imminent, present in the event and the encounter and giving them a mysterious dimension of depth. Christ can therefore assure his own that he will remain with them until the end of the world (Matt. 28:20).

On the day of the ascension Jesus "goes" to the Father whom, as Son, he had never left (John 14:6; 17:11,13). But he does so in order to send his Spirit. More than any human visitor, the Spirit will enlighten the disciples; he will forever be not only *with* them and *at their side* but *in* them (John 14:16–17).[18]

The Visit during the Time of the Church

The Spirit communicates to the Church the prevenient will of God in quest of men to be saved. The disciples are impelled by an irresistible urge to travel throughout the world, spreading the Good News by way of visit and testimony. The same movement which, seen from God's side, is sending—or mission in the active sense—is mandate and task for the one sent—or mission in the passive sense—when it is seen from man's side. For the one to whom he is sent, it is a visit to be received. The dynamism of the apostolic visit prolongs and particularizes, until the end of time, the mystery of the visit of Christ, who never ceases to come: "As the Father has sent me, so I send you" (John 20:21; cf. 17:18); "He who hears you, hears me. He who rejects you, rejects me" (Luke 10:16).

The missionary visit to the pagan world, the pastoral visit within Christian communities, visits of aid, consolation, or simple presence to all men, are one of the most basic requirements of the Church's mission. In each of these actions the various means of communication complement each other in a single, unified effort to be present so as to give witness to the Savior who comes. If prisoners, the afflicted, the sick, and the aged were no longer to be visited, they and the world would be deprived of a sign of the kingdom to which they have a right.

But what a strange reversal is here: he who visits men through the mediation of his emissaries stands before these emissaries in the person of those to whom they have been sent. Because he fully makes his own the reciprocity between us men, Christ is present in the person of the one visited no less than in the person of the visitor. Consequently, a faith-inspired "going to see" another *promotes* him to a superhuman dignity. On the last day each person will be judged by his readiness to serve every man and the Master himself in this way: "I was . . . sick and you visited me, in prison and you came to see me" (Matt. 25:35,JB).

Such visits are not only acts of assistance; they are acts of worship. The apostle James insists that visiting orphans and widows in their distress is an act of pure and unspoiled religion (James 1:27). In the person of others, each individual can *return* to the Lord the saving visits which the Lord is constantly making to him.

Every man is in fact visited in countless ways during that intermediate period which runs from the ascension to return in glory. By countless secret invitations, which theology calls "actual graces," Christ graciously visits each of his fellow men and solicits a welcome: "Here I stand, knocking at the door. If anyone hears me calling and opens the door, I will enter his house" (Rev.3:20).[19] The individual must recognize such visits of his Lord in the passing moment: "Now is the acceptable time! Now is the day of salvation!" (2 Cor. 6:2). Doesn't the Christian therefore ask God each evening at Compline to visit his house and bring him peace and blessing?[20]

The Visit on the Last Day

If the believer ought to live his life in watchful faith, the reason is that the last visit of the Master will come unexpectedly. With this definitive encounter in mind, Christ uses every kind of pedagogical means to bring home to his disciples the need for vigilance: the parables of the servants who await their master's return (Luke 12:35–40), of the steward (Luke 12:42–48), of the thief in the night (Matt. 24:42–44),[21] of the ten virgins (Matt. 25:1–13); lessons drawn from the story of

Noah (Matt. 24:37–42); explicit and frank exhortations (Luke 21:34–36). In their turn, the apostolic letters give the Christian concrete instructions and practical applications. This vigilance, which is necessary particularly in view of the enterprises of the Enemy that must be resisted (1 Pet. 5:8–9), is to be achieved through moderation and prayer (l Pet. 4:7; Col. 4:2; 1 Thess. 5:6). Moderation keeps the heart free, while prayer is an appeal for God's presence and an anticipation of it. Thus the whole life of the Christian and the Church becomes a vigil: militant, confident, and joyful. Does not the liturgical season of Advent come each year to reawaken and stimulate the watchfulness of faith?

A day will come when the visits of God, multiplied over the course of history, will give way to the definitive visit. That day will be the "Day" beyond all days which will bring the coming of the Son of Man and thus put an end to history.[22] It will be a genuine visit, for the glorious Christ will not be an end-product of historical development but will come to meet his own (Matt. 24:30–31; Acts 1:11; cf. Rev. 1:7; 21:2). It will be a supremely prevenient and gracious visit, for the work of salvation, undertaken out of love alone (John 3:16; Rom. 3:24; Eph. 2:8), will be brought to fulfillment on that day. It will be a visit that will carry to its ultimate consequences the ambiguity which has characterized all the visits made by God in the course of history: for some it will be a visit of chastisement, for others a visit of grace, according to the merits of each person (Matt. 25:31–46). The visit will be a more *revelatory* one than any other, since it will complete the revelation of Christ, of God, and of the redemptive plan.[23] Finally, the visit will begin, for the elect, the face-to-face *vision* which cannot be eclipsed and the definitive *presence*. In short, the visit will be at once *apocalypse*, *vision*, and *parousia* forever.[24]

NOTES

1. The analyses of "at home" that were given in *The Humanity of Man*, pp. 289–98, can also be used to study the theme of "God's house" (temple, church, heavenly dwelling) and even to penetrate more deeply into the meaning of "the keys of the kingdom of heaven" (Matt. 16:19), of "Christ the Door" (John 10:7–9), etc.

2. The remainder of this psalm should be read. On the stirring of creation at God's visit, cf. Ecclus. 16:18–19.

3. On absence, cf. *The Humanity of Man*, pp. 34,258, and 300.

4. Without entering into a philological study, we may recall that the Hebrew Bible expresses the idea of visiting in the verb *paqad* and its derivatives; at times it also uses the verb *baqar* (Ezek. 34:11–12, with the meaning "pass in review"). The LXX and the New Testament use *episkopeisthai* and *episkope*.

5. The believer can say that every event is, in a broader sense, a visit from God, just as he can say that everything is grace, etc.

6. Cf. Jer. 2:3: "Sacred to the Lord was Israel, the first fruits of his harvest."

7. Cf. verse 34 (JB): "on the day of my visitation, I will punish them for their sins."

8. This is the perspective we must adopt if we are to understand, e.g., the dream of Jacob (Gen. 28:16) and, in the New Testament, the dreams of Joseph (Matt. 1:20–24; 2:13–19) and the Magi (Matt. 2:12).

9. The verb *paqad* often has the meaning "to punish." The Vulgate translates it literally as *visitare*, whereas modern versions have "to chastise" or "to punish" (e.g., Exod. 20:5; cf. 32:34; Ps. 89:33; Isa. 10:3,12; 13:11; 24:21; 26:21; 27:1; 29:6; Jer. 6:15 [=8:12]; 14:10; 21:14; Amos 3:2,14; Zeph. 1:9).

10. On the date of the return, cf. Jer. 29:10; cf. 32:5.

11. On the meaning of this "coming," cf. above, Chapter 1, note 23. St. Bernard, *Sermons on the Song of Songs*, 57:1 (PL 183:1050) notes the increasing intimacy of God's visits as we move from the one covenant to the other: "Note the progress of grace and the stages in God's condescension. . . . He comes, hastens, draws near, is present, gazes on, speaks to. . . . He comes in his angels, hastens in the patriarchs, draws near in the prophets, is present in the flesh, gazes on us in his mysteries, speaks to us in the apostles."

12. Cf. St. Leo the Great, *Sermons on the Lord's Birth*, 1:1: "A virgin . . . is chosen to bear the sacred child; she would conceive him in her mind before conceiving him in her body"; cf. St. Augustine, *Sermo* 215:4 (PL 38:1074).

13. Cf. St. Ambrose, *In Lucam*, II:19–29 (PL 15:1640–43); Origen, *Homilae super Lucam*, 7 (PG 13:1817–19); *In Joannem commentarium*, 6:30 (PG 14:286–87).

14. The splendid protest of the centurion: "Sir, I am not worthy to have you under my roof" (verse 8) has become part of the ritual for Eucharistic communion.

15. Cf. *The Humanity of Man*, pp. 307–08.

16. On the connection between the ideas of "Day" or "time" and "visit," cf. also Isa. 10:3; 1 Pet. 2:12. First Peter 5:6 is quite significant here: after the words *en kairo* ("at the appointed time") several Greek mss. add *episkopes* ("of visitation"); the Vulgate follows this reading *(in tempore visitationis)*. Cf. the Johannine idea of the "hour" of Jesus, pp. 107–08.

17. The verb *theorein* means more than the verb *horan* ("to see"); it signifies an act of prolonged looking (inspection, contemplation, etc.).

18. The English translations wrongly render both *meta* and *para* by the one English word "with."

19. St. Bernard, *Sermons on the Song of Songs*, 31:1 (PL 183:940) brings out well the way in which the many visits received in faith are ordered to the visit on the last day: "The Word and Spouse often makes himself known to eager hearts, and in various guises. Why so? Because he cannot yet be seen *as he is*. The final vision is not yet given because the form in which he will then be seen is not yet given to us." Cf. *Serm.* 74:5 (PL 183:1141).

20. Prayer at Compline in the Roman Breviary: "Visit this house, we pray you, Lord."

21. On the visit of the thief and his power to break in, cf. *The Humanity of Man*, p. 310.

22. Cf. above Chapter 2, section 11, "The End of Time."

23. Cf. above Chapter 5, section 17, "The Epiphany of Glory."

24. Cf. *ibid.* and note 75.

CHAPTER 7

THE MEAL OF GOD

The visits of God take on their full meaning in the most social of all activities: the meal. Throughout the history of salvation numerous signs prefigure, promise, and anticipate the definitive communion of the messianic banquet.

I. THE OLD TESTAMENT

The Original Communion and Its Disruption

In the beginning, an untroubled communion with God enabled man in his state of innocence to enjoy an abundance of earthly food. "God also said: 'See, I give you every seed-bearing plant all over the earth and every tree that has seed-bearing fruit on it to be your food' " (Gen. 1:29). More than this, the Creator entrusted to man a food that produced immortality: "Out of the ground the Lord God made various trees grow that were delightful to look at and good for food, with the tree of life in the middle of the garden" (Gen. 2:9).

Because dominion over the earth has been delegated to him, man can take its edible produce wholly to himself by eating. The reservation with respect to the forbidden fruit is the sign of the sovereign dominion of God over all things: "The Lord gave man this order: 'You are free to eat from any of the trees of the garden except the tree of knowledge of good and bad. From that tree you shall not eat; the moment you eat from it, you are surely doomed to die' " (Gen. 2:16–17). At the instigation of the Tempter and in the hope that the forbidden fruit will raise them to an equality with God (Gen. 3:5), the human couple divide and eat the enticing fruit. The image of a fatal act of eating expresses the depth of the evil contained in the act and the inner reality of the downfall it entailed. Sin enters into the very being of the woman and the man like a poisoned food. From now on suffering and death are at work in the tissues of humanity, permanent threats of the disaster that will some day overwhelm mankind.

Furthermore, just as the use of the fruits of the earth had hitherto been a seal on man's communion with God, now the fatal meal breaks that communion; the sentence of excommunication and the rejection from Paradise will simply make it clear that the break has occurred (Gen. 3:19, 23–24). Still more surprising: the sharing of the fruit, far from bringing man and woman into a closer relationship, introduces a seed of division between them, for Adam shifts onto Eve the responsibility for the wrongdoing in which he has in fact taken part. In a dreadful reversal of meaning, the sharing of food has broken the original communion.

The Fall thus reaches to the very life-principle of the human pair. In addition to the disordering of carnal desire and the suffering involved in childbearing (Gen. 3:16), the task of obtaining daily nourishment will scar the body: "To the man he [God] said: 'Because you have listened to your wife and ate from the tree of which I had forbidden you to eat, cursed be the ground because of you! In toil shall you eat its yield all the days of your life. . . . By the sweat of your brow shall you get bread to eat' " (Gen. 3:17–19). Finally, the fiery sword of the cherubim bars man from the path to the tree of life, which had been his pledge of immortality.

Henceforth the dependence of man on the God who nourishes him—a dependence which remains after human toil has done its utmost, after the invention of all those instruments of "progress" still in man's future—will no longer be simply that of the creature on his Creator: it will be also the dependence of the mortal in relation to the Eternal, of the sinner in relation to the Holy One. Hunger and fasting and their opposites, enjoyment and abundance, will consequently have new meanings: punishment, repentance, joy in salvation.

After the Flood, which is a punishment for sin, a new human race will receive even broader powers over the lower orders of creation. In this new dispensation, the prohibition concerning blood will be the sign of the sovereignty of divine power (Gen. 9:1–4).

Passover and Unleavened Bread

When the Hebrews, now summoned to become the people of Yahweh, are leaving Egypt, the meal acquires a new and specific ritual value. Whatever the remote origins of the feasts of Passover and of Unleavened Bread, these become at Yahweh's command a festive communal meal which signifies and effects the unity of the chosen people. The rite is to be celebrated by "the whole assembled community of Israel" (Exod. 12:3,6,47). Furthermore, although the meal is not formally a covenant meal, the celebration of it does have a religious meaning: "it is a passover in honor of Yahweh" (Exod. 12:11,14,JB).

In addition, the blood of the lamb, smeared on the doorposts, will protect the first-born of the Hebrews from divine punishment (Exod. 12:7,12–13,22–28). Once the event itself has occurred, the rite will be celebrated annually as a perpetual memorial of it (Exod. 12:14).

The feast of Unleavened Bread, like the Passover, was connected with the memory of the Exodus. According to a Yahwist tradition, the Hebrews, as they hastened to set out, had no time to let the dough rise and therefore they took unleavened bread with them: food produced by chance that is all the more precious for being acquired on the eve of departure (Exod. 12:33–34).[1]

By means of these annual meal rituals the memory of God's great deeds becomes inscribed in Israel's life. The act of eating here acquires its full meaning, for *by eating the lamb and unleavened bread the chosen people feeds upon the memory of its deliverance*. The people incorporate into themselves the event being celebrated, assimilating it into their very being; they receive it as food for a new life of fidelity to the law of Yahweh (Exod. 12:14,17, 24–27,42; 13:3–10; cf. 13:14–16).

Food in the Desert

During the nomadic years the daily necessity of finding food became for Israel the occasion of a discovery and, for God, of a revelation.

It is in time of privation that men learn the true value of the blessings of daily life and the limitations of their own power. Thus the thirst and fasting which are inescapable in the wilderness make Israel aware of the priceless value of the simplest foods: water and bread. At the bitter springs of Marah (Exod. 15:22–25) and at the encampment of Massah and Meribah (17:1–7), Yahweh intervenes at Moses' prayer to quench the people's thirst. Thus he reveals himself as the All-powerful, as the one who alone can open to his people the springs of life. Moreover, the unbelieving people who asked: "Is the Lord in our midst or not?" (17:7) received the dazzling revelation of his attentive presence.

The desert is the place of hunger as well as of thirst. Hunger leads the people to regret the cooking-pots and the bread which they had enjoyed in Egypt. Murmuring starts against Moses, Aaron, and even Yahweh himself. "Then the Lord said to Moses, 'I will now rain down bread from heaven for you. Each day the people are to go out and gather their daily portion. . . . On the sixth day, however, when they prepare what they bring in, let it be twice as much as they gather on the other days' " (Exod. 16:4–5).

The event confirms the prediction, and Yahweh's hand keeps the promise his word has made (cf. Num. 11:23). In the evening a flight of quail falls into the camp, and next morning manna covers the ground (16:13–14). Any attempt to hoard for the future is useless, for maggots get into the manna and it spoils (16:19–20). Only the extra amount kept in view of the sabbath rest can be preserved, as God had indicated (16:22–25).

The revelatory power attaching to every sharing at table reaches a special intensity in the meals taken in the desert. Always coming to the table famished, Israel discovers its own weakness, its own subjection to death, its radical and constant dependence on Yahweh as giver of food. Prayer must daily be addressed to God for daily bread, as Jesus will later teach his disciples (Matt. 6:11). On the other hand, these meals—so improbable from a purely human standpoint—reveal the beneficent power of God at the service of his people. Moses and Aaron had foretold the providential food in these terms: "At evening you will know that it was the Lord who brought you out of the land of Egypt; and in the morning you will see the glory of the Lord" (Exod. 16:6–7). And God himself had declared to Moses: "In the evening twilight you shall eat flesh, and in the morning you shall have your fill of bread, so that you may know that I am the Lord, your God" (16:12).[2]

Tradition will celebrate this manifestation of God's kindness which can set a table in the wilderness and cover it with bread and wine to fill men to satiety (Ps. 78:17–29; cf. 105:40–41) and even to satisfy the taste of each individual (Wisd.16:20–21). But, necessary as bodily food was, there was another food that God dispensed to his people in the wilderness: the Word which preserves those who believe (Deut. 8:3; Wisd.16:26).

The Covenant Meal

Word and meal: there is an intimate relationship between the two; there is a constant exchange of meaning between them, and therefore they shed light on the account of the making of the covenant.

A unanimous verbal agreement of the people to the law given Moses by God was not enough. Nor was it enough to celebrate holocausts at the foot of the mountain or to sprinkle the people with the blood of the victims (Exod. 24:3–8). The covenant had to be sealed by a sacred meal. "Moses went up with Aaron, Nadob and Abihu, and seventy elders of Israel. They saw the God of Israel. . . . They gazed on God. They ate and drank" (Exod. 24:9–11, JB).[3] The mysterious encounter at table, the sharing of food in the presence of Yahweh, are what seal the covenant. Between the two parties to it an intimate, holy union is established forever. Later on, the setting of loaves before Yahweh, which may be eaten only by Aaron and his sons (loaves called "of the face"; in the Vulgate, loaves "of setting before") will be motivated by the perpetual covenant (Exod 25:30; Lev. 24:5–9).[4]

The Hope of the Messianic Feast

The land once promisesd to Abraham's posterity (Gen. 12:7; 17:8), then to Moses and the Israelites, is described in words indicating abundance: "a good and spacious land, a land flowing with milk and honey" (Exod. 3:8; Deut. 8:7–10; 11:10–17). The scouts whom Moses sends out to reconnoiter Canaan find the wonderful prediction fulfilled (Num. 13:20–27; cf. Jer. 2:7).

It was clear that the messianic age, prefigured by the entrance into Canaan, was represented as a time of abundance as well as of peace. The blessings of the Palestinian earth: cheese, new wine, oil, and honey (Gen. 27:28; Ps. 4:8; 81:17), become symbols of the awaited happiness (Hos. 2:24; Joel 2:19–27; 4:18; Amos 9:13–15). That happiness will be pictured as a lavish banquet at which the friendship of men with each other and with God will be forever sealed. Here is how Isaiah describes the messianic happiness: "On this mountain the Lord of hosts will provide for all peoples a feast of rich food and choice wines, juicy, rich food and pure, choice wines" (25:6).

The table that God thus sets up on Sion recalls the meal that the elders took on Sinai. But, far from being reserved to a few persons in authority, the eschatological banquet is open to all the nations. Moreover, it is specified that the poor will be the privileged guests: "All you who are thirsty, come to the water! You who have no money, come, receive grain and eat. Come, without paying and without cost, drink wine and milk! . . . Heed me, and you shall eat well, you shall delight in rich fare" (Isa. 55:1–2). The psalmist speaks in the same vein: "The lowly shall eat their fill; they who seek the Lord shall praise him" (Ps. 22:27; cf. 132:15).

At the final judgment idolaters will be excluded from the feast; only the faithful servants of God will be admitted to it: "Lo, my servants shall eat, but you shall go hungry; my servants shall drink, but you shall be thirsty; my servants shall rejoice, but you shall be put to shame" (Isa. 65:13).

According to the Book of Proverbs, divine Wisdom even now prepares a feast and invites to her table all who pass by (Prov. 9:1–6); according to Sirach she offers to feed anyone who desires her food (Ecclus. 24:19–21). Finally, the psalmist uses terms borrowed from the celebration of a feast in order to describe the favors which God heaps upon his faithful ones; he thanks Yahweh for being a generous host who anticipates every desire: "You spread the table before me in the sight of my foes; you anoint my head with oil; my cup overflows" (Ps. 23:5).

Such abundance, tasted in the course of daily life, becomes for the believer the promise, pledge, and anticipation of the messianic blessings.

II. THE NEW TESTAMENT

In entering into the human condition, the Son of God takes to himself a fragil body subject to the daily need of food; he knows the ceaseless alternation of hunger and thirst and having a meal. As an infant at the breast and as a child, he lives in total dependence in this respect; later on, he has one of the most human of all experiences: earning his bread by the work of his hands. Thus nourished by the fruits of the earth, Jesus becomes ever more deeply rooted in the soil of Israel and in the world of men.

However, even if Christ unresistingly accepts these daily needs, he issues a solemn challenge, before beginning his public ministry, to the relationship, natural in origin but disordered by egoism, which exists between man and food. His forty-day fast in the wilderness brings out a refusal to focus his life on the blessings of the earth.[5] The fast also expresses his will to assert himself as the true Israel who, far from succumbing to sensual desire, triumphs over it in the name of the whole chosen people. Finally, it expresses his determination to make it clear that, above all earthly food, there is the unconditioned Word of God, which is a far more necessary food for man: "Not on bread alone is man to live, but on every utterance that comes from the mouth of God" (Matt. 4:4).[6]

On another occasion Jesus again challenges the priority given to bodily food. During the journey in Samaria the disciples press him: "Rabbi, eat something," but the Master answers: "I have food to eat of which you do not know. . . . Doing the will of him who sent me and bringing his work to completion is my food" (John 4:31–34). And elsewhere we are told that his eagerness to welcome the crowds and to distribute the Word to them deprives Christ even of the time needed for eating, so that people around him said: "He is out of his mind" (Mark 3:20–21).

Meal and Revelation

Now that he has come to visit mankind and is fully involved in the play of interpersonal relations, the Son of God seems to show a kind of predilection for the human action par excellence: the meal. Thus, through the prevenient movement of word, hand, and face, Christ encounters man in the place and time of his authentically social experience.

In the sharing of food, nearness to others and close dependence go together. The dependence is especially felt in certain circumstances. At the well of Jacob, for example, Christ does not hesitate to ask the Samaritan woman for a drink as he waits for the disciples, who have gone off to look for food in the village (John 4:7–8); on the occasion of a crossing over the lake, he is deprived of food because the disciples have forgotten to bring it (Matt. 16:5); in ordinary circumstances he is dependent on the good or bad will of a Judas (cf. John 13:28–29). At the cost, then, of such renunciations as these, the daily sharing of food strengthens the community which exists between the Master and the disciples; it tightens the bonds of friendship and love with a view to the common task.

On the other hand, food provides Christ with the occasion for proclaiming the Good News. This is the case with the various situations just described. At Shechem his own thirst provided Jesus with an opportunity for speaking of the living water (John 4:1–14). When it is discovered that the disciples have forgotten the loaves which will be needed on the voyage across the lake, on which they have already embarked, the Master takes advantage of the situation to put them on guard against the "yeast" (that is, the doctrine) of the Pharisees and Sadducees (Matt. 16:5–12).

Christ makes practice of using the community which comes into existence around a table and the customs of the table as the occasion for teaching, and this in a very decisive way. In the human space created by the guests at table, where mutual presence reaches a special intensity, the actions and gestures of the Master take on exceptional implications. When he is invited to dine at a Pharisee's table, the customary ablutions, which the invited guest has failed to practice, provide a point of departure for a lesson in morality: true purity is internal, not external (Luke 11:37–44). When it comes to the choice of a place at table, the human prudence which suggests that a man take the last place for himself is transposed into a saying of humility: "Everyone who exalts himself shall be humbled and he who humbles himself shall be exalted" (Luke 14:11). The choice of guests, too, should be made in a completely disinterested fashion: to the relatives and the rich people who can return the favor, a man should prefer "beggars and the crippled, the lame and the blind," who cannot return it (Luke 14:12–14). On another occasion, the parable of the evil rich man and poor Lazarus bases itself on the universal experience of meals in order to inculcate the fundamental law that is to determine the new relationships between men: the law of sharing (Luke 16:11–31). Finally, at the Last Supper, the custom of having a servant wash the feet of the guests becomes for the Master a means of teaching a practical lesson—and what a moving one!—on the duty of the most humble mutual service (John 13:1–17).

We have noted elsewhere[7] how a shared meal favors self-manifestation. This natural means of expression becomes for Christ a means of revelation.

The wedding feast at Cana becomes especially important because it occurs at the beginning of the public ministry. On such a festive and joyous occasion[8] the attitudes which each person adopts are particularly revelatory. The changing of water into wine is undoubtedly, for Jesus, a way of relieving his hosts of embarrassment. But we nonetheless put the primary stress (without prejudice to the variety of other useful remarks that would be inopportune here) on the deeper meaning which the evangelist sees in the incident: "Jesus performed this first of his signs at Cana in Galilee. Thus did he reveal his glory, and his disciples believed in him" (John 2:11).

Thus it is within the community established around a table, in the course of a wedding banquet (similar to the awaited messianic feast: cf. Luke 14:15–24; Matt. 9:14–15; 22:1–14), that the Messiah works his first "sign." His Glory, the incommunicable property of the divinity, is unveiled and declared. With an unexpected gesture this extraordinary guest manifests (verse 11: *ephanerosen)* the mystery which is in him. His fellow guests whose hearts are disposed for faith interpret his action as a "sign"; they recognize the divinity of this man who shares the joy of the banquet with them. On this occasion the revelatory power attaching to the meal and the table reach a climax.[9]

The invitation to Levi's house has a different meaning (Luke 5:29–32). The former tax-collector, now a disciple, offers Jesus a great banquet in his home. The Master unhesitatingly accepts a familiarity which is straightway suspect in the eyes of the Pharisees (5:30). Even to enter the house of a pagan (given the significance of "at home")[10] constituted a legal impurity (cf. John 18:28–29,33–38); in a similar fashion, to sit at table with tax-collectors and sinners was regarded as a sign of complicity in the evil they did, or at least of culpable tolerance! Scribes and Pharisees therefore ask reproachful questions of the disciples. Then, following a familiar pattern, the Master answers a question which they dare not address directly to him: "The healthy do not need a doctor; sick people do. I have not come to invite the self-righteous to a change of heart, but sinners" (Luke 5:31–32).[11]

To sinners, then—that is, those who are spiritually sick—the presence of the Savior, his remarks and looks, the meal shared with him, all are a call to an inner change of personal existence. His nearness is a spiritual remedy and an elevation to a new spiritual dignity. Far from being an act of complicity with evil, Christ's intimacy with the guests is intended to bring them to a communion in what is good. Because of Jesus' own holiness, the community around the table undergoes a radical change of meaning.

Although the account of the vist to Zacchaeus makes no mention of a meal, we can hardly doubt the hospitality offered was complete. Moreover, the scandal given the Pharisees suggests it. Here, once again, intimacy with Jesus has its salvific effects of revelation, spiritual advancement, and spiritual communion.

The meal at the house of Simon the Pharisee presents a situation the opposite of the two we have been describing. The host is not a tax-collector but someone who is "pure." Jesus does not refuse to enter and take a place at table (Luke 7:36–50). But presently a sinful woman intrudes herself upon the room, and the network of personal relations—the dynamics of the group— are immediately altered. The attention of the guests is concentrated on Jesus and the woman, as protagonists, and on Simon as witness and judge of what goes on in his house. In the Pharisee's view, the Master's acceptance of the woman's approach—her tears, her ointment poured out on him—constitutes an unclean contact. Jesus, who seems to be ignorant of the woman's identity, cannot be a prophet! The Master responds to these hidden thoughts with the parable of the two debtors who are freed of their unequal debts: he who testifies to the greater love for the generous creditor is, on the evidence, the one who experiences a greater liberation. Applying the parable to the present situation,

Christ stresses the marks of love which have been shown to him by the sinful woman and which, according to contemporary custom, should have been shown to him by Simon himself. To this lesson on hospitality Jesus adds another. Since the love shown is in the measure of the grace received, the woman can be assured that "her many sins are forgiven—because of her great love" (7:47). This lets the hearers understand that Simon, who has shown but little eagerness, is still heavily in debt. Then Jesus gives the woman a direct confirmation: "Your sins are forgiven" (7:48), and leaves the other guests to ask themselves: "Who is this that he even forgives sin?" (7:49).

Without dealing with the exegetical problems to which this text has given rise, we may note how the virtues belonging to the community of the table are exercised here.

There is a strange reversal in the whole situation, for none of the three main characters leaves the table with the same moral identity that had earlier been ascribed to him. Simon is no longer irreproachable in regard to hospitality or, above all, in regard to God. By failing to welcome Jesus as he should, the Pharisee has been guilty of a lack of love which gives evidence of an unconverted heart. Behind the outward appearances of strict fidelity, one has an inkling of a conscience that is perhaps heavily burdened. A hitherto unknown moral state is revealed, and a call to genuine conversion is issued.

The spiritual identity of the woman, too, is unveiled. For the unqualified judgment passed on her by public opinion and repeated in his heart by Simon: "a sinful woman!" Jesus substitutes another which reaches into the depths of her being. The visitor is in reality a penitent who has been wholly forgiven and is all the more loving because of that; she is a new soul. The Master's words: "Your sins are forgiven. . . . Your faith has been your salvation. Now go in peace" (7:48,50) reveal to the woman herself and to the other guests the invisible change which has taken place in the hidden depths of the heart. When the woman leaves the area around the table, she has been advanced, in the eyes of all, to a new identity.

Jesus has also manifested himself under cover of the meal. Believing that his guest has made a mistake with regard to the woman's identity, Simon had concluded that whatever anyone said, so blind a man could not be a prophet. But the Master soon showed that he read the woman's heart just as well as he did Simon's, that he knew the generous pardon she had merited and the debts which still weighed on the Pharisee. It is, however, the words of authority above all—"Your sins are forgiven"—which, here as elsewhere (cf. Matt. 9:1f.), give an inkling of an identity which is out of the ordinary, indeed quite beyond the human. If that conclusion is not stated, it nonetheless is in the minds of all, for God alone has power to forgive sin. Thus, at the Master's will, the table has served to reveal persons to each other.

The meal in the home of Martha and Mary brings out the personalities of the sisters and the way in which grace draws each of them. The occasion and the setting confirm and illustrate a traditional teaching (Luke 10:38–42).[12] The Lord's word, for which Mary hungers, is given to her in the framework of the meal, for this word is itself a food and is superior in value to any earthly food. Martha's merit is that she is zealous in serving others. But "Man does not live by bread alone" and Mary has been wise enough to choose the better portion. Martha is thus invited to discover new values for herself.

After the raising of Lazarus, Martha and Mary receive Jesus again (John 12:1–8). The man who had been dead has taken his old place at the family table, and the impression given is that the reunion is for celebrating the joy of such an unhoped-for restoration. In a gesture of respectful gratitude, Mary pours a precious perfume over the Master's feet. To the hypocritical protest of Judas, Jesus replies by showing the true significance of the gesture: Mary has been paying her homage of loving faith to the body that must soon be buried, to the Master who must die. Thus a ritual of hospitality, a "table custom," acquires prophetic value.

Let us recall, finally, the cure of the man with dropsy whom Jesus encounters while he is at table in a Pharisee's house on the sabbath (Luke 14:1–6). In the circle formed by the guests, attention reaches a high degree of intensity. They watch the Master with malicious curiosity. Jesus seizes upon the occasion to unmask hypocrisy: "Is it lawful to cure on the sabbath or not?" (14:3). Then, in the midst of the hostile but prudent silence of his hearers, the Master cures the man, sends him away, and justifies what he has done. The sabbath law must yield before the suffering of a human being to be rescued.

Thus, in a variety of circumstance, the community of the table has been useful for the manifestation of persons and the revelation of salvation.

The Proclamation of the Messianic Feast

At times Jesus alludes to the traditional theme of the messianic banquet or develops it in a decisive manner. In the sermon on the mount, for example, the fourth beatitude: "Blessed are they who hunger and thirst for holiness; they shall have their fill" (Matt. 5:6) is outlined against that doctrinal background and takes its whole meaning from it.

The banquets in which Jesus shares signify the nuptial joy of the messianic age which is finally at hand, as contrasted with the austerity of the time of waiting: "John's disciples came to him with the objection: 'Why is it that while we and the Pharisees fast, your disciples do not?' Jesus said to them: 'How can wedding guests go in mourning so long as the groom is with them? When the day comes that the groom is taken away, then they will fast' " (Matt. 9:14–15).

One characteristic of the messianic feast is its universality: God invites all men to it; he will save places for them at the table, if one dare put it that way. Even those who seemed, from the human standpoint, to be too far off—indeed, cut off—from it will come and find a place. That is what Jesus teaches when he cures the centurion's servant. He marvels at this pagan's faith and says: "Mark what I say! Many will come from the east and the west and will find a place at the banquet in the kindgom of God with Abraham, Isaac, and Jacob, while the natural heirs of the kingdom will be driven out into the dark. Wailing will be heard there and the grinding of teeth" (Matt. 8:11–12).

The same teaching is given at the meal at which Jesus praises disinterested hospitality and promises that it will be rewarded "in the resurrection of the just" (Luke 14:12–14). One of the other guests outdoes him with a "beatitude": "Happy is he who eats bread in the kingdom of God" (14:15). Jesus responds with the parable of the invited guests who beg off on various pretexts: "I have bought some land. . . . I have bought five yoke of oxen. . . . I am newly married." (14:18–20). Greatly vexed, the master of the house bids his servants to bring in, instead of those invited, "the poor and the crippled, the blind and the lame," and even anyone found on the road (14:21–23). Several things are stated in this parable: the universal prevenance of God and his anxiety to welcome men to the intimacy of his table and of his very life; his indifference to anyone's social status and the regard of which the individual is the object in the eyes of the world; perhaps the substitution of the Gentiles for the unfaithful Jews; and, finally, the decisive role played by a man's spiritual dispositions, for here—as with the word, the hand, the face, and the visit of God—it is the good or bad will of the individual that determines God's attitude towards him.

The last two of these lessons are set forth with a new certainty and emphasis in Matthew (22:1–14). The parable of the wedding feast belongs to the tradition which portrays the covenant between God and his people, and especially the fulfillment of that covenant, as a wedding. In this ultimate meeting, the covenant will be lived out as a communion of love, in the exultation of a perpetual feast. This nuptial aspect gives greater force to the other features of the parable and to the lessons it teaches. The putting to death of the servants who brought the invitation represents a kind of villainy which justifies both the punishment of the perpetrators and their replacement by whoever could be found on the roads. The passage on the wedding garment expresses in a new way the need of moral dispositions if one is to approach God's table.

The Multiplication of Loaves

The two accounts of a multiplication of loaves in the gospels (Matt. 14:13–21 and 32–38; Mark 6:34–44 and 8:1–10; Luke 9:10–17; John 6:1–15) have recollections of the Exodus as their background and receive part of their meaning from them. However, the accounts are also set in the perspective of messianic hopes, the institution of the Eucharist, and the eschatological banquet.

In both instances the event occurs in the desert, which is the place of mortal deprivation[13] but also the place where the manna was given. In both instances the hungry crowd is quite large: several thousand men, without counting women and children. In the first episode several factors are deliberately calculated to make the witnesses feel the ludicrous inadequacy of human means: the Master's question to Philip: "Where shall we buy bread for these people to eat?" (John 6:5); the impossible assignment given to the disciples: "Give them something to eat yourselves" (Matt. 14:16 and par.); finally, the listing of food supplies: a few loaves and small fish.

After the order has been given to seat the people in groups,[14] Jesus takes the loaves in his hands; he draws these few provisions towards himself, into the space for manipulation which characterizes every piece of work, every transformation of matter; he pronounces the words of the blessing and then, in a gesture which is the opposite of the first, breaks and distributes the food to his disciples and, through them, to the crowd. The place of hunger now becomes the place of satiety: all eat and are filled (Matt. 14:20 and par.); it even becomes the place of superabundance, for the disciples fill many baskets with the leftover pieces.

These unhoped-for meals have revelatory power. God alone had, in the past, been able to feed Israel in the wilderness. The action of Jesus shows that in him God is beginning a new Exodus, a new rescue. Divine providence continues to be attentive to the needs of God's people. "They will collapse on the way!" the Master says (Mark 8:3), and therefore he who in his time of temptation in the wilderness had refused to multiply loaves for himself (Matt. 4:4) now uses his power to meet the needs of the people. The people of God is once again gathered around one table; men are exalted to become table companions of God and to enjoy the fullness and superabundance which are signs of the messianic age.[15]

The crowd does not fail to see the significance of what has happened. They realize that Jesus must be an extraordinary person: "When the people saw the sign he had performed they began to say, 'This is undoubtedly the Prophet who is to come into the world' " (John 6:14). They want to take him and make him king, but Jesus refuses any acceptance of temporal power, just as he had when he was tempted, and, instead, he withdraws to the mountain (John 6:15). And fittingly, for is revelation not made up of alternating declarations and silences, interventions and withdrawals, appearances and disappearances?

Of their nature, then, the two multiplications of loaves declare that the age of the Messiah is at hand. But a decisive further step is taken in the discourse on the bread of life, which John alone gives us (6:22–58). The meal taken the evening before in the wilderness and the memories of the manna which it evokes provide a starting-point for the Master's teaching. The true bread is not the manna but Jesus himself and his word; these are genuine nourishment which men are invited to take in faith (6:32–50). In a second phase of the discourse a new revelatory step is taken. The bread of life is not only the person and the word of Jesus but his very flesh surrendered for the life of the world and his blood given as drink (6:51–58).[16] Far from simply extending earthly life as the manna did, this food and drink communicate to men the eternal life which the Son has from the Father (6:57). The fulfillment of the prophetic figures here goes beyond all expectation and possesses a realism that tests men's faith. The hearers react diversely to the prediction of the mysterious meal (6:60–69).

The Institution of the Eucharistic Meal

The *place* of this event is already significant. Jesus brings the new banquet into existence at Jerusalem, the national and religious center upon which for centuries the faith and hope of the people of the promise have been focused, and the place where the Messiah will tomorrow be put to death.[17] Now, from this point in the world at which Isarel gathers for the Mosaic Passover, the new Passover will go forth into the whole universe.

The *time*, too, is essential. Despite his own eager desire, Jesus has determined to wait for the celebration of the Jewish Passover: "I have greatly desired to eat this Passover with you before I suffer" (Luke 22:15).[18]

The festival provides Christ with the occasion for bringing to fulfillment the whole past of Israel, just as his word has brought the law to fulfillment (cf. Matt. 5:17–20). The Jewish Passover is here brought to completion and transcended, as figures yield to realities. Under the veil of signs God gives his new people all the blessings of the kingdom. The ritual meal instituted by Jesus is, from God's side, the fulfillment of his promises; from man's side it is a thanksgiving for this very fulfillment, it is "eucharist." The one, simple action of Jesus Christ is, to the eyes of faith, both the "Yes" of God to his promises and the "Amen" of man to the salvation offered him (cf. 2 Cor. 1:20).

The Passover rite, which provides the framework for the new institution, makes the Lord's meal an *evening meal*, the "Supper" par excellence.[19] The work of the day is done, and the evening hour is, more than any other, the time for the intimacy, the self-communion, and the relaxation that favor mutual confidences.[20] A further decisive circumstance helps in the same direction: this is, for Jesus, a *farewell meal*.[21] The Master is fully aware of his imminent death as he gathers his disciples around the table, celebrates the old Passover there, inaugurates the new Passover, and gives his final instructions. The force of presence which always makes itself felt in the community of the table receives an extraordinary fullness of being from the sacrifice and the separation which were impending. It is true, of course, that a reading of the Gospel narratives shows us the disciples still unacquainted with the deeper meaning of the Master's words and actions. But though they are slow to understand, the Twelve do perceive from the Master's demeanor the gravity of the hour and the weight of meaning in the moment.

This decisive solemnity asserts itself even in the washing of the feet. The precise moment when this action took place may be open to discussion,[22] but it is clearly a *rite of welcome*, usually carried out by servants, and rendered desirable by the conditions of the journey along the dusty roads of Palestine; it had become an accepted courtesy. The evangelist carefully describes all of Jesus' movements and Peter's naive incomprehension, which reflects that of his companions; above all, he reports the interpretation which the Master gives of his action. A deliberate piece of pedagogy, the procedure is in the line of the prophetic actions of the old dispensation, but with this difference: here we have not the prediction of a future event but the enjoining of a precept: the law of the humblest fraternal service of one another.

If this farewell meal is the prelude to a separation from which it receives a great part of its meaning, it is also ordered towards a banquet of final reunion which will be the eternal fulfillment of the new Passover: "I tell you, I will not eat again until it is fulfilled in the kingdom of God" (Luke 22:16); "I tell you, from now on I will not drink of the fruit of the vine until the coming of the reign of God" (22:18).

The *matter* of the Eucharistic meal is rich in an inexhaustible meaning which Christian tradition has from the very beginning never ceased to explore. Bread and wine, products of the soil, concentrate in themselves material nature and the immensity of the cosmos: in them the universe is gathered up to be offered and consecrated to God. These basic foods of man signify that man recovers his orientation, that he returns to the sources of his life itself in order to thank the

Creator for them. These fruits of his daily toil do not present the value attached to rare and choice dishes but, on the contrary, the inestimable communal value of human work: fruit of the harvest, prepared by the collaboration of many hands, they are a perfect sign of the unity of mankind as something already, in part, existing and, in part, still to be realized. This sign of unity is added to that of the table and reinforces it. And finally, unlike the sacrifices of the old covenant, heavy with the flesh and blood of animals, the matter of this new sacrifice and meal is of the utmost lightness; it exhausts its materiality to become no more than a support wholly devoted to meaning.

The biblical tradition brings a new richness to the natural symbolism of bread and wine. In choosing these materials, Christ is harking back, beyond the Mosaic dispensation, to the sacrifice of Melchisidech, a priest of cosmic religion, and in him to the best religious efforts of the pagan world (cf. Gen. 14:17–20).[23] Since, moreover, the Eucharistic food is intended as the wayfaring food of the new people of God on its journey from time to eternity, it is the reality to which the unleavened bread and the providential manna of the old dispensation point. The Eucharist is a fulfillment.

Above all, the new Passover meal receives its transcendent meaning from the *gestures* and *words* of Jesus. Usually the study of the Eucharistic rite is concerned too exclusively with the symbolism of the bread and wine, to the detriment of the action itself. But these elements are the object of an action which takes account of the their natural import but also takes possession of it and transcends it. The community of the table and the circumstances of the meal prepare, in their turn, for this supreme action and wholly surrender their own meaning to it.

In Jesus here present, between his words, his gestures, and his looks, a meaning which is unique, simple, and mysterious circulates and unfolds. In the familiar gesture of so many hosts at table, Christ takes the bread and then the cup in his hands—an act of choosing, of mastering, of appropriation. Here are the elements, brought into that space, at once corporal and spiritual, in which free will, the exertions of the hands, and the word transform things. But it is not an act of selfish taking. If Jesus draws the bread and wine towards himself, it is in the first place to give thanks to the Father for them: to the divine blessing that spreads its gifts over the world and man, the inverse, ascending movement of human blessing responds; the blessings received are carried back to their source on the movement of prayer, in the gaze that is lifted upwards.[24] The blessing is followed by the breaking of the bread. Jesus breaks the one loaf into as many pieces as there are guests to eat it: love multiplies its gifts, recognizing no limit but repletion and superabundance. Then, in a gesture which is the reverse of the taking in hand, the Master gives up the bread and wine, offering them and distributing them to his disciples. At the same time his words indicate the meaning of his action: "Take this and eat it. This is my body. . . . This is my blood" (Matt. 26:28 and par.).

If the hand that distributes the food is eloquent of its own action, the divine word, which never returns to God without having produced its effect (Isa. 55:10–11), *manipulates* the things themselves. Bread and wine are henceforth signs that are eloquent for the senses, the mind, and the faith of man: their appearance, which remains untouched by change, signifies that God gives himself to man as nourishment. But these foods do not acquire only a new finality or a new meaning. Christ's words pronounce a sovereignly efficacious ontological decree: "This is. . . . " The reality effectively given is the body soon to be handed over, this blood soon to be shed.

Here the gesture of distribution takes on a signification of unique realism, a meaning it can never possibly have again in history. Not only is Christ giving up these foods to divide them among his disciples, he is giving up himself in an act of the most total disappropriation. Here the gesture of the hand opening and giving signifies that the whole body of Jesus is in some way detached from itself and surrendered. What the Master is offering to his disciples is not a piece of bread and a little wine, *part of what he possesses*, but his *whole being*, body and soul, humanity and divinity. Here the movement of saving love reaches its fulfillment: the Word once made flesh, today made bread, gives itself to be *consumed.*

Christ's words state in fact, in a very explicit way, the *sacrificial nature* of the Eucharistic meal: "This is my body to be given for you" (Luke 22:19); "This is my blood, the blood of the covenant, to be poured out on behalf of many" (Mark 14:24).[25] The Mosaic Passover had already established an essential connection between the sacrifice of the lamb and the meal at which the victim was eaten (Exod. 12:1–10). From the nature of the rite, the immolation preceded the eating. At the Supper the order is reversed: the Eucharistic meal precedes and points forward to the sacrifice of Christ on Calvary. But the eating of the bread and wine anticipates here and now the sacrificial act in which Christ is to "reach his end" (Luke 13:32). The texts give formal expression to the here-and-nowness of the body given and the blood poured out.[26]

In this respect we must lay stress on another parallel between the Mosaic Passover (taken as a whole which includes both immolation and the meal) and the Lord's Supper. Just as the first Passover rite was instituted *before* the event of Israel's exodus from Egypt, which the rite was to commemorate, so too the Eucharistic rite, left us by Jesus as a memorial, precedes his immolation. Thus in both cases God indicates his mastery of time and the transcendence of his plan in relation to history. Moreover, Jesus hands himself over, under the sacramental signs, before being handed over to his enemies. He is wholly free and his gift is spontaneously given: no one takes his life from him, he gives it of his own accord (John 10:18). The death on Calvary will translate into reality an immolation already offered.

Like every table community, this one makes it possible for the participants to *manifest* their personalities. The evangelical narratives are, of course, not interested in anecdotal detail; everything in the accounts is subordinated to the handing on of the mystery. Nonetheless character traits can be seen from time to time, and they show how, at this extraordinary meal, human truth and transcendent action intermingle. Thus the native spontaneity of Peter bursts forth at the washing of the feet. First the disciple objects to the self-humiliation of the Master; then, when the latter says that the washing is required for any communion with him, Peter does an about-face and, with just as much vehemence as he had shown in refusing to have his feet washed, now asks that his head and hands be washed as well (John 13:6–9). The apostle shows the same impulsive generosity again later on: not understanding the "departure" to which Jesus refers, Peter declares that he is ready to follow Christ into danger and even to give his life for him (13:36–38). The prediction of his imminent denial leaves Peter disbelieving, for he like his companions is very sure of his own fidelity (Matt. 26:33–35). The same good will and the same lack of understanding of the Master's words appear again in the short conversation of Jesus with Thomas and Philip concerning his proximate departure and the road to be taken. According to a recurrent pattern of misunderstanding that characterizes the accounts in the fourth Gospel, the hearers take Christ's symbolic language in an entirely empirical sense (John 14:1–11). The characters of the various people involved emerge clearly.

The community of the table also reveals, but in a highly dramatic way, the spiritual choice made by one of the guests: Judas. If there has been any uncertainty up to this point on the real dispositions of his heart, the meal brings them out into the open. Satan had already given Judas the idea of handing Jesus over (John 13:2). Some of the Master's words, not understood by the other apostles, are heard by Judas as a warning and a final call to a still possible conversion: "You are [cleansed]; though not all. . . . Not all are washed clean" (13:10–11); "My purpose here is the fulfillment of Scripture: 'He who partook of bread with me has raised his heel against me' " (13:18, citing Ps. 41:10); "I tell you solemnly, one of you will betray me" (13:21).[27]

The scene that follows this declaration, the shock felt by those present, the question put to Jesus by the beloved disciple at Peter's urging—it all restrains Judas for the time being. But his acceptance of the morsel dipped in the dish by Jesus shows that the traitor is now irrevocably committed to his plan. In itself this gesture of a share offered and accepted signifies a communion in love; on Jesus' part it is a final appeal for friendship; for Judas it is only a pretense, for his heart is bent on betrayal. The subjective intention perverts the objective meaning of the gesture. Likewise at Gethsemani, the kiss which is a gesture of love and respect will point the Master out to his enemies (Matt. 26:47–50; Mark 14:43–46; Luke 22:47–48).

This must be insisted upon: the community of the table confers on Judas's betrayal the character of very special perfidy.[28] Murderous hatred wears the mask of friendship and communion in the same values in life. Of the two hands joined in the sharing, one is already accomplishing the death of the other. Jesus stresses this with insistence: "I give you my word, one of you is about to betray me, yes, one who is eating with me. . . . It is one of the Twelve—a man who dips into the dish with me" (Mark 14:18–20).[29] "The hand of my betrayer is with me at this table" (Luke 22:21).

Judas's impudent question—"Surely it is not I, Rabbi?" (Matt. 26:25)—only makes his presence and his actions more hypocritical still. But above all it is the identity of the victim—the Son of

Man—that gives the crime its unfathomable depth of malice: "Accursed be that man by whom the Son of Man is betrayed. It were better for him had he never been born" (Mark 14:21).

Certain actions are decisive spiritual choices. In consuming the dipped bread, Judas consummated his sin interiorly. The Gospel text suggests the idea of a communion with Satan: "At that instant after Judas had taken the bread, Satan entered him" (John 13:37,JB). Since the decision is now irrevocable, Jesus presses the traitor to finish his work. Judas leaves the table and goes out into the night. Here at least is a "logical" gesture. He who betrays cannot continue to share the meal. Taking his sin fully upon himself, Judas excommunicates himself.

After his departure, the community around the table, freed of a latent obstacle, draws closer together and opens itself more profoundly to communion with the Master. The unanimity of hearts makes possible a *circulation of meaning* by way of gestures and words. Christ has chosen the meal as the occasion for handing over to the Eleven—the Church to come—some of his most precious revelations. Jesus, who has already shown his unwearying forbearance with regard to Judas, now declares the tender affection he feels for the Eleven, his all-embracing will to save all men at the cost of his blood, his total, loving abandonment to the Father's will in which all his other motivations have their source and their goal. As for the content of Christ's discourse, truly a spiritual testament and a privileged act of revelation,[30] it would be out of the question to analyze or summarize it here. It is enough to note that the warnings, instructions, and assurances given to the Eleven, together with Christ's final prayer to his Father, embrace the divine plan for the world and for man and the whole mission of the Church in time and its consummation in eternity. Never again in history will a community at table be the framework and the means of a comparable revelation. The meaning that circulates across all the elements of the gathering attains a richness, depth, and sublimity quite without equal.

Mysterious too is the increment of spiritual dignity received by those who participate in this new Passover meal. We have observed elsewhere that to nourish another is to treat him as one's own body, to incorporate him into oneself: the guests become "the larger I" of the host.[31] But what Christ is offering to his friends is not ordinary food but his own body and blood. Because of this the disciples are incorporated into Jesus Christ, becoming, without any loss of their own personality, living members of the one Head; they thus constitute the larger body of Jesus and live with his life. Each of them, is thereby *promoted* to a new dignity, caught up in the surge of love which carries the Son towards the Father (cf. John 6:57; 17:2,22–28).

Finally, the Eucharistic meal is a *covenant meal.* The blood that Jesus hands over to his friends is "the blood of the covenant," according to Matthew (26:28) and Mark (14:24). Luke's formulation is still more striking: "This cup is the new covenant in my blood, which will be shed for you" (22:20).

The body and blood distributed at the Supper are the same that will be offered to God in the agony on the cross. In a prophetic anticipation Jesus celebrates his sacrifice as if it were already taking place now in the present moment of the community at the table. The guests are drawn into the sacrifice of the Master. Mankind is thus reconciled with God and with itself by a sacrificial meal; the unity broken of old in Paradise by the eating of the food which brought death is now restored. Better than any other rite, the meal signifies the new and eternal covenant in Jesus Christ who is "our peace" (Eph. 2:14) and who has reconciled all things, making peace by the blood of his cross (Col. 1:20).

Let us note, finally, that in spite of the imminence of separation, the Supper is a *joyous meal;* it is a solemn joy but nonetheless real, though it is most probable that the Eleven at that moment were unable to sound its depths. Joy, for Christ, that his mission is accomplished, the world is overcome, the covenant sealed, and the Father glorified (John 16:33; 17 *passim).* He can therefore invite the disciples to keep their courage up in trial, in the expectation of a joy which no one can take from them (John 16:20–24).

The Paschal Meals

The risen Christ is not content to manifest himself to the eyes of his disciples, to submit himself to the testing of their hands, and to address himself to them in prolonged conversations. He also shares food with them. We may imagine the revelatory power such an action had! The person who has died is one who can no longer eat, who has left an empty place at the daily table. But look! The Master has once again become their companion at table, that is, he is "living with" his friends again, taking part in that most essential of all the acts of the living—eating. This sign reveals in a manner that is quite decisive Christ's victory over death.

The disciples traveling along the road to Emmaus regained their courage by listening to the wayfarer who was a stranger to them. His words have rekindled, then nourished, their faith. In a spirit of outgoing friendliness, they invite him to share their meal. The intimacy which belongs to all community around a table is heightened by the endeavor in which they had engaged together on the road—the exchange of thoughts, the sharing of the sense of disillusionment at first and then the fervor they had experienced upon the unveiling of the Scriptures—and finally by the contemplative spirit which comes with evening. Each of the three persons at table gives himself fully to the other two with a special intensity of presence. "When he had seated himself with them to eat, he took bread, pronounced the blessing, then broke the bread and began to distribute it to them. With that their eyes were opened and they recognized him; whereupon he vanished from their sight" (Luke 24:30–31).

The movement of the hands, the act of giving thanks, the breaking and distribution of the bread, opened the disciples' eyes. In the lightning-flash of a look the wayfarers recognized the stranger. He whom they believed to be swallowed by death is here, now, with them, taking part in the vital act of sharing a meal! But just as on the day when he multiplied the loaves the master slipped away from the crowd (John 6:14–15), so here he vanishes from the gaze of his two companions. Their uncertainty, remaining even after the conversation on the road, is overcome. They have come to a new level of existence in faith. Thus, whether or not the meal is to be regarded as a Eucharist, the table exercised its revelatory power.[32]

The appearance to the Eleven recounted immediately thereafter by the third Gospel corroborates the testimony of the two disciples: "He said to them: 'Have you anything here to eat?' They gave him a piece of cooked fish, which he took and ate in their presence" (Luke

24:41–43).[33] It is no longer necessary to seek among the dead someone who is so obviously alive (cf. Luke 24:5). Eating completes the witness given by the eyes and the testing hands. Jesus is indeed risen, for he engages in that daily act which is the humblest necessity of our existence.

The appearance beside the lake and the miraculous catch of fish with the meal that follows it are set within the same perspective. The Lord, who is recognized first by the beloved disciple and by Peter (John 21:7), is on the shore, where he has gotten ready the fire, the fish to be broiled, and the bread. As an additional courtesy, he invites the fishermen to contribute to the menu by bringing some of their catch. Then he says to them: "Come and eat your meal" (21:12). By this time each of them has recognized the Master, but there is a kind of residual uneasiness because no "introductions" have been made. It seems, however, that Christ's manner overcame all embarrassment: "Jesus came over, took the bread and gave it to them, and did the same with the fish" (21:13).

The simple actions of sharing bring home to the disciples a superhuman truth: the Son of God made man has conquered death; he shows himself as present to his followers in the most everyday reality of work, failure or success, the frugal brotherly meal. Beyond this revelation, the community between the Master and the disciples is re-created by virtue of the sharing. The Eleven, who had shown so little courage during the passion, have once again been made the table companions of the Lord and thereby drawn into the mystery of his resurrection. It is highly significant that after the meal Peter is solemnly constituted shepherd of the flock (21:15–19).

The Book of Acts is careful to note that the risen Jesus shared meals with his disciples; it was during a meal that he gave them his final instructions: to stay at Jerusalem and await the gift of the Spirit (Acts 1:4–5,JB; cf. Luke 24:49).

Reunions of this kind complete the process of strengthening the disciples' faith, for in them Christ manifests with power his recovered vitality.[34] Later on, therefore, when Peter wants to give the real grounds for the privileged role of the apostles as witnesses, he rightly appeals to the appearances of the risen Jesus: he was "seen, not by all, but only by such witnesses as had been chosen beforehand by

God—by us who ate and drank with him after he rose from the dead" (Acts 10:41). It was therefore through sharing with Christ and through the revelation and communion which such sharing brings that the apostles were made privileged witnesses to the resurrection.

The Eucharist, Passover of the Church

After the ascension, Christ's presence in the world continues to be signified by the people of God and, at the center of the Church's life, by the sacrament of bread and wine.

Our earlier analyses of the institution of the sacrament make it necessary here only to point out what is characteristic of the Eucharist during the time of the Church.

The Christian Eucharist commemorates the redemptive sacrifice which the Supper had anticipated. Indeed Jesus instituted the rite precisely as a memorial: "Do this as a remembrance of me" (Luke 22:19; 1 Cor. 11:24–25). Just as in eating the Passover the Israelites had nourished themselves with the memory of their earthly liberation, so the Eucharistic people feeds on the ever-present reality of its own spiritual liberation. We need not be afraid here of a realism that was intended by Christ himself: the living mystery of his own salvation is what the Christian incorporates into himself in order to live by it. Or, to put it better: the Savior incorporates his members ever more fully into himself in order to give them an abundance of life (John 10:10).[35] The unworthy believer who does not recognize the Lord's body "eats and drinks a judgment on himself" (1 Cor. 11:29), but the Christian who has first honestly examined himself eats and drinks his own salvation. In the sacramental act the redemptive reality once brought into being at great cost is communicated here and now. The Eucharistic celebration does not, of course, add anything to the sacrifice of the cross and is not a second sacrifice alongside it, for Christ died only once (Rom. 6:10; Heb. 9:26–28; 1 Pet. 3:18). But the redemptive reality is proclaimed and made present in the moment of liturgy: "Every time, then, you eat this bread and drink this cup, you proclaim the death of the Lord until he comes!" (1 Cor. 11:26). This statement means that the Eucharistic mystery gathers up and condenses into a moment the agelong history of salvation. For the Christian Passover commemorates the mystery of the Supper and Calvary, celebrates its present reality, and anticipates its definitive fulfillment at the Lord's return. It is the Christ once immolated and now glorified who is given here and now: such is the limitless reality that fills the Eucharistic moment.

The Eucharistic Table

The Book of Acts tells us how devoted the first believers were to "the breaking of bread" (Acts 2:42). The rite was celebrated in the course of the fraternal meals taken in private homes; it was the Christian agape or love-meal, the sign and bond of mutual love in Jesus Christ. (It will be recalled that this kind of celebration was also the occasion of abuses which St. Paul was forced to condemn: 1 Cor. 11:20–34; cf. Acts 2:46.)

This is not the place to study, even in the most summary way, the history of the Eucharistic rite.[36] We need only, for our purposes, take note of the important meaning of the table or altar.[37]

As the social furnishing beyond all others, the table is for the Church the place of gathering. Here each day, but especially on the Lord's day, the visible sign of unity is made once again; here the people of God, like a family which is daily scattered by its diverse tasks, declares that it is the assembly which is ever anew called together: *ecclesia.* As the piece of furniture that promotes dialogue, the altar table enables the gathered Church to hear once again the word that summons and nourishes it, and to answer its God, through prayer and song, with the living "Amen" of faith. Revelation ended with the death of the last apostle, but every Christian generation in its turn must discover the God who reveals himself, and each must pass judgment on itself in the light of the summoning word. Then, having been fed with the word, the Christian people can, like the men who once gathered on the lake shore (Mark 6:34–44; Luke 9:11–17), like the apostles at the Supper, like the disciples on the way to Emmaus, receive the bread and wine which are the body and blood of Christ distributed once again. The table of dialogue is also the table of the sacrifical meal, and at it each person is drawn into the Passover of his Lord and the union of all and each with Jesus Christ is perfected in communion: "Because the loaf of bread is one, we, many though we are, are one body, for we all partake of the one loaf" (1 Cor. 10:17).[38]

Around this most unusual of tables the intensity of presence, which is to be experienced only in faith, reaches mysterious depths. Christ is present by various means: in those assembled, in the priest, in his word, and, finally and above all by way of his very body and blood. Each believer is present to his Lord and his brothers, because unanimity in faith and love gives a single meaning to all the gestures and words and to the action in its entirety. The *distribution of bread and wine*, the complete *circulation of meaning*, and the *intimate mutual presence*—all these bring unity to its fullness. The gathered community therefore celebrates the Eucharist in a festive spirit and in the joy of renewed communion with God and with one another.

God's table thus becomes man's table. The original sin had divided man from God, from his fellows, and from himself, but the reconciliation effected by Christ's sacrifice now overcomes that threefold division. It would be equally destructive, therefore, to minimize either the believer's filial relationship to God or his fraternal relationship to other men in the Eucharist. At the Eucharistic table, on the contrary, we find the first and second commandments brought home with equal force. It is here that Christ's instruction becomes most imperative: to be reconciled with one's brother before presenting one's gift (Matt. 5:23–24). It is here that love of God and love of man are subject to no danger of mutual opposition or dualism. It is here that the God-ward thrust of faith, hope, and love exalts and transfigures the whole order of interpersonal and social relationships. It is here finally that we see most clearly how the cultivation of the values of contemplation and adoration is necessary if the relationship of man to man is to be authentically Christian.

The Eucharistic mystery, therefore, signifies and brings to fruition, day after day, the mystery of God's universal presence and his plan to "recapitulate" everything, that is, to "bring all things . . . into one under Christ's headship" (Eph. 1:10). The immense reaches of the universe and its energies are brought to focus in the material for the sacrificial meal. The whole history of the world and mankind as well as the history of salvation with its varied stages are concentrated in a festive action, in a moment that gathers up the past and anticipates the temporal and eternal future. The words God has spoken throughout history are summed up in him who is the Word and makes himself present under the eloquent signs of bread and wine. The powerful interventions of the divine hand under both covenants, and especially the Passion, Resurrection, and Ascension of the Lord, and the Pentecost of his Spirit are concentrated into the gesture of breaking and distributing bread. The manifestations of God, become visible to our eyes in the face of Jesus Christ, and God's repeated visits to men, are all brought together in this mystery of presence through which God is gradually becoming "all in all" (1 Cor. 15:28).[39]

The Heavenly Banquet

The gospel insists on the eschatological significance of every human meal. The kingdom of God is presented to us in the guise of a festive meal in which God and men take part; consequently any table community is a daily prophetic anticipation of the promised blessedness. This connection lies behind Jesus' advice to anyone preparing a banquet: go out of your way to invite those who cannot repay your invitation, and you will receive your reward at the resurrection of the just (Luke 14:14).

According to another theme of revelation, the final judgment will turn in a very special way on how men have shared the most necessary thing of all: daily bread. The parable of the evil rich man and the poor Lazarus teaches with great emphasis that a man risks being condemned if he refuses a fellow man the food he needs (Luke 16:19–31).[40] And according to the great parable of judgment, some will hear the words addressed to them: "Come. You have my Father's blessing! . . . For I was hungry and you gave me food, I was thirsty and you gave me drink" (Matt. 25:34–35), while to others the Judge will say: "Out of my sight, you condemned, into that everlasting fire. . . . I was hungry and you gave me no food, I was thirsty and you gave me no drink" (25:41–42). For, in the persons of others it is to Christ himself that the Christian is asked to give food and drink. A man will be judged by how he shares his bread, for it is in sharing or not sharing it that he ratifies or rejects God's basic will, which is that *man should be* (cf. Gen. 1:26) *and should live* (cf. Ezek. 3:18; 18:23)![41]

Let us recall, finally, that Christ uses the community of the table as a way of presenting an image of messianic blessedness. Indeed even the familiar friendship which the believer now enjoys with Christ through faith is described in this fashion in the Apocalypse: "Here I stand, knocking at the door. If anyone hears me calling and opens the door, I will enter his house and have supper with him and he with me" (Rev. 3:20). Then, according to Luke, at the Last Supper Jesus promises his disciples that their fidelity will be rewarded in the intimacy of the heavenly banquet: "In my kingdom you will eat and drink at my table" (Luke 22:30). He is speaking of the community of the messianic table: there the people of God will be forever gathered; there revelation, which is necessarily imperfect, will make way for face-to-face encounter (1 Cor. 13:12); there the guests are assured of being forever the intimates of God (cf. Eph. 2:19); there the covenant will be made perfect. That will be "the wedding day of the Lamb" (Rev. 19:7), celebrated with the banquet of the eternal Passover: "Happy are they who have been invited to the wedding feast of the Lamb" (Rev. 19:9).

NOTES

1. Cf. verse 34: (NAB): "The people picked up their dough before it was leavened, wrapped their kneading troughs in their cloaks, and slung them on their shoulders."

2. Later on, the prophet Elijah, who is bent on maintaining the covenant, walks across the wilderness to the mountain of God, Horeb. Divine intervention provides him with food (1 Kings 19:1–8).

3. Among other examples of covenants sealed by a meal, cf. those of Isaac and Abimelech (Gen. 26:26–31) and of Laban and Jacob (Gen. 31:45–46, 53–54).

4. But cf. 1 Sam. 21:2–7 and note 37, below. Because of the significance of a meal, certain kinds of eating are prohibited as amounting to alliances with idolatry: Tob. 1:10–11 (cf. 2:13); 2 Macc. 1; cf. 1 Cor. 8:10 and, on food offered to idols, Rev. 2:14.

5. Cf. above, p. 75.

6. Cf. above, Chapter 3, section 13, "God's Word as Man's Food."

7. Cf. *The Humanity of Man* pp. 329–32, "Sharing and Revelation."

8. Cf. *ibid.*, pp. 334–35.

9. Consequently the Roman liturgy sets this passage to be read during the season of Epiphany (second Sunday).

10. Cf. *The Humanity of Man*, pp. 289–98, "The 'Home.' "

11. Cf. Luke 7:33–35. Jesus denounces the inconsistency and bad faith of those who condemn John the Baptist because he fasts, and the Son of Man because he eats and drinks, and this with sinners! The problem of sharing

meals with pagans arose at the very beginning of the new Church. In Acts 10:1–49 Peter accepts the hospitality of Cornelius the centurion; his action will be criticized by the Judeo-Christians (cf. 11:1–18). But Gal.2:12–14 shows that in some circumstances Peter was hesitant. Cf. also the well-known question of food offered to idols: 1 Cor. 8–10.

12. Cf. above, Chapter 3, section 13, "God's Word as Man's Food."

13. Cf. *The Humanity of Man*, p. 47.

14. In 9:14 Luke deliberately uses the term *klisiai* [a place for lying down; a couch or bed; a company of people sitting at meals]: the people lie down so that they form "beds for table."

15. In addition to texts cited earlier in this chapter ("The Hope of the Messianic Feast"), recall the superabundance of wine at Cana (John 2:6), of the miraculous catch of fish (Luke 5:4–10; John 21:6), of living water (John 4:14), of life (John 10:10), and of the Spirit (John 3:34; 7:37).

16. Note the use in verses 54–58 of the Greek verb *trogein* ("to gnaw, chew") which is more realistic than the simple *phagein* ("to eat").

17. Cf. above, pp. 52–53.

18. We cannot here discuss the precise chronological relationship between the celebration of the Passover and the institution of the Eucharist.

19. This is true, whatever one may think was the precise day of the celebration.

20. Cf. *The Humanity of Man*, p. 326.

21. Cf. *ibid.*, p. 335.

22. The grammatical construction in John 13:2 (genitive abosolute in Greek: "during supper") hardly allows us to decide the question. The custom was to perform this ritual of welcome before or at the beginning of the meal (cf. Luke 7:44); but John 13:4 expressly says that Jesus "rose from supper." Perhaps they had not actually begun to eat. In any event, by rising from table the Master makes the disciples even more aware of his action and its lesson.

23. The reader will be aware of the importance given to the priesthood of Melchisedech in the theology of Christ's priesthood as elaborated in the Letter to the Hebrews.

24. Cf. Xavier Léon-Dufour, ed., *Dictionary of Biblical Theology*, trans. P. Joseph Cahill *et al.* (New York: Desclée, 1967), art. "Blessing"; Louis Bouyer, *Eucharist: Theology and Spirituality of the Eucharistic Prayer*, trans. Charles Underhill Quinn (Notre Dame, Ind.: University of Notre Dame Press, 1968).

25. Cf. the minute description of Christ's gestures in St. Ephraem, *Sermones in hebdomadam sanctam*, 4:4 and 6.

26. It is noteworthy that the text of Luke on the body has the present participle *dedomenon* ("being given") and that the three Synoptics have the present participle *ekchunnomenon* ("being poured out") with reference to the blood. The present tense is the present of prophetic anticipation. The translations show variations between present and future tenses. In Luke 22:19 the Vulgate has the present ("quod pro vobis datur"); in 1 Cor. 11:24 it adds "tradetur" to the Greek; in the Synoptic texts on the blood the present

participle is translated by the future verb "effundetur" or simply "fundetur" (Luke 22:20).

27. The next verses highlight the simplicity and closeness to Jesus of "the disciple whom he loved."

28. Cf. *The Humanity of Man*, p. 334.

29. We may recall that the table gives the hands of the guests a field of communal action; cf. *The Humanity of Man*, p. 321.

30. Cf. Charles Hauret, *Les adieux du Seigneur* (Paris: Gabalda, 1951).

31. Cf. *The Humanity of Man*, p. 328. We may note here that the practice of "self-service" fosters standoffishness and deprives participants of an obvious means of access to an understanding of the Eucharistic mystery.

32. Cf. St. Gregory the Great, *Sermons on the Gospel*, 23:1 (PL 76:1182–83): "They had not recognized God in the exposition of sacred Scripture but they recognize him in the breaking of the bread."

33. The Vulgate and some Greek mss. add a very realistic detail: "and, taking the remnants, he gave them to them."

34. Some writers devise empty subtleties on the physiology of this eating; we prefer the point constantly made by the Fathers: by eating and drinking Christ intends to strengthen the faith of the disciples in the physical reality of the resurrection. Thus St. Gregory the Great, *Sermons on the Gospels*, 29:1 (PL 76:1213) (On Acts 1:4 and 9: "eating with them . . . he was lifted up"): "He ate and then ascended, so that the eating might prove the reality of his flesh." Similarly, St. John Chrysostom, *In Matthaeum homiliae*, 82 (83):2 (PG 58:739–40); cf. Leo IX, *Symbolum fidei* (Denz. 681 [344]; St. Thomas Aquinas, *Summa theologiae*, III, q. 54, a. 3, ad 3. The real mystery is not the meals or the shifts in spatial location but the resurrection itself.

35. On the Eucharist as food of the soul cf. Tertullian, *The Resurrection of the Flesh*, 8 (PL 2:806): "The flesh is fed with the body and blood of Christ, so that the soul may be nourished." The Eucharist is also a medicine for eternity: cf. St. Ignatius of Antioch, *Letter to the Ephesians*, 20:2: "medicine for immortality, antidote against death"; a food and pledge of resurrection: St. Irenaeus, *Adversus haereses*, IV: 18,5 (PG 7:1027); V:2,2 (PG 7:1124). On the incorporation of the believer into Christ through the Eucharist, cf. St. John Chrysostom, *In Joannem homiliae*, 46:3 (PG 59:260); *In Mattaeum homiliae*, 82:5 (PG 58:743); and especially *In Epist. I ad Corinthios*, 24:2 (PG 61:200); St. Leo the Great, *Sermo* 63:7 (PL 54:357); St. John of Damascus, *De fide orthodoxa*, 4:13 (PG 94:1144).

36. On this point cf. Louis Bouyer, *Eucharist* (cf. note 24, above).

37. Cf. *The Humanity of Man*, pp. 319–22.

38. We must realize that there is genuine communion, that is, an effective sign of unanimity in faith, only where *all* the participants give the *same* meaning to the *same* words and the *same* gestures. Otherwise there is only an illusion of communion. This point must be kept in mind when we are engaged in the ecumenical quest. Some texts on the Eucharist as effective sign of ecclesial unity: *Didache*, 9:4; St. Ignatius of Antioch, *Letter to the Philadelphians*, 3:4; *Letter to the Ephesians*, 20:2; *Letter to the Smyrneans*, 8:1; St. Augustine, *In*

Joannis evangelium, 26:13 (PL 35:1612–13); *Sermo* 227 (PL 38:1099). In *Sermo* 272 (PL 38:1246–47) St. Augustine goes so far as to tell the faithful that, since they are members of Christ, their own mystery is laid on the table: "If then you are Christ's body and his members, it is your own mystery that is laid on the Lord's table, and it is your own mystery that you receive. You answer 'Amen' to what you yourselves are, and answering you ratify it. You hear 'The Body of Christ' and you answer 'Yes, it is so.' Be truly a member of Christ's body, then, so that your Amen may be true." Cf. also St. Cyril of Jerusalem, *Mystagogical Catecheses*, 4:1 (PG 33:1097 A): "You have become one body and one blood with Christ"; St. Cyril of Alexandria, *In Joannem commentarium*, 10:2 (PG 74:341).

39. We must emphasize, however, the fact that, expressive though it is, the Eucharistic table is part of the sacramental economy of the Church. This means that the Christian people need to have a proper appreciation of signs. In the past a disastrous lack of interest in sign-things and sign-gestures led to an attenuation of them, even though their organic connection with each other is constitutive for a truly living celebration. The understanding of signs was defective. In our own day the response to that situation has been arbitrarily to suppress the signs instead of reviving them. But the opposite abuse also crops up: too much is demanded of the signs; more is expected of them than they can give. People forget that the Church lives by faith, not by vision; that no lucky find can change the present dispensation in which salvation is only signified; and that signs are both a support and a test of faith. These opposite abuses indicate that a true understanding of man, of signs, and even of the the mystery has been lost. If the Eucharistic table is to signify the loving nearness of God to his people (the divine "immanence"), it must also declare the absolute uniqueness (or "transcendence") of this extraordinary meal. To foster a confusion of this meal with a purely human meal by modifying the place, garb, material accessories, and ritual of celebration is to be in danger of not "recognizing the body" of the Lord (cf. 1 Cor. 11:29). The locale, the garb of the celebrant, the accessories, the attitudes and functional differentiation of those present should proclaim that the act done wholly transcends any action that originates solely in man and can be treated as "his." We have here an act of Christ: accessible to faith by reason of the "humanity" of the signs, but transcending the human in its source, nature, and finality.

40. The duty of sharing is already clearly taught in the Old Testament: cf. Isa. 58:6–7; Ezek. 18:7,16; Prov. 25:21 (cf. Rom. 12:20).

41. On the other hand, Christ teaches that the precept of sabbath rest, as well as the prohibition concerning the holy bread, must yield when men are hungry (Mark 2:23–28).

CONCLUSION

Now that we have come to the end of this study the reader may feel some uncertainty with regard to its precise implications. Is there not a danger that in stressing the "credibility" of the revealed datum and its accessibility to the man of yesterday, today, and tomorrow we shall blur the elements of gratuity and risk in the act of faith?

The difficulty deserves examination. We cannot say too often that a "horizontal" Christianity in which the relationship of the believer to a Wholly Other God would be attentuated almost to the breaking point would be a caricature. Conversely, to deprive the Christian God of his "humanity" would be no less disastrous. In opposition to a scruple of this kind, however noble, stands the very fact of revelation, begun of old in the prophets and completed now in Jesus Christ. As we have said, the divine pedagogy is a philanthropy in its source and in its means as well. Anthropological categories and the humanity of Christ itself belong to the created order and are subject to its limitations. In us, moreover, the human is exposed to the attack of sin.

Yet, given the necessary purification and the transcendence of its limitations, such language can nevertheless be at the service of the God who reveals and the man who is evangelized. Likewise, human motherhood and fatherhood are exposed to the possibility of terrible deviations, and yet the Holy One does not fear to have recourse to these human relationships in expressing the mystery of his love.[1] That God is "the Father of our Lord Jesus Christ" (Eph. 1:3) and calls all men to adoptive sonship in Christ (Eph. 1:5) is one of the key statements of the New Testament. Despite all the infirmities of human fatherhood, God calls himself Father and draws men to himself. This fatherhood is very real, but it is unique; capable of being grasped by analogy, free of all human weaknesses, trancendent: God is "the Father of glory" (Eph. 1:17).[2]

We must go a step further. It is not only *despite* their ambiguities that God makes use of human mediations but, in part, *because* of these very ambiguities. Paradoxically, the ambiguities all too evident in the human render it suitable to become a *sign* of God. A created reality, after all, acquires a sign value only through the free choice of a heart open to grace. A mathematical equation is not a sign in that sense because its evidential character forces the assent of the mind. It is the very *ambiguity of the sign* that *makes possible the freedom of the act of faith.* The weakness of the human, the transcendence of the message, and the freedom of the act of faith form an indivisible whole.

The alternatives proposed here have to do with the interpretation of the "humanness" of Christianity. For some, this humanness militates against faith, for it would prove that the message—according to Feuerback, for instance, the idea of God—was the work of men, the projection of their needs and not the product of a revelation. For the believer, God has entered personally into the world and into the interplay of human relations with the intention of bringing salvation; he renders himself thus present to man only to associate him with the transcendent mystery of the divine inner life; the humanity of God makes Christianity singularly accessible with the help of grace; a man can be a Christian today inasmuch as he is a man;[3] an anthropological approach to the mystery imposes neither belief nor unbelief but leaves man "in the hand of his own counsel" (Ecclus. 15:14–17, lit.). It is between these two possible readings of the "humanity of God" that the decision of faith must be made.

The choice of faith does not have either as its intention or as its effect the uprooting of man from the world or from himself. Quite the contrary, for the incarnation, in revealing God to us in Jesus Christ, reveals man to himself and is his salvation. It is all the more urgent today to recognize this truth, for by the deadly logic of unbelief man is in the process of denying himself. If atheist humanism removes from man the ultimate guarantee of his dignity and his rights, atheist anti-humanism, which is more consistent, decrees the death of man after the death of God. According to Christianity, on the other hand, man and God are both forever alive in Jesus Christ.

The essays that make up this book have shown that the Christian is man interpreted anew and that Christ is the Mediator, the "hermeneut," the prophet of this new meaning. Or rather, the incarnate Word is himself the absolute, universal Meaning. A mysterious meaning, conceived by God and wrapped in silence for many ages (cf. Rom. 16:25–26). A meaning that embraces earth and heaven, the infinitely great and the infinitely small, space and time, man and history. A meaning that begins to find expression with the dawn of the world and mankind, and then is specified, confirmed, and matured in the life of the Israelite people. A meaning that circulates throughout the Scriptures (cf. Luke 24:27, 44–45) but is proclaimed in the fullness of time, is manifested in the flesh (1 Tim. 3:16), and is made explicit in the countless words and signs that manifest God's glory (cf. John 2:11). A meaning that seems to be swallowed up in the non-sense on Golgotha but reappears in glory on Easter morning, in the sign of Jonah (Matt. 12:39–40). A meaning that confronts and overcomes all the absurdity of sin, suffering, and death. A living meaning, not a dead letter. A meaning that is not something but Someone. A personal, deathless meaning. A meaning that must be made known to all the nations, be received in faith, and be unveiled in its full radiance on the last day. A meaning that recapitulates and restores all things and hands them over to God. A meaning that is all-embracing and unique, simple and inexhaustible. Christ is *absolute meaning*, for it has pleased God to make the whole fullness of meaning dwell in him (cf. Col. 2:9).

NOTES

1. References to maternal love in Isa. 49:15; 66:13; more humble, the solicitude of the hen for her chickens in Matt. 23:37.

2. The text of Matt. 7:9–11 shows how Christ uses human fatherhood to reveal the mystery of divine fatherhood: "Would one of you hand his son a

stone when he asks for a loaf, or a poisonous snake when he asks for a fish? If you, with all your sins, know how to give your children what is good, how much more will your heavenly Father give good things to anyone who asks him!" Such a text is a model, for it indicates the threefold movement of negation, affirmation, and transcendence which traditional theology will use in enunciating the attributes of God; cf. St. Thomas Aquinas, *Summa theologiae*, I, q. 13, aa. 2–3. Let no one suggest, then, that we should stop speaking of God's fatherhood on the grounds that Freud has shown us the potential ambiguities of paternal love! Mankind did not, unfortunately, have to wait for Freud to know about unworthy fathers; they existed even in Christ's day. Whatever their defects and faults, parents are caught up in a mystery that goes far beyond them. Similarly, the despotic abuse of authority cannot force us to be silent about God's omnipotence: the latter not only puts up with the freedom of man, it creates it at every moment and in all of its acts. The ambiguity attaching to signs is found even in the humanity of Jesus (cf.,e.g., John 1:45–46) and, for other reasons, in the Church which is a prolongation of that humanity.

3. We are therefore following a procedure the opposite of that found in John A.T. Robinson, *But That I Can't Believe!* (London: Collins, 1967). Robinson exaggerates the difficulties of belief, even (by his own admission) to the point of caricature, and consequently empties the faith of its content in order to make it acceptable. Our effort here has been to bring out as one of its aspects, the deeply human meaning of Christianity. The revealed meaning is thus made more accessible without losing any of its transcendence.